THE INTERNATIONAL DICTIONARY OF DESSERTS, PASTRIES, AND CONFECTIONS

To Linda,

Have a delicious journey through the world of sweets!

Carole Bloom
3/96

THE INTERNATIONAL DICTIONARY OF DESSERTS, PASTRIES, AND CONFECTIONS

A Comprehensive Guide with More Than 800 Definitions and 86 Classic Recipes for Everything from Cheesecake to Churros, Financiers to Filo Dough, and Seven-Minute Icing to Semifreddo

Carole Bloom

HEARST BOOKS · NEW YORK

This book is dedicated to my husband, Jerry, with love and gratitude
for helping me to achieve my goals,

and

to all my students.

———————————

It is the policy of William Morrow and Company, Inc., and its imprints and affiliates,
recognizing the importance of preserving what has been written, to print the books
we publish on acid-free paper, and we exert our best efforts to that end.

Bloom, Carole.
The international dictionary of desserts, pastries, and
confections / Carole Bloom.
p.   cm.
Includes bibliographical references and index.
ISBN 0–688–12725–8
1. Desserts.   2. Desserts—Dictionaries.   I. Title.
TX773.B615   1995
641.8′6′03—dc20   94–28419
                                                            CIP

Printed in the United States of America

First Edition

1 2 3 4 5 6 7 8 9 10

BOOK DESIGN BY CHARLES KRELOFF

ACKNOWLEDGMENTS

My biggest thanks go to my husband, Jerry Olivas, who is a constant source of encouragement and support for everything I do. He is always there to help me, whether it's research, fine tuning a sentence, tasting, washing the dishes after a long day of recipe testing, or just making me laugh. I am lucky to have married such a patient man. Without his help throughout this monumental project, it would have taken me much longer to complete.

I am happy to have the opportunity here to warmly thank the many people who have helped me with the work involved in this book. Merci to good friend and colleague Kitty Morse for her shoulder and wit and for the many hours of shared anecdotes about our work. Sincere thanks to dear friend and colleague Lily Loh for believing in me and this project from the very beginning, and for unfailing support and good humor.

Good friend and adviser Betz Collins was always there to lend me her ear and shoulder, to give sound advice, to use her unfailing ability to analyze and see what is really important, and to enthusiastically cheer me on.

Marie Santucci, proprietress of The Kitchen Witch Gourmet Shop in Encinitas, California, where I have taught pastry, dessert, and confectionery classes for many years, helped me enormously with the research on equipment by answering so many of my questions and graciously gave me use of the shop's kitchen to further my research.

Kira Kane, owner of The Cook's Bookshop in San Diego, and her invaluable assistant, Judy Butler, allowed me to use the shop as a library and cheerfully found the answers to my many questions.

My sincere appreciation to Susan Notter of the Notter International School of Confectionery Arts in Gaithersburg, Maryland, who so generously assisted me with the descriptions of the equipment for pulled and blown sugar.

My good friend Jan Bos Meyers shared many of her ideas and recipe suggestions. Thanks to my mother, Florence Bloom, for her encouragement and for being so proud of me.

Special thanks to my terrific agent, Jane Dystel, for being everything I could hope for in an agent and for finding the right home for this book with my talented editor, Harriet Bell.

Many thanks to Harriet for carefully guiding this project through the

many channels necessary to become a book and for choosing copy-
editor Judith Sutton, whose keen eye and meticulous work on my man-
uscript helped make the information in this book clear and accurate.
Thanks also to the staff at Hearst Books for their diligence in the many
different stages of work it took to produce this book.

I'm also delighted that this book has provided me with the opportunity to work with expert publicist Lisa Ekus.

CONTENTS

INTRODUCTION

Eating a delicious dessert, pastry, or confection has to be one of life's most pleasurable experiences. Even thinking about a favorite dessert, pastry, or confection can make you feel good. Some people love cakes, others love tarts. Almost everyone loves chocolate, especially chocolate candies.

Being able to make the best desserts, pastries, and confections is the desire of just about any cook. In order to make the best, it is important to have accurate and thorough information about desserts, pastries, and confections, as well as information about the equipment, ingredients, and techniques needed to make them. This book provides that information, along with seventy-six recipes for classic international desserts, pastries, and confections.

People are often confused about the difference between a dessert, a pastry, and a confection. Even the most experienced chefs use these three terms interchangeably. *Dessert* is a general term that encompasses several different types of sweets, including cakes, tortes, ice creams, puddings, custards, soufflés, and fresh or cooked fruit. A dessert can be either hot or cold and is usually served after a meal, although, on occasion, desserts are eaten as snacks between meals. A *pastry* is usually made with dough and is sweet—such as a pie, a tart, a cream puff, a Napoleon, or a Danish pastry. A *confection* is generally a delicate and fancy sweet that is small and can be eaten in one or two bites, such as a piece of candy.

When I was first learning about desserts, pastries, and confections, I had to consult many different sources to find the answers to my questions. It was a cumbersome and often frustrating process. I would discover part of an answer in one book but need to look in several other books for the rest of the answer. Sometimes I was not able to find the answer at all.

What I needed was a book that was a quick, concise, and thorough reference on desserts, pastries, and confections—with recipes, so I could try out my newly acquired knowledge. As a student in culinary schools and, later, as an apprentice, I needed such a book to answer my questions clearly. As a teacher of desserts, pastries, and confections, I wished many times that I had a good reference book to share with my students. But I never found that book—so I decided to write it.

This book is for both novice cooks and professional chefs. If you know the name of a dessert, pastry, or confection but are not sure what the ingredients are, the answer is in these pages. Likewise, if you know the name of a component part of a dessert, pastry, or confection, but are uncertain as to what it is made of, or how it is used, this too can be found here.

The definitions in this book are written in easy-to-understand, everyday English. They are, for the most part, short; however, if a definition required more explanation in order to be clear, I included more extensive information. Almost nine hundred international terms are defined in alphabetical order.

Where appropriate, the country of origin follows the definition for a dessert, pastry, or confection. Many of the terms are cross-referenced, an especially important consideration because of the similarity and overlap of many dessert, pastry, and confectionery terms.

Recipes for eighty-six classic desserts, pastries, and confections, with their many component parts, are given so that you can learn how to prepare scrumptious delicacies. Each recipe includes step-by-step preparation instructions. The various recipes demonstrate how to use a wide variety of equipment, ingredients, and techniques.

Several appendixes provide quick information. The Batterie de Cuisine provides a list of equipment, divided into three sections: "basic," "nice to have," and "extra." If you like, take the list with you when shopping to outfit your kitchen. The Table of Sugar Temperatures and Stages is a quick reference for the temperature ranges (in both Fahrenheit and Celsius), the stages, and the characteristics of cooked sugar. The Table of Temperature Equivalents for Fahrenheit and Celsius shows the corresponding temperatures in each system, with an easy formula for translating temperatures from one system to another. The Table of Weight and Measurement Equivalents provides information about liquid and dry measures, as well as various ingredients such as nuts and butter, in both avoirdupois and metric measurements. The Comparative Volume of Standard Baking Pan Sizes provides information on various pans and their capacities. This makes it easy to determine which pan sizes can be substituted or interchanged. Converting to and from Metric gives formulas for how to do that, making it easy to translate amounts in recipes from foreign countries.

Also included is a list of Professional Pastry and Confectionery Schools for those wishing to further their skills and knowledge. Major Sources for Equipment and Ingredients Worldwide provides information on mail order sources for equipment and ingredients that may be hard to find worldwide.

My research for this book involved using a good deal of secondary research materials to verify and expand my own knowledge. Most of this material, which is listed in the Bibliography, required extensive analysis and synthesis to translate it into a clear, easy-to-understand format. Much of the information in this book, however, including the recipes, comes from my many years as a pastry chef, teacher, and food writer.

This book can be used in several ways. It can serve as a reference source to locate essential information on desserts, pastries, and confections. It can be used to supplement other cookbooks and recipes by providing you with a clearer and fuller explanation of equipment, ingredients, and techniques. For cooks who want to create their own recipes, the book provides accurate and thorough practical information that will be of value.

For those of you who are just starting out learning about desserts, pastries, and confections, this book will serve as a basic course. It will allow you to find the answers to your questions quickly and easily, and you won't have to consult many sources, as I did. For those of you with some knowledge in this field, the book will allow you to enhance and fine-tune your skills. The recipes do not have to be made in any particular order. Make your favorites, or try them all.

My hope is that this book will encourage you to delve farther into the world of desserts, pastries, and confections. It is a fascinating world full of some of the most satisfying tastes you could ever imagine.

acidulated water A mixture of water and a small amount of an acid such as lemon, lime, or orange juice used for dipping or sprinkling on cut fruits to prevent them from turning brown when exposed to air. To make acidulated water, add 1 part lemon, lime, or orange juice to 5 parts cold water. See also: apple and pear.

active dry yeast See yeast.

aebleskiver A small Danish puffy cake or doughnut made in a specially designed pan that has cavities for individually deep-frying several at the same time. The dessert is garnished with confectioners' sugar and often served with strawberry jam. Denmark.

agar-agar A thickening agent extracted from seaweed. Agar-agar can replace gelatin in desserts, although it has more thickening power than gelatin. Agar-agar is available as powder, transparent sheets, and strands. It is soaked first, then boiled briefly before using. When set, it remains firm and does not melt or lose its shape at room temperature. Agar-agar is widely used in Asian cuisines. It is available at health food stores.

air pump A small oval rubber pump is one of the main tools used in blowing sugar. The pump has a long slender nozzle that fits into a ball of cooked, cooled sugar. It is squeezed by hand to force air into the sugar through the nozzle to form various shapes, such as fruits or animals. There is a valve that ensures that the air will not escape after it has been blown into the sugar. See also: blown sugar.

à la mode The French term for "in the manner of," which refers to the method of preparation of a dish. In the United States, the term refers to a slice of pie topped with a scoop of ice cream.

alchermes A bright red Italian liqueur with a spicy flavor. The red color comes from cochineal, a naturally occurring dye extracted from insects such as ladybugs. Alchermes is used to color and flavor some Italian desserts, dessert sauces, pastries, and confections. Italy.

alcohol burner One of the main tools used for working with pulled sugar, this is a squat round burner filled with spirit alcohol. It is used to heat or melt pieces of pulled sugar, such as ribbons or leaves, so they can be attached together. See also: pulled sugar.

alfajore Classic South American pastries. Sweet or flaky pastry dough is rolled out thin, cut into 4-inch circles, pierced, and baked until lightly golden. When cool, the circles are sandwiched together with a cold filling of a thick, cinnamon-flavored, cooked milk pudding. The pastries are dusted with confectioners' sugar just before serving. Peru and Ecuador. See also: manjar blanco.

alkali Alkali is used to neutralize acids, such as those in buttermilk, molasses, and sour cream, and as a leavener in cakes and breads. When combined in a batter with any of these acid ingredients, it helps to release carbon dioxide gas, which forms air bubbles, causing the batter to rise. This reaction gives the baked goods a tender texture and makes them light and airy instead of dense and heavy. Bicarbonate of soda, also called baking soda, is the most frequently used alkali in cooking. See also: baking soda.

allspice The berry of the *Pimenta dioica* tree, which is native to the West Indies and Central and South America. The berries of the tree are sun-dried for about a week. During this time, they turn a reddish-brown color. Allspice has an aromatic scent and a pungent taste, and it is often mistakenly assumed to be a combination of cinnamon, nutmeg, and cloves. Its primary use is in cookies, cakes, and pies—especially pumpkin. It is used most often during the Thanksgiving and Christmas holidays. Allspice is available both whole and ground. It is best stored whole because once ground, it tends to lose its flavor. Both whole and ground allspice should be stored in tightly sealed glass jars in a cool, dry place.

Allspice was originally found in Jamaica, hence its alternative name, Jamaican pepper. Allspice was introduced to Europe by the Spanish in the sixteenth century.

allumette A small strip of puff pastry with either a sweet topping of royal icing or a savory filling, such as cheese or shrimp. Allumettes are served as a dessert or an appetizer, depending on the filling or topping. They can be served hot or cold. The name derives from the French word for match, because originally they were made in long rectangular matchstick shapes. France. See also: royal icing.

almendras garrapiñadas These candied almonds are a Spanish delicacy prepared for celebrations and festivities. Toasted almonds are cooked in a caramelized mixture of sugar, honey, and water. The mixture is spread out on a marble surface to cool, then broken up into individual nuts. Spain.

almond The seed of the fruit produced by an almond tree. Almond trees are grown primarily in California, Sicily, Asia, South Africa, and the Provençal region of France. There are two primary varieties of almonds, bitter and sweet. Bitter almonds contain lethal traces of hydrocyanic acid, which is destroyed when the almonds are processed. Because of the strong taste of bitter almonds, they are used sparingly to flavor cakes, pastries, and confections. The popular Italian amaretti cookies are flavored with bitter almonds. Sweet almonds are used dried and come in many forms: whole, blanched, sliced, slivered, chopped, smoked, and as a paste, as well as ground into almond meal. Almonds are widely available. They are best stored in the freezer in a tightly covered container or wrapped in a plastic bag to retain freshness. Almonds originated in Asia and were widely used in the Middle Ages, primarily for dessert dishes. See also: almond cream, almond extract, almond meal, almond paste, amaretti, marzipan, nut, and praline.

almond cream A rich, thick, uncooked mixture made with finely ground almonds, pastry cream, eggs, butter, confectioners' sugar, and a flavoring such as a liqueur or extract. It is used primarily as a filling in tarts, cakes, and pastries. See also: pastry cream.

almond extract A concentrated flavoring made from bitter almond oil and alcohol. Almond extract should be used in small quantities because it has a very strong flavor. It has an indefinite shelf life if stored in a cool, dark place and kept tightly closed. Almond extract is widely used in desserts and pastries. See also: almond and extract.

almond flour See almond meal.

almond meal Also called almond flour, almond meal is a fine powder made from very finely ground almonds and sugar. It is most commonly used as an ingredient in desserts and pastries. To yield 1 cup almond meal, which weighs 4 ounces, grind 1 cup plus 1 tablespoon sliced almonds with 1 tablespoon sugar in a food processor until very fine. Almond meal is also made commercially and can be bought at specialty nut stores or some health food stores. See also: almond.

almond paste A confection made of equal parts of finely ground blanched almonds and confectioners' sugar, mixed with glucose, corn syrup, or egg white. It is a pliable substance that is used extensively in pastry making and confectionary both as a decoration and as a flavoring. Almond paste has a sweet almond flavor and a slightly grainy texture. It is often colored and formed into shapes such as flowers, animals, and fruits. It is sometimes used to cover cakes and pastries. Pastries and confections made with almond paste should be kept covered until they are served because the almond paste will turn hard and crusty if exposed to air for very long. Almond paste should be stored tightly covered with plastic wrap in the refrigerator, where it will last for up to 6 months. Almond paste is less firm and pliable than marzipan, although they are essentially interchangeable. Almond paste is available in most major supermarkets and gourmet stores, or it can be easily made. It originated in the Middle East, where it has been used in confectionery for centuries. See also: almond and marzipan.

amande The French word for almond. See also: almond.

amaretti Italian macaroons. There are many varieties of amaretti, but the most well-known are the amaretti di Saronno, made from bitter almonds. Lazzaroni di Saronno is the most popular brand of amaretti. The cookies are usually 1¹/₂ inches in diameter and are wrapped in pairs in colored paper that is twisted at each end. Amaretti are often dipped in sweet dessert wine or served with ice cream. They are also finely ground and used as an ingredient in desserts and pastries. Amarettini are miniature amaretti. Italy. See also: almond and Chocolate Amaretti Torte (page 304).

amarettini See amaretti.

amaretto An Italian liqueur flavored with almonds that is used as a flavoring in desserts, pastries, and confections. There are many brands available, the most well known of which is Amaretto di Saronno from Italy.

angel food cake A light, airy, delicate cake composed of sugar, flour, egg whites, cream of tartar, salt, and flavoring, such as vanilla or lemon extract. **Angel food cake** contains no egg yolks or other fats. The cake depends completely on the air that is beaten into the egg whites for its ability to rise. The egg whites must be beaten to the point where they are stiff, but not dry. This consistency allows the other ingredients to be gently folded into the egg whites, ensuring that the amount of air beaten in will be maintained. Angel food cake doubles in size during baking. It is best baked in a deep tube pan, which conducts heat to the center of the cake so that it bakes evenly. Angel food cake is traditionally positioned upside down to cool, which helps prevent it from sticking to the pan and from falling. It is frequently served plain, but it is also served with whipped cream, fruit sauce, fresh fruit, or a light sugar glaze as a garnish. See also: tube pan.

ANGEL FOOD CAKE

One 10- by 3½-inch round cake; 14 to 16 servings

1 cup sifted cake flour
1½ cups superfine sugar
¼ teaspoon salt
12 large egg whites, at room temperature
1 teaspoon cream of tartar
2 teaspoons vanilla extract
½ teaspoon almond extract
1 teaspoon freshly squeezed lemon juice

Position a rack in the center of the oven and preheat to 325°F.

In a 1-quart bowl, thoroughly blend the flour, ¾ cup of the sugar, and the salt. Place the remaining ¾ cup sugar in a measuring cup near the mixer.

In the grease-free bowl of a stand mixer, using the wire whip attachment, or in a grease-free mixing bowl, using a hand-held mixer, whip the egg whites on low speed until they are slightly frothy. Add the cream of tartar and whip the egg whites until they begin to mound. While whipping on medium speed, slowly sprinkle on the remaining ¾ cup sugar, 2 tablespoons at a time, and then continue whipping until the whites are stiff, but not dry. Beat in the extracts and lemon juice.

Sprinkle the dry ingredients over the whipped egg whites, 3 tablespoons at a time, and gently fold them into the whites, using a long-handled rubber spatula.

Turn the batter into an ungreased 10- by 4-inch tube pan, preferably with a removable bottom. If the pan does not have a removable bottom, cut a round of parchment paper to fit the bottom of the pan, around the center tube. Use the rubber spatula to smooth and even the top. Gently tap the pan on the countertop a few times to eliminate any air bubbles.

Bake the cake until it is golden brown and springs back when lightly touched, and a cake tester inserted near the center comes out clean, about 40 minutes. Remove the pan from the oven and immediately invert it onto its feet, or hang it by the center tube over a large funnel or the neck of a bottle. Let the cake hang for several hours, until it is completely cool.

To remove the cake from the pan, run a thin-bladed knife around the inside of the pan and around the tube. Gently loosen the cake from the sides and if the pan has a removable bottom push the bottom of the pan up, away from the sides, then run the knife between the bottom of the cake and the bottom of the pan. Invert the cake onto a plate. If using parchment paper to line the bottom of the pan, remove it, then reinvert onto another plate, so it is right side up. To serve, slice the cake with a serrated knife, using a sawing motion.

The cake will keep at room temperature, well wrapped in plastic, for 3 days, or it can be frozen for up to 3 weeks. If frozen, defrost in the refrigerator overnight before serving.

angelica An aromatic herb native to Scandinavia and northern Europe, angelica has bright green stems that are candied and used in pastry making for both flavoring and decoration. The fresh stems and leaves are also used to flavor custards, puddings, jams, and marmalades. Angelica has a slightly bitter, musky taste and therefore is best used sparingly. It is expensive and not widely available in the United States.

anise seed Commonly called anise and aniseed, anise seed comes from an herb that is a member of the parsley family and is native to Egypt, Greece, Spain, and Mexico. Anise has a pronounced licorice flavor and is used widely in Europe to flavor breads, pastries, and candies. It is also found as a flavoring in liqueurs, such as anisette, pernod, and ouzo. Anise is known to have been used by the ancient Greeks and Romans, who prized it highly for its medicinal uses. See also: Anise and Almond Biscotti (page 19).

Anjou pear A winter pear with thin, yellow-green skin and off-white, creamy-textured, very sweet flesh. Anjou pears are oval with short necks. They are used as an ingredient in desserts, pastries, and confections. Anjou pears are a favorite choice for baked goods and baking or poaching whole because they hold their shape well. They are available from

October to late May. Choose fragrant, evenly colored, blemish-free, firm fruit with stems attached. Pears should give slightly when pressed at the stem end. Slightly underripe Anjou pears will ripen at room temperature within a few days. To speed up the process, place them in a tightly closed but perforated paper bag with an apple. Store ripe Anjou pears in the refrigerator for up to a week. See also: fruit and pear.

ankerstock An oblong Scottish sweet bread made with rye flour, spices, and currants. Ankerstock is a type of gingerbread that was particularly popular in the nineteenth century, although it is still made today. The name derives from the Dutch *anker*, meaning a measure. Scotland.

apple The fleshy, round fruit of the apple tree. There are over seven thousand varieties of apples grown in temperate climates throughout the world. Apples range in color from pale yellow to green, from yellowish-red to bright red, and they vary from very tart to very sweet in flavor. They are used raw or cooked as an ingredient in many desserts, pastries, and confections and are made into sauce, butter, and preserves as well. Several types of apples are preferred for use in desserts and pastries, including Granny Smith, Gravenstein, Jonathan, Newtown Pippin, Rome Beauty, Winesap, and York Imperial. These are valued for their flavor and their quality of not becoming mushy when cooked or baked. Apples are naturally high in pectin, a jelling substance found in plants. Apples are available year-round, but are best from September through March. Choose firm, fresh-smelling fruit with smooth, even-colored, unblemished skin. Brown patches, called russets or scald, which have a tougher texture, do not mean the fruit is not good. When cut and exposed to air, the flesh has a tendency to turn brown. Acid helps to prevent this. Either rub the surface of the apple with a sliced lemon or lime or place it in water mixed with a little lemon, lime, or orange juice. Store apples in a cool, dark place at room temperature or in the refrigerator. They will last longer if they don't touch each other during storage. See also: acidulated water, Granny Smith, Gravenstein, Jonathan, Newtown Pippin, pectin, Rome Beauty, Winesap, and York Imperial.

apple corer See corer.

apple parer/corer/slicer See corer.

apricot The round, golden-colored fruit of the apricot tree, which is native to China and was cultivated as early as 2000 B.C. Apricots are in the same family as peaches and plums and their flavor resembles them both. They are small, usually 1 to 2 inches in diameter, with an almond-shaped pit in the center of tender, succulent flesh. The pit releases easily from the fruit when it is cut in half. Apricots are used raw, cooked, and dried as an ingredient in many desserts, pastries, and confections.

Canned apricots are available year-round. Fresh apricots are in season in June and July. Choose fruit that gives slightly when pressed and has evenly colored, soft, downy skin and a fresh aroma. To ripen apricots, place them in a tightly sealed paper bag at room temperature. Store ripe apricots in a plastic bag in the refrigerator for 3 to 4 days. To peel apricots, drop them into boiling water for 30 seconds, remove with a slotted spoon or strainer, and immediately place them in a bowl of cold water. The skin will slip off easily. See also: blanch and fruit.

arrowroot A fine white powder derived from the underground stems, or rhizomes, of the tropical arrowroot plant. The stems are dried, then finely ground. Arrowroot is used as a thickener in desserts and glazes and often replaces cornstarch. It thickens more efficiently than other starches and does not become chalky when cooked at low temperatures. Arrowroot has a neutral flavor and becomes clear when cooked. It is usually packaged in glass jars and is available in the spice section of most supermarkets. Arrowroot has an indefinite shelf life if kept well covered in a cool, dry place.

Asian pear A round fruit with smooth skin that ranges from pale green to soft tan in color, occasionally speckled with russet flecks. Asian pears are firm, crisp, and juicy, with a mildly sweet flavor that is a cross between that of an apple and a pear. They are used both raw and cooked as an ingredient in desserts, pastries, and confections. There are over twenty-five varieties of Asian pears, but only a few are widely available. Asian pears are available from August through January. Choose fragrant, firm fruit with no blemishes. Store ripe Asian pears in the refrigerator for up to a month and wash just before use. See also: fruit.

awwam A Lebanese yeast-risen, deep-fried pastry ball. The balls are cooked in hot oil until golden brown, drained, and then dipped immediately into a cold honey or sugar syrup flavored with lemon and rose water. Lebanon. See also: rose water.

baba A light, rich, yeast-risen cake, also called baba au rhum, loaded with raisins and infused with a rum or kirsch syrup after baking. Babas are baked in tall cylindrical individual molds. The same dough, but without raisins, is baked in a shallow ring mold to make a savarin. Savarins can be either individual or large size. Babas and savarins are traditionally decorated with candied cherries and angelica. Babas are said to have originated in the seventeenth century in Lorraine, France, at the court of the exiled Polish King Leszcsynski. Finding the kugelhopf cake there too dry, he soaked it in rum to improve its flavor and named the result after Ali Baba, the legendary hero of fairy-tale fame. France. See also: angelica, kugelhopf, and savarin.

babka A Polish specialty cake similar to a baba, but made without yeast. There are many variations of babka, both sweet and savory. A popular sweet version uses ground almonds and stiffly beaten egg whites in the batter, another includes raisins and candied orange peel, and a savory variation has cream cheese and puréed chicken liver mixed with the batter before baking. Poland. See also: baba.

babovka A classic Czech cake that has alternating layers of chocolate-flavored dark batter and vanilla-flavored light batter. Babovka is richly flavored with nuts and rum and baked in a tall round pan. The Czech Republic.

Bagatelle Also known as Le Fraisier, **bagatelle** is called the French an-swer to American strawberry shortcake. Bagatelle is composed of a génoise that is split in half and filled with a rich mixture of pastry cream and sweetened whipped cream, called Diplomat cream. Fresh cut strawberries are placed between the two layers, and a row of straw-berries cut lengthwise faces out, set upright on the edge of the cake. The cake is topped with a thin layer of pale green marzipan and a green-and-pink marzipan ribbon that is wound around the top outside edge. France. See also: Diplomat cream, génoise, marzipan, and pastry cream.

BAGATELLE

One 9-inch round cake; 12 to 14 servings

2 tablespoons granulated sugar
¼ cup water
One 9-inch round Génoise (page 138)
¾ cup heavy whipping cream
¾ cup Pastry Cream (page 221)
1 envelope (1 scant tablespoon) powdered gelatin or
    3 leaves gelatin
2 pints fresh strawberries, washed, dried, hulled, and cut in
    half lengthwise
¼ cup apricot preserves
1 tablespoon water
1½ rolls (10 ounces) marzipan
Red paste food coloring
Green paste food coloring
Confectioners' sugar for dusting

Combine the sugar and water in a small saucepan and bring to a boil over medium heat to dissolve the sugar. Remove from the heat and let cool.

Slice the génoise in half horizontally. Place the bottom layer on a 9-inch cardboard cake circle.

In the bowl of a stand mixer, using the wire whip attachment, or in a mixing bowl, using a hand-held mixer, whip the cream until it holds firm peaks. Fold the whipped cream into the pastry cream, blending well. Refrigerate while you prepare the gelatin.

If using powdered gelatin, sprinkle it over 2 tablespoons cold water and let stand for 5 minutes. Then transfer the mixture to the top of a double boiler and melt over low heat, stirring occasionally with a rubber spatula. If using gelatin leaves, soak them in cold water to soften for 10 minutes. Squeeze out the excess liquid, and melt the gelatin in a small saucepan over low heat.

Pour the liquid gelatin into the cream mixture in a steady stream, whisking constantly and thoroughly until well blended.

Brush the bottom génoise layer with the cooled sugar syrup. Spread half of the cream mixture over this layer. Make a tight circle of strawberries around the edge of the génoise, standing the berries on their stem ends with the cut sides facing out. Then cover the cream with the remaining strawberries, cut sides down.

Spread the remaining cream over the tops of the berries, leaving the tops of the outer row of cut berries clean. Place the top layer of the génoise on top of the cream and brush it with the remaining sugar syrup.

Place the apricot preserves and water in a small saucepan and bring to a boil over medium heat. Strain the glaze, pushing through as much of the fruit pulp as possible. Brush the top of the cake with the glaze.

Take one third of the marzipan and use a toothpick to dab 2 or 3 drops of red paste food coloring into it. Sprinkle a work surface with confectioners' sugar. Knead the marzipan to distribute the color evenly, using confectioners' sugar to keep it from sticking. Color the remaining marzipan with green paste food coloring.

Set aside one third of the green marzipan. On a smooth work surface sprinkled with confectioners' sugar, roll out the remaining green marzipan to a thickness of ⅛ inch. Using a 9-inch cardboard cake circle as a guide, cut a circle out of the marzipan. Place the marzipan circle carefully on top of the génoise and if necessary, trim it to fit the cake.

Roll the remaining green marzipan into a long, thin rope about 14 inches long. Do the same with the pink marzipan. Then wind them together to form a twisted rope. Lightly brush the outside top edge of the marzipan circle with water. Place the rope of marzipan around the outside top edge of the cake, tucking in the ends, or trimming them off if necessary. Lightly dust the top of the cake with confectioners' sugar.

Serve the cake immediately, or refrigerate until ready to serve. The cake will keep for 6 hours, covered, in the refrigerator.

bain-marie The French term for water bath. See also: double boiler and water bath.

bake blind The technique for baking an unfilled pastry shell. The unbaked shell is pierced evenly with a fork to keep it from puffing up, covered with aluminum foil or parchment paper, and weighted with specially designed aluminum or ceramic pie weights or with rice or beans. The pastry shell is baked with the weights until it is set, about 12 minutes. Then the foil and weights are removed and the pastry baked until it is browned and either partially or completely baked, as needed. See also: pie weights.

bake cup A fluted paper or foil cup used to line muffin or cupcake pans. Bake cups hold the batter and make it easy to release baked goods from the pan. They are available in a variety of colors and seasonal designs, such as red or brown, white with holly leaves and berries, or white with hearts. Standard size is 2 inches wide and 1¼ inches deep. The mini size, used mostly to hold petits fours or finished candies, is about 1 inch wide and ¾ inch deep, and the medium size measures 1¼ inches wide and 1 inch deep. Bake cups come in packages of twenty-four, fifty, and one hundred and are available at cookware shops, supermarkets, and cake decorating and candy making supply shops, and through mail order cookware catalogs.

baked Alaska This dessert is composed of a firm slab of ice cream that sits on a layer of liqueur-soaked sponge cake, all covered and decorated with meringue. The meringue, which insulates the ice cream and keeps it from melting, is browned in the oven rapidly just before serving. Various flavors of ice cream are used. United States. See also: meringue and sponge cake.

Baker's Joy A combination of vegetable oil and flour in a spray, Baker's Joy is used to help release baked goods easily from their pans. It replaces butter or margarine and flour for greasing and flouring pans. By combining two steps in one, Baker's Joy saves cleanup and time. Baker's Joy is available in cookware and gourmet shops and supermarkets.

baker's yeast See yeast.

baking chocolate Also called bitter or unsweetened chocolate, baking chocolate is pure chocolate liquor, pressed from the cocoa bean during processing, with the addition of lecithin, which acts as an emulsifier, and vanilla. Baker's chocolate is used in many desserts, pastries, and confections. See also: chocolate.

baking pan Baking pans come in many different sizes and shapes: round, square, rectangular, and a variety of specialty and novelty shapes. They are usually a minimum of ¾ inch high with straight sides. The most efficient pans are made of aluminum or heavy-gauge steel, because these materials conduct heat efficiently and evenly. Black steel pans conduct heat more efficiently than aluminum pans; therefore, a crust may develop on the outside of the baked good, which is not always desirable. The best baking pans are 2 inches high, deep enough to hold most batters. See also: Bundt pan, cake pan, langue de chat plaque, loaf pan, madeleine pan, springform pan, tube pan, and the table of Comparative Volume of Standard Baking Pan Sizes (page 341).

baking powder Used as a leavener in cookies, cakes, and quick breads, baking powder is made up of 2 parts of a baking acid, such as cream of tartar, and 1 part baking soda. A small amount of cornstarch is also added, to absorb moisture and stabilize the mixture. There are three types of baking powder: single-acting, slow-acting, and double-acting. Single-acting reacts when mixed with liquid, while slow-acting reacts when heated. These types are hard to find in the United States. The most common type of baking powder is double-acting. This type releases a limited amount of carbon dioxide when moistened and a greater amount of carbon dioxide when heated, causing gas bubbles to increase—and cookies, cakes, and quick breads to rise. Baking powder is perishable and should be stored in a cool, dry place. Check the bottom of the can for the expiration date and replace every 6 months. To test if baking powder is still effective, combine 1 teaspoon baking powder with $1/2$ cup hot water. If it bubbles energetically, it is still good.

baking sheet A flat, firm sheet of metal with either open sides, in which case it is called a cookie sheet, or a 1-inch-high rolled rim, called a jelly-roll pan. Baking sheets are used for a variety of tasks in the kitchen including holding batters for jelly-roll cakes and roulades, acting as the bottom for flan rings or forms, and holding cookies as they bake. The best choice of material for baking sheets is aluminum, because it conducts heat efficiently. Black steel pans conduct heat faster than aluminum, but cause the outside of baked goods to develop a crust and to brown rapidly. Air-cushioned baking sheets sandwich a layer of air between two layers of aluminum, protecting the bottoms of baked goods from browning too fast.

baking soda Also called bicarbonate of soda, baking soda is a leavener of baked goods. It helps to release carbon dioxide gas when combined in a batter with an acid ingredient, such as molasses, sour cream, or buttermilk, resulting in rising. Because baking soda reacts when wet, it should always be sifted or combined with the dry ingredients before the liquid is added. The batter should be baked immediately after it is mixed. Too much baking soda in a batter will result in a soapy, chalky flavor. Baking soda has an indefinite shelf life. See also: alkali.

baklava A pastry of Middle Eastern origin. Many layers of buttered phyllo pastry dough are filled with a mixture of chopped nuts, sugar, and spices. The pastry is assembled in a rectangular baking pan and scored into triangles before it is baked. When the baklava is removed from the oven, a spicy honey and lemon syrup is poured over it, which infuses the pastry. Greece. See also: phyllo dough.

balushahi An Indian confection of sweet pastry dough deep-fried in clarified butter until crisp, then immediately dipped in sugar syrup. India.

banana The fruit of the banana tree, native to India and Malaya, grown in tropical climates throughout the world. The long, thick, yellow- or red-skinned fruit grows in compact clusters that hang from the top of the tree. Naturally sweet, ripe bananas are used raw or cooked as an ingredient in many pastries, desserts, and confections. Bananas are available year-round. They are picked when green and continue to ripen at room temperature. Choose firm, plump fruit with evenly colored, unblemished skin. Their bright yellow or red skins will darken and show spots with age. When peeled, bananas turn brown from exposure to air. To prevent this, rub them with a cut lemon or lime or soak them in water mixed with a little lemon, lime, or orange juice; pat them dry with a towel before use. Bananas are naturally high in pectin, a jelling substance found in plants. See also: fruit and pectin.

banana cream pie A custard pie with thinly sliced bananas mixed with the filling. It is also a variation of Boston cream pie. United States. See also: Boston cream pie.

bananas Foster This impressive flaming dessert originated in New Orleans at Brennan's Restaurant in the 1950s, where it was named for a regular patron of the restaurant, Richard Foster. It is made by splitting a banana lengthwise and sautéing it briefly in butter, with sugar, spices, rum, and liqueur. The banana is served with the sauce, accompanied by a scoop of vanilla ice cream and flambéed. United States.

banana split A rich, whimsical American dessert composed of a banana split lengthwise and placed in a boat-shaped glass dish. Traditionally the banana is topped with three scoops of ice cream—vanilla, strawberry, and chocolate—which are covered with sweet sauces such as butterscotch, strawberry, and chocolate. The dessert is further embellished with whipped cream, chopped nuts, and maraschino or candied cherries. United States.

Banbury cake A regional specialty of Banbury, Oxfordshire, Banbury cake is made from two layers of oval-shaped sweet pastry dough, often puff pastry, that enclose a filling of dried fruits and spices. The smaller round Eccles cake is the same except for size and shape. The origins of Banbury cake are said to date back to the thirteenth century, when the Crusaders returned from the Holy Land with tales of a cake made from pastry wrapped around a mixture of fruits and spices. United Kingdom. See also: Eccles cake.

Banbury tart A variation of Banbury cake in the form of a tart. A sweet pastry shell is filled with a mixture of raisins, sugar, eggs, lemon juice, lemon zest, butter, and chopped candied fruits, then baked. After cooling, the tart is garnished with whipped cream. United Kingdom. See also: Banbury cake and tart.

banh troi Translated from Vietnamese as "floating cakes," bahn troi are sweet rice dumplings. Mung beans are soaked, steamed, puréed to a paste with sugar, and then chilled until firm. A paste of sesame seeds is combined with the chilled bean paste, and the mixture is formed into small balls. A dough of glutinous rice flour is rolled into a circle, a ball of bean and sesame seed paste is placed in the center, and the dough is pinched together to enclose the ball. The dumplings are briefly boiled in water, drained, and then simmered in a syrup of fresh ginger and sugar. The dumplings are cooled, sprinkled lightly with toasted sesame seeds, and served in the warmed sauce. Vietnam.

bannock A Scottish round, sweet bread made with oats, rye, or barley meal. Bannock was traditionally baked on a griddle, but today it is usually baked in the oven. Oven-baked bannock is called Selkirk, named after the town where it originated. Pitcaithly is a sweeter type of bannock that includes chopped candied orange peel and chopped almonds. Although it originally was a specialty of the Christmas season, these days bannock is available year-round at Scottish bakeries. In ancient times, bannock was regarded as a symbol of the sun. Scotland.

bar cookie Bar cookies are made by baking a soft batter or dough in a square or rectangular baking pan, cooling it, and cutting it into bars or squares. See also: batter, cookie, and dough.

barfi An Indian fudgelike candy made from milk that is cooked slowly over low heat until it is thick and has the consistency of cream, then sweetened. Almonds or pistachio nuts are added, and the confection is flavored and colored with rose water or almond extract. Occasionally cocoa or coconut is added instead of nuts. The mixture is poured into a shallow baking pan or pie pan and left to cool before being cut into squares or diamonds. Other variations of barfi are made with coconut or ground cashews cooked slowly with water and sugar until thick. Occasionally barfi is decorated with *vark*, silver leaf. India. See also: silver leaf.

bark An irregularly shaped flat chocolate candy that usually contains toasted nuts. Often chopped dried fruits such as apricots and raisins are added. Any type of chocolate can be used to make bark. It is a popular candy that is broken into uneven pieces and eaten out of hand. The name probably derives from the appearance of the candy, which slightly resembles the rugged outer covering of a tree. United States.

barquette The French word for small boat, meaning a boat-shaped tart-let. The barquette shell is made from sweet pastry dough, puff pastry, or short pastry dough. Barquettes are often baked blind, without a filling, and the filling is added after the shells cool. Barquettes hold either sweet or savory fillings. See also: bake blind, pâte brisée, pâte sablée, pâte su-crée, puff pastry, and tartlet.

barquette mold A boat-shaped individual tartlet mold. The molds are available with either fluted or plain sides. They are generally 3 to 4 inches long, 1³/₄ inches across at their widest, and ¹/₂ inch deep. See also: barquette and tartlet.

barriga de freira The name of this classic Portuguese sweet translates as "nun's belly," probably because in the seventeenth century nuns made and sold many delicious sweets to raise money for their convents. Sugar and water are cooked together to make a thick syrup. Butter and bread crumbs are added, then beaten eggs are stirred into the syrup, and the mixture is cooked until thickened. It is turned into a serving dish, deco-rated with nuts and crystallized and dried fruits, and cooled to room temperature before serving. Portugal.

Bartlett pear Also called Williams pear, a Bartlett is a summer pear. The bell-shaped pears have smooth yellow skin and creamy off-white flesh. Their skin is occasionally streaked with red. Tender, sweet, and juicy, Bartletts are used both raw and cooked as an ingredient in desserts, pas-tries, and confections. They are available from July to November. Choose fragrant, evenly colored, blemish-free, firm fruit with stems at-tached. Bartlett pears should give slightly when pressed at the stem end. Slightly underripe pears will ripen at room temperature within a few days. To speed up the process, place them in a tightly closed but perfo-rated paper bag along with an apple. Store ripe Bartlett pears in the re-frigerator for up to a week. See also: fruit and pear.

basboosa A sweet Egyptian semolina cake with lemon and rose water syrup. The cake batter is spread in a baking pan and scored into a dia-mond pattern. A whole blanched almond is pressed into the center of each diamond, then the cake is brushed with melted butter and baked until lightly browned. While still warm, the cake is sprinkled with a sweet rose water and lemon syrup. Variations of this cake made with co-conut or almonds are found throughout the Middle East. Egypt. See also: rose water.

Bath bun A sweet, yeast-risen roll, packed full of candied citrus peels, currants, and, occasionally, saffron. Bath buns are traditionally topped with crushed sugar and sometimes caraway seeds. They originated in the town of Bath, England, in the mid-eighteenth century, during the town's heyday as a fashionable spa. Some sources say the creator of Bath buns was Dr. W. Oliver of Bath. United Kingdom.

batter An uncooked mixture that is the base for such baked goods as cakes, quick breads, muffins, and crêpes. It can be either thick or thin. Batter is usually composed of flour, eggs, and a liquid such as milk. Often sugar, butter, and flavorings such as vanilla extract are added to the mixture.

batterie de cuisine This French term can be translated as "the complete set of kitchen utensils." It refers to all kitchen equipment and tools, including the pots, pans, knives, spatulas, bakeware, cookware, measuring devices, specialized utensils, and other implements necessary for preparing desserts, pastries, and confections. See page 331.

Baumé scale See Brix scale.

baumkuchen A traditional German Christmas cake, only made by specialty bakeries, composed of many thin concentric rings that resemble the rings of a tree trunk. Baumkuchen is not baked but is broiled on a rotating horizontal rod that turns over a hot grill. A thin layer of batter is brushed over the turning rod. When that layer is set, another layer is applied over it. Continuing in this manner produces the many layers that make up the cake. While the cake is still warm and soft, a long wooden comb is pressed into the sides, which gives baumkuchen its characteristic indentations that resemble the threads of a screw. Traditionally the cake is glazed first with apricot, then with chocolate or a clear sugar icing. Germany.

Bavarian cream This classic cold dessert is a molded custard to which gelatin, whipped cream, and flavoring have been added. Bavarian cream is light, creamy, and velvety in texture. Chocolate, vanilla, and orange are popular flavors for Bavarian cream, but fresh fruit purées are also often used for flavoring. France.

beat The technique of rapidly mixing ingredients in a circular motion, in order to transform their consistency. Beating makes batters smooth, and it adds volume to egg whites and cream by incorporating air into them.

beignet The French word for fritter. Beignets are deep-fried yeast-risen pastries, similar to doughnuts, dusted with confectioners' sugar. They are a specialty of New Orleans. Beignet may also refer to a dough made with ground almonds that is used as the basis for petits fours. See also: fritter and petit four.

beijos de anjo Translated from Portuguese as "angel kisses," this is a classic light Brazilian dessert. Egg yolks are beaten until they are thick and hold a ribbon, then stiffly beaten egg whites are folded in. This mixture is poured into greased muffin tins and baked until set. The beijos are unmolded when slightly cool and poached in a syrup of sugar, water, vanilla, and cloves. They are served in bowls with spoonfuls of the syrup. Brazil.

bejinhos de coco A Brazilian confection, these little coconut kisses are made from sweetened condensed milk combined with butter and cooked slowly until thick. This blend is cooled slightly, then freshly grated coconut is added. The mixture is kneaded on a buttered surface, shaped into balls, rolled in confectioners' sugar, and decorated with whole cloves. Brazil.

belle-hélène A cold dessert of pears, poached in syrup, served on vanilla ice cream, and topped with hot chocolate sauce. Sometimes the chocolate sauce is served separately on the side. France.

bench scraper This useful hand-held tool has a rigid rectangular stainless steel blade held on one long side by a wood or plastic handle. The handle may also be a rolled steel extension of the blade itself. The blade is wide and flat with sharp edges, measuring 6 by 3 inches. A bench scraper is used for cleaning and scraping surfaces—for example, for removing hardened chocolate or brittles from marble—and for lifting, pushing, cutting, and portioning dough. This tool is known by many other names, including pastry scraper.

Bénédictine A sweet liqueur made at the Abbey of Fécamp in Normandy, France. Bénédictine is named after the monks of the abbey who first made it in the sixteenth century. It is made with Cognac flavored with a variety of herbs, spices, and fruit peels. Bénédictine is used to flavor desserts, pastries, and confections. France. See also: Cognac.

benne See sesame seed.

berry The small, pulpy fruit of a variety of plants. Berries are stoneless, but contain seeds. They grow both singly and in clusters. Many berries are used raw or cooked in desserts, pastries, and confections, including blackberries, blueberries, boysenberries, cranberries, fraises des bois, gooseberries, olallieberries, raspberries, and strawberries. When choosing fresh berries, make sure the bottom of the wooden or plastic basket is not stained with juice, which indicates crushed or bruised fruit. Look for plump, firm berries with even, deep color. Spots on the fruit indicate mold or rot. Most berries are best stored in a single layer in the refrigerator for a few days. They should not be rinsed until just before use, or they will rot. Berries can be frozen on baking sheets in a single layer, then placed in a plastic bag when firm. They will keep in the freezer for 6 to 9 months. See also: blackberry, blueberry, boysenberry, cranberry, fraise des bois, fruit, gooseberry, olallieberry, raspberry, and strawberry.

Betty Also called brown Betty, this classic American dessert is a baked bread pudding with alternating layers of buttered bread crumbs and fruit mixed with sugar and spices. The most familiar Betty is apple brown Betty, made with apples and sweetened with brown sugar. United States. See also: bread pudding.

bicarbonate of soda See baking soda.

Bing cherry See cherry.

biscotti The dough for these Italian cookies is shaped into a loaf about 1 inch high and baked. Then the loaf is cut on the diagonal into cookies, which are baked again until crisp and dry. This second baking makes biscotti very crunchy. The most common biscotti are **anise and almond biscotti**, made with anise seed and almonds. Nuts, especially almonds and hazelnuts, are commonly used in biscotti. Chocolate-dipped biscotti are very popular, as are chocolate biscotti, made with cocoa. Biscotti are traditionally dipped into sweet dessert wine or espresso before eating. *Biscotti* is also the Italian word for the general category of slightly dry cookies, but the precise definition of the word is "twice baked": *Bis* is the Italian word for twice, and *còtto* means baked. Italy. See also: anise seeds.

~~~~~~~~

ANISE AND ALMOND BISCOTTI

3 dozen biscotti

2¾ cups all-purpose flour
1¾ cups granulated sugar
1 teaspoon baking powder
¼ teaspoon salt
1 tablespoon plus 1 teaspoon anise seed
3 large eggs, at room temperature
3 large egg yolks, at room temperature
2 teaspoons vanilla extract
1⅔ cups (8 ounces) unblanched whole almonds

continued

Position the oven racks in the lower and upper thirds of the oven and preheat to 350°F. Line two baking sheets with parchment paper.

Combine the flour, sugar, baking powder, salt, and anise seed in the bowl of a stand mixer or in a mixing bowl. Mix together with the flat beater attachment or with a hand-held mixer at low speed.

In a separate bowl, combine the eggs, yolks, and vanilla extract and whisk lightly to break up the eggs. With the mixer at low speed, slowly add this mixture to the dry ingredients. Then add the almonds and mix just until the dough holds together.

Divide the dough into 4 pieces. Form each piece into a log about 8 inches long, 2 to 3 inches wide, and 1 inch high by rolling it under your palms on a smooth work surface. Place 2 logs on each of the prepared baking sheets.

Bake the biscotti for 10 to 15 minutes, then switch the positions of the pans and bake for 8 to 10 minutes longer until the biscotti are lightly browned and set. Remove the baking sheets from the oven, transfer to racks, and let the biscotti rest for 10 minutes. Lower the oven temperature to 325°F.

Carefully slice each log on the diagonal into ½-inch-thick slices, and place the slices on their sides on the baking sheets. Bake for 10 minutes, then switch the positions of the pans and bake for 10 to 12 minutes longer, until the biscotti are very firm. Transfer the pans to racks to cool.

Biscotti will keep for up to a month stored in an airtight container at room temperature.

biscuit A small sweet or savory quick bread made from a soft dough, with leaveners such as baking powder and baking soda. There are many types of biscuits, such as drop biscuits, dumplings, and the biscuit dough that tops cobblers. Sweet biscuits are most often used as part of a dessert such as strawberry shortcake. Savory biscuits are usually served on their own as an accompaniment to a meal. Biscuits should be light, tender, and fluffy, with a golden crust, and should rise to double their original height during baking. Biscuits are generally round, but they can be cut into squares, rectangles, or other desired shapes. Many different flavorings can be added to biscuits, such as buttermilk, cheese, citrus zest, ginger, or herbs. In the United Kingdom, biscuits refer to small flat cookies or crackers. In France, the word *biscuit* (pronounced bees KWEE) refers to various sponge-type cakes, such as biscuit de Savoie, biscuit roulade, and biscuit à la cuillière, that are light and airy. The eggs for these cakes are separated and the egg whites and yolks whipped separately, then folded together, which results in a light, delicate texture. United States, United Kingdom, and France. See also: fold, ladyfingers, and shortcake.

biscuit à la cuillière See ladyfingers.

bittersweet A term generally used to describe chocolate to which a very small amount of sugar is added during processing, producing a flavor that is both slightly sharp or piquant and sweet.

blackberry A purplish-black, seedy wild berry that grows on thorny bushes. When mature, blackberries are between half an inch and an inch long. They are cultivated throughout the United States and are available fresh from May to September in various regions. Frozen blackberries are available year-round. Blackberries are used as an ingredient in many desserts, pastries, and confections, such as fresh fruit tarts, pies, cobblers, shortcakes, sorbets, and ice creams, and they are used to make dessert sauces, jams, and jellies. Choose fragrant, plump, deeply colored, juicy berries, without their hulls. If the hull is still attached, it means the berries were picked too soon and will be tart. Store fresh blackberries in a single layer in the refrigerator for up to 2 days and rinse just before use. See also: berry.

black bottom pie A rich pie with several flavors and textures, black bottom pie takes its name from the bottom layer of dark chocolate custard. Rich rum- or vanilla-flavored custard tops the chocolate, followed by a layer of sweetened whipped cream. Shaved chocolate is sprinkled over the cream to adorn the top of the pie. United States.

Black Forest cherry torte A classic cake composed of three layers of chocolate génoise that are brushed with kirsch-flavored sugar syrup and filled with sweetened whipped cream and cherries. The cake is covered with whipped cream and decorated with shaved chocolate and cherries. The torte takes its name from the kirschwasser used in it, which is a cherry brandy. The best kirsch comes from the Black Forest region in southern Germany. Germany. See also: génoise and kirschwasser.

blanch A technique for whitening by removing the outer skins of nuts or fruits. The nuts or fruits are plunged into a pan of boiling water and left for approximately 1 minute. Then they are removed with a strainer or tongs and plunged into cold water to stop the cooking process. The skins then easily slip off the nuts or the peel off the fruits.

blancmange A jelled molded almond pudding that is served cold. Originally it was made with both bitter and sweet powdered almonds. However, today it is usually made with cornstarch or gelatin in place of the powdered almonds and served unmolded with fruit or a fruit sauce. This opaque, pale, off-white colored dessert is said to have originated in the Languedoc region of France. France. See also: almond and pudding.

blend The technique for combining ingredients together so they are smooth and uniform in appearance. Blending can be accomplished by hand or using a machine, such as a food processor, electric mixer, or blender. See also: blender, electric mixer, and food processor.

blender This electrical kitchen appliance has short blades in the bottom of a tall narrow container, which sits on top of a motor base. A blender has several speeds, which allow it to handle many kitchen tasks, such as puréeing liquids and chopping small amounts of nuts. As blenders do not whip air into mixtures, they are not useful for whipping cream or egg whites. A blender works best for small quantities.

blintz Similar to a French crêpe, a blintz is a very thin, tender pancake, fried on one side, then filled with a sweet or savory mixture such as fruit, cottage cheese, ricotta cheese, or meat. It is folded into a rectangular packet to enclose the filling, then sautéed or baked until browned and served with sour cream. Blintzes are of Eastern European origin. Germany, Israel, Poland, Russia, and the Ukraine.

blood orange A member of the family of sweet oranges, the blood orange is known for its dark red pulp and juice. Blood oranges are small to medium-sized citrus fruits, with bright-orange skin that is often streaked with red. They are juicy and have a zesty, full-bodied, sweet-tart citrus flavor with hints of raspberry. They are used as an ingredient in desserts, pastries, and confections. In the United States, blood oranges are grown primarily in California. Many varieties are imported. They are available from December to June, depending on the variety. Choose bright-skinned, firm fruit that feels heavy for its size, with no soft spots or discoloration. Russets, rough brown spots on the skin, do not affect the quality or flavor of the fruit. Store blood oranges in a cool, dry place for several days or in the refrigerator for several weeks. See also: citrus fruit, fruit, and orange.

blown sugar To make blown sugar, sugar that has been cooked to just below the hard crack stage is poured out onto an oiled marble slab and worked with a metal spatula until it is cool enough to be handled. It is "satinized" by pulling it and folding it back on itself several times until it becomes glossy and smooth. Then the tube or nozzle of an air pump is inserted into a ball of the sugar and air is gently blown into it. As the ball of sugar expands, it may be formed by hand into various animals, fruits, or other desired shapes. The finished piece is carefully cut from the pump with a sharp knife and left to cool in front of a fan. When cooled, the piece can be hand-painted with food coloring. Blowing sugar is best done in a dry, cool environment. Objects made from blown sugar will last for several months stored in an airtight container at room temperature. See also: air pump.

blueberry A dark purplish-blue, small, juicy, round berry with smooth skin that grows on a bush of the same name. Blueberries are used as an ingredient in many desserts, pastries, and confections, such as fresh fruit tarts, pies, cobblers, muffins, quick breads, shortcakes, sorbets, and ice creams, and they are used to make dessert sauces, jams, and jellies. Frozen and canned blueberries are available year-round. Fresh blueberries are available from May to October. Choose fragrant, firm, plump, dark-colored berries with a silvery frost. Store fresh blueberries in the refrigerator for up to 2 days and rinse just before use. See also: berry.

boiled icing An icing made by beating a cooked sugar syrup into firmly whipped egg whites, then beating the mixture until it is smooth, fluffy, and glossy. It is the same as Italian meringue. United States. See also: meringue.

bombe Also called *bombe glacée*, this is a frozen two-layered dessert composed of two mixtures packed into a round or cylindrical mold. The mold is lined with ice cream or sorbet, which is then frozen until solid. Then the center is filled with a bombe mixture and frozen. The bombe mixture is made of a combination of sugar syrup and egg yolks cooked together until thick and fluffy, cooled, and blended with whipped cream. The bombe is unmolded before serving and decorated with a variety of ingredients, such as candied fruit, crystallized violets, nuts, and chocolate. Specific names are given to bombes that contain particular ingredients: Diplomate, for example, is a bombe lined with vanilla ice cream and filled with a maraschino bombe mixture blended with diced candied fruit that has been marinated in maraschino liqueur. A bombe is also a frozen dessert composed of several layers of ice cream or sorbet. Each layer is softened, added, and frozen before the next is added. After freezing the bombe is unmolded to serve. France.

bonbon The French word for candy, sweetmeat, or confection, usually referring to small one- or two-bite–sized pieces. The category includes such sweets as fondant-centered chocolates, pastilles, mints, marzipan, sugared almonds, pralines, truffles, toffee, chocolates, caramels, nut brittles, licorice, and candied and crystallized fruits. France.

börek, bourek A pastry of Middle Eastern origin that is traditionally made with phyllo dough, although puff pastry is sometimes used. Usually a savory filling such as cheese, spinach, ham, or fish is enclosed in the pastry, but there are sweet variations with a filling of eggs, sugar, and brandy. Traditional shapes include triangles, squares, rectangles, rolls, and coils. The sweet pastries are either deep-fried or baked until crisp and golden brown, then dipped into a warm, sweet syrup and sprinkled with confectioners' sugar. Turkey. See also: phyllo dough.

Bosc pear An elongated, slim-necked winter pear with mottled russet-colored skin and firm, sweet, juicy white flesh. Bosc pears are used both raw and cooked as an ingredient in desserts and pastries. Bosc pears are a favorite choice for baked goods and for baking or poaching whole because they hold their shape. Bosc pears are available from October to May. Choose fragrant, blemish-free, firm fruit, with stems attached. Bosc pears should give slightly when pressed at the stem end. Slightly under-ripe Bosc pears will ripen at room temperature within a few days. To speed up the process, place them in a tightly closed but perforated paper bag along with an apple. Store ripe Bosc pears in the refrigerator for up to a week. See also: fruit and pear.

Boston cream pie This classic American dessert is traditionally called a pie, although it is a cake. It is composed of two layers of sponge cake filled with a rich, thick vanilla pastry cream. The dessert is topped with either a shiny chocolate glaze or a generous sprinkling of confectioners' sugar. A well-known variation called banana cream pie includes sliced bananas in the filling. United States. See also: chocolate glaze, pastry cream, and sponge cake.

bouchée The French word for mouthful. A bouchée is a small round puff pastry case that holds either a sweet or a savory filling, such as crème Chantilly or chicken or seafood. Another type of bouchée is made with a hollowed-out piece of sponge cake that holds a filling of flavored pastry cream and is coated with fondant icing. France. See also: fondant, pastry cream, and puff pastry.

bowl scraper See pastry scraper.

boysenberry A cross between a blackberry, a raspberry, and a loganberry, a boysenberry looks like a large blackberry with a deep purplish-red color. Boysenberries have a rich, sweet taste similar to that of raspberries. They are used as an ingredient in many desserts, pastries, and confections, such as fresh fruit tarts, pies, cobblers, shortcakes, sorbets, and ice creams, and they are used to make dessert sauces, jams, and jellies. Choose fragrant, firm, plump, deeply colored berries of similar size. Store fresh berries in a single layer in the refrigerator for up to 2 days and rinse just before use. See also: berry.

brandy An alcoholic spirit distilled from wine or fermented fruit juice. Brandy is aged in wood, which mellows its flavor and gives it color. Calvados, made from apples, and Cognac are well known types of brandy. The word *brandy* comes from the Dutch word *brandewijn*, which means burnt, or distilled, wine. Brandy is used to flavor desserts, pastries, and confections. See also: brandy snap and eau-de-vie.

brandy snap A thin, crisp wafer cookie that is quickly rolled around a dowel or the handle of a wooden spoon into a tube or a cone shape immediately after it is baked and still warm, before it starts to harden. Either shape can be filled with sweetened whipped cream, buttercream, or ice cream. Brandy snaps are made from a batter that is rich with molasses, spices, and brandy. Unfilled, they will keep for several days in an airtight container at room temperature. Brandy snaps are descended from the French *gaufres*, or wafers, of the fourteenth century. They were originally baked on wafer irons, which evolved into waffle irons after they were brought to the United States by the first colonists. United Kingdom. See also: brandy, wafer, waffle, and waffle iron.

Brazil nut The seed of a wild tree native to the tropical rain forests of the Amazon, a Brazil nut is not technically a nut. The trees yield large, heavy pods that resemble coconuts and hold between twelve and twenty seeds each. The large ivory-colored seeds are surrounded by a papery brown skin, enclosed in a hard, dark brown, three-sided shell. Brazil nuts have a sweet, rich flavor that is enhanced by toasting. They are widely used in desserts, pastries, and confections. Because Brazil nuts have a high natural oil content, they turn racid quickly. They are available unshelled and shelled. Choose unshelled nuts without cracks or holes in the shells. Store unshelled nuts in a cool, dry place for up to 6 months. Shelled nuts are best stored in an airtight container in the refrigerator for up to 3 months, or in the freezer for up to 6 months. See also: nut.

bread pudding An old-fashioned dessert made with slices or cubes of bread soaked in a mixture of eggs, milk, sugar, vanilla, and spices, then baked in a mold. Nuts and candied, dried, and, occasionally, fresh fruits are sometimes added to the pudding. Bread pudding is served either warm or cold with a dessert sauce or cream. There are many variations of bread pudding, including a chocolate version, summer fruit pudding, brown Betty, which is made with bread crumbs and sliced apples, and bread-and-butter pudding, made with bread that is generously buttered before being combined with the liquid. United States.

brioche A very light, slightly sweet, yeast-risen classic French bread that is enriched with eggs and butter. The classic shape, with a fluted base and a round top, is called *brioche à tête* in French. A special mold, a brioche pan, is used to form this shape. Brioche may also be hexagonal or loaf-shaped. Brioche mousseline is made with double the usual amount of butter and is baked into a tall, cylindrical shape. Brioche can be an individual or large size. It is eaten for breakfast and afternoon tea, and it has many savory uses as well. France. See also: brioche pan.

brioche pan The traditional pan for baking classic *brioche à tête* is a deep mold with fluted angled sides. Brioche pans are made of tinned steel and range in size from individual molds 1½ to 3½ inches in diameter to large molds that measure 8 inches in diameter by 2½ inches high.

briouat A Moroccan specialty pastry of phyllo dough stuffed with a rich pastelike filling of ground almonds, confectioners' sugar, cinnamon, butter, and orange flower water. Balls of the filling are placed on strips of phyllo pastry, which are rolled up into cylinders or triangles, then deep-fried in hot oil or baked until golden brown. The pastries are then immersed in a pot of simmering honey and saturated for a few minutes before they are served. Morocco. See also: phyllo dough.

brittle A general category of candy that is made with toasted nuts stirred into a caramelized sugar mixture or with raw nuts cooked in a sugar mixture until it reaches the hard crack or caramel stage. The mixture is turned out onto an oiled surface, such as marble, to cool. During the cooling process, many brittles are stretched by pulling their corners to make them very thin. It is important to work quickly with brittles, because they cool rapidly. When completely cool, the brittle is broken into pieces. **Peanut brittle**, whether clear or the more usual opaque, is the most popular brittle; however, many variations can be created using different nuts. Brittle is very sensitive to humidity and becomes sticky and crumbly when exposed to too much moisture. It should be stored at room temperature in an airtight container. United States. See also: caramelize.

PEANUT BRITTLE

Approximately 4 cups

2 tablespoons flavorless vegetable oil, for the pan

2 cups granulated sugar
½ cup water
½ teaspoon cream of tartar
2 cups roasted salted peanuts *or* 2 cups roasted peanuts plus
    ½ teaspoon salt

Generously coat the back of a baking sheet or jelly-roll pan with the vegetable oil.

Combine the sugar, water, and cream of tartar in a 3-quart heavy-bottomed saucepan. Cook over high heat until the mixture is a medium caramel color, 8 to 10 minutes, brushing down the sides of the pan with a pastry brush dipped in warm water a few times to prevent the sugar from crystallizing.

Add the peanuts, and salt if using unsalted peanuts, and stir quickly with a long-handled wooden spoon to coat completely with the caramelized sugar. Remove the pan from the heat and immediately turn the mixture out onto the oiled baking sheet. Use the wooden spoon to spread out the mixture; work very rapidly, since the mixture begins to set up quickly. Let the brittle cool completely.

Break the cooled brittle into pieces with your hands. Stored in an airtight container between layers of waxed paper, the brittle will keep for a week at room temperature.

Brix scale A scale of measurement for the density of sugar dissolved in water to make a syrup. The scale measures the amount of sugar in relation to the amount of water, to determine whether a syrup is low or high in density. The Brix scale, which is a decimal system, has replaced the older Baumé scale, which was expressed in degrees. Sugar syrups are measured with an instrument called a saccharometer to determine their concentration. See also: saccharometer.

brown Betty See Betty.

brownie A classic American confection that is a cross between a cake and a cookie. Brownies are generally chocolate and usually contain nuts. They are thick and are usually cut into squares or rectangles like a bar cookie. Brownies have various textures: They may be dense, fudgy, and chewy, like **chocolate fudge brownies**, or moist and cakelike. **Blondies** are butterscotch brownies, made without chocolate. United States. See also: butterscotch.

CHOCOLATE FUDGE BROWNIES

Twenty-five 1½-inch-square brownies

1 tablespoon unsalted butter, softened, for the pan
2 teaspoons all-purpose flour, for the pan

4 ounces bittersweet chocolate, finely chopped
4 ounces (1 stick) unsalted butter, cut into small pieces

continued

2 large eggs, at room temperature
1 ½ cups granulated sugar
1 tablespoon instant espresso powder dissolved in
    1 tablespoon warm water
2 teaspoons vanilla extract
¾ cup all-purpose flour
1 cup walnuts, finely chopped

Center a rack in the oven and preheat to 350°F. Generously butter the inside of an 8-inch square baking pan and a square of parchment paper cut to fit the bottom with the softened butter. Dust the inside of the pan with the flour, then shake out the excess. Line the bottom of the pan with the buttered square of parchment paper, buttered side up.

Melt the chocolate and butter together in the top of a double boiler over hot, not simmering, water, stirring frequently with a rubber spatula to ensure even melting.

Remove the top pan from the double boiler and wipe it dry. Lightly beat the eggs with a fork and add them to the chocolate, blending thoroughly. Stir in the sugar in 3 additions, blending thoroughly after each addition, then blend in the espresso and vanilla. Add the flour in 3 additions, blending thoroughly after each addition. Stir in the walnuts.

Pour the batter into the prepared pan. Bake for 30 minutes, or until a toothpick inserted 2 inches in from the edge comes out with moist crumbs clinging to it. Transfer the pan to a rack to cool completely.

Cut the brownies into 1 ½-inch squares (5 rows in each direction). The brownies will keep for up to 4 days in an airtight container at room temperature or for a week in a tightly covered container in the refrigerator. The brownies can also be frozen for up to 4 months. If frozen, defrost them overnight in the refrigerator before serving.

brown sugar See sugar.

broyage The Swiss name for a flat disk of nut meringue, such as dacquoise and Succès. Switzerland. See also: dacquoise, meringue, and Succès.

brune kager Translating as "little brown cakes," these are Danish spice cookies that are traditionally served during the Christmas holiday season. They are richly flavored with dark corn syrup or golden syrup, brown sugar, cloves, cardamom or cinnamon, ginger, and lemon zest and are decorated with blanched almonds. Brune kager are traditionally cut into 2-inch rounds. They can be stored for several weeks in an airtight container at room temperature. Denmark.

bublanina A classic Czech cake. The top of a sponge cake batter is studded with fresh pitted cherries or plums, then baked until golden. The fruity cake is sprinkled with vanilla-scented sugar while warm. The Czech Republic. See also: sponge cake.

buccellato A traditional Sicilian ring-shaped cake loaded with dried figs, raisins, nuts, and spices. This rich cake was traditionally made for Christmas celebrations, but is now served year-round. The name derives from the Latin word for ring or wreath. Italy.

Bûche de Noël The name of this classic French Christmas cake translates literally as "Yule log." It is made from a chocolate génoise cake baked in a jelly-roll pan. The cake is turned out of the pan and while warm it is rolled into its log shape. When cool, the cake is unrolled, filled with a rich chocolate, chestnut, or mocha buttercream, rolled up again, and iced with more buttercream. It is decorated with meringue mushrooms or snowmen, confectioners' sugar, marzipan leaves, and candies that look like holly berries, to resemble a seasonally decorated log. France. See also: buttercream, génoise, and marzipan.

buckle An old-fashioned American deep-dish fruit dessert. A layer of rich cake batter is spread over the bottom of a deep round or square baking pan, and sweetened sliced fruit is placed on top. As the buckle bakes, the cake bubbles up between the fruit slices, and the cake batter combines with the fruit juices to form a sweet, crisp crust. Buckles are best served warm with heavy cream or vanilla ice cream. United States.

budino di riso The Italian version of rice pudding, budino di riso is also called a rice tart, as the pudding is generally baked in a sweet pastry shell. It is very popular in Northern Italy, where rice is used extensively. Italy. See also: rice pudding.

Bundt pan A special, deep cake pan that has a center tube and grooved rounded sides, in a repeating design of six to eight sections, that result in a curved, ridged pattern on the cake. Bundt pans generally measure $3^1/_2$ inches deep and 9 or 10 inches in diameter, with a capacity of 10 to 12 cups. Bundt pans are also available as mini-sized muffin pans.

buñuelo This Mexican sweet is a puffy, round deep-fried pillow of pastry dough sprinkled with cinnamon and sugar. Buñuelos have no center holes, but are hollow in the center, similar to raised doughnuts. They are eaten hot or at room temperature. Mexico. See also: doughnut.

burnt sugar See caramelize.

Bury See simnel cake.

butter A solid-fat dairy product made from churned sweet cream. In order to be called butter in the United States, the product must contain a minimum of 80 percent butterfat, although some brands may exceed this figure. The remaining percentage is water and milk solids. Annatto, a natural coloring agent, is added to some butter seasonally to give it its characteristic deep yellow color.

Butter is graded by the U.S. Food and Drug Administration according to many characteristics, including taste, body, texture, aroma, and color. The grades are AA, which is the highest at 93 points; A, at 92 points; and B, at 90. Grades AA and A must be made from fresh sweet cream. These are the types most often available commercially. Unsalted butter is often inaccurately called sweet butter, but sweet butter actually refers to butter made from sweet cream, which can be either salted or unsalted. Annatto is never added to unsalted butter. Unsalted butter is clearly labeled as such on its package. The addition of salt acts as a preservative, increasing the butter's shelf life and giving it a distinctive flavor. Different manufacturers add varying amounts of salt to their butter, making it difficult to tell how much salt to add to a recipe when using salted butter. For this reason, and because unsalted butter has a fresher, more delicate flavor than salted butter, unsalted butter is preferred for making pastries, desserts, and confections. Unsalted butter has a relatively short shelf life, since it lacks salt's preservative qualities, so it should be stored in the freezer if it is kept for longer than a week. Salted butter can be stored in the refrigerator for up to a month. Whipped butter is butter, either salted or unsalted, that has had air whipped into it, making it easily spreadable directly from the refrigerator. Whipped butter is not recommended for making desserts, pastries, and confections because the air whipped into it changes its volume and makes it hard to be accurate with measurements.

Butter adds flavor and texture to desserts, pastries, and confections. It also helps baked goods rise, because the water in the butter evaporates and turns into steam when it comes in contact with heat, causing the dough or batter to rise. See also: fats and oils.

buttercream A rich, creamy, fluffy mixture used both as a filling and a frosting, or icing, for countless cakes and pastries. Buttercream is generally composed of butter, eggs, and sugar. It can be flavored with melted chocolate, various extracts and liqueurs, fruit purées, candied fruit, nuts, nut butters, nut pastes, or praline. There are many types of buttercream, including cooked and uncooked, whole egg–based, egg white–based, egg yolk–based, and custard-based (called *crème au beurre au lait* in French). **Classic French buttercream**, which is made with a cooked sugar syrup and both whole eggs and egg yolks, is one of the most often used types of buttercream. United States and France.

CLASSIC FRENCH BUTTERCREAM

4 cups

2 large eggs, at room temperature
2 large egg yolks, at room temperature
I cup plus 2 tablespoons granulated sugar
½ cup water
¼ (heaping) teaspoon cream of tartar
14 ounces (3½ sticks) unsalted butter, softened

Optional flavors (choose one):
I tablespoon instant espresso powder dissolved in
   I tablespoon warm water
3 tablespoons liqueur, such as Grand Marnier, Curaçao, or Kahlúa
I to 2 tablespoons extract, such as vanilla, orange, or lemon
⅓ cup fruit purée
½ cup nut butter or paste
¼ cup finely ground praline or nuts
4 ounces bittersweet, milk, or white chocolate, melted and cooled

Combine the eggs and yolks in the bowl of a stand mixer or in a mixing bowl. Using the wire whip attachment, or a hand-held mixer, beat the eggs on medium-high speed until very pale colored and the mixture holds a slowly dissolving ribbon when the beater is lifted, 5 to 8 minutes.

Meanwhile, combine the sugar, water, and cream of tartar in a 2-quart heavy-bottomed saucepan and bring to a boil over high heat. Cook the mixture until it reaches 242°F on a candy thermometer, washing down the inside of the pan with a pastry brush dipped in warm water two or three times to prevent sugar crystals from forming.

When the sugar is at the correct temperature, turn the mixer speed to low and pour the sugar syrup into the egg mixture in a slow, steady stream. Then turn the mixer speed up to medium-high and beat until the bowl is cool to the touch, 5 to 8 minutes.

Beat in the softened butter 2 tablespoons at a time, and continue to beat until the buttercream becomes fluffy and homogenous, 2 to 3 minutes. Beat in the optional flavoring in 2 additions, stopping to scrape down the sides of the bowl with a rubber spatula after each addition.

The buttercream can be refrigerated, covered, for up to 3 days, or frozen for up to 4 months. If frozen, defrost in the refrigerator overnight before using. To rebeat cold or defrosted buttercream, place chunks of it in the bowl of a stand mixer or a mixing bowl and place the bowl in a saucepan of warm water. When the buttercream around the bottom and sides of the bowl begins to melt, remove the bowl from the water and wipe it dry. Beat the buttercream with the flat beater attachment or with a hand-held mixer on medium speed until it is fluffy, 2 to 3 minutes.

buttermilk Originally the milky liquid left over after churning butter, buttermilk today is commercially made by the addition of special bacterial cultures to skim milk. This process produces a thick, creamy texture and a rich, tangy, buttery flavor. Some buttermilk producers add butter flakes to the buttermilk to re-create its old-fashioned style. Buttermilk is used in making many desserts and baked goods. See also: milk.

butterscotch Made from the combination of brown sugar and butter, butterscotch is a flavoring used for candies, cakes, cookies, and ice creams. Butterscotch is also a hard candy, similar to toffee, that is caramel cooked to a high temperature, which contributes to its rich flavor, then butter is added. Butterscotch was first developed in Scotland in the eighteenth century. Scotland. See also: toffee.

butter tart The national dessert of Canada. A butter tart is made with a sweet pastry dough that is lightly baked. A rich, buttery, vanilla-flavored filling sweetened with brown sugar and loaded with raisins is placed inside the tart shell. The tart is baked until golden brown, then cooled before serving. Butter tarts can be made in large or individual round shapes, or in a rectangular pan, then cut into squares. Canada.

butterteig The German word for puff pastry. See puff pastry.

cacao A tree, which is cultivated in tropical climes around the world, and its beans. The beans are dried and partially fermented, then processed to produce chocolate, cocoa butter, and cocoa powder. See also: chocolate, cocoa butter, and cocoa powder.

cake Sweet baked good made from a mixture, or batter, of flour, sugar, liquid, and fat, often including other flavorings and eggs. Cakes are made from complex formulas that have been developed to balance the ingredients, and each ingredient has an important role to play. The structure of a cake would change drastically if one ingredient were re-moved or its proportions changed. Cakes can be individual, such as cup-cakes, or large. There are many types and varieties: Some are simple with no filling or decoration—such as pound cake—and others are elab-orate, embellished creations—such as wedding cakes.

Cakes are categorized either by how they rise, which involves their method of preparation, or by their ingredients. There are two basic cat-egories of raised cakes: shortened cakes, also called butter cakes, and foam cakes. Pound cakes, tea cakes, fruitcakes, and coffee cakes all are butter cakes. Sponge cakes, chiffon cakes, and angel food cakes are foam cakes. Butter cakes are made by creaming fat and sugar until very fluffy, then adding a chemical leavener such as baking powder or baking soda, which releases carbon dioxide and leavens the mixture when it bakes. Foam cakes use the air that is beaten into either whole eggs or egg whites to leaven them. They may or may not contain fat, and they are usually lighter in texture than butter cakes. There is also a category of yeast-risen cakes, such as kugelhopf, baba, and savarin. Chocolate cakes, such as **chocolate almond cake**, and cheesecakes are cakes that are categorized by their ingredients.

Many cakes are regional or national specialties, including Black Forest cherry torte from Germany, Dundee cake from Scotland, and New York cheesecake from the United States. Cakes are called *tortes* in German and *gâteaux* in French. Cakes are often thought of as celebration food. Many cakes are representative of festive occasions, such as the French Bûche de Noël, a Christmas cake. See also: angel food cake, baba, Bûche de Noël, cheesecake, chiffon cake, coffee cake, fruitcake, jelly-roll cake, kugelhopf, pound cake, savarin, sponge cake, torte, and wedding cake.

CHOCOLATE ALMOND CAKE

One 9- by 2-inch round cake; 12 servings

1 tablespoon unsalted butter, softened, for the pan
2 teaspoons all-purpose flour, for the pan

7 ounces bittersweet chocolate, finely chopped
7 ounces (2½ cups plus 1 tablespoon) sliced almonds
8 ounces (2 sticks) unsalted butter, softened
1 cup granulated sugar
5 large eggs, separated, at room temperature
1 teaspoon almond extract
Confectioners' sugar for garnish
12 fresh mint leaves for garnish (optional)
6 fresh strawberries, washed, dried, hulled, and cut in half
    lengthwise, or 12 fresh raspberries, for garnish

Center a rack in the oven and preheat to 325°F. Use the softened butter to butter the inside of the cake pan and a 9-inch parchment paper round. Dust the inside of the pan with the flour and shake out the excess. Place the parchment paper round, buttered side up, in the bottom of the pan.

Combine the chocolate and almonds in the work bowl of a food processor fitted with the steel blade. Pulse the mixture until it is finely ground, about 2 minutes.

In the bowl of a stand mixer, using the flat beater attachment, or in a mixing bowl, using a hand-held mixer, beat the butter until it is light and fluffy, 1 to 2 minutes. Add the sugar and blend well.

Scrape down the sides of the bowl with a rubber spatula. Add the egg yolks 1 at a time, stopping to scrape down the bowl after each addition. Blend in the almond extract, then add the chocolate-almond mixture and blend well.

In a grease-free bowl, whip the egg whites with grease-free beaters until they hold stiff, but not dry, peaks. Fold the whipped egg whites into the chocolate mixture in 4 additions, blending well.

Turn the batter into the prepared cake pan. Bake for 45 to 50 minutes, until a toothpick inserted 2 inches in from the outer edge of the cake comes out clean. Transfer the pan to a rack to cool for 10 minutes. Place a 9-inch cardboard cake circle over the cake pan and invert the pan. Gently lift off the cake pan, and peel the parchment paper off the cake. (The bottom of the cake is now the top.) Place the cake, on the round, on the rack, and let cool completely.

To decorate the cake, dust the top heavily with confectioners' sugar. If using the mint leaves, place them evenly around the outer edge of the cake, then place half a strawberry or a raspberry at the base of each leaf. If not using the mint, arrange the strawberry halves or raspberries evenly around the outer edge of the cake.

The cake will keep for 4 days in an airtight container at room temperature or for up to a week in the refrigerator. If refrigerated, the cake will become firmer and denser. Bring to room temperature before serving.

cake breaker A long-toothed metal comb used to cut angel food cakes and chiffon cakes. It cuts these cakes more cleanly than a knife, which tends to squash them. The thin metal $3^1/2$-inch-long teeth are attached to an offset handle. Cake breakers are available at cookware shops and supermarkets and through mail order cookware catalogs.

cake circle Cake circles are corrugated cardboard cake rounds placed underneath cakes to stabilize and hold them for assembling, decorating, and serving. These circles are available in sizes ranging from 6 to 20 inches in diameter. Corrugated cardboard rectangles are also available in the following sizes: $9^1/2$ by $13^1/2$ inches, 11 by 15 inches, $13^1/2$ by $18^1/2$ inches, 14 by 20 inches, and $18^1/2$ by 26 inches. These can be cut to various sizes to fit a rectangular or square cake. Cardboard cake circles or rectangles can be covered with colorful foil and a paper doily to make an attractive serving plate. They are available at cake decorating supply shops and through mail order catalogs.

cake comb See pastry comb.

cake flour See flour.

cake leveler A utensil used to slice cakes into even horizontal layers. A wide, low, U-shaped metal frame stands on plastic feet, and a thin, sharp serrated cutting blade sits horizontally between the sides of the frame. The height of the blade is adjustable so that cakes of different heights and layers of different thicknesses can be cut. The cake is pushed against the cutting blade or the blade is pushed against the cake to cut the layers. A cake leveler cuts cakes up to 16 inches in diameter. A similar tool called a cake saw, which looks like a carpenter's saw, is made of cast aluminum with a silver steel serrated blade that can be adjusted to various heights to cut different thicknesses. The cake saw is available in two sizes, 14 inches and 22 inches in diameter. These tools can be found at cake decorating supply shops and through mail order catalogs.

cake lifter/decorating stencil A flat round plastic utensil about 9 inches in diameter with a wedge-shaped handle extending out from one side. Designs, such as hearts and flowers, are cut out of the center of the utensil. It is used to lift and move cake layers for icing and assembly. When the tool is placed over the top of the cake, it acts as a stencil. Cocoa or confectioners' sugar is dusted over the top of the cake, then the stencil is removed, leaving the design embossed on the cake. This inexpensive item is available at cookware and cake decorating supply shops.

cake marker Made of either metal or plastic, this utensil is used to score the top of a cake into equal wedge-shaped slices. It looks like a bicycle wheel: round, about 1 inch high, with a center circle. Vertical spoke blades that radiate from the center circle to the outside edge mark off the cake slices. The cake marker is available in 10- and 12-inch diameters to cut 12, 14, 16, and 18 portions. The cake marker is set on the top of the cake and gently pressed down to mark the lines for cutting the cake into slices. This tool is available at cookware shops and through mail order catalogs.

cake pan There are many shapes and sizes of cake pans. Layer cake pans are generally round with straight sides. They are available in a wide range of sizes, from 3 inches in diameter to 24 inches in diameter. There are square cake pans, rectangular pans, jelly-roll pans, loaf-shaped pans, and specialized pans that are used for baking particular types or shapes of cakes, such as angel food cake pans, springform pans, and Bundt pans. Some cake pans have removable bottoms, which makes removing a cake from the pan an easy task. Cake pans are made in a variety of materials: aluminum, tin, coated steel, and stainless steel. The most efficient pans are those made of aluminum or heavy-gauge steel, because these materials conduct heat efficiently and evenly. Black steel pans conduct heat more efficiently than aluminum pans, causing a crust to develop on the outside of the cake, which is not always desirable. The best cake pans are at least 2 inches high. Many of the specialty cake pans, such as cheesecake pans, are 3 to 4 inches high, depending on their use. Most cakes can be baked in pans of a different shape from the one the particular recipe calls for, as long as the volume of the pans is the same. A good general guide to follow is to use a cake pan that is as high as the cake will be at its greatest height during baking. If the pan is too large for the amount of batter, the cake will be dry. If the pan is too small, the batter will spill over the edge as it bakes. See also: baking pan, baking sheet, Bundt pan, cheesecake pan, springform pan, tube pan, and Comparative Volume of Standard Baking Pan Sizes (page 341).

cake ring See entremet ring.

cake saw See cake leveler.

cake slicer Also called a cake knife or a baker's knife, this is a 12- to 14-inch-long narrow serrated-edge knife, with a blunt round tip. It is invaluable for slicing cakes, such as génoise, into thin layers. It is important to use a knife with a blade that is longer than the diameter of the cake, so it is visible while slicing the cake. If the blade is not visible, it is too easy to make rough cuts in the cake, resulting in uneven layers.

cake strip A 1^1/$_2$-inch-wide by 30-inch-long strip of heat-resistant metallic fabric. The strip is moistened and wrapped around the outside of a cake pan before the cake is baked. Its purpose is to maintain an even temperature, keeping the edges of cake pans from heating more rapidly than the center. This even heat produces an evenly baked, level cake, which is easier to frost and decorate than a domed one. Cake strips are available in packages of two for 8- and 9-inch round cakes and in packages of four for 10-, 12-, 14-, and 16-inch round cakes or square and rectangular cakes. They can be found at cookware shops and cake decorating supply shops and through mail order cookware catalogs.

cake tester A very thin, long, firm metal wire with a small ring at the top, used to pierce a baked cake to test for doneness.

calisson A centuries-old confection from Aix-en-Provence in the South of France. Shaped like a diamond, it has a delicate flavor from its ingredients of almond paste or ground almonds flavored with candied fruits and orange flower water. The confection is topped with royal icing. France. See also: almond paste and royal icing.

Calvados A dry apple brandy distilled from cider, made in Calvados, in the Normandy region of northwest France. It is used to flavor desserts, pastries, and confections, particularly those made with apples. France. See also: brandy.

candied fruit Fruit that is preserved by cooking or steeping it in a concentrated sugar syrup, which penetrates the fruit. After cooking, the fruit is dried, and then usually dredged in granulated sugar. Orange, lemon, and grapefruit rinds, cherries, angelica, ginger, and pineapple are among the candied fruits that are readily available. Candied fruits are used in baked goods, especially fruitcakes, and candies. They are also used to decorate desserts, pastries, and confections. Some candied fruits, such as **candied citrus-fruit peel**, can be eaten as a confection on their own. Candied fruits are available at specialty food shops and some supermarkets; many can be homemade. They are best stored in unopened packages in a cool, dark place or in an airtight container in the refrigerator for up to 4 months.

CANDIED CITRUS-FRUIT PEEL

6 cups

6 to 8 large thick-skinned oranges, 12 large lemons, 14 limes,
　　12 tangerines, or 4 grapefruits
6 cups granulated sugar
¼ cup orange-flavored liqueur

　　Cut the ends off the fruit and discard. Cut the fruit into quarters, and cut off all but ½ inch of the pulp from the peel.
　　Place the citrus fruit quarters in a 6-quart *nonreactive* saucepan and cover them with cold water. Bring the water to a boil over medium-high heat, and boil for 5 minutes. Drain off the water and repeat the process twice with fresh cold water.
　　Drain the fruit quarters, and rinse them in cold water. Remove any pulp that is still attached. Slice the quarters into thin slices. Combine the fruit slices, 3 cups of the sugar, and the orange liqueur in the saucepan and cook over low heat, stirring constantly, until the sugar is dissolved, about 5 minutes. Then cook, stirring frequently, for about 1½ hours. Most of the sugar will be absorbed by the slices as they cook.
　　Spread the remaining 3 cups sugar on a sheet of waxed paper. Remove the saucepan from the heat and, using a wooden spoon, transfer spoonfuls of the hot citrus slices to the sugar. Roll the slices

in the sugar, separating them and coating them completely. Transfer the slices to another sheet of waxed paper and let them air-dry, about 30 minutes.

The peel will keep for up to 4 months in a tightly covered container in the refrigerator.

candy The name for both a particular confection made primarily from sugar and a broad category of confectionery, referring to individual sweets made from various ingredients such as chocolate, nuts, sugar, and marzipan. Candy is divided into different types, such as truffles, chocolates, fudge, nougat, divinity, fondant, caramels, taffy, brittles, marzipan, fruit candies, hard candies, and soft candies. *To candy* is a technique for preserving food, such as fruit or flowers, by cooking or steeping in a concentrated sugar syrup. The fruit or flowers are drained and dried, then dredged in sugar. Candying preserves flavor, color, and shape. See also: candied fruit and confectionery.

candy bar A rectangular block of candy, usually coated with chocolate, or a rectangular bar of chocolate. A candy bar often contains nuts, nougat, or caramel as a filling. Regular candy bars have several bites; miniature candy bars have only one or two bites. Candy bars are very popular and are often eaten as snack food.

candy coffee beans These commercially produced candies are shaped like coffee beans and taste like coffee. There are also chocolate-dipped espresso beans. Candy coffee beans are used to decorate desserts, pastries, and confections. They are available at cookware and gourmet specialty food shops.

candy dipper See chocolate dipping forks.

candy thermometer A thermometer designed specifically for registering the temperature of cooked sugar and candy mixtures. It registers temperatures in the range of 100° to 400°F and is marked for the various stages of cooking sugar. It is important for a candy thermometer to be marked in at least 2-degree gradations, so that small changes in the temperature of the sugar can be detected. A candy thermometer is essential for accuracy when cooking sugar for desserts, pastries, and confections. Miscalculating by a few degrees in either direction can mean disastrous results. A thermometer should be read at eye level for accuracy. The best candy thermometers are those made with mercury, because it is the most consistently reliable material for registering heat. Store a candy thermometer where it will not be jostled by other utensils, which can cause the mercury to separate or the glass to crack. See also: Table of Sugar Temperatures and Stages (page 335).

cannoli A classic Sicilian dessert composed of a deep-fried sweet pastry horn or tube filled with a mixture of sweetened whipped ricotta cheese, candied citron or orange peel, chocolate pieces, and chopped pistachio nuts. Italy. See also: cannoli form.

cannoli form A tinned-steel or aluminum tube about 1 inch in diameter and 6 inches long. It is used for shaping cannoli by wrapping the dough around the form, which holds the dough as it cooks. When the cooked dough is cool, the form is removed, leaving the dough in its characteristic tube shape. Cannoli forms are available in sets of four at cookware shops and supermarkets and through mail order cookware catalogs. See also: cannoli.

canola oil Also called rapeseed oil, canola oil is pressed from the seed of the rape plant, a European herb of the mustard family. Monounsaturated canola oil is naturally low in cholesterol, and the lowest of all oils in saturated fat. Canola oil is virtually flavorless and is used as an ingredient in desserts, pastries, and confections. It can be substituted for other vegetable oils, such as corn, olive, peanut, safflower, soybean, and sunflower. Because canola oil has a high smoke point, it is one of the preferred oils for frying. Canola oil is best stored tightly capped in the refrigerator. If it becomes cloudy, let it stand at room temperature to clarify. Canola oil is widely available in supermarkets. See also: fats and oils and smoke point.

cantaloupe A melon developed in the fifteenth century in the papal gardens at the Castle of Cantaloupo, outside of Rome, the true cantaloupe is not exported. The American cantaloupe is a type of muskmelon with a hard, yellowish-green rind covered with a raised cream- to tan-colored net. The juicy, sweet, reddish-orange flesh encloses a center cavity filled with seeds, pulp, and juice. Cantaloupes are used raw as an ingredient in desserts and pastries such as fruit salads, ice creams, sorbets, and parfaits. Cantaloupes are available practically year-round, from foreign imports, with the peak in the summer months. Choose very fragrant, firm melons that feel heavy for their size, with no soft spots or bruises. A ripe cantaloupe should give slightly at both ends when pressed. The stem end should be smooth, indicating that the melon broke naturally from the stem when it was ripe and was not picked green. An underripe cantaloupe will not ripen at room temperature, but it will become softer and juicier. Store ripe cantaloupe in the refrigerator for up to a week. See also: fruit and melon.

carambola Also called star fruit, carambola is the fruit of a tropical tree native to India and Malaya, although today it is grown in tropical climates throughout the world. The fruit is oval, about 2 to 5 inches long, with five evenly spaced ribs that run lengthwise down its body. When the fruit is sliced, the slices are star-shaped. Shiny yellow, slightly waxy, thin skin covers pale yellow, translucent, juicy flesh. There are two types of carambolas, sweet and sour. The taste of a sweet carambola is a cross between sweet plums, juicy Concord grapes, and McIntosh apples. The sour variety has a taste similar to lemon, but not as tart. Carambolas are used as an ingredient in desserts and pastries, including Bavarian creams, fresh fruit tarts, fruit salads, ices, mousses, and sorbets. They are available from August to February. Choose firm, full fruits with plump ribs and a sweet, fruity fragrance. Ripen green fruit at room temperature. Store ripe carambolas in the refrigerator for up to 2 weeks. See also: fruit.

caramel Sugar cooked, usually with water, until it is a rich dark brown color, used for coloring and flavoring desserts, dessert sauces, and candies. Caramel has a full, rich, intense flavor. It is the basis for nut brittles since it becomes very hard when it cools. Dry caramel, which is made by cooking sugar with no liquid except a few drops of lemon juice, is the basis for nougatine. Caramel is also a type of candy, firm but moist and chewy, that is made from sugar, corn syrup, honey, milk or cream, and butter. Nuts and other ingredients, such as chocolate, are often added for texture and to enhance the flavor of caramels. See also: brittle and nougatine.

caramelize To cook sugar to a very high temperature, causing it first to melt into a thick syrup, then to become a thinner liquid and darken in color. The color ranges from light golden to dark brown, depending on the temperature to which it is cooked. Caramelization takes place between 310° and 360°F (a candy thermometer can be used to determine the correct temperature). It produces a full, rich, intense flavor. Caramelized sugar is also called burnt sugar. See also: caramel and caramel sauce.

caramel rulers Also called caramel bars, chocolate rulers, and chocolate bars, these are 1/2-inch square stainless steel or chromed steel bars of varying lengths (20 to 30 inches). They are used to contain hot caramel, chocolate, or fondant mixtures while they cool. Since they are separate pieces, the rulers can be adjusted to form squares or rectangles of different sizes, as needed. The bars are either lightly oiled or dusted with cornstarch to keep them from sticking and set on top of a marble board, then the hot mixture is poured into the space they create. After the mixture is cool, the bars are removed, leaving a square or rectangle to be cut into pieces. Caramel rulers are sold in sets of four and are available through mail order catalogs.

caramel sauce Cooked caramelized sugar with the addition of water, butter, and/or cream to make it fluid and pourable. Caramel sauce is used to accompany desserts. It can be served either hot or cold. See also: caramel and caramelize.

cardamom A member of the ginger family, cardamom is native to the Middle East and India, where it has been in use for thousands of years. Cardamom was brought to Europe by the spice traders and was used by the Romans as early as the fourth century B.C. It is widely used in baked goods in Scandinavia, Russia, and Eastern Europe, and in desserts in India. In the Middle East, cardamom is added to strong cof-fee to enrich its flavor. After saffron and vanilla, cardamom is the third most expensive spice in the world because it is very labor-intensive to harvest and process. The small green seed pods of the flowering shrub must be collected by hand. Each pod contains up to twenty of the sticky, brown, highly aromatic seeds. Cardamom pods are either green or white; the white pods are green pods that have been bleached. Brown cardamom pods are a related vari-ety, not true cardamom. Cardamom has a pungent, spicy flavor, which gave it its alternative name, "grains of paradise." It is best bought in its pods and ground fresh for use, since ground cardamom loses its flavor rapidly. Either ground or in pods, cardamom is best stored in a tightly cov-ered container in a dark, dry place.

carob Also called Saint John's bread and locust bean, carob is the pod of the evergreen locust tree, native to the Mediterranean. The long pod produces a sweet pulp high in protein, which can be eaten fresh, and hard red seeds, which are usually not eaten. The pulp is also dried, then ground to a fine powder and used to flavor desserts, pastries, and confec-tions. It has a sweet, slightly chocolatey flavor and is used as a chocolate substitute. Carob pods and carob powder are available primarily in health food stores.

casaba melon A member of the same family of melons as cantaloupe, casaba is a large, round melon with a thick, slightly wrinkled, golden-yellow rind. The creamy-white, juicy, sweet flesh has a mild flavor rem-iniscent of cucumber. Casaba can be used like cantaloupe as an ingredient in desserts and pastries such as fruit salads, ice creams, sor-bets, and parfaits. Casabas are available from July to December, with the peak in September and October. Choose fresh-smelling, deeply colored melons that are firm and heavy for their size, with no soft spots or blemishes. They should give slightly at the blossom end when pressed. Store underripe casaba melons at room temperature for a few days so they will become softer and juicier. Store ripe casaba melons in the refrigerator for up to a week. See also: cantaloupe, fruit, and melon.

cashew The fruit of the cashew tree, which is native to South America, but now is widely cultivated in India, East Africa, and Southeast Asia. The kidney-shaped, pale tan–colored nut is enclosed in a hard shell that is toxic. The shells must be removed and the nuts carefully cleaned before they are marketed. Cashews have a crunchy texture and a sweet, rich, buttery flavor, which is enhanced by roasting. They are used to flavor and decorate desserts, pastries, and confections. Because of their high natural oil content, they turn rancid quickly. Store them in an airtight container in the freezer for up to 9 months. See also: nut.

cassata There are two types of this classic Italian dessert. Sicilian cassata is a celebration cake traditionally served at holidays and weddings. It is usually made in a rectangular shape, although round and domed versions are also found. Liqueur-soaked slices of génoise cake are used to line a mold that is filled with a rich mixture of ricotta cheese, shaved chocolate, and candied fruit. The cake is unmolded and decorated with pale-green–tinted marzipan and candied fruits or whipped cream and chocolate. The other version of cassata is a rectangular-shaped molded ice cream dessert that comes from Naples. Various flavors of ice cream are used to line the mold and hold the filling of ricotta cheese, whipped cream, and candied fruits. The cassata is unmolded and sliced into pieces for serving. The word *cassata* translates as "little case," which refers to the rectangular shape. Italy. See also: génoise and ice cream.

castagnaccio A rustic Italian cake made with chestnut flour and baked in a round shallow pan. The cake is sprinkled with dark and golden raisins, pine nuts, and fresh rosemary before baking. Castagnaccio is a Florentine specialty. Italy.

caster sugar See sugar.

cat's tongues See langues de chat.

cenci Translated from the Italian as "rags and tatters," cenci are pastries made from thinly rolled strips of sweet rum- or brandy-flavored dough that are tied into knots and deep fried. Cenci are served warm, sprinkled with confectioners' sugar. Cenci, also called lover's knots, are eaten during the Carnival celebrations in Italy. Italy.

chamanju Japanese bean paste dumplings made from a sweet paste of adzuki beans, sugar, and arrowroot mixed with salt and more sugar and cooked over low heat in a saucepan to form a stiff paste. After cooling, the paste is formed into small balls. A mixture of flour, baking soda, and brown sugar is mixed with water into a stiff dough, then rolled out on a floured surface and cut into circles. A ball of the bean paste is placed in the center of each circle of dough and the dough is pinched together to enclose the balls. These dumplings are steamed, then cooled slightly before serving. The dumplings are traditionally served with afternoon tea rather than after a meal. Japan. See also: arrowroot.

Chambord A plum-colored, sweet, black-raspberry–flavored French liqueur. Chambord is widely used to flavor desserts, pastries, and confections. France.

charlotte A molded dessert usually assembled in a special deep cylindrical flared mold, although almost any mold can be used. Charlottes are unmolded before serving. The charlotte mold is lined with ladyfingers, madeleines, cake, or, occasionally, bread, and filled with mousse, custard, cream, or fruit.

Charlottes can be either hot or cold. Buttered bread lines the mold for apple charlotte, which is traditionally served hot. Charlotte Russe, also called charlotte à la parisienne, is one of the most famous cold charlottes, created by Antonin Carême, the great nineteenth-century French pastry chef. For this charlotte, ladyfingers line the bottom and sides of the mold and vanilla Bavarian cream fills the center. Another cold charlotte variation, called Charlotte Royale, lines the mold with tightly coiled spirals of jam-filled jelly roll or strips of jam-filled génoise. Many charlotte variations can be created by choosing different linings for the pan and different fillings.

There is little agreement on how the dessert was named. Some food historians speculate that it was named after Queen Charlotte, the wife of George III of England, or Princess Charlotte, their daughter. Others feel that it was named for a character in a Goethe novel that was popular in the eighteenth century. Still others feel that it was actually the mispronunciation of the Yiddish word for apple pudding that gave the dessert its name. France. See also: Bavarian cream, charlotte mold, jelly-roll cakes, ladyfingers, madeleine, and mousse.

charlotte mold The classic French charlotte mold is deep and cylindrical with tapered sides and a handle on each side. It is made of tinned steel and is available in graduated sizes from 6 ounces to 2 quarts. Brioche pans, cake pans, soufflé dishes, rounded glass bowls, or any other container with either straight or flared sides can be used to mold charlottes. See also: brioche pan, cake pan, charlotte, and soufflé dish.

che chuoi A classic Vietnamese dessert, this is a sweet pudding. It is usually served as an afternoon snack or as a sweet with tea. Coconut milk, sugar, and water are simmered together, then sliced bananas and tapioca are added. The mixture is cooked for a short while, then served in bowls with toasted sesame seeds sprinkled on top. Vietnam.

cheesecake A rich, creamy, dense cake baked in a springform pan or a specially designed cheesecake pan. It generally has a bottom crust of crushed wafers, gingersnaps, or graham crackers or finely ground nuts, although often cheesecakes are baked with no crust at all. The filling for cheesecake is made with cream cheese or cottage cheese, or with ricotta cheese, to create the Italian version of the cake. Often sour cream is used to top the cheesecake. New York–style cheesecake, made with cream cheese and usually sour cream, is the richest, densest version. Cheesecake is baked, cooled, and then chilled for several hours before it is unmolded to be served. There is also an unbaked version of cheesecake, which uses gelatin to set the filling. Cheesecakes, such as **hazelnut white chocolate cheesecake**, will last for up to 4 days in the refrigerator if kept well covered or can be frozen for up to 4 months. If frozen, the cake should be defrosted for at least 24 hours in the refrigerator before serving. Because cheesecake tends to stick to the knife, it is easiest to cut with a knife that is dipped in hot water and dried between each slice. Dental floss or heavy thread can also be used to make neat slices. Italy and United States. See also: cheesecake pan and springform pan.

HAZELNUT WHITE CHOCOLATE CHEESECAKE

One 10-inch round cake; 12 to 14 servings

Praline and hazelnuts
¾ cup unblanched hazelnuts
1 tablespoon flavorless vegetable oil
½ cup granulated sugar
¼ cup water

1 tablespoon unsalted butter, softened, for the pan

Crust
8½ ounces (about 22) Marie Lu Wafers (butter biscuits) or other biscuits au beurre, broken into pieces

continued

2 tablespoons granulated sugar
1 teaspoon ground cinnamon
2½ ounces (5 tablespoons) unsalted butter, melted and cooled

Hazelnut praline filling
1 pound top-quality white chocolate, finely chopped
2 pounds cream cheese, softened
4 large eggs, at room temperature
1 large egg yolk, at room temperature
4 ounces (1 stick) unsalted butter, cut into pieces, softened
1 tablespoon vanilla extract
3 tablespoons Frangelico or other hazelnut liqueur
Hazelnut Praline (see above)
¼ teaspoon freshly grated nutmeg

Raspberry sauce
1 cup fresh raspberries or frozen raspberries, defrosted and drained
2 tablespoons Framboise or Chambord
1 tablespoon granulated sugar
2 teaspoons freshly squeezed lemon juice

Center a rack in the oven and preheat to 350°F.

Place the hazelnuts on a jelly-roll pan and toast them in the oven for 15 to 18 minutes, until the skins split and the nuts turn light golden brown. Transfer the pan to a cooling rack, and let cool for 10 minutes. Then rub the nuts between your hands or in a towel to remove most of the skins.

For the praline, coat the inside of a pie plate or cake pan with the vegetable oil. In a 1-quart heavy-bottomed saucepan, combine the sugar and water and bring to a boil over high heat. Brush down the sides of the pan with a pastry brush dipped in warm water, and continue cooking until the mixture turns a light caramel color, about 8 minutes. Immediately add ½ cup of the hazelnuts, and stir with a long-handled wooden spoon to coat them completely with the caramel. Turn the mixture out into the pie plate or cake pan and let cool completely. Then pulverize the mixture in the work bowl of a food processor fitted with a steel blade.

Use the softened butter to coat the inside of a 10-inch springform pan.

For the crust, in the work bowl of a food processor fitted with the steel blade, combine the wafers, the remaining toasted hazelnuts, the sugar, and cinnamon. Pulse until finely ground, about 1 minute. With the machine running, pour the melted butter through the feed tube, and process to blend thoroughly. Pat the mixture into the bottom and about 1 inch up the sides of the springform pan. Refrigerate the crust while you prepare the filling.

Position a rack in the center of the oven and preheat to 300°F.

Melt the white chocolate in the top of a double boiler over hot, not simmering, water, stirring frequently with a rubber spatula, until very smooth.

For the filling, in the bowl of a stand mixer, using the flat beater attachment, or in a mixing bowl, using a hand-held mixer, beat the cream cheese until light and fluffy, 2 to 3 minutes. Beat in the eggs and egg yolk 1 at a time, stopping to scrape down the beater and bowl after each addition. Beat in the butter, until well blended, then beat in the melted white chocolate. Add the vanilla extract and liqueur and beat the mixture until very smooth, about 1 minute. Add the praline and nutmeg, and blend thoroughly.

Place the springform pan on a jelly-roll pan and pour the filling into the crumb crust. Bake the cheesecake for 1½ hours, or until the cake has puffed up over the top of the pan and the top looks slightly cracked around the edges. Transfer the springform pan to a rack and cool completely. (As the cake cools, the top will sink back to the level of the pan.)

Cover the cake and refrigerate for at least 6 hours or, preferably, overnight before serving. The cake will keep for up to a week, well covered, in the refrigerator.

For the raspberry sauce, place all the ingredients in the work bowl of a food processor fitted with the steel blade and purée for 1 minute. Strain the mixture through a fine sieve to remove the seeds. The sauce will keep for a week in a tightly sealed container in the refrigerator.

Serve slices of the cheesecake in pools of the raspberry sauce.

cheesecake pan A straight-sided deep round cake pan with a removable bottom. The bottom pushes up and the sides drop away, which makes it easy to remove the cake from the pan. The pans are available in a range of sizes, from 2 to 3½ inches deep and from 3 to 16 inches in diameter. Cheesecake pans are made of sturdy aluminum. See also: springform pan.

cheesecloth An inexpensive natural white cotton cloth, available in various weaves from coarse to fine. Some of the best features of cheesecloth are that it is lint-free, maintains its shape when wet, and does not import any flavor to foods. It is used for straining jams, jellies, and the delicate cheese mixture for coeur à la crème. Cheesecloth is available in supermarkets, cookware shops, and cookware sections of department stores. See also: coeur à la crème.

chef's knife Also called a cook's knife, this versatile and useful kitchen tool is used for cutting, chopping, and slicing. It has a wide, thin triangular-shaped rigid metal cutting blade that is straight along the top edge. The bottom sharp cutting edge of the blade is tapered toward the point. In good-quality knives, the base, or tang, of the blade extends into the handle, where it is held by rivets, lending weight and balance to the knife. There is a widening or thickening of the blade, called the bolster, where it meets the handle. It protects the cook's hands from slipping into the blade and adds extra weight to improve the balance of the knife. The blades are made of carbon steel, which discolors easily, or high-carbon stainless steel, which does not rust but maintains the softness of carbon steel, allowing it to be sharpened easily. Inexpensive, poor-quality knives are also made of stainless steel, which does not hold an edge and must be sharpened for each use. The blades are available in lengths ranging from 6 to 13 inches; 8 to 10 inches is the most practical, useful, and popular size for home cooks. The blades can be either stamped or forged; forged knives are better-quality and longer-lasting. The handles may be natural hardwood, resin-impregnated wood, or plastic. Knives should be washed and dried immediately after use. To prolong their life, they are best stored in a slotted knife rack or drawer, or on a magnetic bar, which protects the blades. A good knife should be well balanced and heavy enough that its weight does much of the work. Choose a knife by how it feels in the hand and how it will be used.

cherry A relative of roses, apricots, peaches, and plums, the cherry is the small, round stone fruit of the cherry tree. Cherries have been cultivated in Europe since the Middle Ages, when they arrived from Asia Minor. The skin of cherries ranges in color from pale yellow to deep, dark, reddish-purple. There are two main types of cherries: sour and sweet. Morello and Montmorency are sour cherries that are used extensively for making pies and other pastries and desserts. They are more readily available canned than fresh. Royal Anne, Bing, and Tartarian cherries are the sweet varieties most often found in the United States. Cherries are used raw, cooked, or dried as an ingredient in many desserts, pastries, and confections. They are also used to make dessert sauces, syrups, jams, jellies, and preserves. Kirschwasser, which is cherry brandy, and Maraschino, an Italian cherry liqueur, are used in many desserts, pastries, and confections. Canned cherries are available year-round. Fresh cherries are available from May through August, with the peak in June. Choose shiny, plump, firm fruit with even, deep color. Store fresh cherries in the refrigerator for no longer than a few days. Wash and pit them just before use to prevent rot. See also: Black Forest cherry torte, cherry pitter, clafouti, dried fruit, fruit, kirschwasser, and Maraschino.

cherry pitter A utensil used to remove the pits from cherries, this tool looks like a large pair of metal tweezers with an L-shaped (or V-shaped) strip of metal above a plunger at the wide end. The plunger sits above a small cup, which holds a cherry. When the device is squeezed together, the metal strip pushes the plunger into the cherry and removes the pit. An automatic version has a funnel to hold the cherries that sits above the plunger mechanism. When the plunger is raised, a cherry drops into place. The plunger pushes out the pit into a bottom container, and the cherry slides out into another container. Cherry pitters are available at cookware shops.

chess pie A regional specialty of the American South, chess pie has a rich, satiny, translucent filling of sugar, eggs, and butter mixed with a little flour. Originally, molasses was the sweetener used for this pie. As refined sugar became more available in the early nineteenth century, it replaced the molasses, first in the form of brown sugar, then as granulated sugar. Different flavorings, such as vanilla, buttermilk, pineapple, or bourbon, can be added to make many variations of the basic chess pie. United States.

chestnut A distant relative of the acorn, the chestnut has been cultivated for centuries in many parts of the world. Currently, France is one of the biggest chestnut-producing countries. The tan-colored nuts are surrounded by a bitter, reddish-brown skin, enclosed in a hard, dark-brown shell. Chestnuts must be cooked to be edible. They are available in many different forms. To be eaten whole, they are toasted and peeled. Preserved in sugar, they are called *marrons glacés* in French and are available either whole or in pieces. If they are puréed with sugar, they become *crème de marrons*. Unsweetened chestnut purée is called *purée marrons*.

The various chestnut products come in cans and tubes and can be found at gourmet food shops and supermarkets. They are widely used in desserts, pastries, and confections. Dried chestnuts and chestnut flour are also available at some ethnic and specialty markets. Fresh chestnuts are available in the fall. Choose firm nuts with unbroken shells. Store unshelled nuts at room temperature in a dry place. Store shelled nuts in an airtight container in the refrigerator for several days. See also: Mont Blanc and nut.

Chiboust cream Vanilla pastry cream lightened by the addition of stiffly beaten egg whites. Chiboust cream is named after the pastry cook who created Gâteau Saint-Honoré. The cream is the traditional accompaniment for the cake, although whipped cream is often used in its place. France. See also: Gâteau Saint-Honoré and pastry cream.

chiffon cake A light, airy, delicate-textured cake leavened with a combination of whipped egg whites and baking powder or baking soda. Chiffon cake is a cross between the characteristic richness of a butter cake and the delicate quality of an angel food cake. It uses vegetable oil instead of solid shortening, which contributes to the cake's soft texture and gives it extra moistness. It also makes the batter thinner than that for angel food cake. Chiffon cake, which is baked in an angel food cake pan, is richer and less sweet than angel food cake. It can be flavored in a wide variety of ways, using extracts, chopped fruit, chocolate, cocoa powder, finely ground nuts, fruit juices and zests, and spices, as in **lemon-spice chiffon cake**. A sugar glacé icing or just a dusting of confectioners' sugar is the classic way to finish chiffon cake. Chiffon cake was developed in the 1920s as an easy variation of the angel food cake. It did not become known to the public until the late 1940s, when the recipe was bought by General Mills. United States. See also: angel food cake, baking powder, cake, and sponge cake.

LEMON-SPICE CHIFFON CAKE

One 10- by 4-inch round cake; 16 servings

½ cup water
½ cup flavorless vegetable oil, such as canola or safflower
¼ cup freshly squeezed lemon juice
1 teaspoon lemon extract
1 teaspoon vanilla extract
2¼ cups sifted cake flour
1 tablespoon baking powder
½ teaspoon ground cinnamon
¾ teaspoon ground ginger
¼ teaspoon freshly grated nutmeg
1½ cups superfine sugar
¼ teaspoon salt
Finely minced zest of 1 large lemon
6 large eggs, separated, at room temperature
½ teaspoon cream of tartar
Confectioners' sugar for garnish

Center a rack in the oven and preheat to 325°F. Cut a round of parchment paper to fit the bottom of a 10- by 4-inch tube pan, with a removable bottom, cutting a center hole out of the paper to fit over the tube of the pan. Place the round in the bottom of the pan.

In a small bowl or a 2-cup liquid measure, mix together the water, oil, lemon juice, and extracts. Sift together the flour, baking powder, and spices into the bowl of a stand mixer or a large mixing bowl. Stir in 1 cup of the superfine sugar and the salt. Make a well in the center of the mixture, and add the lemon zest, egg yolks, and the lemon juice mixture. Using the flat beater attachment or a hand-held mixer on low speed, or a wooden spoon, blend the ingredients together until smooth and well combined, about 1 minute.

In a grease-free mixing bowl, using grease-free beaters, whip the egg whites with the cream of tartar on medium-high speed until frothy. Gradually sprinkle on the remaining ½ cup sugar, and continue to whip the egg whites until they are glossy and hold stiff, but not dry, peaks. Using a large rubber spatula fold a large scoop of the egg whites into the egg yolk mixture. Then gently fold in the remaining egg whites in 4 or 5 additions, until thoroughly blended.

Pour the batter into the prepared pan and use a rubber spatula to smooth and even the top. Bake the cake until it is golden brown and springs back when lightly touched, and a cake tester inserted near the center comes out clean, 55 to 60 minutes. Remove the pan from the oven, and immediately invert it onto its feet over a cooling rack, or hang it by the center tube over a large funnel or the neck of a bottle. Let the cake hang for several hours, until it is completely cool.

To remove the cake from the pan, run a thin-bladed knife around the inside of the pan and around the tube. Gently loosen the cake from the sides and push the bottom of the pan up, away from the sides. Run the knife between the bottom of the cake and the bottom of the pan. Invert the cake onto a plate, and peel off the parchment paper. Then reinvert the cake onto a serving plate, so it is right side up. Dust the top of the cake heavily with confectioners' sugar. Slice the cake into serving pieces with a serrated knife.

The cake can be stored well wrapped in plastic, at room temperature for up to 3 days or frozen for up to 2 months.

chiffon pie A pie with light, fluffy, delicately textured filling in a sweet crust. The texture of the filling is achieved by folding either whipped cream or stiffly beaten egg whites into an egg yolk base; it is flavored in a wide variety of ways, including mocha, chocolate, rum, or lemon, and with candied and crystallized fruit, liqueurs, and honey. Sometimes gelatin is added to the filling as a stabilizer. A crumb crust is traditionally used for chiffon pies because it absorbs less moisture than a flaky crust and so the pie can be held longer while filled without getting soggy. Chiffon pies can be made in advance and kept refrigerated or frozen.

chocolate Called *xocoatl* by the Aztecs and dubbed *Theobroma*, meaning "food of the gods," by Linnaeus, the Swedish botanist, chocolate has been in use for centuries. The Maya had cocoa plantations as early as 600 A.D. Columbus was the first European to discover the cocoa bean, during his search for the route to India. Hernán Cortés observed the Aztecs' use of chocolate during his encounters with them and brought chocolate back to the Old World in 1519. Chocolate comes from cocoa beans, which grow in large pods on cocoa trees in countries close to the equator. There are two primary types of cocoa trees, criollo and forastero. The criollo tree, which is native to Equador and Venezuela, is small and hard to cultivate, but produces the best quality beans. The forastero tree produces a harsher, more bitter bean, and accounts for about 90 percent of the world's production of cocoa beans. Forastero trees are grown primarily in Brazil and Africa.

When the beans arrive at the chocolate factory, they are first roasted at a temperature ranging from 250° to 350°F for about an hour. This is when the beans begin to smell like chocolate. The length of time that the beans are roasted is one of the factors that determines the flavor of the chocolate. After roasting, the beans go through a process called winnowing. This process cracks the bean's outer hull and blows it away, leaving the inner nib or kernel, which contains approximately 50 to 56 percent cocoa butter.

At this point different types of beans are blended. Even though there are just two types of cocoa beans, the different growing locations produce hybrid beans and contribute different qualities to the bean's flavor. The blending proportion is another major factor that determines the flavor of the chocolate. After blending, the nibs are ground and become a rich, dark liquid called chocolate liquor, the basis of all chocolate.

Cocoa butter is extracted from the chocolate liquor by pressing it in large hydraulic machines, leaving dry cakes of cocoa called presscakes. These are crushed, ground, and sifted to make cocoa powder, which tends to be acid. Adding alkali to the cocoa powder neutralizes its acidity, darkens its color, and mellows and enriches the flavor. This process was discovered in 1828 by a Dutch chemist named Coenraad van Houten and the result is known as Dutch-processed cocoa.

If no sugar, flavoring, or cocoa butter is added to pure chocolate liquor, it is bitter, or unsweetened chocolate, also called baker's or baking chocolate. Semisweet or bittersweet chocolate, also called dark chocolate, is made from chocolate liquor with the addition of cocoa butter, sugar, vanilla, and occasionally, lecithin, which acts as an emulsifier. The only difference between semisweet and bittersweet chocolate is the amount of sugar. They are almost always interchangeable in recipes. To make milk chocolate, milk solids are added to the mixture. Milk chocolate is not interchangeable with dark chocolate because of their different compositions. White chocolate is made from cocoa butter, milk solids, sugar, vanilla, and lecithin. According to the U.S. Food and Drug

Administration white chocolate cannot be called chocolate since it does not contain chocolate liquor. It is usually labeled "confectioners' coating." It is often confused with another product called "summer coating" or "compound coating," which is made with a vegetable fat other than cocoa butter as its base. Since summer coating has a higher melting point than white chocolate it does not need to be tempered, making it easy to handle in warm weather. The drawback is that summer coating does not taste like chocolate since it lacks cocoa butter. White chocolate is not interchangeable with either dark chocolate or milk chocolate because it has less body than either type. Couverture is another type of chocolate that has a higher percentage of cocoa butter than regular chocolate. This makes it perfect for the smooth, thin coatings for dipped candies and truffles. It is available in bittersweet, semisweet, milk, or white chocolate. Couverture is the primary type of chocolate used by professionals. It must be tempered to stabilize the cocoa butter before use. Besides dipping, couverture can be used for baking, candy making, pastry making, and eating out of hand.

After the ingredients are blended, the chocolate mixture is "conched," or stirred for several hours. This process was developed by Rodolphe Lindt in the late nineteenth century. Conching involves stirring the liquid chocolate constantly with heavy rollers that break down any remaining solid particles of cocoa butter, producing velvety smooth, melt-in-the-mouth chocolate. How long chocolate is conched depends on the manufacturer. It is another factor that determines the quality of the chocolate. Top-quality chocolates are conched for as much as seven days, some lesser-quality chocolates for as little as 4 hours. It is easy to tell good-quality chocolate. It breaks cleanly, is smooth and not grainy, and has a shiny, unblemished appearance.

To choose chocolate, taste a piece. The flavor does not change when chocolate is used for baking, pastry making, or candy making. There are many brands on the market, so it is easy to find one that you like.

Chocolate must be handled with care. Water or any liquid is its enemy. A few drops of liquid can cause it to "seize up," or thicken to the point that it is like mud. If this happens, there is little that can be done to rescue it. Adding vegetable oil to it can make it smooth again, but then it no longer tastes like chocolate, and cannot be used as pure chocolate. Therefore, prevent any moisture from coming into contact with chocolate, unless it is specifically called for in a recipe. Make sure all utensils are completely dry. Low humidity and a temperature of 65°F are the perfect environment for working with chocolate. Try to avoid working with chocolate during foggy and rainy days or on hot summer days. Air-conditioning can help when it's hot, as can a dehumidifier when it's humid.

To melt chocolate, cut or chop it into small pieces and place it in the top of a double boiler over hot, not simmering, water. Be sure the top pan fits snugly over the bottom pan, so that no water or moisture from the steam can enter the top pan. Melt chocolate slowly, do not allow it to come in direct contact with the heat, and do not heat it above 120°F (115°F for white chocolate). If it is heated higher than this, it will burn, which affects its taste and texture. Overheated chocolate will seize up and become grainy. As chocolate is melting, stir it often with a rubber or plastic spatula. (Wooden utensils are porous and hold the flavors of food, whereas plastic does not.) When the top pan of the double boiler is taken off the water, be sure to wipe the bottom and sides of it completely dry. This will prevent a stray drop of water from running down the side of the pan as the chocolate is being transferred to another container, which would let the water mix with the chocolate and cause it to seize up. Alternatively, chocolate can be melted in a microwave oven. Place the chopped chocolate in a glass dish and set the oven on low power. Check the chocolate every 15 seconds and stir it each time. It is extremely easy to burn chocolate when melting it in a microwave oven.

Store chocolate at room temperature, wrapped in foil, not plastic wrap, which holds moisture. Because it will pick up moisture from condensation, which will mix with the melted chocolate, do not store chocolate in the refrigerator or freezer. Dark chocolate has an extremely long shelf life (many years), if stored properly. Milk chocolate and white chocolate can last no longer than a year, because of the milk solids they contain. Buy them in small quantities and use them quickly. If you detect an unappealing aroma from your chocolate, don't use it.

If any chocolate is left over after dipping candies or truffles, transfer it to a clean container, cover, and store it at room temperature. As long as nothing else has been mixed with it, it is still pure and can be chopped and melted again. (If the chocolate has been tempered, it will go out of temper as it cools, and must be tempered again before it is used for dipping or molding.)

Chocolate is widely used to flavor desserts, pastries, and confections. Chocolate is available in bars, squares, and chips in supermarkets. High-quality chocolate and couverture are available at cookware shops, at gourmet food shops, and through mail order cookware catalogs. Cocoa powder is readily available in supermarkets and gourmet food shops. See also: chocolate bloom, Dutch-processed, and tempering chocolate.

chocolate bloom Also called fat bloom, this condition occurs when the cocoa butter in chocolate has separated out, floated to the top, and crystallized. It appears as a dull, gray film or white dots and streaks on the surface of chocolate. It does not mean that the chocolate has spoiled; it merely looks unpleasant. When the chocolate is melted, the cocoa butter will melt back in. See also: chocolate.

chocolate dipping forks Also called truffle dippers and candy dippers, these European hand tools are designed to hold truffles and candies for dipping into chocolate. There are several shapes and sizes available: oval, round, spiral, grid, and various long-tined forks. Each is used for a particular candy, according to the candy's shape and size. These dippers are made of thin stainless steel, with $3^1/_2$-inch-long wooden handles. Dipping forks are available singly or in sets, ranging from six to ten pieces. There are also domestically made plastic dipping tools available.

chocolate glaze A fluid, pourable mixture of melted chocolate and cream or butter used to coat cakes, pastries, and confections. The mixture should be liquid enough that it will pour smoothly and coat evenly, but not so thin that it runs off without clinging to the cake, pastry, or confection. Chocolate glaze gives cakes, pastries, and confections a sleek, glossy surface. Occasionally sugar is added to the glaze for extra sweetness, or corn syrup is added to help keep the glaze shiny. Instant espresso powder dissolved in a small amount of water may be added to make a mocha flavor.

chocolate modeling paste See chocolate plastic.

chocolate mold There are two types of chocolate molds: shallow molds that are used for solid molding and two-part molds that are used for both hollow molding and filled chocolates. The flat shallow molds are generally made of plastic and are very flexible. Each mold is for a particular shape or design, with twelve to eighteen cavities per mold, depending on its size. There are myriad designs available, ranging from mini to large size. Tempered chocolate is piped into the cavities up to the top. The mold is chilled briefly to set the chocolate, then the candies are turned out of the mold. The two-part molds are made of either metal or sturdy plastic and are available in many shapes and sizes, such as rabbits and snowmen. They are filled with tempered chocolate, left to set very briefly, and then the still-liquid chocolate is poured out, leaving a thin coating of chocolate in the mold. If the chocolates are to be filled, the filling is inserted at this point. In either case, the two pieces of the mold are clipped together and left to set completely. Chocolate molds should be handled with care. Chocolate will not release from a mold if it is scratched. To prevent this, wash the molds in warm, soapy water and dry them with a soft towel. Do not use abrasive cleansers or cleaning pads. The molds should be stored in a cool, dry place. They should be completely dry before they are used. See also: tempering chocolate.

chocolate plastic Also called chocolate modeling paste, **chocolate plastic** is a pliable decorating paste made from a mixture of chocolate and corn syrup, similar in texture to marzipan. Chocolate plastic is used to wrap around the outside of cakes and confections and to make ribbons, ruffles, various flowers, leaves, and stems for decorating desserts, pastries, and confections. A variety of designs and shapes can be cut and fashioned from thinly rolled-out chocolate plastic. Chocolate plastic can be made with dark, white, or milk chocolate. United States.

CHOCOLATE PLASTIC

Approximately 9 ounces; enough to cover a 9-inch round cake

7 ounces bittersweet chocolate, finely chopped
¼ cup light corn syrup

Melt the chocolate in the top of a double boiler over hot, not simmering, water, stirring frequently with a rubber spatula to ensure even melting.

Remove the double boiler from the heat, remove the top pan from the water, and wipe the outside very dry. Stir the chocolate for a few minutes to cool slightly. Pour in the corn syrup and stir until the mixture is smooth and thick; it will look dull.

Scrape the chocolate mixture into a mound onto a large piece of plastic wrap. Wrap tightly, and leave it to stand at room temperature for 6 hours, or refrigerate it for 2 hours, to firm.

Knead the chocolate plastic on a smooth surface until it is smooth and pliable, then roll it out on a smooth surface lightly dusted with cocoa powder. Chocolate plastic can also be rolled out through a pasta machine.

Store chocolate plastic tightly wrapped in plastic in an airtight container at room temperature for up to 1 year. If it becomes too firm, add a drop or 2 of corn syrup when you knead it.

Variations: Chocolate plastic can also be made with other types of chocolate. If using white chocolate, decrease the corn syrup to 1½ tablespoons. If using milk chocolate, decrease the corn syrup to 2½ tablespoons. If using semisweet chocolate, decrease the corn syrup to 3½ tablespoons.

chocolate sauce A fluid, liquid, pourable mixture of melted chocolate and cream and/or butter, often sweetened and flavored with an extract or a liqueur, that is used to garnish and accompany desserts and pastries.

chocolate thermometer This specially designed long glass mercury thermometer has clear markings and reads in 1-degree gradations in the range of 40° to 130°F. It is used primarily during the process of tempering chocolate, when extreme accuracy is necessary. This thermometer should be handled very carefully and stored where it will not be jostled by other utensils. See also: tempering chocolate.

chocolate truffle This rich, elegant, and highly treasured confection is considered to be the ultimate in chocolate candy. Chocolate truffles are made up of about 80 percent chocolate. Their centers are composed of ganache, which is a mixture of chocolate and cream, shaped into balls. They are finished with an outer coating of tempered chocolate, cocoa powder, confectioners' sugar, shredded coconut, or finely chopped nuts. Chocolate truffles have countless variations, made with the addition of butter, liqueurs, extracts, coffee, nuts, fruit purées, and/or candied fruit. **Classic chocolate truffles** are generally two-bite–sized and should literally melt in your mouth. They take their name from the similarly shaped, much-sought-after fungi that grow around the roots of trees in France and Italy. France. See also: chocolate dipping forks, ganache, paper candy cup, paper pastry cone, pastry bag, pastry tip, and tempering chocolate.

CLASSIC CHOCOLATE TRUFFLES

Sixty 1-inch truffles

1 pound bittersweet chocolate, finely chopped
1½ cups heavy whipping cream
3 to 4 tablespoons Dutch-processed unsweetened cocoa powder
1½ pounds bittersweet chocolate to be tempered (see page 297).

Melt the chopped chocolate in the top of a double boiler over hot, not simmering, water, stirring frequently with a rubber spatula to ensure even melting.

Meanwhile, in a 1-quart saucepan, bring the cream to a boil over medium heat.

Remove both pans from the heat. Remove the top pan from the double boiler and wipe the bottom and sides dry. Pour the cream into the melted chocolate and stir until thoroughly blended. Transfer the mixture to a bowl, cover tightly with plastic wrap, and let cool to room temperature. Refrigerate until thick but not stiff, 2 to 3 hours.

Line 2 baking sheets with parchment or waxed paper. Fit a 12-inch pastry bag with a #5 large plain tip and fill with the truffle cream. Holding the pastry bag 1 inch above the paper, pipe out mounds about 1 inch in diameter. Cover the mounds with plastic wrap and chill in the freezer for 2 hours or in the refrigerator for 6 hours.

Dust your hands with cocoa powder, and roll the piped mounds into balls to be the truffle centers. Cover and chill the centers for another 2 hours in the freezer or 6 hours in the refrigerator.

Temper the 1½ pounds chocolate.

Line 2 baking sheets with parchment or waxed paper. Remove the truffle centers from the freezer, one sheet at a time. Place a truffle center into the tempered chocolate, coating it completely. With a chocolate dipper or a plastic fork with the two center tines broken off, lift the center from the chocolate, carefully shake off the excess chocolate, and place the truffle on a paper-lined baking sheet. Repeat with the remaining truffles.

After dipping the truffles, place 4 to 6 tablespoons of the remaining tempered chocolate in a paper pastry cone, and snip off a tiny opening at the pointed end. Pipe parallel lines across the tops of the truffles. Place the baking sheets in the refrigerator to set the chocolate for 10 to 15 minutes.

When the truffles are set, place them in paper candy cups.

Stored in a tightly covered container wrapped in several layers of aluminum foil, the truffles will keep for 1 month in the refrigerator or 2 months in the freezer. Truffles are best served at room temperature.

Variations: For classic white chocolate truffles, substitute white chocolate for the bittersweet chocolate in the centers and reduce the whipping cream to ¾ cup. Dip the centers into, and decorate the tops of the truffles with, tempered white chocolate. For classic milk chocolate truffles, substitute milk chocolate for the bittersweet chocolate in the centers, and reduce the whipping cream to 1 cup. Dip the centers into, and decorate the tops of the truffles with, tempered milk chocolate.

choux pastry A classic pastry dough that is one of the foundation doughs of pastry making. It is unusual in that it is first cooked in a pan on the stove top, then baked in the oven. **Choux pastry** is made with water or milk, butter, and flour that are cooked together. The mixture is slightly cooled, then eggs are beaten in, creating a pastelike dough. The dough is piped through a pastry bag to form various shapes that rise during baking. The baked shapes are split open when cooled and filled with various mixtures, such as whipped cream or pastry cream. Choux pastry is very versatile and is used for both sweet and savory dishes. The most notable examples are cream puffs, croquembouche, éclairs, Gâteau Saint-Honoré, Paris-Brest, profiteroles, and religieuse. Choux pastry has been in use since the sixteenth century. France. See also: cream puff, croquembouche, éclair, Gâteau Saint-Honoré, Paris-Brest, profiterole, and religieuse.

CHOUX PASTRY

Approximately 3 cups, makes enough for 100 profiteroles, 50 cream puffs, or 30 éclairs

1 cup water
4 ounces (1 stick) unsalted butter, cut into 1-inch pieces
2 tablespoons superfine sugar
Pinch of salt
1 cup all-purpose flour
4 large eggs, at room temperature

Combine the water, butter, sugar, and salt in a 2-quart heavy-bottomed saucepan and bring to a boil over medium-high heat.

Add the flour all at once, and stir vigorously with a wooden spoon until the flour is completely mixed into the mass, 1 to 2 minutes. The mixture will form a ball around the wooden spoon.

Remove the saucepan from the heat, and transfer the mixture to the bowl of a stand mixer or a mixing bowl. Using the flat beater attachment or a hand-held mixer, beat the mixture on medium speed until steam stops rising from it, about 4 minutes. Add the eggs 1 at a time, mixing well after each addition, and stopping frequently to scrape down the sides of the bowl with a rubber spatula. Beat for 1 to 2 minutes longer, until the mixture is smooth.

Choux pastry is best used immediately after it is prepared. However, if necessary, it can stand, covered, for 30 minutes before using.

PROFITEROLES

1 recipe Choux Pastry (above)
1 large egg lightly beaten with 1 teaspoon milk
3 cups vanilla, coffee, or chocolate ice cream, softened
6 ounces bittersweet chocolate, finely chopped
¾ cup heavy whipping cream

Position the oven racks to the upper and lower thirds of the oven and preheat to 400°F. Line 2 baking sheets with parchment paper.

Fit a 12- or 14-inch pastry bag with a #5 large plain tip and fill with choux pastry. Holding the pastry bag 1 inch above the baking sheet, pipe out 1-inch mounds of choux pastry, leaving 1 inch of space between them.

Brush the top of each mound with the egg wash mixture. Bake for 10 to 12 minutes. Switch the positions of the baking sheets and bake another 10 to 12 minutes, until the profiteroles are golden and firm. Check one profiterole by splitting it open. If it is still damp inside, bake the profiteroles another 3 to 5 minutes, until dry. Transfer the baking sheets to racks to cool completely.

To fill the profiteroles, use a serrated edge knife to split them open lengthwise. In the chilled bowl of a stand mixer, using the flat beater attachment, or in a mixing bowl using a hand-held mixer, whip the ice cream on medium speed until it holds firm peaks. Fit a pastry bag with a #4 large star tip and fill with the whipped ice cream. Pipe ice cream into the cavity of each puff until it mounds slightly over the top. Cover each profiterole with its top. Place the profiteroles on a baking sheet in a single layer, cover tightly with plastic wrap and freeze until ready to serve. The profiteroles can be frozen up to a week once they are filled. Unfilled profiteroles can be kept wrapped in foil at room temperature for 2 days before filling or they can be frozen, unfilled, for up to 4 months. If frozen, defrost overnight before filling.

For the chocolate sauce, melt the chopped chocolate in the top of a double boiler over hot, not simmering, water, stirring frequently with a rubber spatula to ensure even melting. In a $^1/_2$-quart saucepan, heat the cream over medium heat, until just before the boil. Remove the top pan from the double boiler and wipe the outside dry. Pour the cream into the chocolate and stir until smooth and completely blended. Let the sauce cool until it is warm, stirring frequently so it does not form a skin on top.

To serve the profiteroles, place 5 of them in a serving bowl, stacked in a pyramid shape. Drizzle about 2 tablespoons of the warm chocolate sauce over each serving of profiteroles.

CREAM PUFFS

1 recipe Choux Pastry (page 59)
1 large egg lightly beaten with 1 teaspoon milk
2 cups heavy whipping cream
2 teaspoons superfine sugar
1 teaspoon vanilla extract
$^1/_4$ cup confectioners' sugar for garnish

Position the oven racks to the upper and lower thirds of the oven and preheat to 400°F. Line 2 baking sheets with parchment paper.

Fit a 12- or 14-inch pastry bag with a #5 large plain tip and fill with choux pastry. Holding the pastry bag 1 inch above the baking sheet, pipe out 2¼-inch mounds of choux pastry, leaving 2 inches of space between them.

Brush the top of each mound with the egg wash mixture. Bake for 12 to 15 minutes. Switch the positions of the baking sheets and bake another 12 to 15 minutes, until the cream puffs are golden and firm. Check one cream puff by splitting it open. If it is still damp inside, bake the puffs another 3 to 5 minutes, until dry. Transfer the baking sheets to racks to cool completely.

To fill the cream puffs, use a serrated edge knife to split them in half horizontally. In the chilled bowl of a stand mixer, using the wire whip attachment, or in a mixing bowl, using a hand-held mixer, whip the cream on medium speed until it is frothy. Slowly sprinkle on the superfine sugar and continue whipping until the cream holds soft peaks. Blend in the vanilla. Fit a pastry bag with a #4 large star tip and fill with the whipped cream. Pipe cream into the cavity of each puff until it mounds slightly over the top. Cover each puff with its top. Dust the tops of the cream puffs with confectioners' sugar. Serve the cream puffs immediately or refrigerate for up to 3 hours before serving.

Baked cream puffs can be kept wrapped in foil at room temperature for 2 days before filling or they can be frozen, unfilled, for up to 4 months. If frozen, defrost overnight before filling.

ÉCLAIRS

1 recipe Choux Pastry (page 59)
1 large egg lightly beaten with 1 teaspoon milk
1 recipe Pastry Cream (page 221), can be optionally flavored
        with 5 ounces melted bittersweet chocolate or 2 tablespoons
        instant espresso powder dissolved in 2 tablespoons warm water
6 ounces bittersweet chocolate, finely chopped
⅔ cup heavy whipping cream

Position the oven racks to the upper and lower thirds of the oven and preheat to 400°F. Line 2 baking sheets with parchment paper.

Fit a 12- or 14-inch pastry bag with a #5 large plain tip and fill with choux pastry. Holding the pastry bag 1 inch above the baking sheet at a 45° angle, pipe out 4-inch-long fingers of choux pastry, leaving 2 inches of space between them. Or pipe the pastry into the cavities of an éclair plaque. *continued*

Brush the top of each éclair with the egg wash mixture. Use the tines of a fork to lightly score the tops of the éclairs. Bake for 12 to 15 minutes. Switch the positions of the baking sheets and bake another 12 to 15 minutes, until the éclairs are golden and firm. Check one éclair by splitting it open. If it is still damp inside, bake the éclairs another 3 to 5 minutes, until dry. Transfer the baking sheets to racks to cool completely.

To fill the éclairs, use a serrated edge knife to split them horizontally, leaving the top attached on one long side. Use the pastry cream flavored with vanilla or stir one of the other flavorings into the pastry cream. Fit a 12- or 14-inch pastry bag with a #5 large plain tip and fill with the pastry cream. Hold each éclair open with one hand while piping the filling into it up to the edge. Replace the top over each éclair.

For the chocolate sauce, melt the chopped chocolate in the top of a double boiler over hot, not simmering, water, stirring frequently with a rubber spatula to ensure even melting. In a $1/2$-quart saucepan, heat the cream over medium heat, until just before the boil. Remove the top pan from the double boiler and wipe the outside dry. Pour the cream into the chocolate and stir until smooth and completely blended. Let the sauce cool until it is warm, stirring frequently so it does not form a skin on top. Place about 1 tablespoon of chocolate sauce along the center top of each éclair. Serve the éclairs immediately or refrigerate for up to 3 hours before serving.

Baked éclairs can be kept wrapped in foil at room temperature for 2 days before filling or they can be frozen, unfilled, for up to 4 months. If frozen, defrost overnight before filling.

chuoi chien A Vietnamese dessert of bananas stuffed with a sweet filling such as pistachio or hazelnut paste, then dipped in batter of flour, cornstarch, sugar, and salt and deep-fried until golden brown. The stuffed bananas can also be flambéed. They are dusted with confectioners' sugar just before serving and served warm. Vietnam.

churro A Mexican deep-fried pastry, similar to a doughnut. Churros are made from a dough similar to choux pastry that is flavored with cinnamon. They are shaped using a pastry bag and tip into long, twisted strands and deep-fried in hot oil until golden brown and crisp outside. They are rolled in a mixture of cinnamon and sugar while warm. Mexico. See also: choux pastry and doughnut.

ciambella Translated from the Italian as "ring-shaped," ciambella is a buttery-rich, lemony pound cake baked in a pan with a center hole, such as a tube pan or Bundt pan. There are many variations of ciambella throughout Italy; some are made with raisins soaked in rum or brandy, others are made with cornmeal. Italy.

cinnamon This ancient spice is used extensively to flavor desserts, pastries, and confections. It is made from the interior bark of a tropical evergreen tree. The bark is dried and formed into tight curls, called quills, more commonly known as cinnamon sticks. The bark is also ground to a fine powder. There are two varieties of cinnamon: Ceylon cinnamon from Sri Lanka, which is true cinnamon, and cassia from China, which is a relative of cinnamon. Cassia has a dark reddish color and a more robust, aromatic, sweet flavor than the pale tan, more delicate Ceylon cinnamon. Most cinnamon sold in the United States is cassia. Cinnamon is widely available in supermarkets and gourmet shops. It should be stored in an airtight glass container in a cool, dark, dry place. Stick cinnamon has an indefinite shelf life. Ground cinnamon should be replaced every 6 months for maximum flavor.

citron A citrus fruit that looks like a very large, misshapen, yellow-green lemon. Citron has a hard, thick peel and very tart flesh. It is not eaten raw, because it is too sour and bitter. The peel is candied and used as an ingredient in desserts, pastries, and confections, particularly fruitcakes. Candied citron peel, which comes either chopped or in strips, is available in specialty and health food stores, and in some supermarkets, although the supermarket type usually contains preservatives. If candied citron is unavailable, substitute an equal amount of candied lemon peel with the addition of a teaspoon of lemon extract. Store candied citron in the freezer for up to 6 months. See also: citrus fruit and fruit.

citrus fruit A family of fruit native to Southeast Asia and now grown in warm climates all over the world. Noted for its skin and juicy, pulpy flesh, the citrus family includes the citron, clementine, grapefruit, lemon, lime, mandarin, orange, pomelo, tangelo, tangerine, and ugli fruit. Citrus fruits have a slightly acid flavor. Citrus fruits and their juices are used both raw and cooked as ingredients in many desserts, pastries, and confections. They are also used to make jams, marmalades, and several liqueurs. Choose fragrant fruit that is heavy for its size with smooth, unblemished skin. See also: citron, clementine, fruit, grapefruit, lemon, lime, mandarin, orange, pomelo, tangelo, tangerine, and ugli fruit.

citrus juicer See juicer.

citrus reamer A hand-held utensil used to extract the juice from citrus fruits. A reamer is a ribbed, pointed cone attached to a handle. The pointed end is pushed into the center of half a lemon, lime, orange, or grapefruit and twisted, releasing the juice from the fruit. Reamers are made of either wood or plastic. They are available at cookware shops and supermarkets.

clafouti A rustic type of fruit tart baked without a bottom pastry crust, **clafouti** originated in the Limousin region of France. Traditionally the fruit used to make a clafouti is dark, sweet cherries, unpitted, but almost any fruit can be used. A thick pancakelike custard batter is poured over the fruit in a deep buttered baking dish. The batter puffs when baked, forming a crust over the fruit. A clafouti is best served warm, dusted with confectioners' sugar and accompanied by ice cream or whipped cream. France.

CLAFOUTI

One 8-inch square clafouti; 8 to 10 servings

2 teaspoons unsalted butter, softened, for the pan
2 teaspoons granulated sugar, for the pan

1 pound fresh dark sweet cherries, pitted
1 teaspoon cornstarch
4 large eggs, at room temperature
¼ cup superfine sugar
¼ cup all-purpose flour, sifted
1⅔ cups milk
Pinch of salt
1 teaspoon vanilla extract

Confectioners' sugar for garnish

For serving
1 cup heavy whipping cream
2 tablespoons superfine sugar
1 teaspoon vanilla extract
or
1 pint vanilla ice cream

    Center a rack in the oven and preheat to 350°F. Generously butter the inside of an 8-inch square cake pan or other shallow 2-quart baking pan with the softened butter, then dust the inside with the sugar.

Arrange the cherries in a single layer in the baking pan. Sift the cornstarch over them.

In the bowl of a stand mixer, using the wire whip attachment, or in a mixing bowl, using a hand-held mixer, beat the eggs with the sugar until they are very thick and pale-colored and hold a slowly dissolving ribbon when the beaters are lifted, about 5 minutes. With the mixer on low speed, gradually sprinkle the flour onto the mixture, blending well.

Combine the milk, salt, and vanilla in a 2-cup measure. Add to the egg mixture in a steady stream with the mixer on low speed, stirring to blend well. Pour the custard over the cherries.

Bake the clafouti until the top is puffed and brown and a toothpick inserted in the center comes out clean, 45 to 50 minutes. Transfer to a rack to cool for 10 to 15 minutes before serving.

Meanwhile, if using the cream, whip it in the chilled bowl of a stand mixer, using the wire whip attachment, that has been chilled or in a chilled mixing bowl, using a hand-held mixer with chilled beaters, until frothy. Add the sugar and vanilla and continue to whip until the cream holds soft peaks.

Lightly dust the top of the clafouti with confectioners' sugar.

Scoop portions of the clafouti onto serving plates and top with a dollop of the whipped cream or with a scoop of vanilla ice cream.

Store the clafouti, covered with plastic wrap, for up to 2 days in the refrigerator. Warm it in a 350°F oven for 10 minutes before serving.

clementine A seedless citrus fruit hybrid created in North Africa in 1902 by Father Clément, by crossing the tangerine and the Seville orange. The clementine is a type of mandarin, noted for its thin, easily removed skin. Round, orange-colored, and tiny, the firm-skinned clementine is sweet and juicy. Clementines are used like oranges as an ingredient in many desserts, pastries, and confections. They are cultivated primarily in the countries of the Mediterranean basin, including Spain, Italy, Morocco, and Algeria, and are available from November to April, with the peak in December and January. Choose fragrant, plump, evenly colored fruit with firm skin that feels heavy for its size. Store clementines at room temperature for a few days or in the refrigerator for up to 2 weeks. See also: citrus fruit and fruit.

clotted cream Also called Devonshire cream, clotted cream is a rich, thick, scalded cream produced by slowly heating, cooking, and skimming cream or unpasteurized whole milk. The thickened cream rises to the surface, and after cooling it is removed. The treatment improves the keeping qualities of the cream by destroying the bacteria that would cause it to become sour. Clotted cream is made commercially primarily in the western regions of Devon, Cornwall, and Somerset, England. The cream used to make clotted cream is generally 55 percent cream. Clotted cream is traditionally served with scones and fresh fruit for breakfast and tea. United Kingdom.

clove The dried unopened bud of a tropical evergreen tree that is native to the Spice Islands of Indonesia. The name comes from the Latin *clavus*, meaning nail, which the buds resemble. Cloves were in use in China many centuries before they were discovered and enthusiastically embraced by Western cultures. Cloves add a sweet, warm, pungent flavor to gingerbread, cakes, and cookies. Cloves are available both whole and finely ground, the best form to use for desserts, pastries, and confections. Ground cloves are best stored in an airtight container in a cool, dark, dry place. They should be replaced every 6 months for maximum flavor.

coat a spoon A technique that tests whether a mixture, such as a cooked custard, is ready: If the mixture is cooked enough, it will leave a uniform coating and cling to a spoon. To make the test, a spoon is dipped into the custard and held aloft, then a line is drawn with a finger across the spoon. If the custard holds its shape and does not obliterate the line, it is done.

cobbler A popular American deep-dish fruit dessert with a rich, thick, biscuit-type dough on top of the fruit. The dough is often drizzled with melted butter and sprinkled with sugar before baking. Often the dough is placed on the top of the fruit in small mounds, which results in a cobblestone look after it is baked. Cobblers are usually made in square or rectangular pans that are a minimum of 2 inches deep. Cobblers, such as **fresh mixed berry cobbler**, are often served with either vanilla ice cream or sweetened whipped cream and are best eaten warm. United States. See also: buckle, grunt, pandowdy, and slump.

FRESH MIXED BERRY COBBLER

One 8-inch square cobbler; 8 to 10 servings

7 cups fresh berries, such as blueberries, blackberries, raspberries, olallieberries, or boysenberries
¾ cup granulated sugar

2 tablespoons freshly squeezed lemon juice
2 ounces (4 tablespoons) unsalted butter, softened

Biscuit dough
1 cup all-purpose flour
2 tablespoons granulated sugar
2 teaspoons baking powder
1/4 teaspoon salt
2 ounces (4 tablespoons) unsalted butter, chilled, cut into pieces
1/4 cup plus 2 tablespoons milk or light whipping cream

1 ounce (2 tablespoons) unsalted butter, melted
1 to 2 tablespoons granulated sugar
1 cup heavy cream, whipped to soft peaks

Position a rack in the center of the oven and preheat to 425°F.

Place the berries in an 8-inch square baking pan and sprinkle them with the sugar. Drizzle the lemon juice over the berries, then dot them all over with the softened butter.

For the biscuit dough, combine the flour, sugar, baking powder, and salt in the work bowl of a food processor fitted with the steel blade. Add the chilled butter and pulse until the butter is cut into very tiny pieces. Add the milk or cream, and mix until the dough forms a ball, about 30 seconds.

Roll the biscuit dough out on a lightly floured work surface to approximately a 9-inch square and a thickness of about 1/4 inch. Very gently roll the biscuit dough up around a rolling pin, then lift the rolling pin over the baking pan and gently unroll the dough over the berries. Trim the excess dough with a sharp knife, and lightly push the edges of the dough down into the pan with your fingertips to create a tight fit.

Drizzle the melted butter over the dough and sprinkle 1 or 2 tablespoons of sugar evenly over it. Place the baking pan on a baking sheet, and bake for 35 to 45 minutes, until the juices are bubbling and the biscuit crust is light golden brown. Transfer to a rack to cool slightly.

Serve the cobbler warm, cutting it into squares and scooping each square out onto a plate, with the fruit up. Place a large dollop of whipped cream on the fruit.

The dough will become soggy if the cobbler stands, so it is best eaten within a few hours of preparation.

cocada amarela A yellow coconut pudding from Mozambique. Sugar, water, and cloves are simmered together until a thick syrup is formed, then coconut is added. Egg yolks are beaten with sugar and added to the coconut mixture, and it is cooked until thick. The pudding is poured into shallow bowls or dishes, sprinkled with ground cinnamon, and chilled for a few hours, until set. Mozambique.

cocoa butter The ivory-colored naturally occurring fat in cocoa beans, cocoa butter is extracted from the beans during the process of producing chocolate and cocoa powder. It is added to chocolate liquor to give chocolate its smooth texture and rich flavor. Cocoa butter is the base of white chocolate. See also: chocolate and cocoa powder.

cocoa powder The cocoa bean, which produces both chocolate and cocoa powder, grows on the tropical evergreen tree Theobroma cacao. The beans are removed from the large pods that grow on the branches and the trunk of the tree, fermented, and dried. Then the beans are sent to chocolate factories, where they are roasted, the outer hulls removed, and the inner nibs ground to produce chocolate liquor. Most of the cocoa butter is extracted from the chocolate liquor, leaving a dry cake called press cake, which is further processed into unsweetened cocoa powder. If the cocoa is treated with alkali to produce a dark, mellow-flavored powder, it is called Dutch-processed. See also: chocolate and Dutch-processed.

coconut The fruit of the coconut palm tree, native to Malaysia. Coconuts are widely cultivated in Africa, South America, India, Southeast Asia, the Pacific Islands, and other tropical countries. Coconuts are large and round or oval-shaped with a hard, fibrous, brown outer shell. On one end they have three small round "eyes." Fresh coconut is available year-round, although the peak period is September through January. Choose a coconut that feels heavy and sounds full of liquid when shaken. The outer shell of the coconut must be cracked open with a hammer or another strong tool to reach the milky-white meat, which is covered by a thinner brown skin. To accomplish this, pierce one of the eyes to drain the liquid inside, then crack open the shell and pry the meat away from the shell. To help release the meat from the shell more easily, dry the coconut in a 350°F oven for about 20 minutes. After the thin brown skin attached to the meat is removed with a knife or vegetable parer, the meat can be cut into pieces or grated by hand or in a food processor.

Coconut has a rich, sweet, slightly nutty flavor. It is widely used in desserts, pastries, and confections in cuisines throughout the world. It is available in many forms, including dried grated, shredded, and flaked, either sweetened or unsweetened. It is also available frozen. Often coconut is toasted to enhance the flavor. Fresh coconut is also used to thicken and flavor many desserts. Coconut milk and cream made from fresh coconut are used in desserts in many Asian cuisines. Coconut milk and cream can also be made by soaking dried coconut in milk or water, then squeezing out the liquid. Coconut cream is made from the rich liquid that floats to the top of the milk after the first pressing—or by increasing the amount of dried coconut added to the liquid. Coconut cream and coconut milk are unsweetened and available in cans in many major supermarkets and Asian markets. Homemade coconut cream and milk must be stored in the refrigerator and used within a day. Once opened, the commercial varieties will last up to a week tightly covered in the refrigerator. Dried coconut will last for several months stored in a tightly covered container in the refrigerator.

coconut cream See coconut.

coconut milk See coconut.

coconut oil See fats and oils.

coeur à la crème This is a classic cheese dessert composed of a blend of cream cheese and sweetened whipped cream or crème fraîche. Occasionally cottage cheese and sour cream are used as ingredients in the dessert. **Coeur à la crème** is molded in either a heart-shaped wicker basket lined with cheesecloth or a porcelain mold with bottom holes, both of which allow the whey (liquid) to drain off. This gives a firmer texture to the crème. The dessert is chilled for several hours, then unmolded and served with fresh berries or a berry sauce. France. See also: coeur à la crème mold.

∾∾∾∾∾∾∾∾∾∾

COEUR À LA CRÈME

6 servings

8 ounces cream cheese, softened
2 tablespoons confectioners' sugar, sifted
Pinch of salt
1/2 teaspoon vanilla extract
2/3 cup crème fraîche (see page 86) or 1/2 cup heavy whipping
    cream, whipped to soft peaks
2 cups fresh raspberries or strawberries
1 tablespoon granulated sugar
1 teaspoon freshly squeezed lemon juice   *continued*

Cut a double piece of cheesecloth to fit a 2-cup heart-shaped coeur à la crème basket or mold, with enough extra length so it can be doubled over the top. Dampen the cheesecloth and wring it out. Line the basket or mold with the cheesecloth, letting the excess hang over the edges.

In the bowl of a stand mixer, using the flat beater attachment, or in a mixing bowl, using a hand-held mixer, beat the cream cheese until it is light and fluffy, about 2 minutes. Add the confectioners' sugar and salt and beat to blend well. Stir the vanilla into the crème fraîche or whipped cream, then fold the crème into the cream cheese mixture in 3 additions, blending well after each addition.

Turn the mixture into the basket or mold, and smooth the top. Cover the top with the overlapping ends of the cheesecloth. Place the basket or mold on a shallow plate to catch the drippings, and refrigerate for 8 to 12 hours.

Pour off any liquid that has accumulated on the plate. To unmold the coeur, fold the edges of the cheesecloth back, place a serving plate over the basket or mold, and invert the coeur onto the plate. Remove the cheesecloth.

Place 1 cup of the raspberries or strawberries in the work bowl of a food processor fitted with the steel blade, add the sugar and lemon juice, and purée the mixture. Strain to remove any seeds.

Arrange the remaining berries around the coeur. Place a pool of sauce on each individual plate, then slice the coeur and set it on top of the sauce.

The coeur will keep for 2 days tightly covered in the refrigerator.

coeur à la crème mold A heart-shaped wicker basket or a heart-shaped porcelain mold about 1 inch high with holes in the bottom is the traditional mold used to shape this classic dessert. The wicker or the holes allow the excess liquid to drain off, giving a firmer texture to the crème. The molds and baskets are available in both individual and large size, ranging from 3 to 7 inches in length and diameter. They can be found at cookware shops and through mail order cookware catalogs. See also: coeur à la crème.

coffee cake A sweet, rich, yeast- or baking powder-leavened cakelike bread that often contains nuts and fruits, coffee cake is traditionally served with afternoon coffee or tea, for breakfast, or brunch. Coffee cakes are sometimes frosted or given a streusel topping. They can be served with no adornment, but are often spread with butter or jam. Coffee cake is best served warm. See also: streusel.

Cognac French brandy distilled from the white wine made from select grapes grown in and around the town of Cognac in the west of France. After it is heated twice to specific temperatures, the wine is aged in Limousin oak barrels, where it develops its characteristic flavor. The stars on the label indicate the number of years the brandy has been aged, with one star corresponding to 3 years. The categories V.S. (very special) and V.S.O.P. (very special old pale) indicate brandies that have been aged longer than 5 years. The term "Fine Champagne" on the label indicates that over half of the grapes come from the area around Cognac known as Grande Champagne, considered to produce the best grapes. The richly flavored, clear, pale-orange brandy is used extensively to flavor desserts, pastries, and confections. France.

Cointreau A clear, colorless liqueur flavored with natural orange essence and orange peels, Cointreau has been made in France since 1849. Cointreau has a sweet, slightly piquant orange flavor. It is used to flavor desserts, pastries, and confections. France.

colomba Translated literally from the Italian as "dove," colomba is a traditional Easter cake made in the shape of a dove. Colomba is made from a rich yeast-risen dough, similar to panettone, that is full of candied fruit and flavorings and topped with crystallized sugar and toasted unblanched almonds. Italy. See also: panettone.

Comice pear A round, stocky winter pear with practically no neck, the Comice is the most flavorful of all the pears. Its skin ranges in color from brownish-green to yellow, often streaked with red. The creamy white flesh is very fragrant and sweet with a buttery texture. Comice pears are used both raw and cooked as an ingredient in desserts, pastries, and confections. It is a favorite pear for baked goods and baking and poaching whole because it holds its shape. Comice pears are available from October through January. Choose very fragrant, firm, blemish-free fruit. The pears should give very slightly when pressed at the stem end; if they are soft, they are overripe. Store ripe Comice pears in the refrigerator for up to a week. See also: fruit and pear.

compote A dessert of fresh or dried fruit, either whole or cut into pieces, cooked in a sugar syrup flavored with cinnamon, vanilla, cloves, and orange or lemon zest. If dried fruit is used, it is usually soaked before cooking. The fruit is cooked slowly so it holds its shape. The dessert is served slightly warm, accompanied by whipping cream, or chilled and served cold, lightly sprinkled with kirsch or brandy. A compote can also be used as an ingredient in other desserts—for example, as the filling for turnovers or tarts—or to garnish an ice cream sundae. France and United States.

conch, conching Conching is the technique for stirring liquid chocolate during the manufacturing process to make it extremely smooth and palatable. The liquid chocolate is poured into a deep container, then a heavy roller moves back and forth over the liquid mixture continuously, breaking down any particles and thoroughly mixing the ingredients. The result is a mellow-tasting, melt-in-the-mouth chocolate. Conching may last as long as 72 hours. Both the technique and the machine used for it were developed by the pioneer Swiss chocolate manufacturer Rodolphe Lindt, in the late nineteenth century. The name comes from the Spanish word for shell, *concha*, the shape the first conching troughs resembled. See also: chocolate.

confection A prepared sweet dish, a sweetmeat, or a candy.

confectioners' foil Brightly colored foil used to wrap candies, individual pastries, or pieces of cake for an attractive presentation. The foil is stronger than aluminum foil and does not tear easily, but it conforms very well to the shape of the item that it wraps. Confectioners' foil comes in many colors, in squares in a variety of sizes. It is available at cake decorating and candy making supply shops and through mail order catalogs.

confectioners' sugar See sugar.

confectionery The general category of sweets and of food products based on sugar, such as marzipan, caramels, and other candies, including chocolates. Confectionery is also the term for a candy shop, for the art of sweet making, and for the techniques and processes for producing sweets and candies.

confectionery coating A substitute for pure chocolate, confectionery coating is made with a vegetable fat other than cocoa butter, sugar, milk solids, and a variety of flavorings. Confectionery coating is used for dipping candies and for molding. Because it does not contain cocoa butter, it does not need to be tempered; however, for the same reason, it lacks the rich flavor of real chocolate. Confectionery coating is also called summer coating. See also: chocolate, cocoa butter, and tempering chocolate.

confiserie The French word for confectionery. See also: confectionery.

confiture The French word for jam, jelly, marmalade, and fruit preserves. See also: jam, jelly, marmalade, and preserves.

conserve A mixture of at least two fruits cooked with sugar, raisins, and nuts until thick. Citrus fruit, often in the form of zest, is usually added to the mixture. Conserves are used as a spread on quick breads, scones, and muffins, as a topping for ice cream, as a sauce for desserts, and as a filling in cakes and cookies. See also: jam, jelly, marmalade, and preserves.

convection oven A fan that evenly and consistently circulates the hot air throughout is the unique feature of this oven. It is generally regarded as the best oven for baking and pastry making because it bakes evenly, rapidly, and efficiently. A convection oven bakes at least 30 percent faster than a conventional oven, and at a lower heat. It also allows many items to be baked at the same time, since very little air space is needed between them. Convection ovens are available as compact stand-alone countertop models that are a little larger than the standard toaster oven and as large freestanding models for use in commercial kitchens.

cookie From the Dutch word *koekje*, meaning small cake, cookies are small, sweet, flat or slightly raised cakes. Called biscuits in England and biscotti in Italy, cookies are universal. Each country has its own classic cookies, whether they are elegant or earthy. Cookies come in a variety of textures, crisp and crunchy or soft and chewy, and in a multitude of shapes and flavors. There are many types of cookies, classified by how they are made. For drop cookies, a soft batter is dropped from a spoon onto a baking sheet. For rolled cookies, the dough is rolled out with a rolling pin and cut with a cookie cutter or a decoratively carved rolling pin. Bar cookies are formed by baking the batter in a square or rectangular pan, then cutting into bars after baking. Molded cookies are formed by fitting the dough into molds, then tapping the dough out before baking. Hand-formed cookies are shaped by hand into balls, logs, or crescents. Pressed cookies are made by pressing the dough through a cookie press or through a pastry bag, forming different shapes. Refrigerator cookies are made by shaping the dough into logs, chilling it, then slicing and baking. Eaten as snacks, for afternoon tea, and for dessert, many cookies, such as kourambiedes from Greece and Swiss **pofer cookies**, are traditionally served during special celebrations and holidays. See also: biscotti, cookie cutter, cookie mold, cookie press, cookie sheet, cookie stamp, gingerbread, kourambiedes, langues de chat, macaroon, madeleine, mandelbrot, rolling pin, shortbread, speculaa, and springerle.

∽∽∽∽∽∽∽∽∽∽

POFER COOKIES

3½ dozen cookies

10½ ounces (1 stick plus 5 tablespoons) unsalted butter, softened
1 cup granulated sugar
2 cups finely ground almonds
¼ teaspoon ground cinnamon
½ teaspoon vanilla extract
2 large eggs, at room temperature, lightly beaten
4 cups all-purpose flour
Pinch of salt
1¼ cups apricot or raspberry preserves
½ cup confectioners' sugar, for garnish

In the bowl of a stand mixer, using the flat beater attachment, or in a mixing bowl, using a hand-held mixer, beat the butter until light and fluffy, about 3 minutes. Add the sugar and cream the mixture until light, about 1 minute. Scrape down the sides of the bowl with a rubber spatula. Add the finely ground almonds in 3 additions, blending well after each addition. Beat in the cinnamon and vanilla. Add the lightly beaten eggs and blend well.

Mix the flour with the salt, and beat into the almond mixture in 3 additions, stopping to scrape down the sides of the bowl with a rubber spatula as necessary. Then beat the dough until it is smooth, about 2 minutes. Gather the dough together and wrap in plastic. Chill for at least 3 hours, or until it is firm enough to roll out. (The dough can be kept in the refrigerator for up to 3 days, or it can be frozen. If frozen, defrost it overnight before using.)

Position the racks in the upper and lower thirds of the oven and preheat to 350°F. Line three baking sheets with parchment paper. Roll out half of the dough on a lightly floured work surface to a thickness of ¼ inch. Using a fluted 3-inch round cutter, cut circles out of the dough. Using a fluted 1-inch round cutter, cut out the centers of half of the circles.

Place the circles on the baking sheets, with 1 inch of space between them, and bake for 6 minutes. Switch the positions of the baking sheets and bake for 6 to 8 minutes longer, until the cookies are light golden colored and set. Transfer the baking sheets to the racks to cool completely. Repeat with the remaining cookie dough.

Place a teaspoon of jam in the center of each of the cookies without a center hole. Heavily dust the cookies with the holes with the confectioners' sugar, and place these on top of the cookies with the jam, forming sandwiches.

The cookies can be kept for up to 4 days in an airtight container at room temperature before they are assembled. Once they are assembled, they will keep for 1 day wrapped tightly in foil at room temperature.

cookie cutter Made of either plastic or metal with sharp edges, about 1 inch deep, and usually open on top as well as bottom—although some have handles—cookie cutters are available in numerous shapes and sizes. They are used to cut rolled-out cookie dough or other doughs into various shapes before baking. Cutting the dough is easier if they are first dipped in flour. Cookie cutters can be purchased separately or in sets. The sets may have graduated sizes of the same shape, or they may be theme-related; for example, for a particular holiday. There is also a rolling cookie cutter that is a metal drum or cylinder mounted on a short wooden handle. The cylinder is imprinted with a series of raised designs that leave no wasted space. When the cutter is rolled over the dough, it cuts the designs into the dough repeatedly. The big advantage to this type of cutter is its efficiency, since it uses all of the dough and is quicker.

cookie mold Cookie molds are usually wood or ceramic and come in many shapes and sizes. They are used to make decorative designs in cookie dough. The cookie dough is pressed or rolled into the floured mold and flattened out. The mold is then inverted and tapped to release the dough. Springerle, German anise seed Christmas cookies, are traditionally molded, as is Scottish shortbread. Molds are also available for forming gingerbread houses. These are heavy rectangular cast-iron molds with indentations that form the shape of the houses and their different parts, such as windows, doors, and roofs. Gingerbread cookie house molds and other types of cookie molds are available at cookware shops and through mail order cookware catalogs.

cookie press This tool is also called a cookie gun. It has a cylindrical barrel with several different round templates or nozzles that fit at one end. At the other end is a trigger or plunger mechanism that, when pushed, forces the soft cookie dough out through the template, forming various shapes.

cookie sheet See baking sheet.

cookie stamp Made of glass, ceramic, plastic, or wood, a cookie stamp is usually round or square and only a few inches in diameter. It has a small knob handle on top and a decorative design is etched into the underside. The cookie stamp is used to press a small ball of unbaked cookie dough flat, giving the cookie its shape and imprinting the design into the dough. Dipping the cookie stamp into flour between pressings keeps it from sticking to the dough. Cookie stamps are available in many different designs at cookware shops and through mail order cookware catalogs.

cooling rack A kitchen utensil used to cool baked cakes, cookies, and breads. The flat rack is made from closely spaced parallel metal wires that rest on small feet (about 1/2 inch high), which suspend it above the counter. The rack allows air to circulate around the baked goods so steam does not build up, which would cause them to become soggy on the bottom. Cooling racks are available in round, square, or rectangular shapes and several sizes. They should be sturdy so they will not collapse from the weight of the pans or baked goods they hold.

copper egg white bowl With a rounded bottom and sloping sides, this spherical unlined copper bowl is the classic choice for whipping egg whites by hand with a wire balloon whisk. It is a large deep bowl available in sizes ranging from 9 to 14 inches in diameter. The top has a rolled rim with a hanging ring set just below the rim. A copper bowl insert is also available for the bowls for some brands of heavy-duty electric mixers. Copper has a chemical reaction with the albumen (protein) in egg whites that helps to stabilize them, allowing them to hold more air, and thereby increasing their volume by at least one third more than any other method of whipping. For that reason, a copper bowl for whipping egg whites is very highly regarded by cooks and chefs. To care for a copper bowl, clean it thoroughly with warm soapy water or a mixture of coarse salt and lemon juice, rinse clean, and wipe it thoroughly dry before using. See also: whisk.

corer A hand-held utensil designed to remove the center, or core, from fruit. There are several different corers designed for use with specific fruits. Most have stainless steel blades with wood handles. An apple corer has either a long, hollow, cylindrical shaft or a short (1/2-inch-long) ring at the end of a metal shaft. The edges are sharp and may be either plain or serrated. To use, plunge it into the center of the apple from the stem to the bottom, removing the core in one piece. An apple corer is also used to core other fruits, such as pears. However, there is a corer that is designed specifically for pears. It has a short wooden handle with a sharp, pointed loop of metal at the other end. To use, slice the pear in half lengthwise. Press the corer against the center of the pear and gently pull downward. A pineapple corer resembles a doughnut cutter, but it is taller, to fit the height of a pineapple. It has both a center and an outer sharp serrated metal ring, held together by U-shaped handles that are joined at the top. First the top and bottom must be cut off the pineapple, then the cutter is pushed down into the fruit with a twisting motion, removing the outer skin and the core at the same time.

Another utensil, frequently called a fruit or apple slicer/corer, cores and slices fruit at the same time. It is round and flat with sharp spokes that radiate from a ¹/₂-inch center circle. The sides of the tool flatten out to form handles. It is pushed down into the fruit from the top, neatly removing the core and cutting uniform slices. This tool is used most often for apples or pears.

Still another tool is called a parer/corer/slicer or a peeler/corer/slicer. It is made of cast iron or stainless steel and clamps onto a table or coun tertop. It has a U-shaped frame with a hand-cranked handle at one side, which turns a shaft that pushes an apple against two cutting blades on the opposite side. Another blade hits the bottom of the fruit. As the handle is turned, the apple rotates against the blades, which simultaneously core, peel, and slice it. All of these corers are available at cookware shops and supermarkets and through mail order cookware catalogs.

coriander A member of the carrot family, the coriander plant is native to the Far and Middle East and the Mediterranean basin. Its culinary use has been traced as far back as seven thousand years, documented in Sanskrit writings. The Romans spread the use of coriander throughout Europe and it was brought to the New World with seventeenth-century explorers and settlers. The dried seeds of the coriander plant have a warm, sweet, pungent taste, slightly like orange peel. The seeds are widely used to flavor desserts, breads, and pastries, particularly in Scandinavia. The tiny cream, green, or brown seeds are used both whole and finely ground. Whole coriander seeds will keep indefinitely stored in a tightly sealed glass jar in a cool, dry place. Once ground, the seeds rapidly lose flavor. Ground coriander should be stored tightly sealed in a dark, dry place and replaced every 4 to 6 months for maximum flavor.

corne See pastry scraper.

cornmeal Ground from dried corn to a fine, medium, or coarse texture, cornmeal is used as an ingredient in desserts and pastries. Most cornmeal is made from either yellow or white corn, but blue cornmeal is available in some specialty shops. There are two main types of cornmeal: stone-ground, which retains the bran and germ, and steel-ground, from which the bran and germ have been removed. Stone-ground cornmeal is available in bulk in many health food stores. It is perishable and should be stored in an airtight container in the refrigerator for no longer than 4 months. Steel-ground cornmeal is sold in boxes in most supermarkets. It can be stored in a covered container in a cool, dry place for up to a year. When used in baked goods, cornmeal is usually mixed with flour.

corn oil A flavorless oil processed from corn kernels. Polyunsaturated corn oil has no cholesterol and is a major ingredient in many brands of margarine. Because corn oil has a high smoke point, it is particularly good for frying. Corn oil is used as an ingredient in desserts, pastries, and confections. It is virtually interchangeable with other vegetable oils, such as canola, olive, peanut, safflower, soybean, and sunflower. Corn oil is widely available in supermarkets. Store corn oil tightly capped in a dark place at room temperature for up to 6 months or in the refrigerator for up to a year. If it becomes cloudy in the refrigerator, let it stand at room temperature to clarify. See also: fats and oil and smoke point.

cornstarch A fine white powder milled from the inner grain, or endosperm, of corn. Cornstarch is most often used as a thickening agent for custards and sauces. It works best when first mixed with a small amount of cold water, then heated. This technique prevents it from forming lumps. Since cornstarch contains no protein, it thickens more rapidly than flour, and when heated, it becomes clear rather than opaque. Generally, 1 tablespoon of cornstarch has the thickening capacity of $1^1/_2$ to 2 tablespoons of all-purpose flour. Cornstarch is also mixed with flour in many recipes for European cakes and cookies, to give them a fine, light texture, similar to the result when using cake flour. The British term for cornstarch is *cornflour*. Cornstarch is widely available in boxes at supermarkets. It will keep indefinitely if stored in a cool, dry place.

corn syrup A thick liquid syrup sweetener derived from mixing cornstarch with acids or enzymes. Corn syrup is available both light and dark. Light corn syrup has been clarified to remove any color, and dark corn syrup has either refiners' syrup or caramel color and flavor added. Corn syrup is highly valued in confectionery and baking because it is an interfering agent, meaning that it inhibits crystallization during the process of cooking sugar, thereby preventing candies from developing a grainy texture. It also helps prevent moisture loss, which gives confections and baked goods a longer shelf life. Corn syrup is widely available in glass bottles in supermarkets. It will last indefinitely if stored tightly capped in the refrigerator after opening.

cotignac A French confection from the city of Orléans, cotignac has been made for hundreds of years. It is reported to have been presented to Joan of Arc on her triumphant entry into Orléans. Cotignac is made from a sweetened quince paste, which turns pink naturally from its exposure to air. The paste is cut into rounds or pressed into molds engraved with the image of Joan of Arc and packed into thin, round wooden boxes, then air-dried. France.

coulis A thick sauce of puréed raw or cooked fruit, used as a garnish for desserts, ice creams, and pastries. Originally this term referred to thickened meat juices. Today it applies to the juices of vegetables, fish, chicken, and fruit. France.

coupler A two-piece plastic device used to attach a pastry tip to a pastry bag. A coupler allows the tips to be changed without having to change the pastry bag. A cylindrical piece that has threads in the center fits into the pastry bag. Its wide top keeps it from falling out of the pastry bag, while the bottom protrudes from the bag. The pastry tip is placed onto the bottom of the coupler and a plastic ring with inside threads fitted over the pastry tip and is secured by screwing it onto the other half of the coupler. Couplers are available in both small and large sizes to fit pastry tips of different sizes. They are most often used with small decorating tips. See also: pastry bag and pastry tip.

couverture A type of chocolate that has a minimum of 32 percent cocoa butter, which is higher than regular chocolate, making it ideal for the thin, smooth, shiny coatings for dipped truffles and candies. Couverture is used for coating by professional confectioners. Because of its high cocoa butter content, it must be tempered before use. Besides coating candies and truffles, couverture can be used for molding, baking, dessert making, candy making, pastry making, and eating out of hand. See also: chocolate, cocoa butter, and tempering chocolate.

cranberry A small, round, smooth-skinned, bright red berry with tart, acidic flavor. Cranberries are native to northern Europe and North America. They are grown on low vines in large flooded areas, called cranberry bogs. Cranberries are used raw, cooked, and dried as an ingredient in desserts, pastries, and confections such as cobblers, quick breads, muffins, pies, custards, candies, and a classic Russian dessert, kissel. They are also used to make compotes, jams, and jellies. Frozen cranberries are available year-round. Fresh cranberries are available from September to December, packed in plastic bags. Choose firm, bright, evenly colored berries. Store cranberries in their plastic bags in the refrigerator for up to 2 months or in the freezer for up to a year. Wash them just before use. See also: berry.

cream The fat part of milk that rises to the top. In modern dairies, machines use centrifugal force to bring the cream to the top. There are several types of cream available. Whipping cream, also called light whipping cream, is between 30 and 36 percent butterfat; heavy whipping cream, also called manufacturing cream, is between 36 and 40 percent butterfat; and light cream, also called table cream or coffee cream, is between 18 and 30 percent butterfat. Half-and-half is a blend of half cream and half milk that contains about 10$\frac{1}{2}$ percent butterfat. Ultrapasteurized cream is made by briefly heating cream to 300°F to kill the bacteria that cause cream to sour. This process gives the cream a longer shelf life, but it will not whip as well and its taste is affected.

Sour cream, which is thick and fluffy, it made by adding an acidifier, either lactic acid–producing bacteria or vinegar, to cream and letting it stand for several hours, until the cream curdles. This process produces sour cream's characteristic tangy flavor. Sour cream contains about 18 percent butterfat. Light sour cream, made with half-and-half, has about half the fat of regular sour cream.

Cream is widely used in desserts, pastries, and confections, both as an ingredient and as an accompaniment. Cream provides a smooth, satiny texture and a rich, buttery taste to a vast variety of desserts, pastries, and confections. It also gives body and tenderness to baked goods. Because of the large amount of fat it contains, cream holds its shape when whipped. For stability, chill the cream, bowl, and beater before whipping. Cream is highly perishable and should be kept refrigerated until used.

The term "to cream" refers to a technique for mixing or beating together fat and other ingredients, such as sugar, until they are smooth, creamy, and well blended. The mixture should be so well combined that it is not possible to distinguish the individual ingredients. Creaming is best done when the fat is at room temperature, so that it can fully incorporate the sugar without graininess. Creaming also traps air that expands when heated in the oven, helping to leaven the baked goods. See also: crème fraîche.

cream cheese A soft, delicate, creamy, unripened cheese made from cows' milk. Cream cheese has a mildly acid flavor and a smooth, spreadable texture. It lends itself well to other flavors, and it is widely used as an ingredient in many types of cheesecake, pastry dough, tarts, and cookies, as well as other desserts and confections. Cream cheese is made from milk cultured with bacteria, salt, and stabilizers. It comes in two styles: regular, made from whole milk, and light, also called neufchâtel style, made from skim or low-fat milk. Light cream cheese has one third less fat and 30 percent fewer calories than regular. Cream cheese is available in 8-ounce and 3-ounce packages in supermarkets. Soft cream cheese is softer than regular cream cheese, and whipped cream cheese has air whipped into it to make it fluffy. Because of the different texture of soft cream cheese and the added air in whipped cream cheese, they cannot be substituted for regular or light cream cheese in baking. Cream cheese is highly perishable and should be kept refrigerated. It should be used by the pull date on the package.

cream horn An individual pastry made of a thin strip of puff pastry that is wound around a cone-shaped metal form, brushed with beaten egg, dredged in sugar, and baked until crisp and golden brown. When cool, the pastry horn is slipped from the metal form and filled with crème Chantilly. France. See also: cream horn mold, crème Chantilly, and puff pastry.

cream horn mold A tapered tinned-steel tube about 1 inch in diameter and 6 inches long. A strip of puff pastry is wrapped around the form and baked to make a cream horn. When the baked dough is cool, the mold is removed, leaving the dough in a cone shape to hold its cream filling. A similar but more pronounced cone-shaped form that tapers to a point at one end is called a ladylock form. Cream horn molds are available in sets of six at cookware shops and through mail order cookware catalogs. See also: cream horn.

cream of tartar Tartaric acid is a fast-acting fine white crystalline acid salt that is a by-product of the wine-making industry. This powdery substance, which is deposited on the inside of wine casks after fermentation, is refined to produce commercial cream of tartar. In candy making, cream of tartar is used to prevent crystallization of sugar mixtures as they cook because it gets in the way of the movement of sucrose and slows down the crystallizing process. This action prevents graininess in finished candies. Cream of tartar is a component of baking powder, which is used as a leavening agent in many baked goods. When added to egg whites during whipping, cream of tartar stabilizes them and allows them to reach maximum volume. It also accelerates coagulation in eggs during cooking. Cream of tartar will last indefinitely if stored in an airtight container in a cool, dry place. See also: baking powder and crystallization.

cream puff An individual pastry made from choux pastry dough, a cream puff is a round, hollow, baked shell. When cool, the puff is split open and filled with a variety of creams or custards, such as crème Chantilly and crème pâtissière. Miniature cream puffs are called profiteroles. They are most often stacked in a shallow bowl and drizzled with chocolate sauce to create a favorite dessert. Cream puffs are also used to make Gâteau Saint-Honoré, croquembouche, and religieuse pastries. France. See also: choux pastry, croquembouche, Gâteau Saint-Honoré, pastry cream, profiterole, and religieuse.

cream puff pastry See choux pastry.

crème anglaise The French term for a rich, pourable, stirred custard sauce used to accompany cakes, desserts, and fruit. **Crème anglaise** can be served warm or cold. Variations include orange, lemon, raspberry, chocolate, coffee, caramel, and praline, and it can be flavored with various liqueurs. It is also used as the base for many chilled or frozen desserts, such as Bavarian cream and ice cream. France. See also: Bavarian cream and ice cream.

⌇⌇⌇⌇⌇⌇⌇⌇⌇⌇⌇

CRÈME ANGLAISE

1 ½ cups

1 cup milk
1 vanilla bean
4 large egg yolks, at room temperature
⅓ cup granulated sugar

Optional flavorings
⅓ cup praline paste
4 ounces bittersweet chocolate, melted
2 tablespoons liqueur
2 teaspoons instant espresso powder dissolved in 2 teaspoons
    warm water
⅓ cup fresh fruit purée, such as raspberry
Finely minced zest of 1 large lemon
Finely minced zest of 1 medium orange

Place the milk in a 2-quart heavy-bottomed saucepan. Using a sharp knife, split the vanilla bean lengthwise. Scrape out the seeds and add them and the bean to the milk. Heat the milk over medium heat to just below the boiling point.

Meanwhile, in the bowl of a stand mixer, using the wire whip attachment, or in a mixing bowl, using a hand-held mixer, beat the egg yolks and sugar together until they are pale yellow and hold a slowly dissolving ribbon when the beater is lifted, about 4 minutes.

Turn the mixer speed to low and slowly add about half of the hot milk to the egg yolk mixture, blending well. Then pour this mixture back into the saucepan. Place the pan over low heat and cook, stirring constantly with a wooden spoon, until the custard has thickened and registers 175° to 180°F on a candy thermometer, or until steam is rising from the pan, 6 to 8 minutes. At this point, a line drawn through the custard with the back of the spoon should leave a clearly defined path.

Strain the custard into a glass or metal bowl. Stir in the optional flavorings if desired. Cover the custard, cool to room temperature, then chill in the refrigerator. The custard will thicken slightly as it chills. Crème anglaise will keep for up to 3 days, well covered, in the refrigerator.

⌇⌇⌇⌇⌇⌇⌇⌇⌇⌇⌇

crème au beurre The French term for buttercream. See also: buttercream.

crème au beurre au lait A French variation of buttercream, made with the addition of pastry cream, which produces a softer, less rich buttercream than the classic version. See also: buttercream.

crème brûlée Translated as "burnt cream," **crème brûlée** is a cold custard that is sprinkled with sugar just before serving, then placed under a broiler or a crème brûlée iron is heated and placed on top to caramelize the sugar. This creates a brittle topping over the rich, creamy custard, giving the dessert its renowned textural contrast. Although its origins are cloudy, crème brûlée is thought to have been created at Trinity College in Cambridge, England. United Kingdom.

CRÈME BRÛLÉE

6 servings

2 cups heavy cream
½ cup granulated sugar
1 vanilla bean, split lengthwise
6 large egg yolks, at room temperature

¼ cup plus 2 tablespoons granulated sugar, for topping
Fresh mint sprigs for garnish (optional)
Fresh strawberries or raspberries for garnish (optional)

Place the cream, sugar, and vanilla bean in the top of a double boiler over hot, not simmering, water. Stir often with a wooden spoon until the mixture is hot, about 30 minutes.

Remove the double boiler from the heat, remove the top pan from the double boiler, and wipe the outside dry. Remove the vanilla bean and reserve it. Whisk the egg yolks into the cream until thoroughly blended. Strain the custard into a bowl or a plastic container. Add the vanilla bean, cover, and refrigerate for at least 4 hours.

Preheat the oven to 350°F. Place 6 individual custard cups or ramekins in a flat rectangular baking pan.

Whisk the custard briefly, then strain it into a pitcher or a large measuring cup. Pour the custard into the cups, filling them to just below the top edge. Place the baking pan on the center oven rack and pour boiling water into the baking pan to come two thirds of the way up the sides of the custard cups.

Cover the baking pan with foil and bake the custards for 40 minutes. Remove the foil and gently tap or shake the custard cups. The custard should be firm. If it is not, cover with the foil and bake for 5 to 10 minutes longer, until set.

Remove the baking dish from the oven, remove the foil, and let the custard stand in the water bath for 30 minutes to cool. Cover each custard with plastic wrap and refrigerate at least 4 hours.

Just before serving, preheat the broiler.

Sprinkle the top of each custard with 1 tablespoon sugar in a thin, even layer. Place the custard cups in the baking pan and surround them with ice cubes. Place the custards under the broiler for a few minutes, just until the sugar begins to bubble and caramelize. Let the custards cool on a rack to room temperature before serving. (An alternative method for caramelizing the tops of the custards is to use a propane torch, aimed directly at the sugar or heat a crème brûlée iron and place it on top of the sugar until it caramelizes.)

If desired, decorate the top of each custard with a sprig of fresh mint and a few fresh strawberries or raspberries.

crème caramel A light egg custard that is baked in a caramel-lined mold in a water bath. After the custard is baked, it is chilled and then turned out of the mold. The caramel forms a topping and a sauce for the custard. **Crème caramel** is usually served cold. In Spain, it is called flan and in Italy, crema caramella. France. See also: water bath.

CRÈME CARAMEL

8 servings, one 1-quart soufflé dish or ovenproof mold, or 8 4-ounce ramekins or ovenproof molds

Caramel
½ cup granulated sugar
¼ cup plus 2 tablespoons water

Custard

1 vanilla bean
2½ cups milk
3 large eggs, at room temperature
3 large egg yolks, at room temperature
½ cup granulated sugar

Center a rack in the oven and preheat to 350°F.

For the caramel, combine the sugar and ¼ cup of the water in a 1½-quart heavy-bottomed saucepan. Bring to a boil stirring to dissolve the sugar, then cook without stirring. Cook the mixture over high heat until it turns a rich golden brown, about 8 minutes. Remove the pan from the heat, and carefully stir in the remaining 2 tablespoons water. Return the pan to the heat and, using a long-handled wooden spoon, stir the mixture for a minute or 2 to dissolve any lumps. Have ready a 1-quart mold or eight 4-ounce molds. Pour the caramel into the ovenproof mold or molds and tilt the mold or molds so the caramel completely covers the bottom.

For the custard: With a sharp knife, split the vanilla bean lengthwise. Scrape out the seeds, and place the seeds and bean in a 2-quart heavy-bottomed saucepan with the milk. Heat the milk over medium heat to just below the boil. Remove the pan from the heat, cover it, and set aside to infuse.

In the bowl of a stand mixer, using the wire whip attachment, or in a mixing bowl, using a hand-held mixer, whip the eggs and egg yolks together until frothy. Slowly beat in the sugar. In a steady stream, add the hot milk, blending well.

Strain the custard into the caramel-coated mold or molds. Place the mold or molds in a large roasting pan. Set the roasting pan on the center oven rack and fill it with hot water to reach halfway up the sides of the mold or molds. Turn the oven temperature down to 325°F and bake the custard for 40 minutes, or until a toothpick inserted in the center comes out clean.

Remove the pan from the oven, and transfer the custard mold or molds to a rack to cool.

To unmold, run a thin-bladed sharp knife around the edges of the mold to loosen the custard. Place a serving plate over the top of the mold and invert the custard onto the plate. Refrigerate the custard until ready to serve.

crème Chantilly The French term for whipped cream that is lightly sweetened with sugar and flavored with vanilla.

crème fraîche A thick, tangy cream with a nutty, slightly sour taste and a velvety smooth texture. In France, **crème fraîche** is made from unpasteurized cream, which naturally contains the bacteria necessary to thicken it. In the United States, it is made by adding a lactic bacteria culture, such as buttermilk, to our pasteurized heavy cream. The ingredients are combined at room temperature, or the mixture is slowly heated to 95°F, then left to stand at room temperature for 12 to 24 hours to thicken. Crème fraîche is used in pastry making and candy making as a filling, an ingredient, and a decoration. It is also used in a sauce or as an accompaniment to desserts and pastries. France.

CRÈME FRAÎCHE

I cup

I cup heavy cream plus I tablespoon cultured buttermilk
  or ½ cup heavy cream plus ½ cup sour cream

Combine the cream with the buttermilk or sour cream in a mixing bowl and blend well. Pour the mixture into a glass jar or plastic container and cover tightly. Let stand in a warm, draft-free place for 12 hours, or overnight, to thicken.

Stir the crème, cover tightly again, and refrigerate for at least 4 hours before using. The crème will keep for up to a week in a tightly sealed container in the refrigerator. When the crème has passed its prime, it will taste bitter.

crème pâtissière The French term for pastry cream. See pastry cream.

crème pralinée Crème pâtissière blended with powdered praline, used as a filling in pastries and confections. See also: crème pâtissière and praline.

crème renversée Another French term for crème caramel. See also: crème caramel.

Crenshaw melon Also called cranshaw, this large melon has slightly fur-rowed, speckled gold-and-green skin with bright salmon-colored flesh. Crenshaw melons can weigh up to 9 pounds. They are oval-shaped with a slightly pointed stem end. Crenshaw is one of the sweetest and juiciest of all the melons, with a spicy aroma. Crenshaw melons are used like cantaloupes as an ingredient in desserts and pastries such as fruit salads, ice creams, sorbets, and parfaits. They are available from July to No-vember, with the peak in August and September. Choose very fragrant, firm melons that feel heavy for their size, with no soft spots or bruises. A ripe Crenshaw melon should give slightly at both ends when pressed. Store underripe Crenshaw melons at room temperature for a few days so they will become softer and juicier. Store ripe Crenshaw melons in the refrigerator for up to 2 weeks. See also: cantaloupe, fruit, and melon.

crêpe French for pancake, a crêpe is a small, paper-thin, flexible pan-cake made from a batter. Various flours are used to make crêpes, which are used for both sweet and savory dishes. Dessert crêpes, made with a sweetened batter, are spread with jam, a mixture of cream and fruit, chocolate, honey, or butter and may be sprinkled with sugar or a liqueur. They can also be wrapped around ice cream. The crêpes are sometimes folded into quarters and may be flamed with a liqueur or brandy, or they can be rolled around the filling and baked in the oven. They can even be stacked with a filling of crème Chantilly to form a cake. Savory crêpes are rolled around a filling of cheese, meat, seafood, or vegetables, baked, and served for a main course, occasionally with a sauce. France.

crêpes Suzette A famous French dessert composed of sweet crêpes heated in a chafing dish with an orange-butter sauce and flamed with or-ange liqueur. France.

crimp A technique for sealing the edges of pastry or pie shells by pinch-ing or pressing them together. Crimping also forms an attractive, deco-rative, fluted edge. It is done with a fork, the back of a knife blade, a crimper, or fingers. To crimp a single-crust pie or pastry, the edge is turned under, forming a raised rim, which is then fluted or shaped into a design. A crimper can also be used to imprint designs into the edges of the pastry. See also: crimper and flute.

crimper This hand-held tool is used to imprint decorative designs into and to seal the edges of pastry shells and pies. Crimpers look like a large pair of tweezers, ranging from 4 to 6 inches long, and $3/4$ inch wide. They may be made of chrome, stainless steel, brass, or silver. The ends are grooved and are made in various designs. Miniature crimpers, about 2 inches long and between $3/16$ and $3/4$ inch wide, are used for decorative detail work on marzipan, gum paste, and rolled fondant. See also: crimp, gum paste, marzipan, and rolled fondant.

Crisco See solid shortening.

crisp A baked deep-dish fruit dessert with a crisp, crunchy topping, a crisp is a relative of cobblers, grunts, pandowdies, and slumps. The fruit is placed in the pan and covered with a crumbled topping made from a mixture of flour, brown sugar, granulated sugar, spices such as cinnamon and nutmeg, and butter. Crisps are best served warm with whipped cream. Apples are the most popular fruit to use in crisps, but just about any fruit can be used. United States. See also: cobbler, grunt, pandowdy, and slump.

croissant A classic crescent-shaped roll made from a rich, buttery, yeast-risen dough. **Croissants** are typically eaten for breakfast in France and other European countries. Croissants are often filled with jam or marzipan. The same dough is filled with chocolate and rolled into a rectangular shape to make a pain au chocolat. Savory variations are made with fillings such as ham or cheese, or a croissant may be split open and used as bread to hold a sandwich filling.

Croissants originated in Austria in 1686 during the war between Austria and Turkey. A group of bakers who were in their bakery during the night heard Turkish troops tunneling under them and sounded the warning, which led to the Turks' defeat. The bakers' reward was the right to create a pastry in the shape of the crescent on the Turkish flag. Originally the dough for croissants was similar to bread dough. The French refined it and developed a dough similar to puff pastry that is used today to make croissants. France.

CROISSANTS

Approximately 30 croissants

¾ cup milk
¾ cup water
2 packages quick-rise or active dry yeast
4 cups plus 2 tablespoons all-purpose flour
3 tablespoons granulated sugar
2 teaspoons salt

2 teaspoons unsalted butter, softened, for the bowl

10½ ounces (2 sticks plus 5 tablespoons) unsalted butter,
    cut into small pieces and chilled
1 egg yolk beaten with 1 teaspoon milk, for glaze

In a small saucepan heat the milk and water over low heat until lukewarm. Remove the pan from the heat, sprinkle the yeast over the liquid, and stir gently. Set aside for 5 minutes.

Place 4 cups of the flour in the bowl of a stand mixer or in a mixing bowl and add the sugar and salt. Using the flat beater attachment or a hand-held mixer, blend briefly on low speed. Slowly beat in the yeast mixture. Turn the mixer speed up to medium and mix for about 1 minute. Scrape down the sides of the bowl and beaters and beat for 30 seconds, or until the dough leaves the sides of the bowl and wraps around the blade or beaters.

Lightly butter the inside of a 2-quart bowl with the softened butter. Turn the dough out into the bowl and cover the bowl with a damp kitchen towel. Set the bowl in a warm, draft-free place and let rise for 20 minutes if using quick-rise yeast, 40 minutes if using regular yeast.

Deflate the dough by knocking or punching it lightly on top. Cover it again with the damp towel and let rise until it is doubled in bulk, about 1 to 1½ hours with quick-rise yeast, 2 to 3 hours with regular. (The dough can be refrigerated for several hours or overnight at this point. Cover the damp towel with plastic wrap so the dough does not dry out.)

Place the chilled butter in the bowl of a stand mixer or in a mixing bowl. Add the remaining 2 tablespoons flour and, using the flat beater attachment or a hand-held mixer, mix for 30 seconds. Scrape down the bowl and beater with a rubber spatula and repeat the mixing process several times, until the butter is pliable, but not soft. There should not be any hard spots left in the butter.

Roll the dough out on a lightly floured work surface to a 15-inch square. Make a line down the center of the dough with your finger. Spread the butter evenly over half the dough, leaving an outside border of 1 inch. Fold the other half over the butter, matching the edges evenly. Press the edges together to seal.

Turn the dough so that the fold faces you, and roll the dough out to a large rectangle. It is important to keep the edges square and even. Fold the ends of the rectangle over into even thirds as if you were folding a letter. Place the dough on a floured baking sheet, cover with a damp cloth, and let rest in the refrigerator for at least 15 minutes.

Repeat the rolling and folding process twice, being careful to place the dough on the work surface so that the fold faces you. This helps ensure that the dough is worked and turned evenly. Be sure to chill the dough during the rest periods, or the butter will soften and seep out.

Cut the dough crosswise into three equal pieces. Work with 1

piece at a time, and keep the remaining dough covered in the refrigerator.

Roll out each piece of dough to a large rectangle about 12
inches long by 6 inches wide and ¼ inch thick. Cut the rectangle
lengthwise in half. Cut each strip into even triangles. Brush off any
excess flour, then, starting from the wide end, roll up each triangle
into a tight roll.

Place the rolled croissants on the lined baking sheets, placing
them so they sit on the "tongue." Curl the ends in toward the center, with the point of the "tongue" toward the inside so the croissants have a "claw" shape. Lightly press the ends down, if necessary,
to help them hold their shape.

Cover the croissants with a cloth and let rise in a warm place for
15 to 30 minutes.

Position the oven racks in the upper and lower thirds of the oven
and preheat to 400°F. Line two baking sheets with parchment
paper.

Beat the egg glaze well, then lightly brush the top of each croissant with the mixture. Bake the croissants for 18 to 20 minutes, until they are risen and golden brown. Let cool slightly before serving.

After the croissants are shaped, they can be refrigerated
overnight or, if well wrapped, frozen. If frozen, defrost overnight in
the refrigerator before baking.

croissant cutter This cutter looks something like a small hollow rolling
pin. It has angled stainless steel blades that form triangles, which are attached to round blades at each end. The round blades are connected to
wooden handles. As the cutter is rolled across the dough, it cuts out uniform triangular shapes that are then rolled up to form croissants. Croissant cutters are available in various sizes, from mini to extra-large. There
is also a triple croissant cutter, which cuts three triangles simultaneously.
Croissant cutters are available at cookware shops and through some mail
order cookware catalogs.

croquant The French word for crunchy, referring to a type of almond
brittle candy. See krokant.

croquembouche A traditional French dessert composed of profiteroles
(miniature cream puffs) stacked in a tall pyramid. The profiteroles are
first dipped in caramel so they will stick together. The outside of the

pyramid is often decorated with spun sugar and, occasionally, pulled sugar flowers. For more elaborate versions, nougatine is formed into an elevated base for the croquembouche. Croquembouche is a traditional celebration cake and is often served at weddings. France. See also: caramel, choux pastry, nougatine, profiterole, pulled sugar, and spun sugar.

croquembouche mold A tall cone-shaped stainless steel form used as a base for stacking small cream puffs, called profiteroles, to make croquembouche. It is made in various heights ranging from 10 to 24 inches. This mold is available at cookware shops and through mail order cookware catalogs. See also: croquembouche.

crostata The Italian word for pie or tart, often indicating a pastry with a bottom crust, filling, and a lattice crust topping. See also: pie and tart.

croustade A baked square puff pastry case that holds a filling, such as pastry cream or mixed fresh fruit or berries, for a dessert. A croustade can be made in any size from individual to large. A croustade can be served with a dessert sauce, such as crème anglaise or a fruit coulis. Croustades are also filled with savory mixtures and served as appetizers or first courses. France. See also: coulis, crème anglaise, pastry cream, and puff pastry.

cruller A small cake usually made from a doughnut type of dough, with the addition of nutmeg, ginger, lemon, and buttermilk. Some crullers are made with a yeast-raised dough. Crullers are shaped into long twisted strips, deep-fried in hot oil, and served warm, sprinkled with sugar or brushed with a sugar glaze. The name derives from the Dutch *krulle*, which means twisted cake. United States. See also: doughnut.

crumpet A small, round, flat, straight-sided, yeast-raised bread made from a thin batter cooked in a ring mold on a griddle on top of the stove. Crumpet rings, which are shallow metal rings with no top or bottom, are necessary to define the crumpet's shape because the batter is so thin. Crumpets are smooth on the bottom and full of tiny crevices and holes on top. They are toasted, spread with butter and jam, and served for afternoon tea. United Kingdom.

crust The pastry dough used for pies and tarts is known as the crust. Crust also means the firm, compact outer layer of baked goods and a hard outer shell or covering, such as the top of a baked custard like crème brûlée and the top of a mixture that has hardened from exposure to air. See also: dough.

crystallization The process of forming sugar crystals. Crystallization occurs when sugar particles clump together because the liquid, such as water, they are mixed with has been saturated to its fullest point and has no more room to absorb sugar. Crystallization can also be triggered by agitating a sugar syrup as it cooks and by introducing foreign matter, such as a dirty spoon, into the solution. Brushing down the sides of the pan with a pastry brush dipped in water when cooking a sugar syrup pushes any sugar crystals back into the solution to dissolve. In candy making, crystallization can cause problems by throwing the delicate formulas out of balance. However, the process of crystallization can be controlled to create desired textures. One of the ways to do this is by choosing the point at which a mixture is stirred. Generally, large crystals, which result in a grainy, coarse texture, form when a mixture is stirred while it is hot. Small crystals, which result in a smooth, creamy texture, form when a mixture is stirred while cool. Fudge is an example of a candy whose texture is determined by choosing when it is stirred, thereby controlling the crystallization. Other ingredients, such as honey, corn syrup, and cream of tartar, known as interfering agents, help to inhibit crystallization. They are often used in candy recipes for this reason. Fondant and taffy are other examples of candies that have crystallized under controlled circumstances, resulting in the desired effect. See also: corn syrup, cream of tartar, fondant, fudge, honey, and taffy.

crystallized flowers A fresh flower that has been coated with egg white, then either dipped in superfine sugar or cooked in a sugar syrup and dried. Crystallized flowers, such as violets and rose petals, are used for decorating desserts, pastries, and confections. They are available in cookware shops, in gourmet food shops, or through mail order cookware catalogs. The commercially made flowers and petals will last indefinitely if stored well wrapped in a cool, dark, dry place. If made in your kitchen using fresh egg white, the flowers will last for 2 to 3 days in a dry place or in the refrigerator. See also: candy.

crystal sugar Also called sanding sugar, crystal sugar is white sugar that has been processed into small oblong grains resembling pellets about $1/16$ inch in size, four to six times larger than grains of granulated sugar. Crystal sugar is used for garnishing cookies, and other baked goods, pastries, and confections. It is often colored with food coloring and called rainbow sugar. See also: sugar.

cupcake An individual cake baked in a cup-shaped mold, such as a muffin pan. The muffin pan is usually lined with fluted paper bake cups, which make it easy to release the cupcakes from the pan. Cupcakes are usually frosted with icing or dusted with confectioners' sugar. United States. See also: bake cup and muffin pan.

cupuaçu A relative of cocoa, cupuaçu is the fruit of the tree of the same name that is native to the Amazon rain forest in Brazil. A cupuaçu pod is about the size and shape of a football, with skin that resembles the skin of a kiwifruit. The seeds are buried in the moist pulp of the fruit inside the pods. The seeds are dried, then processed like cocoa beans to produce a light-colored chocolate that has a mellow, mild bittersweet flavor with fruity undertones. Cocoa butter is present in cupuaçu as it is in chocolate. Cupuaçu is processed into both powder and bars and is used in the same way as cocoa powder and chocolate. Brazil. See also: cacao, chocolate, cocoa butter, and cocoa powder.

Curaçao A liqueur made from the dried peel of sour and bitter oranges, originally from those grown on the island of Curaçao in the Caribbean. Curaçao is also known as Triple Sec. The orange-flavored liqueur is most often clear, but can be golden-colored or blue. It is used to flavor desserts, pastries, and confections.

curdle Curdling occurs at the point at which a mixture coagulates or a liquid separates into its liquid and solid elements. Curdling occurs in milk and milk products, custards, and sauces. The addition of liquid, such as eggs, to butter that has been beaten can cause curdling. If this occurs, scrape down the sides of the mixing bowl and slowly beat the mixture until it is smooth. Lemon juice and other acids can cause some mixtures to curdle. Heat causes the liquid in eggs, milk, and cream to cook and thicken or gel into clumps, which results in a curdled mixture. Constant stirring and cooking over low heat help to prevent this from occurring. Another method of prevention is to slowly stir a small amount of hot liquid into eggs before mixing them with the remainder of the liquid; this brings the eggs up to the temperature of the liquid without curdling. See also: custard.

currants See raisins.

cuscus dolce Italian for sweet couscous, a specialty of the Santo Spirito Monastery in Agrigento, Sicily. This specialty has been made at the monastery since the thirteenth century. To make cuscus dolce, freshly blanched, unsalted green pistachio nuts are combined with almond extract, ground cinnamon, and almond oil or vegetable oil in the workbowl of a food processor fitted with a steel blade and processed until the mixture forms a paste. This paste is kneaded into cooked couscous (semolina), the mixture is steamed briefly in a couscous pan, then spread out in a rectangular pan to cool. A cooked sugar syrup is worked by hand into the cooled couscous, keeping the grains fluffy and separate, then the mixture is air dried for several hours. To serve, the couscous is mounded on a platter and sprinkled evenly with grated chocolate followed by confectioners' sugar. The mound is decorated with a few pieces of candied fruit. See also: seffa.

custard A puddinglike, smooth-textured, sweet mixture made with eggs, sugar, milk, and various flavorings and baked until firm or cooked until thick. Custards must be cooked or baked slowly, with low heat, to prevent the eggs from curdling. In the oven, a custard is baked slowly in a water bath, and on top of the stove, it is cooked in a double boiler. Stirred custards, such as crème anglaise, have a softer texture and less body than baked custards. Stirred custard is a dessert on its own, and it is also used as a sauce to accompany other desserts or fresh fruit or as a base for ice cream or Bavarian cream. Custards are eaten either warm or cold. France. See also: Bavarian cream, crème anglaise, crème brûlée, crème caramel, and pastry cream.

custard cup A deep, flat-bottomed individual-sized cup with slightly flared sides, about 2 inches deep and 3 inches wide at the top. Custard cups have no handles. They are used to hold the mixture for custards or puddings while they bake in a water bath. The cups are smooth on the inside and often ribbed on the outside. Custard cups are usually made of porcelain or glazed earthenware. A pot de crème cup is a similar type of cup, usually rounder, with a lid and with a small loop handle on each side. It may also be used for baking and serving custards or puddings. Pot de crème cups are available in sets of six. Both pot de crème and custard cups are available at cookware and restaurant supply shops.

cut in The technique for combining solid fat such as butter and margarine, with dry ingredients such as flour, until the mixture is in small pieces. This is accomplished using a pastry blender, a fork, two knives, fingers, a food processor, or a stand mixer with the flat beater attachment. Use chilled fat and utensils and work quickly when cutting in, so the fat will not melt and lose its shape. See also: electric mixer, food processor, and pastry blender.

dacquoise This classic French cake is composed of two or three disks of crisp hazelnut or almond meringue filled and decorated with rich buttercream. The buttercream is usually coffee-flavored, although mocha, a combination of coffee and chocolate, is also popular. The top of the cake is dusted heavily with confectioners' sugar, and ground toasted hazelnuts, toasted almonds, or shaved chocolate is pressed into the sides. **Dacquoise** can be made in both individual and large sizes. Dacquoise is also the name of the crisp nut meringue layer used to make the cake. The meringue layer is also know under various other names, including broyage, progrès, japonaise, and Succès. France. See also: broyage, buttercream, meringue, mocha, and Succès.

MOCHA DACQUOISE

One 9-inch round cake; 12 to 14 servings

Hazelnut meringue disks
  1 cup unblanched hazelnuts
  2 tablespoons granulated sugar
  2 tablespoons cornstarch

5 large egg whites, at room temperature
½ teaspoon cream of tartar
¾ cup superfine sugar

Assembly
1 recipe Classic French Buttercream (page 31), flavored with
    1 tablespoon instant espresso powder dissolved in 1 table-
    spoon water *and* 4 ounces bittersweet chocolate, melted
¼ to ⅓ cup confectioners' sugar

Center a rack in the oven and preheat to 350°F.

Place the hazelnuts on a jelly-roll pan and toast them in the oven for 15 to 18 minutes, until the skins split and the nuts turn light golden brown. Transfer the pan to a cooling rack, and let cool for 10 minutes. Reduce the oven temperature to 200°F.

Rub the nuts between your hands or in a towel to remove most of the skins. Place the nuts in the work bowl of a food processor fitted with the steel blade, add the granulated sugar, and pulse until the nuts are very finely ground. Measure out 1 cup of the ground hazelnuts for the meringue disks, and set the rest aside for the final decoration. Combine the cup of ground hazelnuts with the cornstarch and toss to blend well.

Line three baking sheets with aluminum foil. Using a 9-inch cardboard cake circle as a guide, trace a circle onto the dull side of each piece of foil, then turn the foil over on the baking sheets.

In the bowl of a stand mixer, using the wire whip attachment, or in a mixing bowl, using a hand-held mixer, whip the egg whites at medium-high speed until frothy. Add the cream of tartar and whip until the whites form soft peaks. Gradually sprinkle on the superfine sugar, and continue to whip until the egg whites hold firm peaks.

Fold in the hazelnut-cornstarch mixture.

Fit a 14-inch pastry bag with a #5 large plain tip. Fill the pastry bag with the meringue mixture, and pipe concentric circles of the mixture into the traced circles on the aluminum foil, filling in each circle completely.

Place the baking sheets in the oven and dry for 2 hours. Then turn the oven off and leave the meringues in the oven until they are cool.

Gently peel the aluminum foil off the meringue disks. (The meringue disks can be made up to a week in advance and stored at room temperature, covered with foil. They are subject to humidity and may soften if it is too humid or damp; they can be redried at 200°F for 1 hour if they become too soft.) Only 2 meringue disks are needed for the cake. Set aside the third disk for another use.

Place 1 hazelnut meringue disk on a 9-inch cardboard cake circle, and carefully trim the edges to make them even. Using a flexible-blade spatula, spread 2¹/₂ cups of the mocha buttercream evenly over the meringue layer. Carefully trim the edges of the second meringue layer, and place it, bottom side up, on top of the buttercream. Reserve ¹/₃ cup of the remaining buttercream and use the rest to cover the sides of the cake.

Heavily dust the top of the dacquoise with confectioners' sugar, completely covering the meringue disk. Place the reserved ground hazelnuts on a sheet of waxed or parchment paper. Use a flexible-blade spatula to lift up the cake, and carefully hold up the cake with one hand. With your other hand, press the ground hazelnuts into the sides of the cake just up to the top edge. Gently set the cake down on a work surface.

Fit an 8- or 10-inch pastry bag with a #3 or #4 large closed star tip. Place the reserved buttercream in the pastry bag, and pipe a border of shells around the top outer edge of the cake. Pipe a large rosette in the center.

Refrigerate the dacquoise for at least 2 hours to mellow. Let it stand at room temperature for 30 minutes before serving. Cut the cake with a sharp serrated knife. The dacquoise will keep for up to 3 days, well covered, in the refrigerator.

dadar An Indonesian specialty dessert of stuffed crêpes. The crêpes are made from a mixture of rice flour and cornstarch or all-purpose flour mixed with coconut milk and salt, then cooked briefly in a hot pan. The filling of freshly grated coconut, brown sugar, cinnamon, salt, and vanilla is fried in a hot skillet briefly to toast the coconut, then rolled up inside the crêpes. The crêpes are served warm accompanied by coffee or tea. Indonesia.

Danish pastry A yeast-risen, butter- and egg-enriched, sweet pastry dough made using the same techniques as puff pastry and croissants. The dough is rolled out into a large rectangle and the butter is placed on half or a third of it. The dough is folded over, rolled out, and folded again. Repeating the process several times results in hundreds of flaky layers of dough. The pastry dough is made into sweet rolls of various shapes with different fillings, such as fresh and dried fruits, cheese, nuts, almond paste, custard, or jam. Often, Danish pastry is iced after baking. **Danish pastry** is usually served for breakfast. The Danes call the pastry Vienna bread because when the Danish bakers went on strike in the late nineteenth century, they were replaced by Viennese bakers who made a light, flaky pastry dough. When the Danish bakers returned to work, they adopted the dough, improving on it by adding their own variations and fillings, and making it uniquely theirs. Denmark. See also: croissant and puff pastry.

DANISH PASTRY

2 pounds, 4 ounces dough

2 envelopes (I tablespoon plus I ½ teaspoons) active dry yeast
½ cup lukewarm water
½ cup granulated sugar
5 to 6 cups all-purpose flour
½ cup milk
2 large eggs, at room temperature, lightly beaten
I tablespoon unsalted butter, softened
¼ teaspoon freshly grated nutmeg
½ teaspoon ground cardamom
½ teaspoon salt
I teaspoon vanilla extract
I pound cold unsalted butter

In a measuring cup, sprinkle the yeast over the lukewarm water. Stir in I teaspoon of the sugar, and let the mixture stand in a warm, draft-free place for 5 to 8 minutes, until the yeast is bubbly.

Place 4 cups flour in the bowl of a stand mixer or in a large mixing bowl. Make a well in the center of the flour and add the remaining sugar, milk, yeast mixture, eggs, butter, spices, salt, and vanilla. Using the flat beater attachment or a hand-held mixer mix on low speed to blend the mixture, then beat until it is smooth, about I minute, stopping to scrape down the sides of the bowl several times.

Turn the dough out onto a floured work surface and knead it for several minutes, until it is smooth and pliable. Dust a baking sheet with flour, transfer the dough to the sheet, and dust the top of the dough with flour. Cover the dough with plastic wrap, and let rest in the refrigerator for at least 30 minutes.

While the dough is resting, let the butter stand at room temperature so that it becomes pliable, but not too soft. Then place the sticks of butter closely together on a large piece of floured waxed paper, lightly flour the top of the butter, and cover it with another piece of waxed paper. Roll the butter out between the waxed paper to a large rectangle measuring about 8 by 12 inches. Cut the rectangle in half crosswise to form 2 rectangles, each measuring 8 by 6 inches. Transfer the waxed paper—covered butter to a baking sheet and refrigerate.

On a floured work surface, roll out the chilled dough to a large rectangle measuring about 9 by 18 inches, keeping the edges very straight and even. Place 1 of the butter rectangles lengthwise down the center of the dough, and fold one short end of the dough rectangle over the butter. Brush off excess flour from the dough. Place the remaining butter rectangle on top, and fold the other end of the dough over the butter, enclosing it and forming alternating layers of dough and butter. Dust the top of the dough with flour, return it to the baking sheet, cover with plastic wrap, and refrigerate for at least 20 minutes.

Remove the dough from the refrigerator and place it on a floured work surface with a narrow end facing you. Roll out the dough to a large rectangle about 8 by 18 inches, making sure to keep the edges straight and even. Brush off any excess flour from the dough. Fold each short end over to meet in the center, brush off any excess flour, then fold the dough in half at the center point to make 4 layers. Return the dough to the floured baking sheet, dust the top with flour, cover with plastic wrap, and chill for 20 minutes. Repeat this process once more, and chill the dough for 20 minutes.

Roll the dough out to an 8- by 18-inch rectangle. Brush off any excess flour and fold the dough crosswise in half. Transfer the dough to the floured baking sheet, dust the top with flour, and cover it securely with plastic wrap. Let rest in the refrigerator for at least 3 hours, or overnight.

You will need one quarter recipe of this dough to make each of the following recipes; cut the dough rectangle crosswise to form 4 10- by 2½-inch rectangles, and proceed as directed in the individual recipe.

If desired, freeze the unused portions of the dough. To freeze, wrap the dough tightly in several layers of plastic wrap covered with aluminum foil. Defrost the dough overnight in the refrigerator before using.

CURRANT-NUT RINGS

Approximately 21 pastries

¼ recipe Danish Pastry dough (page 98)
1 egg white lightly beaten with 1 teaspoon water, for egg wash
1 cup finely chopped walnuts
3 tablespoons currants

continued

1 tablespoon plus 1 teaspoon granulated sugar mixed with
      1 tablespoon plus 1 teaspoon ground cinnamon

Position the oven racks in the upper and lower thirds of the oven and preheat to 400°F. Line two baking sheets with parchment paper.

On a floured work surface, place the dough with the long side facing you and roll the dough out to a large rectangle about 16 by 9 inches. Brush the dough all over with the egg wash. Sprinkle the walnuts, currants, and sugar-cinnamon mixture evenly over the dough. Lightly press the mixture into the dough with your fingertips or the rolling pin.

Starting from one long end, roll up the dough tightly, like a jelly roll. With a sharp knife, cut the roll into ³/₄-inch-wide slices. Lay the slices on the lined baking sheets, leaving 1 inch between them.

Bake the pastries for 10 minutes, then reduce the oven temperature to 350°F and switch the positions of the baking sheets. Bake the pastries for 12 minutes longer, or until golden brown. Transfer the pastries to cooling racks to cool.

The pastries can be heated in a 350°F oven for 10 minutes before serving. They will keep for 3 days in an airtight container at room temperature, or they can be frozen for up to 4 months.

ALMOND RINGS

Approximately 21 pastries

3 ounces (6 tablespoons) unsalted butter, softened
1 roll (7 ounces) almond paste
2 tablespoons all-purpose flour
Finely minced zest of ¹/₂ lemon
¹/₄ recipe Danish Pastry dough (page 98)
1 egg white lightly beaten with 1 teaspoon water, for egg wash

Position the oven racks in the upper and lower thirds of the oven and preheat to 400°F. Line two baking sheets with parchment paper.

In the bowl of a stand mixer, using the flat beater attachment, or in a mixing bowl, using a hand-held mixer, beat the butter until light and fluffy, about 2 minutes. Break the almond paste into small pieces and add to the butter. Beat until smooth, stopping occasionally to scrape down the sides of the bowl. Add the flour and lemon zest and blend thoroughly.

On a floured work surface, roll the dough out to a large rectangle about 16 by 9 inches. Spread the almond paste mixture evenly over the dough leaving a ½-inch border at the bottom and top. Starting from one long end, roll up the dough tightly, like a jelly roll. Brush the top of the dough lightly with the egg wash. With a sharp knife, cut the roll into ¾-inch-wide slices. Lay the slices on the lined baking sheets, leaving 1 inch space between them.

Bake the pastries for 10 minutes, then reduce the oven temperature to 350°F and switch the positions of the baking sheets. Bake the pastries for 8 minutes longer, or until light golden. Transfer the pastries to cooling racks to cool.

The pastries can be heated in a 350°F oven for 10 minutes before serving. They will keep for 3 days in an airtight container at room temperature, or the pastries can be frozen for up to 4 months.

BEAR CLAWS OR COCKSCOMBS

Approximately 15 pastries

3 ounces (6 tablespoons) unsalted butter, softened
1 roll (7 ounces) almond paste
2 tablespoons all-purpose flour
Finely minced zest of ½ lemon
¼ recipe Danish Pastry dough (page 98)
1 egg white lightly beaten with 1 teaspoon water, for egg wash
3 to 4 tablespoons coarse (pearl) sugar

Position the oven racks in the upper and lower thirds of the oven and preheat to 400°F. Line two baking sheets with parchment paper.

Prepare the almond filling according to the instructions for the Almond Rings on page 100.

On a floured work surface, roll the dough out to a large rectangle about 18 by 10 inches, making sure the edges are straight and even. Spread the almond filling lengthwise along the bottom half of the dough, then fold the top half of the dough over the filling. With your fingertips, press the edges of the dough together to enclose the filling. Cut the dough crosswise into 2½-inch-wide strips. Cut 3 slits three quarters of the way into each strip, starting at the open side, leaving the strip attached at the top. Open the strips slightly, and transfer the pastries to the paper-lined baking sheets. Brush the pastries lightly with the egg wash, then sprinkle liberally with coarse sugar.

Bake the pastries for 10 minutes, then reduce the oven temperature to 350°F and switch the positions of the baking sheets. Bake the pastries for 8 minutes longer, or until light golden. Transfer the pastries to cooling racks to cool.

The pastries can be heated in a 350°F oven for 10 minutes before serving. They will keep for 3 days in an airtight container at room temperature, or they can be frozen for up to 4 months.

JAM TWISTS

Approximately 10 pastries

1 cup jam or preserves, such as apricot, raspberry, or blackberry
¼ recipe Danish Pastry Dough (page 98)
1 egg white lightly beaten with 1 teaspoon water, for egg wash
3 to 4 tablespoons coarse (pearl) sugar

Place the jam or preserves in a heavy-bottomed saucepan and cook over medium heat, stirring frequently, until reduced by one third, about 15 minutes. Strain the jam to remove any seeds if necessary, and let cool.

Position the oven racks in the upper and lower thirds of the oven and preheat to 400°F. Line two baking sheets with parchment paper.

On a floured work surface, roll the dough out to a large rectangle about 20 by 10 inches, making sure the edges are straight and even. Spread half the jam or preserves lengthwise along the bottom half of the dough, then fold the other half of the dough over the filling. With your fingertips, press the edges of the dough together to enclose the filling, then gently roll the rolling pin over the dough strip to secure the filling.

Cut the strip of dough crosswise into 2-inch-wide strips. Make a 3-inch-long slit in the center of each strip, leaving the dough attached at each end. Fold one of the ends under the slit and push it up through with your fingertips. Place the twist on a lined baking sheet and repeat with the remaining pieces of dough. Brush the tops of the twists with the egg wash, and sprinkle liberally with coarse sugar.

Bake the pastries for 10 minutes, then reduce the oven temperature to 350°F and switch the positions of the baking sheets. Bake the pastries for 12 minutes longer, or until light golden. Transfer the pastries to cooling racks to cool.

The pastries can be heated in a 350°F oven for 10 minutes before serving. They will keep for 3 days in an airtight container at room temperature, or they can be frozen for up to 4 months.

JAM OR CUSTARD POCKETS

Approximately 10 pastries

¼ recipe Danish Pastry dough (page 98)
⅓ cup jam or preserves, such as apricot, raspberry, or blackberry,
   or Pastry Cream (page 221)

Position the oven racks in the upper and lower thirds of the oven and preheat to 400°F. Line two baking sheets with parchment paper.

On a floured work surface, roll the dough out to a large rectangle about 8 by 20 inches, making sure the edges are straight and even. Cut the dough lengthwise in half, making 2 strips about 4 by 20 inches. Cut each strip into 4-inch squares. Fold the corners of the square into the center, and press down lightly to secure them. Place a teaspoon of jam or preserves or Pastry Cream in the center of each pastry.

Bake the pastries for 10 minutes, then reduce the oven temperature to 350°F and switch the positions of the baking sheets. Bake the pastries for 12 minutes longer, until light golden. Transfer the pastries to cooling racks to cool.

The pastries can be heated in a 350°F oven for 10 minutes before serving. They will keep for 3 days in an airtight container at room temperature, or they can be frozen for up to 4 months.

darázsfészek A Hungarian yeast-raised coffee cake made of several individual pinwheels of dough, each enclosing a rich filling of walnuts, raisins, butter, sugar, and milk. The pinwheels puff as they bake. The traditional way to eat the cake is not to cut it, but to break off the puffs, working from the outside in. The cake is best made a day or 2 before serving so the flavors of the filling can permeate the dough. Hungary.

dartois A classic French pastry made from two rectangular sheets of puff pastry enclosing an almond cream filling. After baking, the pastry is cut crosswise into individual pieces. Other sweet fillings such as jam, pastry cream, or fruit purées occasionally replace the almond cream. Savory versions of dartois, with fillings such as chicken, anchovies, or foie gras, are served as appetizers. France. See also: frangipane, pastry cream, and puff pastry.

date The oblong-shaped, glossy fruit of the date palm tree, which grows in clusters on the trees. Date palms are native to North Africa and Asia and have been cultivated in the Mediterranean area for thousands of years. Today date palms are widely cultivated in the hot, dry climates of California and Arizona. There are several varieties of dates, but the ones most widely available in the United States are the Medjool, Deglet Noor, Empress, and Khadrawi. Fresh dates are about 1 to 2 inches long, with a long, narrow seed and a thin, golden-colored skin. They are naturally sweet, consisting of over 50 percent sugar when fresh. As the fruit dries, the sugar becomes more concentrated and the color of the dates darkens. Dried dates are available year-round in bulk and packaged, both whole, pitted or unpitted, and chopped. Fresh dates are occasionally available in specialty markets from late summer through early spring. Choose plump, moist dates with a smooth, even color. Store fresh dates in a plastic bag in the refrigerator for up to 2 weeks. Store dried dates in a sealed bag or container in the refrigerator for up to a year. Dates are eaten as a sweet on their own and are widely used as an ingredient and flavoring in desserts, pastries, and confections. They are also ground to a powder when dried to make date sugar, which is used as a sweetener to sprinkle on cereal or ice cream.

Demerara sugar See sugar.

Desdemona A pastry named for the wife of Othello, who is the tragic character in Shakespeare's *Othello*. Desdemonas are composed of two 3-inch round biscuits, similar to ladyfingers, sandwiched together with vanilla-flavored whipped cream, brushed with apricot glaze, and covered in kirsch-flavored white fondant. Desdemonas are usually served on a platter accompanied by other similar pastries, Iagos, Othellos, and Rosalindas, all named for Shakespearean characters. United Kingdom. See also: fondant, glaze, Iago, ladyfingers, Othello, and Rosalinda.

dessert A sweet that is traditionally served after the last course of a meal. Desserts include pastries, cakes, tarts, pies, confections, ice creams, cookies, puddings, custards, soufflés, and fresh or cooked fruit. A dessert can be either hot or cold.

détrempe The French term for a mixture of flour and water that is the foundation mixture for pastry dough such as puff pastry. The remaining ingredients are added after the détrempe has had a chance to rest. France.

devil's food cake An American classic, devil's food cake is a rich, moist, dark, and very chocolatey two-layer cake filled and iced with rich, fudgy chocolate frosting. The cake takes its name from its dark reddish-brown color, which comes from the baking soda used to neutralize the acid of the chocolate and to leaven the cake. The dark color is the opposite of the delicate whiteness of angel food cake. United States. See also: cake and leaven.

Devonshire cream See clotted cream.

dextrose A naturally occurring form of glucose, dextrose is also called grape sugar and corn sugar. See also: glucose and sugar.

Diplomat cream A mixture of equal parts of chilled vanilla pastry cream and sweetened vanilla flavored whipped cream. See also: Bagatelle and pastry cream.

Diplomat pudding A cold molded dessert. Rum- or kirsch-soaked ladyfingers or slices of brioche line a mold that is filled with alternating layers of Bavarian cream, crystallized fruits, and apricot jam. After chilling, the pudding is unmolded and served with fruit sauce or custard or glazed with apricot jam and decorated with crystallized fruit. France.

divinity A confection made from cooked sugar syrup beaten into firmly whipped egg whites. The mixture is beaten until cool and firm, then shaped into mounds and left to set at room temperature. Divinity can be flavored in many different ways: with praline or ground nuts, with orange or lemon, with ginger, or with chocolate. When divinity is sweetened with brown sugar, it is called seafoam. Divinity is very sensitive to humidity. It is best stored in an airtight container at room temperature and eaten within 4 days. United States.

Dobostorte, Doboschtorte This world-famous classic cake is of Hungarian origin. It consists of seven very thin round layers of chocolate génoise or sponge cake that are filled and frosted with rich chocolate buttercream. The cake is topped with a shiny crisp caramel glaze that is marked into serving pieces. Dobostorte was created in Budapest in the late nineteenth century by chef József Dobos. Hungary.

docinhos de amendoim Roasted peanuts and freshly grated coconut are combined with sugar and eggs and cooked slowly until thickened to make these Brazilian sweet peanut cakes. The mixture is poured onto a buttered surface or into a buttered pan, cooled, and cut into squares. The squares are rolled in confectioners' sugar and each one is decorated with a roasted peanut. These bite-sized sweets are served in paper candy cups. Brazil.

docker A tool for piercing holes in pastry dough, particularly puff pastry, so the steam can escape as the dough bakes. A docker resembles a paint roller. It is made of a 6-inch-wide roller, with numerous protruding short metal or reinforced plastic spikes, attached by metal strips on each side to a short wooden or plastic handle. An all-plastic docker is also manufactured. Dockers are available at cookware shops and through mail order cookware catalogs.

dolce The Italian word for sweet and for sweets, including desserts, candies, pastries, and cakes.

dollop A small scoop or mound, generally referring to whipped cream or a custard sauce used as a garnish for a pastry or dessert.

double boiler A pot consisting of two pans that fit together snugly. The bottom pan, which is slightly larger than the top pan, is used to hold a small amount of hot water. A snug fit between the two pans is important so that no water or steam from the bottom pan can escape and mix with the ingredients in the top pan. A double boiler insulates and provides a consistent source of heat for melting ingredients evenly, such as chocolate and butter, and for holding them at a constant temperature without burning and for cooking delicate mixtures like custards, zabaglione, and lemon curd. A double boiler can also be devised using a heatproof bowl, such as one of stainless steel, that fits tightly over a saucepan. See also: water bath.

dough An uncooked mixture of flour and liquid, such as water, milk, or eggs, that is the basis of many baked items, including breads. Most types of dough contain salt, which enhances flavor. A dough is thick enough to knead or roll, unlike a batter, which is poured or dropped from a spoon. Raised doughs are made with yeast or another leavening agent such as baking powder. Pastry dough usually contains fat, such as butter, and eggs, which act as a binding agent. Soft doughs contain more liquid in proportion to the dry ingredients than do stiff doughs.

dough divider Also called an expanding pastry cutter, this stainless steel tool is used to cut dough into many strips at once. It has either five or seven wheels attached to metal bars with X-shaped bars between them, which form an expandable, accordion-style frame. The bars can be pulled out or pushed in sideways to create more or less space between the cutting wheels. The divider will cut strips from $1/2$ inch to 5 inches wide. The cutting wheels may be either plain or fluted. There is also a dough divider/cutter that has seven cutting wheels mounted on a long metal bar, with wooden handles at each end; the space between the wheels cannot be changed. The divider or divider/cutter is rolled over rolled-out dough in the same way as a rolling pin and cuts the dough simultaneously into strips of equal size. A dough divider and divider/

cutter are available through mail order cookware catalogs and at restaurant supply shops.

doughnut, donut A small individual cake or pastry of sweetened dough leavened by yeast or baking powder that is deep-fried or baked. Doughnuts are shaped with either a specially designed doughnut cutter or two biscuit cutters. One cutter is used to cut the cake or pastry, the other to cut out the center, which is called the doughnut hole. The holes are also fried and treated as pastries. Doughnuts are dusted with sugar or glazed after frying or baking and are eaten hot or at room temperature. Round doughnuts are generally filled with jam before frying.

Cake doughnuts are made with baking powder and are of various flavors, such as spice or chocolate. The dough for cake doughnuts is chilled before frying to prevent the cakes from absorbing too much oil when they are fried. They have a slightly crunchy outside and a soft cakey inside. They are usually best served warm. Crullers are lemon- and spice-flavored doughnuts usually made with a baking powder–raised dough, although some variations are made with yeast. To make crullers, two strips of dough are twisted together into a long rope shape before frying. The dough for raised doughnuts is made with yeast; this is the dough used to make jam-filled doughnuts. Raised doughnuts come in many shapes: round, square, oblong, and twisted. French doughnuts are made from choux pastry. They are lighter and more delicate than cake or yeast doughnuts. Churros are a type of Mexican doughnut made from strips of choux pastry. Buñuelos, also of Mexican origin, are pillows of deep-fried sweet dough, usually with hollow centers. United States. See also: buñuelo, choux pastry, churro, cruller, and doughnut cutter.

doughnut cutter This utensil is made of two 1-inch high rings of aluminum or stainless steel. In a standard doughnut cutter, a small ring fits in the center of a larger ring, held together by a U-shaped handle at the top. The inner ring is about 1½ inches in diameter and the outer ring is 3 to 4 inches in diameter. The cutter may have either plain or fluted edges. A convertible doughnut cutter has a removable center ring, making two individual cutters. To use a doughnut cutter, first dip it in flour to prevent sticking, then press it down on the rolled-out dough, cutting out the characteristic inner-tube shape. Doughnut cutters are available at cookware shops and supermarkets.

dragée There are two types of dragées: tiny shiny silver or gold balls, made mostly from sugar, which are used for decorating desserts, pastries, and confections; and candies that have an almond or other center covered with a hard, shiny, colored sugar coating. Pistachio nuts or hazelnuts are sometimes used rather than almonds. Nougat, chocolate, fondant, almond paste, or liqueur may all be used for the centers; these fillings are molded before they are coated with the sugar. The word *dragée* derives from the Greek word for honey-coated almonds. Almond dragées have been recorded as far back as the thirteenth century. They became popular in the seventeenth century, when sugar came into widespread use in Europe. Traditionally, almond dragées are served at weddings and religious celebrations in France. France.

Drambuie Considered to be the oldest Scottish liqueur, Drambuie is made from a secret formula that is based on Scotch whiskey. The pale golden liqueur is flavored with a variety of herbs and spices and sweetened with heather honey. Its name comes from a Gaelic expression, *an dram buidheach,* meaning "the liqueur that satisfies." Drambuie is used as a flavoring for desserts, pastries, and confections. Scotland.

dredger A type of sifter that looks like a large saltshaker, about $3^{1}/_{2}$ inches high and $2^{1}/_{2}$ inches in diameter with an arched mesh screen on top. Dredgers are made of either aluminum or plastic and some have a handle on the side. Dredgers are used to sift small amounts of confectioners' sugar or cocoa powder or to dust them over the top of a cake, pastry, or other confection.

dried fruit Fruit that has had most of its water removed through evaporation. The process intensifies the fruit's sweetness and taste and preserves the fruit, thereby increasing its shelf life. Fruit can be sun-dried or dried commercially in mechanical dehydrators. Many fruits are dried with sulfur dioxide, which aids in preserving both color and nutrients. A wide variety of fruits is dried, including apples, apricots, bananas, blueberries, cherries, cranberries, currants, dates, figs, mangos, peaches, pears, persimmons, pineapple, prunes, raisins, and strawberries. Dried fruit is widely used in desserts, pastries, and confections. It can be soaked in liquid to reconstitute it before adding it to baked goods, or it can be used as it is. Dried fruit is available in most major supermarkets, health food stores, and stores that specialize in nuts and dried fruits. It can be stored at room temperature until opened; once opened, the fruit should be stored tightly covered in the refrigerator, where it will keep for several months.

drizzle To lightly pour a liquid over a surface in a thin, slow, steady stream. Some coffee cakes, cookies, and other baked goods are drizzled with a thin sugar glaze or icing or with piping chocolate as a decoration after baking, or they may be drizzled with melted butter before baking.

drop cookie A cookie formed by dropping a soft batter from a spoon onto a baking sheet. See also: batter and cookie.

drum sieve Also called a tamis, this is a type of sifter. It has a straight-sided round wooden frame, 2 to 3 inches high, that is open at the top. A piece of fine metal or nylon mesh is stretched across the bottom. The ingredients to be sifted are placed into the drum sieve and can be pushed through the mesh by hand, or the tamis can be moved back and forth to agitate the ingredients and sift them through. Drum sieves range from 3 inches to 16 inches in diameter. The most practical and commonly used size is 9 inches in diameter. A drum sieve is used to sift flour, confectioners' sugar, and other dry ingredients and to make some purées. Drum sieves are available at cookware shops and through mail order cookware catalogs.

dumpling Dessert dumplings are made of fruit baked inside a sweet, rich, biscuitlike pastry dough and are served with a sauce. Dumplings may also be baked or poached in a sweet sauce and served with heavy cream or vanilla ice cream. United States.

Dundee cake A classic Scottish cake, Dundee cake is a light-textured, rich cake loaded with candied orange peel, currants, lemon and orange zest, ground and slivered almonds, and spices. Its top is completely covered with whole blanched almonds. The cake takes its name from the town of Dundee near the eastern coast of Scotland, where it originated in the early nineteenth century. Scotland.

dust The term for lightly sprinkling or coating pastry dough, pastries, cakes, confections, or baking pans with a powdery substance such as flour, confectioners' sugar, cocoa powder, or finely ground nuts.

Dutch-processed During the manufacturing of chocolate and cocoa powder, either the inner nibs of the cocoa bean or the chocolate liquor, the liquid pressed from the nibs, is treated with an alkaline solution. The alkaline reduces the acid in cocoa powder, giving it a more mellow flavor, making it darker in color, and more soluble in liquid. This process was invented in 1828 by the Dutch chemist Coenraad van Houten. See also: chocolate and cocoa powder.

eau-de-vie A strong, colorless brandy or liqueur distilled from fermented fruit, such as kirschwasser, made from cherries, and framboise, made from raspberries. Eau-de-vies are used to flavor desserts, pastries, and confections. *Eau-de-vie is* is the French term for "water of life," derived from Latin. France. See also: framboise and kirschwasser.

Eccles cake An individual-size British cake made from a small circle of shortcrust pastry that is heaped with a mixture of currants, candied orange or lemon peel, sugar, and spices. A second larger circle of pastry is placed on top of the filling and the edges of the pastry circles are twisted together to form a decorative ropelike border. Slits are made in the top of the cake before it is baked in a hot oven. Eccles cake is traditionally served with afternoon tea. United Kingdom. See also: Banbury cake.

éclair An individual pastry made from cream puff pastry that is piped through a pastry bag, onto a baking sheet, into a long finger shape. After baking and cooling, the pastry is split open horizontally and filled with plain, coffee, or chocolate pastry cream or sweetened whipped cream. The top of the éclair is coated with plain glaze, chocolate glaze, or fondant that is the same flavor as the filling. Unfilled éclairs can be kept at room temperature for 2 days or frozen for several months. Filled éclairs should be refrigerated until served. They are best if eaten within 4 hours of preparation. France. See also: chocolate glaze, choux pastry, fondant, and pastry cream.

éclair plaque A flat rectangular tinned-steel pan with twelve 3-inch-long and 1-inch-wide shallow indentations that help form the finger shape of éclairs. The choux pastry for éclairs is piped into the indentations in the pan, then baked. This pan can also be used to form ladyfingers and langues de chat cookies. See also: éclairs, ladyfingers, and langues de chat.

egg The hard-shelled oval or round reproductive body produced by female birds. Eggs are extremely versatile and nutritious. They contain many vitamins and minerals and are a complete protein. The white is primarily composed of water, with some protein, while the yolk contains protein, fat, cholesterol, vitamins, and minerals. Although there are many types of eggs available, hens' eggs are the most commonly used for making desserts, pastries, and confections. Eggs are graded for both quality and size. The gradings reflect the size of the air pocket between the egg and the shell, the firmness of the yolk, and the thickness of the white. AA- and A-graded eggs are the most commonly available. These high-quality eggs have round yolks, thick whites, and small air pockets. The color of the shell is determined by the breed of hen and has no bearing on the flavor, quality, or nutritive value of the egg. Size classifications for eggs are determined by a specific minimum weight per dozen: Jumbo eggs weigh 30 ounces per dozen; extra large, 27 ounces; large, 24 ounces; medium, 21 ounces; small, 18 ounces; and peewee, 15 ounces. Most recipes use large eggs. If a different size is used, the recipe must be adjusted.

   Buy eggs as fresh as possible. They should be stored in the refrigerator in their cardboard carton, with their pointed ends down. Eggs can be kept in the refrigerator for up to a month, but are usually best if used within 10 days. To determine if an egg is fresh, place it in a bowl of cold water. A fresh egg will sink to the bottom, while an older egg will float— this is caused by the evaporation of moisture that takes place as an egg ages. Egg whites can be stored in the refrigerator in a tightly covered container for up to a week, or they can be frozen for up to 8 months. Defrost them completely before using and they will whip as well as if they were fresh. An ice cube tray is a good way to freeze egg whites individually. Egg yolks can be stored covered with water in an airtight container in the refrigerator for up to 3 days. They can also be frozen if stirred slightly and mixed with ¼ teaspoon sugar per yolk. Eggs are widely used in desserts, pastries, and confections as a leavening agent, for thickening, to add tenderness, to bind ingredients together, and to impart flavor, color, and richness.

egg wash Egg wash is made from a whole egg, an egg yolk, or an egg white beaten together with milk, cream, or water. Egg wash is brushed on the top of baked goods before they are baked to aid in even browning and to give them a shiny, crisp outer surface. Egg wash also helps hold toppings, such as almonds or poppy seeds, in place.

electric mixer There are two basic types of mixers: hand-held and stand mixers. The hand-held mixer has a small motor inside a plastic housing with a handle. Two removable beaters are set into the housing. A hand-held mixer is portable and easy to store, but it is not as powerful as a stand mixer and, therefore, its uses are more limited. A stand mixer has a solid base, which sits on a countertop, with the motor housing at the top. The motor is a heavy-duty type, allowing the mixer to mix heavy doughs and batters without wearing out or burning out. The motor housing may or may not tilt back, depending on the model and manufacturer. There are several adjustable speeds and the mixing bowl is removable and interchangeable with a second bowl. The beater spins while the bowl is stationary (in some inexpensive mixers the bowl rotates), allowing the beater to reach all areas of the bowl, resulting in efficient mixing. Stand mixers usually come with stainless steel bowls and three different removable beaters: a wire whip used for whipping air into mixtures; a flat beater, also called a paddle, used for blending ingredients; and a dough hook, used to mix bread doughs. Extra bowls and beaters can be purchased, as can other accessories, such as a pouring shield, for adding ingredients without spilling, and a water jacket, which sits underneath the work bowl to hold either hot or cold water, keeping the work bowl hot or cool. The two most popular brands of stand mixers are KitchenAid and Kenwood. KitchenAid is available with both a $4^{1}/_{2}$-quart- and a 5-quart-capacity bowl. The $4^{1}/_{2}$-quart model has a motor housing that tips back for changing the beaters and removing the mixing bowl. The 5-quart-capacity mixer is a small version of commercial KitchenAid mixers. The motor housing is stationary and the two arms that hold the mixing bowl move up and down. Which mixer is used is a matter of personal preference. Kenwood makes a 5-quart- and a 7-quart-capacity mixer. Both of these mixers have a motor housing that tips back and bowls that lock into place on the bases.

Engadine nut torte A classic Swiss tartlike cake composed of a two-layer pastry shell filled with a rich mixture of walnuts caramelized in cream, sugar, and honey. The torte is named for the mountainous Engadine region in southeastern Switzerland. Because **Engadine nut torte** is rich and compact, it provides sustaining energy and is considered ideal for the picnic basket or for carrying in a backpack while hiking. It is found in elegant pastry shops as well. Switzerland.

@@@@@@@@@@

ENGADINE NUT TORTE

One 9½-inch round torte; 12 servings

1 recipe Pâte Sucrée (page 225)
1¼ cups granulated sugar
¼ cup water
⅔ cup heavy whipping cream
1 tablespoon honey
2 cups walnuts, roughly chopped, plus 12 walnut halves
1 large egg, at room temperature, lightly beaten
1 ounce bittersweet chocolate

Divide the pâte sucrée in half, and cover and refrigerate one half. On a lightly floured work surface, roll out the other half to a ⅛-inch-thick 12-inch diameter round. Gently roll up the pastry around the rolling pin, and carefully unroll it into a 9½-inch fluted tart pan with a removable bottom. Fit the pastry into the bottom and up the sides of the pan without stretching the dough, and trim off the excess pastry. Chill the pastry shell while you prepare the filling.

Center a rack in the oven and preheat to 425°F. Combine the sugar and water in a 2½-quart heavy-bottomed saucepan and bring to a boil over high heat, brushing down the sides of the pan with a pastry brush dipped in water twice, to prevent crystallization. Then cook until the mixture is a light caramel color, about 12 minutes.

Meanwhile, heat the cream to a boil in a 1-quart saucepan over medium heat. Remove from the heat.

Reduce the heat under the caramel to medium, and add the hot cream to the caramel in a steady stream, stirring constantly with a long-handled wooden spoon. Be careful, as the mixture may splatter. Cook, stirring, for a few minutes to dissolve any lumps, then stir in the honey and chopped walnuts. Remove from the heat and stir for 1 minute. Pour the mixture into the chilled tart shell, and place the tart pan on a jelly-roll pan.

Roll out the remaining pastry dough on a lightly floured work surface to a 12 to 13 inch ⅛-inch-thick round. Gently roll up the pastry around the rolling pin, and unroll onto the top of the torte. Press the edges of the pastry dough together to seal. Use a fork to make a decorative design on top of the pastry and to create steam holes. Brush the beaten egg over the top of the torte.

Bake the torte for 25 minutes, or until golden brown. Transfer to a rack to cool.

Melt the chocolate in the top of a double boiler over hot, not simmering, water. Dip half of each walnut half in the chocolate and shake off the excess. Place the walnut halves evenly around the outer edge of the torte.

Wrapped in foil, the torte will keep for 5 days at room temperature or up to 2 weeks in the refrigerator.

entremet ring Also called a cake ring, this is a deep, straight-sided open stainless steel ring that is used to mold cakes and desserts and to bake cakes. For both molding and baking, the ring is placed on a parchment paper–lined baking sheet that acts as its bottom. Entremet rings are available in sizes that range from 1³/₈ to 3 inches high and from 3 to 14 inches in diameter. Adjustable rings are also available; these have two metal strips that straddle the side through which the ring slides. The metal strips regulate the diameter of the ring, from 6 to 12 inches. Entremet rings are available at some cookware shops, at restaurant supply shops, and through some mail order cookware catalogs.

entremets This French word translates literally as "between dishes," but today it means the sweet course and side dishes served after the cheese course. It also refers to composed desserts, those that have more than one component, which are classified into three categories: hot entremets, consisting of soufflés, pancakes, and sweet omelettes; cold entremets, such as charlottes, pastries, meringues, puddings, layer cakes, mousse cakes, and other molded desserts; and iced entremets, such as sorbets and ice creams, bombes, parfaits, vacherins, and mousses. See also: entremet ring.

espresso powder A powder made from dried roasted espresso beans that dissolves instantly in water. It imparts a rich, robust coffee flavor and aroma to desserts, pastries, and confections. Italy.

essence A concentrated flavoring in liquid form derived from natural sources, such as plants, by the process of distillation or infusion. Essences are potent and, therefore, only a small amount is needed. Fruit essences, such as strawberry and apricot, are often used to flavor desserts, pastries, and confections. Essences will last indefinitely stored in tightly covered glass bottles, to prevent evaporation, in a cool, dark, dry place. See also: extract.

essential oil Essential oil has a strong flavor and is extracted from various parts of plants, such as leaves, stems, and flowers. Essential oils are used to impart flavor to desserts, pastries, and confections. They are very powerful and should be used sparingly. They will last indefinitely if stored in tightly covered glass bottles, to prevent evaporation, in a cool, dark, dry place. See also: essence and extract.

evaporated milk Canned homogenized milk that has had half of its water removed through evaporation. Evaporated milk does not have added sugar, but it does have a caramelized taste because it has been sterilized and the heat from that process lightly caramelizes the lactose, the naturally occurring milk sugar. Evaporated milk is available in whole, skim, low-fat, and "lite" or nonfat varieties. By adding an equal amount of water to evaporated milk, you can use it in baking as a substitute for fresh milk. It provides richness and creaminess to custards and other baked goods. Evaporated milk will last indefinitely if unopened. Once opened, transfer the contents to a clean container and store the milk tightly covered in the refrigerator for no more than a week. If frozen slightly, evaporated milk can be whipped and used as a substitute for cream. See also: milk.

extract A pure extract is made from concentrated natural oils, derived from plants, that are mixed with alcohol. Examples of pure extracts are vanilla, lemon, and almond. Imitation extracts are synthesized from chemicals to recreate the flavor of pure extracts or to create flavors that are not available as extracts in natural form, such as coconut, maple, or butterscotch. Because extracts are very concentrated, only a small amount is needed to impart flavor to desserts, pastries, and confections. Extracts are very sensitive to heat and light. The best way to store them is in tightly covered glass bottles, to prevent evaporation, in a cool, dark, dry place. Stored this way, they have an indefinite shelf life. See also: vanilla extract.

fat See fats and oils

fat bloom A condition that occurs when the cocoa butter in chocolate has separated out, floated to the top, and crystallized. Also called chocolate bloom, it appears as a dull, gray film or as white dots and streaks on the surface of chocolate. It does not mean that the chocolate has spoiled; it merely looks unpleasant. When the chocolate is melted, the cocoa butter will melt back in. Fat bloom also occurs often in candies—such as fondant and fudge—that are stored in an airtight container at room temperature to "ripen" for a day or 2 after they are made. During this time, the fat in the mixture comes together and rises to the surface, forming large crystals that appear as a white layer. When fat bloom occurs, the texture of the candy changes from smooth to grainy. See also: chocolate bloom.

fat rascal A Yorkshire, England, regional specialty, a variation of the classic scone. A fat rascal is a large scone, about 6 inches in diameter, that is plump with candied citrus peel, candied cherries, spices, and almonds. Fat rascals are often served hot, split in half, and buttered. United Kingdom. See also: scone.

fats and oils There are many types of fats used in making desserts, pastries, and confections, including butter, margarine, vegetable shortening, lard, and oil. Fats contribute several important qualities to baked goods. They help leaven batters and doughs by creating air pockets, add flavor and color, tenderize, and aid in holding liquids in a mixture, which contributes moisture.

One of the primary contributions of fats is to add texture, richness, and tenderness to pastry doughs, cakes, cookies, and other baked goods. Fat limits the development of gluten in doughs and batters by coating the gluten strands, resulting in a more tender product. The degree of tenderness and richness depends on the type of fat used and the method used to combine it with the other ingredients in a particular recipe. Chilled solid fat is the best for making flaky, tender pastry dough because even when it is cut into tiny pieces, it does not combine with the flour. This creates alternate layers of fat and flour in the dough, which remain separate when the dough is baked, producing a flaky texture. Lard tends to make the flakiest pastry of all the fats, but it has little flavor.

Room-temperature fat that is thoroughly creamed with sugar traps air in a batter, creating light-textured cakes. Liquid fat, whether it is melted butter, margarine, vegetable shortening, or oil, creates a firm crust with a crumbly texture in baked goods. A distinguishing characteristic of chiffon cakes is that oil is the fat used in their preparation.

In making desserts, pastries, and confections, butter gives the best flavor of the many fats. The oils used in desserts, pastries, and confections are derived primarily from vegetables, seeds, and fruits, and they work best if they are delicately or lightly flavored. These oils include canola, corn, olive, peanut, safflower, soybean, and sunflower, which are all low in cholesterol. The oils are essentially interchangeable with each other, except olive oil which has a distinct flavor. Oils are either unrefined or refined, according to the amount of processing they undergo. Unrefined oils are thicker, with a heavy flavor, while refined oils are clear, with a light, delicate flavor. Oils can solidify and/or become cloudy when refrigerated, but will return to liquid and/or clarify when brought to room temperature—except for coconut oil, which is highly saturated and remains solid at room temperature. Solid vegetable shortenings, such as margarine and Crisco are created by hydrogenation. This process forces pressurized hydrogen gas through oils derived from vegetable or animal fats and changes them from liquid to solid.

Fats and oils are categorized as either saturated or unsaturated, according to their chemical makeup and how many carbon and hydrogen atoms they contain. The unsaturated fats are further categorized as either polyunsaturated or monounsaturated, depending on their structure of hydrogen atoms. Saturated fats come primarily from animal fats and are solid at room temperature. Saturated fats have less of a tendency to turn rancid than unsaturated fats. They are best stored tightly wrapped in the refrigerator for up to a month or in the freezer for several months. Unsaturated fats come primarily from plants, seeds, and vegetables and are liquid at room temperature. They are best stored tightly covered at room temperature for up to a month or in the refrigerator for up to 3 months. Hydrogenated vegetable shortening is best stored tightly covered at room temperature for up to 3 months.

Butter and margarine have a low smoke point. Shortening, lard, and oils have a high smoke point and are the best to use for frying. See also: butter, canola oil, chiffon cake, corn oil, gluten, lard, margarine, olive oil, peanut oil, safflower oil, smoke point, solid shortening, soybean oil, and sunflower oil.

feqqas There are many variations of feqqas, which are classic Moroccan cookies. Peanut feqqas, which are very popular, are made from a cream cheese pastry dough that is rolled up around a filling of sautéed peanuts mixed with butter. The roll is chilled, then cut into rounds and baked. Almond and anise feqqas are crunchy, biscottilike, twice-baked cookies, flavored with ground almonds, anise seeds, sesame seeds, golden raisins, and orange flower water. They are often served as an accompaniment to mint tea. Morocco. See also: biscotti.

feuilletage The French word for the process of making flaky puff pastry, called *pâte feuilletée*. See also: feuilletée and puff pastry.

feuilletée The French word for turning over of a leaf, referring to the leafy, flaky, multilayered puff pastry dough called *pâte feuilletée*. To make this dough, layers of fat, usually butter, are rolled out between layers of dough and folded over many times to create hundreds of thin, leafy layers. See also: feuilletage and puff pastry.

fig The pear-shaped edible fruit of the fig tree that is native to Asia Minor. Use of figs in Egypt has been documented as far back as six thousand years. They were brought to the United States by Spanish Catholic missionaries in the late seventeenth century. The skin of figs ranges in color from pale cream to green to dark purplish-black, with flesh ranging from pale gold to dark red. Figs are naturally sweet with moist flesh. There are many varieties of figs; the most widely available are Calimyrna, also called Smyrna, Mission, and Kadota. Figs are used either fresh, cooked, or dried as an ingredient in many pastries, desserts, and confections. They also are used to make jam. Dried figs are available year-round. Fresh figs are available from June through October, with the peak in August and September. Choose fresh figs that are soft and dry with no blemishes and a sweet fragrance. Underripe figs will ripen at room temperature. Once ripened, they are very fragile. Store ripe figs on paper towels in the refrigerator for no longer than 2 days. Wash and gently dry just before use. See also: dried fruit and fruit.

filbert See hazelnut.

filo dough See phyllo dough.

financier A delicate sponge-type cake made from a mixture of finely ground almonds blended with egg whites and melted butter. **Financiers** are dense, moist, and tender inside with a chewy outer crust. The pans for large-size financiers are lined with sliced almonds, which adhere to the cake as it bakes. Individual financiers, which are very popular, are traditionally made in a rectangular shape, but oval and round ones are also found frequently. They are both eaten as individual pastries and used as the base for small pastries or petit fours. Large financiers are used as layers for more elaborate cakes, or the cake itself may be decorated by icing it with fondant or brushing it with apricot glaze and finishing it with fresh strawberries and mint leaves. France. See also: fondant, glaze, and petit four.

FINANCIERS

Eighteen 2- by 4- by ½-inch rectangular cakes or twenty-four 2½- by 1-inch-high round cakes or nine 3- by 2¼- by 1¾-inch-deep oval cakes.

1½ tablespoons unsalted butter, melted, for the pans

1 cup almond meal or 1 cup unblanched sliced almonds
1⅔ cups confectioners' sugar
⅓ cup plus 2 tablespoons all-purpose flour
6 large egg whites, at room temperature
3 ounces (6 tablespoons) unsalted butter, melted and cooled

Use a pastry brush to butter the insides of eighteen 2- by 4-inch rectangular molds or twenty-four 2½- by 1-inch-deep fluted round tartlet molds or nine 3- by 2¼- by 1¾-inch-deep oval molds with the melted butter.

Center a rack in the oven and preheat to 350°F.

Place the almond meal or sliced almonds in a shallow pan and toast in the oven until light golden, about 6 to 8 minutes, stirring once to prevent them from burning. Let cool. Raise the oven temperature to 450°F.

If using the sliced almonds, place them in the work bowl of a food processor fitted with the steel blade and pulse until they are ground to a fine powder, about 1 minute. If using the almond meal, place it in the bowl of the food processor.

Add the confectioners' sugar to the ground almonds and pulse until well blended, about 1 minute. Add the flour and pulse briefly to blend. Transfer the mixture to a 2-quart mixing bowl.

continued

Stir in the egg whites until thoroughly blended, then stir in the melted butter until blended.

Spoon the mixture into the molds filling them to just below the top if using rectangular and round molds or halfway if using oval molds. Place the molds on a baking sheet or jelly-roll pan. Bake for 6 minutes if using rectangular or round molds, 8 minutes if using oval molds. Reduce the oven temperature to 400°F and bake for 6 minutes for rectangular or round molds, 8 minutes for the oval molds, until golden. Turn off the oven, open the oven door slightly, or prop it open with a wooden spoon, and let the cakes cool in the oven for another 4 minutes. Then transfer the cakes to a rack to cool.

Lightly tap the molds against a firm surface, then slip the cakes from the molds. Financiers will keep for up to a week stored in an airtight container at room temperature.

firm ball stage The stage at which a small amount of hot sugar syrup dropped into cold water forms a firm but pliable, sticky ball that holds its shape briefly when removed from the water, then deflates if left at room temperature for a few minutes. The temperature range for firm ball stage is from 244° to 248°F on a candy thermometer. See also: Table of Sugar Temperatures and Stages (page 335).

firni A classic Indian custard made with rice flour or cream of rice, almonds, milk, cream, and sugar cooked to a velvety smooth texture. Firni is flavored with rose water and garnished with almonds, pistachio nuts, and occasionally, pomegranate seeds. India. See also: rose water.

flan An open-faced pastry shell that holds either a sweet filling, usually custard or fruit, or a savory one. Flans are baked in special straight-sided 1-inch high open metal rings or forms from which they take their name. The flan rings are placed on a lined baking sheet that serves as the bottom of the rings. Flans are made in individual and large sizes. Flan is also the Spanish name for a popular caramel-topped custard dessert. France and Spain. See also: crème caramel, flan ring, and tart.

flan de queso A Peruvian light custard dessert of cottage cheese, condensed milk, water, and eggs. The ingredients are puréed together, then baked in a shallow pan until set. The cheese custard is cooled and served at room temperature or chilled and served with fresh or stewed fruit. Peru.

flan ring Also called a flan form, a flan ring is a bottomless straight-sided 1-inch-high metal form with rolled rims, used to shape open-faced tarts, pastry shells, and candies. A flan ring is always placed on a baking sheet, which serves as its bottom. The baking sheet is lined with parchment paper, aluminum foil, or waxed paper. Flan rings come in many sizes and shapes; round, square, rectangular, and daisy petal. See also: flan.

fleuron A small crescent of puff pastry that is used to garnish both sweet and savory dishes made with pastry dough.

flexible-blade spatula This cooking utensil has a long narrow stainless steel blade with a rounded end and straight sides, set into a wooden handle. The blade is flexible (but not wobbly). This type of spatula has many uses, including icing cakes and pastries; spreading frostings, fillings, and batters; transferring cakes and pastries from one place to another; and releasing desserts from molds. Flexible-blade spatulas come in a large variety of sizes, ranging from a 3-inch-long blade to a 14-inch-long blade. The size of the blade to use depends on the task it is used for and the personal preference of the user.

floating island The "islands" in this cold dessert are composed of egg-shaped mounds of firmly beaten sweetened egg whites that are poached in milk or water. The mounds are served in a pool of thin crème anglaise (custard sauce) and topped with crushed praline or threads of caramel. In France, the dessert is called *oeufs à la neige*, which means "snow eggs." When the meringue mixture is formed into a round cake shape, the dessert is called *île flottante*; hence, the English name. France. See also: crème anglaise, poach, and praline.

Florentine A true confection, a Florentine is a cross between a cookie and a candy. Florentines are unusual in that they are first cooked and then baked. Butter, sugar, honey, cream, almonds, and candied orange peel are combined and cooked to the soft ball stage (248°F), then flour is added to the mixture. Small mounds of the mixture are placed on an oiled baking sheet, flattened with the back of a damp spoon, and baked. When cool, the underside of the Florentine is coated with tempered chocolate, and a pastry comb is run through the chocolate to create a wavy design. France. See also: pastry comb, tempering chocolate, and Table of Sugar Temperatures and Stages (page 335).

flour The finely ground meal of wheat and various other grains, flour is used in countless baked goods for both body and texture. The milling process turns grain into flour. Historically, rotating stones were used for milling. Today most flour is milled between fluted or grooved rollers, which break open the grain to expose the germ and bran, although stone-ground flour is available in some supermarkets and health food stores. The intense heat generated by the milling process would cause the germ and bran to turn rancid if they were not removed. The germ and bran are sifted away, leaving the endosperm, the heart of the grain. The endosperm is ground to various sizes from coarse to very fine, depending on its eventual use and the type of grain. Because wheat flour is naturally yellow after it is milled, it is often bleached with chlorine dioxide to whiten it rapidly. If left alone, however, it would whiten naturally in a month or 2, because of oxidation. Because aging enhances flour for baking, most producers age it chemically with potassium bromate or iodate to speed up the process. Vitamins are added to white flour to replace those that have been removed during milling. Vitamin-enriched flour is labeled as such.

There are several types of wheat flour. The most commonly available is all-purpose flour, which is a combination of high-gluten (protein) hard and low-gluten soft wheats. All-purpose flour is available both bleached and unbleached, which are essentially interchangeable. Bread flour is made from high-gluten hard wheat flour with a low starch content. Bread flour is used for making yeast-leavened breads. Because of its high gluten content, doughs made with bread flour rise substantially. Cake or pastry flour is made primarily from low-gluten soft wheat flour with a high starch content. It produces tender, crumbly baked goods. Pastry flour has slightly more protein than cake flour. Self-rising flour is all-purpose flour with added salt and baking powder. Gluten flour comes from hard wheat flour that has been treated to remove much of its starch, which gives it a high gluten content. It is combined with low-gluten flours or with regular flour to produce gluten breads for people whose tolerance to wheat is low. Whole wheat flour is milled from the entire kernel and has a richer, fuller flavor than white flour. It is available as both all-purpose and pastry flour. Whole wheat flour produces heavier, denser baked goods than white flour.

Flour gives structure to baked goods and batters, and it is used to coat foods for deep-frying and to dust baking pans to keep their contents from sticking. All flour should be stored in airtight containers at room temperature for no longer than 6 months. Whole wheat flour has a tendency to turn rancid rapidly because of the oil in the germ. It should be stored tightly wrapped in the refrigerator or frozen. Many other grains, such as corn, rice, and oats, are also ground into flour. See also: gluten.

flower former Made of plastic, a flower former is an 11-inch-long trough used to hold flowers and leaves made of icing while they dry so they will have a natural, slightly curved shape. The flower former can be used for support on either the inner or outer curve, depending on the flower and the shape desired. Flower formers come in sets of as many as nine pieces of three different widths. They are available at cake decorating supply shops and through mail order cookware catalogs.

flower nail This tool is used extensively in cake decorating to form three-dimensional flowers such as roses. Flower nails are also used to form small icing baskets, arches, and crescents. Flower nails are made of either plastic or metal; they look like long nails or screws with wide, platformlike tops. The top may be flat to curved, depending on the flower or other decorative element that it is used to form. To use a flower nail, a square of waxed or parchment paper is placed on its top, and the nail is held in one hand and rotated slowly while the other hand uses a pastry bag to pipe out icing to form the flower shape. Flower nails are available individually or in sets at cake decorating supply shops and cookware shops and through mail order cookware catalogs.

flute A technique for forming a decorative V-shaped or scalloped design on the outer edge of a pastry shell before it is baked. To form this design, place your forefinger against the inside of the pastry rim and place the thumb and forefinger of your other hand on the outside of the rim, then gently press your fingers toward each other.

foguete *Foguete* translates from the Portuguese as "rocket," and these deep-fried pastries resemble tiny firecrackers. Hollow sweet pastry tubes are deep-fried in hot oil. After cooling, they are filled with a mixture of pineapple, cashews, and raisins or cashews cooked in a sugar syrup until very thick, then flavored with rose water. The pastries are often dipped in a sweet syrup, which helps them to stay crisp for a few days. The pastries are dusted with confectioners' sugar before serving. Sri Lanka. See also: rose water.

foil candy cup These 1-inch wide and ⅝-inch high candy cups have fluted edges and are made of sturdy colored foil. They are ideal for holding truffle creams and candy mixtures that are liquid, since they will retain their shape when a filling is placed in them. The cups come in boxes of forty or sixty, in three colors: red, green, and gold. When they are peeled away from a candy, they leave an attractive fluted design around the sides. Foil candy cups are available at cake decorating and candy making supply shops, at cookware shops, and through mail order catalogs.

fold The technique used to combine a light and a heavy mixture and, in the process, retain the air that has been beaten into the lighter mixture. Folding is accomplished by first sweeping a long-handled rubber spatula around the inner edge of a mixing bowl in a clockwise direction, while gently giving the mixing bowl a quarter turn at a time in the opposite direction, then bringing the spatula up through the center of the mixture from the bottom, which lifts the bottom mixture up to the top. Repeating the process several times results in a thoroughly blended mixture. Folding should be done rapidly, but gently. See also: génoise and mousse.

fondant A confectionery mixture made from sugar syrup cooked to the soft ball stage (234° to 240°F), which is worked with a spatula on a marble or other smooth surface until it becomes a thick, opaque paste. This paste is kneaded until it is soft and pliable. Fondant is variously colored and flavored and used to fill and ice chocolates and other confections; it is used as the center for many candies. Fondant is heated in the top of a double boiler with liquid for use as an icing for cakes, pastries, and confections. Fondant will keep tightly wrapped in an airtight container in the refrigerator for up to 2 months. Commercially made fondant is available at some specialty food shops and cake decorating supply shops. France. See also: knead and Table of Sugar Temperatures and Stages (page 335).

fondant funnel A large stainless steel cone-shaped tool with a handle on the side and a small opening in the pointed end. Either a wooden dowel that blocks the hole, or a trigger mechanism that fits across the top, and works a plastic dowel, controls the flow of the fondant, or chocolate or sauce, out of the opening. The funnel is used to create uniform sizes of candy or portions of sauce. A nipplelike filler tube can be fitted over the bottom hole to make the opening tiny enough to fill 1/2-inch-wide chocolate shells. Fondant funnels are available at cake decorating and candy making supply shops, at cookware shops, and through mail order cookware catalogs.

fondue A dessert fondue consists of melted chocolate, often with the addition of cream and liqueur. The fondue is generally made in a ceramic or copper pan, which is held in a frame over a candle to keep it warm. Cubes of pound cake or angel food cake and pieces of fresh or candied fruit are dipped into the liquid chocolate. France.

food color Food color is used to tint candies, cakes, and frostings. Liquid food colors are the most well known and are available in supermarkets in small bottles in packages of red, green, yellow, and blue. The colors created with liquid food coloring are subtle. Paste food colors come in a wide variety of colors and are available in cake decorating and candy making supply shops. They are very concentrated and are used for tinting ingredients and mixtures that do not mix well with liquid, such as some fats and chocolate. Paste food colors should be used sparingly, added just a drop at a time and blended well before adding more, because the colors they impart are so deep. Powder food colors, also available at specialty shops, are used primarily to tint such mixtures as gum paste and pastillage. They are also very concentrated and a small amount is all that is needed to impart color. All food coloring is best stored tightly capped in a cool, dry place. Liquid food coloring will last for up to 4 years; paste and powder food colorings will last indefinitely. See also: gum paste and pastillage.

food processor This heavy-duty kitchen machine consists of a squat motor base with a central drive shaft upon which sits a sturdy clear plastic work bowl. Often the work bowl has a front handle. A variety of blades and disks fit on the drive shaft and a clear plastic cover with a feed tube fits the top of the work bowl. Ingredients are placed into the bowl either directly or, while the machine is operating, through the feed tube. Some machines have the option of fitting an expanded feed tube, which is large enough to hold a whole apple. When the top is in place, the drive shaft spins the blade at high speed to perform the various functions of chopping, shredding, slicing, grinding, mixing, and puréeing. The larger-capacity food processors have motors that are powerful enough to knead bread dough. The action of most machines is controlled by both an on/off switch and a pulse switch. Pulsing allows more control since the user determines exactly how long the switch will be held down. The standard blades for most food processors are an S-shaped steel multipurpose cutting blade, an S-shaped plastic dough blade, a shredding disk, and a slicing disk. Many other disks and attachments are also available, such as a whip for whipping cream or egg whites. Extra bowls can also be purchased, as can racks for storing disks and blades. Food processors come in many sizes and bowl capacities, ranging from mini, with a 3½-ounce-bowl capacity to extra-large, with a bowl capacity of 4 quarts. The food processor was introduced into the United States by a French company in the 1970s.

fool A classic British dessert, a fool is a chilled sweet made of fruit and whipped cream. Fools are traditionally made with a cooked fruit purée that is chilled and then sweetened, although today they are also made with fresh fruit, as in **kiwifruit fool**. The purée of fruit is folded into whipped cream. Fools are usually served like parfaits, layered in tall glasses. Gooseberries are the most traditional fruit, but fools are also made with many other fruits. Fools have been traced as far back as the fifteenth century. United Kingdom.

KIWIFRUIT FOOL

2½ cups; 4 to 6 servings

5 large ripe kiwifruit
3 to 4 tablespoons granulated sugar, to taste
⅔ cup heavy whipping cream
1 teaspoon vanilla extract

Peel the kiwis, cut them into quarters, and place them in the work bowl of a food processor fitted with the steel blade or in a blender. Pulse until the fruit is reduced to a rough purée. Transfer to a mixing bowl and stir in the sugar.

In the chilled bowl of a stand mixer, using the wire whip attachment, or in a chilled mixing bowl, using a hand-held mixer, whip the cream on medium speed until it is frothy. Add the vanilla extract and whip until the cream holds firm peaks.

Gently fold the cream into the kiwifruit purée, leaving some streaks of white. Pour the mixture into a glass serving bowl or into individual parfait or wine glasses. Cover the fool and refrigerate until serving time. The fool is best served within 3 hours of preparation.

fraise des bois A tiny, very sweet, French wild strawberry. France. See also: fruit and berry.

Fraisier See Bagatelle.

framboise The French word for raspberry. Also a raspberry-flavored eau-de-vie (clear fruit brandy), used as a flavoring in desserts, pastries, and confections, made in the Alsace region in northeastern France. France. See also: eau-de-vie.

Frangelico An Italian liqueur made from hazelnuts blended with an infusion of berries and flowers, Frangelico is a pale straw color. A fanciful legend claims that Frangelico was created by a hermit who lived in the mountains of Northern Italy three hundred years ago. Frangelico is used to flavor desserts, pastries, and confections. Italy.

frangipane Frangipane is a rich almond cream or pastry custard used as a filling in various desserts, tarts, and pastries, such as gâteau Pithiviers and the classic **pear frangipane tart**. Frangipane is also the name of a type of pastry similar to choux pastry, made of a cooked mixture of egg yolks, butter, flour, and milk. Frangipane puffs are filled with meat or poultry and served as an appetizer. France. See also: Pithiviers.

FRANGIPANE

1¼ cups

½ cup almond paste
⅓ cup granulated sugar
2 tablespoons unsalted butter, softened
2 large eggs, at room temperature, lightly beaten
1 teaspoon vanilla extract
1 teaspoon dark rum
1 teaspoon finely diced lemon zest
2 tablespoons all-purpose flour

Combine the almond paste and sugar in the bowl of a stand mixer or in a mixing bowl. Using the flat beater attachment or a hand-held mixer, blend together thoroughly. Add the softened butter and blend until smooth, about 2 minutes.

Add the eggs and all the flavorings, and beat until smooth, about 2 minutes. Add the flour and blend well. The frangipane cream will keep in a tightly covered container in the refrigerator for up to 4 days.

PEAR FRANGIPANE TART

One 9½-inch round tart; 12 to 14 servings

Poached pears
2 cups granulated sugar
4 cups water
Juice of 1 large lemon
2 cinnamon sticks
2 whole cloves
4 ripe but firm pears

Assembly
1 recipe Pâte Sucrée (page 225)
1 recipe Frangipane (above)
½ cup apricot preserves
2 tablespoons Grand Marnier or other orange-flavored liqueur

Combine the sugar, water, lemon juice, cinnamon sticks, and cloves in a large heavy-bottomed nonreactive saucepan and bring the

continued

mixture to a boil. Reduce the heat to low so the mixture is at a simmer.

Meanwhile, peel the pears, slice them in half lengthwise, and remove the stems and seeds.

Add the pears to the simmering liquid and poach until they are soft, but not mushy, about 1 hour.

Transfer the pears to a bowl of cold water. Drain and pat dry with a towel just before using. (The pears can be prepared up to 3 days in advance and stored in the refrigerator, in their poaching liquid, in a covered container.)

Center a rack in the oven and preheat to 375°F.

Roll out the pâte sucrée on a lightly floured work surface to a ⅛-inch-thick, 12-inch diameter round. Loosely roll the pastry dough up over the rolling pin, and unroll gently into a 9½-inch fluted tart pan with a removable bottom. Carefully fit the dough into the bottom and up the sides of the tart pan without stretching. Trim off the excess pastry dough.

Place the tart pan on a jelly-roll pan. Fill the pastry shell with the frangipane cream, spreading it evenly. Thinly slice the poached pears crosswise, keeping the sliced pear halves intact. Press down on the sliced halves gently, then, using a wide spatula, transfer them to the filling, stem ends pointing to the center of the shell.

Bake the tart for 30 to 35 minutes, until puffed and lightly browned. Transfer the pan to a rack to cool slightly.

Combine the apricot preserves and Grand Marnier in a small saucepan and bring to a boil over medium heat. Strain the glaze to remove the fruit pulp. Brush it over the top of the tart.

The tart is best served slightly warm. It will keep for 3 days well wrapped in the refrigerator.

French meringue See meringue.

friandise The French word for a dainty tidbit of pastry or confectionery. Friandises are small confections such as delicate cookies, chocolates, and petits fours. They are usually served with tea or coffee or at the end of a meal, after dessert. France.

frittella The Italian word for fritter. See also: fritter.

fritter Called *beignets* in France, fritters are pieces of fruit, such as apple slices, that are coated with a variety of batters and deep-fried in hot oil. The batter itself, such as choux pastry or a yeast-risen dough also used for doughnuts, can be made into fritters. Dessert fritters are usually served hot, dusted with granulated or confectioners' sugar. Occasionally they are filled with jam before being deep-fried. Edible flowers, such as squash blossoms, are also made into fritters. There are many types of fritters and many regional specialties, such as Mexico's churros, found in countries throughout the world. United States. See also: batter, beignet, choux pastry, churro, and doughnut.

frost To cover a cake or pastry with frosting or icing. See also: frosting and icing.

frosting Made primarily of sugar, frosting is a sweet covering and filling for cakes and pastries used in all types of confectionery. Other ingredients may include butter, eggs, milk, water, and a variety of flavorings. There are many types of frosting, both cooked and uncooked, such as buttercream, boiled icing, and ganache. The term *frosting* is interchangeable with *icing*. See also: buttercream, ganache, and icing.

fructose A sugar that occurs naturally in fruit and honey, fructose, also called levulose, is almost twice as sweet as sucrose (regular granulated sugar), with only half the calories. Fructose is referred to as a simple sugar because it is half of the sucrose molecule, but fructose cannot be substituted directly for sucrose in a recipe. It comes in both liquid and granulated form. See also: sugar.

fruit The edible pod of a woody or perennial plant that is succulent and usually sweet. Fruit is an important component of many desserts and pastries, such as buckles, cakes, compotes, cobblers, fools, fritters, fruitcakes, mousses, pandowdies, pies, shortcakes, sorbets, tarts, turnovers, and ice creams, and fruit is widely used in confectionery. Fruit is used to make some dessert sauces and to make conserves, jams, jellies, and marmalades, which are used as a part of or as an accompaniment to many desserts and pastries. Fruits can be used in desserts, pastries, and confections raw, baked, cooked, or poached, and a number of fruits can be dried and candied. Many ripe fruits can be served as dessert on their own or as part of a fruit salad. The best way to tell if fruit is ripe is by its fragrance and color. To be sure of the best quality, choose fruit that is in season. For use in most pastries, desserts, and confections, choose fruit that is ripe or slightly underripe so it will hold its shape. Fruit that is overripe will have trouble holding its shape, but can be used for a purée or sauce. Most fruit continues to ripen at room temperature, but stops ripening if refrigerated. Gently wash fruit just before using. See also: candied fruit, dried fruit, and specific individual fruits.

fruitcake A rich, buttery, dense, sweet, sometimes spicy batter mixed with a variety of candied fruits and nuts, then baked. Fruitcake traditionally has just enough batter to hold the fruits and nuts together. It is traditionally baked in a loaf shape or in a tube pan and is made several weeks in advance of serving so it can "mellow," by being wrapped in cheesecloth and soaked in rum or brandy. Dark fruitcake is made with molasses or brown sugar and dark fruits and nuts. Light fruitcake is sweetened with light corn syrup or granulated sugar and contains light-colored fruits and nuts. Fruitcake is generally served only at special occasions and holidays, such as Christmas. United States and United Kingdom.

fruit corer/slicer See corer.

fudge A semisoft creamy candy of various flavors, although chocolate is the most popular. Fudge can be smooth, but it often contains nuts, as in the favorite **chocolate walnut fudge**. The main ingredients in fudge are sugar, butter, and cream, which are combined and cooked to the softball stage (234°-240°F). Grainy fudge is the result of beating the mixture before it is cool, which causes large sugar crystals to form. If the fudge is beaten after it is cool, small sugar crystals form, which produce a smoother texture. Fudge is cut into squares after it has cooled and set. United States. See also: soft ball stage and Table of Sugar Temperatures and Stages (page 335).

CHOCOLATE WALNUT FUDGE

Thirty-six 1¼-inch squares

½ tablespoon unsalted butter, softened, for the pan

1 cup granulated sugar
1 cup firmly packed light brown sugar
½ teaspoon cream of tartar
Pinch of salt
¼ cup light corn syrup
¾ cup heavy whipping cream
7 ounces bittersweet or semisweet chocolate, very finely chopped
1½ tablespoons unsalted butter, cut into pieces, softened
2 teaspoons vanilla extract
1½ cups roughly chopped walnuts

Line an 8-inch square baking pan with aluminum foil so that it extends over the sides, and butter the bottom and sides of the foil with the softened butter. Rinse a jelly-roll pan with cold water, shake off the excess, and set the pan near the stove.

In a heavy-bottomed 3-quart saucepan, combine the granulated sugar, brown sugar, cream of tartar, salt, corn syrup, and cream. Cook over medium heat, stirring constantly with a long-handled wooden spoon, until the sugar dissolves, about 3 minutes. Brush down the sides of the pan with a pastry brush dipped in warm water to prevent crystallization.

Take the pan off the heat, and stir in the chocolate in 3 to 4 additions, making sure each addition is melted before adding the next. (This will take 1 to 2 minutes.) Return the pan to medium heat and position a candy thermometer in the pan. Cook, without stirring, until the mixture registers 238°F on the candy thermometer, 20 to 25 minutes.

Remove the pan from the heat and quickly stir in the butter and vanilla just to blend. Immediately turn the mixture out into the jelly-roll pan. Do not scrape out the bottom of the pan. Let the mixture cool until it registers 110°F on an instant-read thermometer, 10 to 15 minutes.

Using a plastic bowl scraper or rubber spatula, scrape the fudge into a mixing bowl or the bowl of a stand mixer. Using a hand-held mixer or the flat beater attachment, beat the fudge on low speed until it thickens and loses its sheen, 5 to 10 minutes, stopping to scrape down the sides of the bowl 2 or 3 times. When the fudge reaches the right point it will thicken, lighten in color, and form peaks. Beat in chopped walnuts just to blend.

Turn the fudge out into the foil-lined pan. Use your fingertips to push the fudge into the corners of the pan and to even the top. Set the pan on a cooling rack and leave the fudge to firm at room temperature for 1 to 2 hours.

Remove the fudge from the pan by lifting out the aluminum foil. Gently peel the foil off the fudge. Cut the fudge into 36 pieces (6 rows in each direction).

Store the fudge between layers of waxed paper in an airtight container at room temperature for up to 10 days.

funnel cake A Pennsylvania Dutch specialty, this pastry is made by pouring batter through a funnel into hot fat and swirling it to form spirals, which are deep-fried until crisp and golden. Funnel cakes are drained and served hot with sugar or maple syrup. United States.

galette A flat round cake made with puff pastry, yeast-risen pastry similar to brioche dough, or sweet pastry dough, such as pâte sucrée. A galette is also a sweet or savory tart with a thin, crunchy dough, which is cut into pie-shaped wedges. There are a wide variety of galettes representing the many regions of France, with myriad toppings, such as jam, candied fruit, marzipan, cream, cheese, meat, and nuts. Galette des Rois, also called Twelfth Night Cake, is a traditional cake served during Twelfth Night celebrations. It is made with puff pastry and baked with a bean or other memento embedded in the filling, which is reputed to bring good luck to the recipient. France. See also: pâte sucrée and tart.

Galliano Blended from a variety of herbs, spices, and berries, this slightly sweet, brilliant yellow Italian liqueur has a pronounced licorice taste, which comes from anise, with a hint of vanilla. Galliano is used to flavor desserts, pastries, and confections. Italy.

ganache A mixture of melted or finely chopped chocolate and heated cream that are blended together until very smooth. The proportions of chocolate and cream can vary: more chocolate than cream, more cream than chocolate, or equal amounts of both. **Ganache** has many uses. It can be shaped into balls to form the soft center for truffles. When liquid and lukewarm, it can be poured over a cake for a smooth, shiny glaze. It can be whipped with soft butter to create ganache beurre, or ganache soufflé (rich chocolate buttercream), which is used as a filling for cakes, prebaked tartlet shells, and petits fours. Rum, Cognac, or a liqueur can also be added to ganache that is then whipped to a fluffy consistency and used for a filling. France.

GANACHE

1⅓ cups

8 ounces bittersweet chocolate, finely chopped
¾ cup heavy whipping cream

Melt the chocolate in the top of a double boiler over hot, not simmering, water, stirring frequently with a rubber spatula to ensure even melting.

Meanwhile, in a ½-quart saucepan, heat the cream over medium heat to just below the boil.

Remove both pans from the heat. Remove the top pan from the double boiler, and wipe the outside dry. Pour the cream into the chocolate, and stir for several minutes, until the mixture is completely blended and smooth. Pour the ganache into a bowl, a jar, or a plastic container and cover tightly. Let the ganache cool to room temperature, then refrigerate until it is the consistency of thick pudding.

Ganache will keep for up to 2 months in a well-covered container in the refrigerator, or it can be frozen for up to 6 months. If frozen, defrost for at least 24 hours in the refrigerator before using. Ganache that is very firm must stand at room temperature to soften before it is used.

Variations: For milk chocolate ganache, use 8 ounces milk chocolate and ½ cup cream. For white chocolate ganache, use 8 ounces white chocolate and ⅓ cup cream.

gâteau The French word for cake.

Gâteau l'Opéra Named in honor of the Paris Opera, this classic rectangular cake is composed of three layers of delicate almond génoise or biscuit, soaked with sugar syrup. The layers are spread alternately with rich coffee buttercream and ganache. The sides of the cake are left unfrosted. The word "L'Opéra" is written on a chocolate plaque the size of the top of the cake, with piping chocolate, and the plaque is set on top of the cake. Flecks of edible gold leaf are often used to decorate the top of the cake. The cake is cut into rectangular pieces for serving. France. See also: buttercream, chocolate glaze, ganache, génoise, gold leaf, piping chocolate, and sugar syrup.

GÂTEAU L'OPÉRA

One 11- by 5-inch rectangular cake; 12 to 14 servings

2 teaspoons unsalted butter, melted, for the pan
1 tablespoon all-purpose flour, for the pan

Cake
1 cup finely ground almonds
1 cup confectioners' sugar, sifted
⅓ cup all-purpose flour
4 large eggs, at room temperature
4 large egg whites, at room temperature
2 tablespoons granulated sugar
2½ tablespoons unsalted butter, melted and cooled

Sugar syrup
¼ cup granulated sugar
½ cup water

Ganache
6 ounces bittersweet chocolate, finely chopped
½ cup heavy whipping cream
4 ounces (1 stick) unsalted butter, softened

Buttercream
2 large eggs, at room temperature
2 large egg yolks, at room temperature
1 cup plus 2 tablespoons granulated sugar
½ cup water
¼ teaspoon cream of tartar
14 ounces (3½ sticks) unsalted butter, softened
1 tablespoon instant espresso powder dissolved in 1 tablespoon water

Assembly
6 ounces bittersweet chocolate to be tempered (see page 297)
1 ounce melted bittersweet chocolate, for piping

Center a rack in the oven and preheat to 400°F. Line a jelly-roll pan with a sheet of parchment paper. Brush the parchment paper with the melted butter, dust with the flour, and shake off the excess.

For the cake, combine the ground almonds, confectioners' sugar, flour, and 2 of the eggs in the bowl of a stand mixer or in a mixing bowl. Using the wire whip attachment or a hand-held mixer, blend together on medium speed for 3 minutes. Add the remaining 2 eggs and beat the mixture until it holds a slowly dissolving ribbon when the beater is lifted, about 3 minutes.

In a grease-free mixing bowl, using grease-free beaters, whip the egg whites until they hold soft peaks. Gradually sprinkle on the sugar and whip the egg whites until they hold stiff, but not dry, peaks. Fold the beaten egg whites into the almond mixture in 3 additions, then fold in the melted butter in 2 additions.

Pour the batter into the prepared pan, and use an offset spatula to spread it evenly and smoothly in the pan. Bake the cake for 8 to 10 minutes, or until it is golden brown and the top springs back when lightly touched. Transfer to a rack to cool.

Loosen the edges of the cake from the pan with a small knife. Place a sheet of parchment paper on top of the cake, place another jelly-roll pan, bottom side down, on top of the parchment paper, and invert the cake onto the pan. Peel off the paper. Trim off the edges of the cake, then slice the cake crosswise into 3 equal strips about 5 inches wide.

For the sugar syrup, combine the sugar and water in a saucepan and bring to a boil over high heat. Remove from the heat and let cool.

For the ganache, melt the chopped chocolate in the top of a double boiler over hot, not simmering, water, stirring frequently with a rubber spatula to ensure even melting.

Meanwhile, in a small saucepan, heat the cream over medium heat to a boil.

Remove both pans from the heat. Remove the top pan from the double boiler and wipe the outside dry. Pour the cream into the chocolate and stir together until smooth and thoroughly blended. Pour the mixture into a bowl, cover tightly with plastic wrap, and chill in the refrigerator until the consistency of thick pudding, 1 to 2 hours.

In the bowl of a stand mixer, using the flat beater attachment, or in a mixing bowl, using a hand-held mixer, beat the butter until it is very soft and fluffy. Add the soft ganache to the butter a few tablespoons at a time, blending well. Cover with plastic wrap and set aside at room temperature.

For the buttercream, combine the eggs and egg yolks in the

bowl of a stand mixer or in a mixing bowl. Using the wire whip attachment or a hand-held mixer, beat on medium-high speed until the mixture is very pale colored and holds a slowly dissolving ribbon when the beater is lifted, 6 to 8 minutes.

Meanwhile, combine the sugar, water, and cream of tartar in a small heavy-bottomed saucepan and bring to a boil over high heat. Wash down the sides of the pan with a pastry brush dipped in warm water after it comes to a boil, then continue cooking. Cook the mixture until it reaches 242°F on a candy thermometer, washing down the sides of the pan with a pastry brush dipped in warm water 2 or 3 times to prevent crystals from forming.

When the sugar syrup is at the correct temperature, with the mixer on low speed, pour it into the egg mixture in a slow, steady stream. Turn the mixer speed to medium-high and beat until the mixture is completely cool and the bowl is cool, 5 to 8 minutes.

Beat in the softened butter a few tablespoons at a time, and continue to beat the buttercream until it is fluffy, 2 to 3 minutes. Add the espresso, stopping to scrape down the sides of the bowl with a rubber spatula as necessary. Cover tightly with plastic wrap and set aside at room temperature.

Line a jelly-roll pan with waxed paper.

Temper the 6 ounces bittersweet chocolate, and pour the chocolate onto the waxed paper. Use an offset spatula to spread it into a large rectangle about 6 by 12 inches. Lift up opposite corners of the waxed paper and shake them gently to smooth the chocolate and eliminate any air bubbles. Refrigerate the chocolate until it is firm, about 15 minutes.

Cut an 11- by 5-inch cardboard rectangle. Using the cardboard as a guide, cut out a chocolate rectangle to fit the top of the cake.

To assemble the cake, place 1 cake layer on the cardboard rectangle, top side up. Brush with some of the sugar syrup, then spread half of the coffee buttercream evenly over the cake layer. Position another layer of cake on top of the buttercream, and brush the cake layer with sugar syrup. Spread the chocolate ganache evenly and smoothly over this layer. Position the third layer of cake on the chocolate cream, and brush with sugar syrup. Spread the remaining buttercream over the cake layer.

Hold the edges of the waxed paper, position the chocolate rectangle on top of the buttercream, and peel off the waxed paper. Use scissors to trim the chocolate rectangle as necessary to fit evenly on the buttercream.

For the piping chocolate, prepare a small parchment paper pastry cone. Stir 1 or 2 drops of water into the melted chocolate until it thickens very slightly. Pour the mixture into the paper pastry cone, fold down the top to secure the mixture, and snip off a tiny opening at the pointed end. Pipe "L'Opéra" on top of the chocolate plaque.

Refrigerate the cake for at least 2 hours. Let stand at room temperature for 30 minutes before serving.

Cut the cake crosswise into 1-inch-wide slices. The cake will keep for up to 4 days, well covered, in the refrigerator.

Gâteau Saint-Honoré This classic cake is made with a round base of either pâte brisée or puff pastry. Choux pastry (cream puff pastry) is piped in concentric circles onto the pastry base, from the center to the outer edge. One-inch-diameter puffs are piped from the remaining pastry, then the cake and puffs are brushed with egg wash and baked until golden brown. When cool, the small puffs are filled with sweetened whipped cream, and their tops are dipped in liquid caramel. They are placed around the outer edge of the cake, using more caramel to hold them in place. The center of the cake is filled with the same cream, or with Chiboust cream, piped in a decorative shell design. The cake can be decorated with candied cherries, crystallized violets, or candied orange peel placed between the small puffs. Saint Honoré is the patron saint of pastry cooks. France. See also: candied fruit, Chiboust cream, choux pastry, crystallized flowers, egg wash, pâte brisée, piping, and puff pastry.

gelatin A colorless, tasteless, natural product derived from collagen, a protein found in the connective tissue and bones of animals. Gelatin is a thickening agent, which activates when moistened. It is used to set fillings, puddings, mousses, Bavarian creams, and other desserts and confections. Gelatin is most commonly sold in the United States in dry powder form, which comes in premeasured envelopes and in bulk. European gelatin, which is also available in the United States, takes the form of clear paper-thin leaves or sheets. Either type of gelatin can be used in any recipe; one package of powder gelatin is equal to three sheets of leaf gelatin. To soften the powder gelatin, sprinkle it over a small amount of cold water (2 tablespoons water for 1 envelope or 1 tablespoon gelatin) and let it sit for a minimum of 5 minutes, then heat it in the top of a double boiler over moderate heat. To soften sheets of gelatin, soak them in cold water for at least 10 minutes, then squeeze out the excess water, transfer to a saucepan, and heat gently over low heat until the gelatin liquifies. Gelatin should be used as soon as it is melted. Both powder and sheet gelatin should be stored wrapped airtight in a cool, dry place, where they will last indefinitely. See also: agar-agar.

gelato Italian for ice cream. Gelato has less air than either American or French ice cream, so it is denser, firmer, and richer. See also: ice cream.

génoise A light, airy, sponge-type cake made of eggs and sugar that are beaten together to incorporate air, which aids in rising during baking. Flour, and sometimes cornstarch, is then folded in, followed by melted butter. Ground nuts, liqueurs, extracts, or citrus zest may be added for flavoring. Génoise is most often baked in a round shape. Before the génoise is used as the base for a dessert, it is usually brushed with a sugar syrup for added moisture. Génoise is extremely versatile and is the basis for many layered cakes and desserts. It is used throughout Europe and the United States. Génoise was developed in Genoa, Italy, and adapted by the French in the fifteenth century. Italy and France. See also: fold.

GÉNOISE

One 9- by 2-inch round cake

1 tablespoon unsalted butter, softened, for the pan
2 teaspoons all-purpose flour, for the pan

3 large eggs, at room temperature
3 large egg yolks, at room temperature
½ cup plus 1 tablespoon granulated sugar
¼ cup all-purpose flour
¼ cup cornstarch
2 tablespoons unsalted butter, melted and cooled

Center a rack in the oven and preheat to 300°F. Using the softened tablespoon butter, butter the inside of a 9- by 2-inch round cake pan and a 9-inch parchment paper round. Dust the pan with the flour and shake out the excess. Place the parchment round in the bottom of the pan, buttered side up.

Place the eggs and yolks in the bowl of a stand mixer or in a mixing bowl. Using the wire whip attachment or a hand-held mixer at low speed, beat the eggs to blend, then beat in the sugar. Turn the speed up to medium and beat until the mixture is very pale colored and holds a slowly dissolving ribbon when the beater is lifted, 5 to 8 minutes.

Sift together the flour and cornstarch, and using a long-handled rubber spatula, fold into the beaten eggs in 3 additions. Fold in the melted butter in 2 stages. Pour the batter into the prepared cake pan and smooth the top.

Bake the cake until golden-colored and the top springs back when lightly touched, 45 to 50 minutes. Transfer to a rack to cool for 10 minutes.

Place a 9-inch cardboard cake circle over the top of the cake pan and invert the cake onto the cardboard. Gently remove the cake pan. Carefully peel off the parchment paper and reinvert the cake onto the cardboard cake circle. Let cool completely on a rack.

The génoise will keep for 4 days well wrapped in the refrigerator, or it can be frozen for several months. If frozen, defrost the génoise in the refrigerator overnight before using. The génoise is easier to cut if made the day before it is to be used.

gianduja A blended mixture of chocolate and hazelnuts that has a unique flavor and velvety-smooth texture. Usually milk chocolate is used, but gianduja can be made from semisweet or bittersweet chocolate. Gianduja chocolate has a short shelf life, between 6 and 8 months. It should be handled and stored the same way as other types of chocolate. Gianduja is also the name of a category of candies and confections that contains chocolate and hazelnuts. See also: chocolate.

ginger Derived from the underground stems of a plant native to Southeast Asia, ginger has a pungent, spicy taste. It is used to flavor and decorate cakes, cookies, breads, ice cream, and candies. The two most common forms for use in sweets are finely ground dried ginger and crystallized ginger, which has been cooked in a sugar syrup and covered with sugar. Ginger was one of the earliest spices imported to Europe by Arab traders. Both ground and crystallized ginger are best stored in tightly sealed glass jars in a cool, dark, dry place. Ground ginger tends to lose its flavor after 4 to 6 months. Crystallized ginger will last indefinitely if stored properly.

gingerbread A favorite sweet worldwide. There are endless recipes and variations for **gingerbread**, ranging from light-colored and mildly spicy to dark and piquant. It ranges in texture from cakelike to as crisp as a cookie. The cookielike version is used during the Christmas holiday season to create gingerbread people and richly decorated gingerbread houses. Many countries have their own classic gingerbread variations: for example, speculaas in Holland, which are cookielike and formed in molds, and pain d'épice in France, which is considered to be a spice cake. The English and American versions of gingerbread are cakelike and use molasses in place of the honey in the European versions. American gingerbread is usually baked in a square pan and served with sweetened whipped cream. Gingerbread has a rich and varied history that can be traced back through the eleventh-century Crusades to the spiced honey cakes of the Middle East. Medieval German bakers were the first to adapt these honey cakes to become gingerbread, but it soon found a place in the cuisine of every European country. Medieval gingerbread was baked in elaborate molds and intricately decorated. Germany.

GINGERBREAD

Sixteen 2-inch squares

1 tablespoon unsalted butter, softened, for the pan
1 tablespoon all-purpose flour, for the pan

2½ cups all-purpose flour
2 teaspoons baking soda
1 tablespoon ground ginger
1 teaspoon ground cinnamon
½ teaspoon ground cloves
¼ teaspoon freshly grated nutmeg
¼ teaspoon salt
4 ounces (1 stick) unsalted butter, at room temperature
¼ cup firmly packed light brown sugar
¼ cup granulated sugar
2 large eggs, at room temperature, lightly beaten
1 cup unsulfured molasses
1 cup boiling water
½ cup heavy whipping cream whipped to soft peaks, for garnish

Center a rack in the oven and preheat to 350°F. Generously butter the inside of an 8- by 2-inch square baking pan with the softened butter, then dust the pan with the flour and shake out the excess.

Sift together the flour, baking soda, and spices onto a large piece of waxed paper, then blend in the salt.

In the bowl of a stand mixer, using the flat beater attachment, or in a mixing bowl, using a hand-held mixer, beat the butter until it is soft and fluffy, about 2 minutes. Add the brown sugar and granulated sugar and beat until well blended, about 2 minutes, stopping to scrape down the sides of the bowl with a rubber spatula twice.

Beat in the eggs and then the molasses, blending well, then beat in the boiling water. Scrape down the sides of the bowl. With the mixer on low speed, add the dry ingredients in 2 or 3 additions, beating well after each addition. Turn the mixture out into the prepared pan.

Bake for 45 minutes, until the top springs back when lightly touched and a cake tester inserted into the center comes out clean. Transfer the pan to a rack to cool. Cut the gingerbread into squares, and top with a dollop of whipped cream.

The gingerbread will keep for 3 days at room temperature, well wrapped in foil.

gingerbread house mold See cookie mold.

gingersnap A thin, crisp, small round cookie flavored with ginger. Flour, eggs, baking soda, molasses, sugar, salt, and cinnamon are the primary ingredients of gingersnaps.

glace The French word for ice cream.

glacé The French word for iced, frozen, frosted, glazed, candied, or crystallized. It also refers to a type of frosting or icing for cakes and pastries.

glaze A thin, shiny coating for desserts, pastries, and confections that is either brushed or poured on. There are several types of glazes. Jam or jelly glazes, such as **apricot glaze**, are made by heating together a jam, jelly, preserve, or marmalade and a liquid, such as water or liqueur, then straining the mixture to remove the fruit pulp. The glaze is cooled slightly, then brushed on the top of fruit tarts or baked goods such as tea breads or coffee cakes. Chocolate glazes are made with melted chocolate blended with cream, butter, or corn syrup to a pourable consistency. They are poured over cakes, petits fours, or individual pastries, which are set on a cooling rack over a baking sheet to catch the excess that drips off. A confectioners' sugar glaze is made by mixing the sugar with a little liquid, such as lemon juice or water, until it is smooth and pourable. A caramel glaze is used to coat the tops of cream puffs for Gâteau Saint-Honoré. Another type of glaze is an egg wash made with a whole egg, an egg yolk, or an egg white mixed with milk or water. Egg wash is brushed on top of baked goods before they are baked to give them a shiny finish and to help them brown evenly. Glazes are applied by pouring, drizzling, or dipping. See also: egg wash and Gâteau Saint-Honoré.

APRICOT GLAZE

½ cup

½ cup apricot preserves
2 tablespoons Grand Marnier or other orange-flavored liqueur
    or water

Combine the preserves and liquid in a heavy-bottomed saucepan. Bring the mixture to a boil over medium heat, stirring occasionally. Press the mixture through a strainer into a small bowl, pushing through as much of the fruit pulp as possible. Cool the glaze briefly before applying it with a pastry brush.

The glaze will keep for up to 3 months in a tightly sealed container in the refrigerator. Reheat it before using to thin it. If the glaze is too thick, stir in up to 1 tablespoon more liquid and heat briefly.

glazirovanniye sirki Russian cheese confections glazed with chocolate. A blend of cream cheese and farmer's cheese is combined with sugar, egg yolks, lemon zest, and lemon juice, then wrapped in cheesecloth and drained overnight. The mixture is formed into balls and chilled, then dipped in melted chocolate and chilled again to set the chocolate. Russia.

glucose A naturally occurring sugar found in fruits, honey, and some vegetables, glucose is also called dextrose. It is half as sweet as granulated sugar. Glucose is a simple sugar that makes up half of the sucrose molecule. Glucose does not crystallize easily and, therefore, is used as an interfering agent in making candies, baked goods, and icings. It also holds moisture, thereby increasing the shelf life of candies and baked goods. Corn syrup, made from cornstarch, is a type of glucose. See also: corn syrup and sugar.

gluten A combination of the naturally occurring substances gliadin and glutenin, gluten is an elastic protein that forms when wheat flour, or flour made from certain other grains, is mixed with liquid and stirred or kneaded. The amount of gluten developed can be determined by how much or how little the mixture is handled. Strands of gluten form as the dough or batter is stirred or kneaded. These strands form an elastic network that traps air and gas released by the leavening agents used. When heated, the air and gas expand, stretching the gluten. During the final stages of baking, the gluten firms up and sets. The process results in lightness and volume in breads, cakes, and other baked goods. Flours that are made from hard wheat and have a high proportion of gluten, such as bread flour, are more desirable for use in baked goods that require a strong structure. Cake and pastry flours are made from soft wheat and have lesser amounts of gluten, so are better for use in delicate, tender biscuits, cakes, and pastries. See also: flour.

glycerin, glycerine Also called glycerol, glycerin is a syrupy, odorless, sweet, clear liquid, derived from fats and oils. It is used in confectionery and icings, such as rolled fondant, to preserve moisture, to add sweetness, and to prevent crystallization.

golden syrup A straw-colored sugar syrup with a thick consistency similar to corn syrup, golden syrup is made from processed sugarcane juice. It has a rich, toasty flavor and can be used in place of corn syrup in baked goods and in candy making. Golden syrup is very popular in Great Britain, where it is widely used as a sweetener. It is also known as light treacle. The most well known brand of golden syrup is Lyle's, which is available in many supermarkets and specialty food stores. United Kingdom.

gold leaf Edible gold leaf is made from pure 22- to 24-karat gold. It comes in packages of twenty-five $3^{1}/_{2}$-inch-square leaves, layered between sheets of tissue parchment paper. There are two main types of gold leaf, loose and patent. The loose variety is paper-thin ($^{1}/_{200,000}$th of an inch) and works best for pastry and confectionery. Patent is thicker than loose and must be cut with a knife or heavy scissors. Golf leaf is also available in skewings, similar to confetti, which can be sprinkled onto desserts, pastries, and confections. Gold leaf has no taste. It dissolves easily from the moisture in one's hands if touched, so it must be handled with a sable brush. Gold leaf is used to decorate special desserts, pastries, and confections in France, India, Southeast Asia, and the United States. Gold leaf is available from gilders' and sign-painters' suppliers and art supply stores. Gold leaf is best stored in a cool, dry place, where it will last indefinitely. See also: gold powder and gold ribbon.

gold powder Edible gold powder is made from 22- to 24-karat gold or nontoxic mica, both of which are ground to dust. Gold powder, which has no taste, is used to decorate desserts, pastries, and confections. It is extremely light and has a tendency to "fly," so it should be handled carefully. A sable brush is the best tool to use to gild a surface with gold powder. Gold and mica powder are available from gilders' and sign-painters' suppliers, art supply stores, and cake decorating supply shops. Gold powder is best stored in a cool, dry place in a well-covered container, where it will last indefinitely. See also: gold leaf and gold ribbon.

gold ribbon Similar to the loose type of gold leaf in texture and thickness, gold ribbon comes in spools ranging from 1/8 inch to 6 3/4 inches wide, about 70 feet in length. Like gold leaf, gold ribbon is backed with a thin layer of tissue parchment paper. To be considered edible, it must be between 22 and 24 karats. Gold ribbon has no taste and is used to decorate desserts, pastries, and confections. It dissolves easily from the moisture in one's hands if touched, so it must be handled by the paper backing or fed through a dispenser, available for use with the 1/8-inch-wide ribbon. Gold ribbon is available from gilders' and sign-painters' suppliers and art supply stores. It is best stored in a cool, dry place, where it will last indefinitely. See also: gold leaf and gold powder.

goldwasser Translated from the German as "gold water," goldwasser is a straw-colored herb-flavored liqueur with tiny flecks of edible gold leaf suspended throughout. Goldwasser is also referred to as Danziger Goldwasser, which is the most well known brand. It is used to flavor desserts, pastries, and confections. It is available at most large liquor stores. Germany.

gooseberry A large round berry, resembling a grape, with taut skin. Gooseberries are either smooth or fuzzy-skinned, depending on the variety. Their color ranges from white to apple-green to yellow to pink, and they are often streaked with red. The most common ones in American markets are the green and yellow-green varieties streaked with white. Crisp, naturally tart gooseberries are used both raw and cooked as an ingredient in desserts and pastries—primarily fools, pies, and tarts—and are used to make preserves. Canned gooseberries are available year-round. Fresh gooseberries are available in the summer months, although they can be difficult to find in the United States. They are very popular in northern Europe. Choose dry, firm, evenly colored, shiny berries. Store gooseberries in the refrigerator for up to 2 weeks and rinse just before use. See also: berry.

goosefeather brush See pastry brush.

Grand Marnier A French liqueur that is a blend of fine old Cognac brandy and oranges. It is clear with a tint of gold. Grand Marnier is used extensively to flavor desserts, pastries, and confections. France.

granita An Italian water ice with a grainy texture, granita is made from a mixture of sugar, water, and flavoring, such as fruit juice, coffee, or wine. The mixture is stirred frequently during the freezing process to produce the characteristic granular texture. Although granita is a type of sorbet, it is not as smooth as sorbet. Granita is usually served slightly softened and slushy, either between courses as a palate cleanser or as a dessert or snack. Italy. See also: sorbet.

Granny Smith apple One of the favorite apples for use in baked goods and for baking whole because it holds its shape. Granny Smith apples have pale green skin and crisp, juicy, sweet-tart flesh. They are available almost year-round because of imports from New Zealand and Australia that alternate seasons with the U.S. crop. See also: apple.

grape Grapes have been cultivated for at least six thousand years. There are about sixty types grown today in temperate climates throughout the world. Grapes grow in clusters on climbing vines. They are small, round, juicy fruits with smooth skin, ranging in color from pale whitish-green to dark red to purplish-black. Many varieties have seeds, but some are seedless. There are three main types of grapes other than those grown for wine: raisin grapes, juice grapes, and table grapes, which are used as an ingredient in many desserts and pastries and for making jams and jellies. Among the many varieties of table grapes are Concord, Thompson, Ribier, Flame Tokay, and Emperor. Fresh grapes are available almost year-round. Choose firm, plump, evenly colored, unblemished fruit that is still attached to the stem, with a sweet aroma. Store grapes in a perforated plastic bag in the refrigerator for up to a week. Grapes taste best at room temperature, so remove them from the refrigerator an hour or more before serving. Wash them and dry gently with paper towels just before using, to avoid rot. See also: fruit.

grapefruit A member of the citrus family, the grapefruit is a hybrid cross between an orange and a pomelo, created in the eighteenth century. Grapefruits are large and round with thick, bitter, yellow skin and acidic, juicy, white or pink pulp. Candied grapefruit peel and raw grapefruit are used as an ingredient in desserts, pastries, and confections such as fruitcakes, compotes, and sorbets, and fresh grapefruit is used to make marmalade. Fresh and canned grapefruit is available year-round, with the peak for fresh grapefruit in the winter months. Choose plump, brightly colored fruit that feels heavy for its size, with thin, smooth skin that gives slightly when pressed. Store grapefruit at room temperature for up to 2 days or in a plastic bag in the refrigerator for up to 3 weeks. See also: citrus fruit and fruit.

Gravenstein apple One of the favorite apples for pies and other baked desserts, Gravensteins tend to lose their shape when baked whole. They have deep green skin blushed with red streaks and crisp, juicy, sweet-tart flesh. Gravenstein apples are available in August and September primarily in California, Oregon, and Washington. See also: apple.

grunt A Colonial American type of cobbler made with berries or other fresh fruit topped with biscuitlike pastry dough, steamed in a kettle covered with a tight-fitting lid, hung over an open fire. Besides the water present in the fruit, a few additional tablespoons of water help the grunt to steam. The water is added to the sugar sprinkled on top of the fruit and forms a syrup as the grunt steams. The name comes from Massachusetts and supposedly derives from the sound the fruit makes as it steams beneath the pastry dough. Modern versions are baked in the oven. Grunts are best served warm with heavy cream or vanilla ice cream. Grunts were originally served for breakfast and gradually became popular as desserts. United States. See also: buckle, cobbler, pandowdy, and slump.

guava Native to Brazil, guavas today are grown in many tropical and semitropical climates throughout the world, including Hawaii, southern California, Arizona, and Florida in the United States. There are over a hundred varieties of guavas. Generally guavas are oval or round and about 2 inches wide. The color of the thin skin ranges from yellow-green to purple, and the flesh ranges from pale yellow to orange to red. The moist flesh is both sweet and tart with a unique flavor that is a combination of banana, strawberry, and pineapple. Some varieties of guavas have tiny black seeds, other are practically seedless. Guavas are usually available fresh only where they are grown both because they are delicate and don't transport well and because they are prone to infestation by fruit flies. Guavas are used raw as an ingredient in desserts, pastries, and confections and are also used to make jams, jellies, pastes, and preserves. Choose highly aromatic fruit with yellow skin that gives slightly when pressed. Slightly underripe guavas will ripen at room temperature in a few days. Once they are ripe, refrigerate and use within 2 days. See also: fruit.

gubana A specialty of the Friuli region of northeastern Italy, gubana is a fruit-and-nut-filled sweet bread traditionally shaped in a spiral, like a snail. The name translates from the local dialect as "snail" or "rolled-up." The rich filling of dried fruits and nuts is spread over the dough, which is then rolled up, shaped into a spiral, and baked. There are many versions of this pastry. Some are made with puff pastry, but the most common is made with an enriched yeast-risen briochelike sweet dough. Gubana, traditionally served for Easter, is often sprinkled with brandy or grappa, a fiery Italian brandy, before it is served. Italy.

gulab jamun A classic confection from northern India, gulab jamun are sweet, sticky balls of dark milk fudge made by boiling milk until it is reduced and very thick. The balls are deep-fried until golden brown, then soaked in a syrup flavored with rose water and cardamom or cinnamon for several hours before serving. India. See also: cardamom, cinnamon, and rose water.

gum paste A modeling paste with the consistency of pie dough, similar to pastillage but more delicate, made of confectioners' sugar, gum traga-canth or gelatin, glucose, water, and flavoring, such as lemon juice. Gum paste is used to make decorations such as ribbons, delicate three-dimensional flowers, and figures such as animals and dolls. Occasionally it is used to make small architectural shapes. It is mixed, kneaded, colored as desired, and allowed to rest. Then it is rolled out on a cornstarch-dusted smooth surface, cut into pieces, fashioned into shapes, and left to air-dry. If the pieces are to be used to assemble an architectural shape, they are dried first, then glued together with royal icing. Gum paste can also be molded into various designs and shapes by using bowls, plates, or other forms as molds. Gum paste forms can be painted with food coloring or cocoa thinned with sugar syrup or water after they are dry. Gum paste can be made and kept sealed in an airtight plastic bag for several weeks before using; it must be kneaded to make it pliable again before using. See also: gelatin, glucose, gum tragacanth, pastillage, and royal icing.

gum paste tools and cutters A variety of tools and cutters designed specifically to cut and shape gum paste into various forms and pieces, which are assembled into flowers or architectural forms and other items. Gum paste tools and cutters are made of either metal or plastic. There are many different tools and cutters, including flower cuppers, leaf cut-ters, trowels, knives, scoops, spears, rollers, and petal cutters in a variety of sizes. They are available at cake decorating supply shops and through mail order cookware catalogs. See also: gum paste.

gum tragacanth A vegetable gum extracted from the astragalus shrub, which is native to Asia, gum tragacanth is an essential ingredient in gum paste. Gum tragacanth is colorless and odorless, has no discernible taste, and is very moist. It is used as a thickener, emulsifier, and stabilizer and to help prevent crystallization in commercially produced ice creams, candies, and jams. See also: gum paste.

hálfmánar Icelandic half-moon–shaped delicate butter cookies flavored with cardamom. The cookies are filled with fruit preserves or lekvar, a prune spread, then sprinkled with crystal sugar before baking. They are traditionally served during Christmas celebrations. Iceland. See also: crystal sugar and lekvar.

halvah A Middle Eastern confection made from ground sesame seeds and honey or sugar. Occasionally pistachio nuts or dried or candied fruits are added. Homemade halvah is often made with almonds instead of sesame seeds and sprinkled with cinnamon. Halvah is very sweet, with a chewy texture. It is available in supermarkets in paper-wrapped bars or in Jewish delicatessens in slabs, which are cut into individual slices. Turkey.

hamantaschen A Jewish specialty, this pastry is traditionally made to celebrate the festival of Purim, commemorating the defeat of the wicked Haman of Persia, who plotted to massacre the Jews. Pastry dough is cut into triangular shapes, filled with a mixture of poppy seeds and honey or with almonds and raisins, cooked apricots or prunes, then deep-fried or baked. While still warm, the pastries are sprinkled with confectioners' sugar. The shape of the pastry symbolizes either Haman's purse or his three-cornered hat. Israel.

hand-formed cookies Cookies made by forming the dough by hand into balls, logs, crescents, or various other shapes before baking. See also: cookie and dough.

hard ball stage The stage at which a small amount of hot sugar syrup dropped in cold water forms a rigid, sticky ball that holds its shape against pressure when removed from the water. The temperature range for hard ball stage is 250° to 266°F on a candy thermometer. See also: Table of Sugar Temperatures and Stages (page 335).

hard crack stage The stage at which a small amount of hot sugar syrup dropped in cold water separates into brittle threads that shatter easily. The sugar is no longer sticky at this point. The temperature range for hard crack stage is 300° to 310°F on a candy thermometer. See also: Table of Sugar Temperatures and Stages (page 335).

hard sauce To make hard sauce, softened butter is beaten until fluffy, then combined with confectioners', granulated, or brown sugar and flavoring. Brandy is the flavoring used most often, but vanilla is also widely used. The mixture is placed in a bowl or formed into a roll, tightly covered, and refrigerated until firm. If shaped in a roll it is thinly sliced and traditionally served with plum pudding. Hard sauce is also shaped into decorative molds and unmolded before serving. United States.

hazelnut Also called filberts, hazelnuts are native to the Northern Hemisphere. They are widely grown in Italy, Spain, and Turkey, and in the northwestern United States. Hazelnuts are small round or oval golden-colored nuts covered with a brown papery skin, enclosed in a hard, dark-brown shell. Because the skin is slightly bitter, it is generally desirable to remove it before use. To do this, toast the hazelnuts on a jelly-roll pan in a 350°F oven for 15 minutes. Remove the pan from the oven, cool the nuts for a few minutes, then rub them between your hands or in a kitchen towel to remove the majority of the skins. The rich, buttery flavor of hazelnuts is also enhanced by toasting. They are widely used whole, chopped, or ground to flavor and decorate desserts, pastries, and confections. Hazelnuts are available shelled and unshelled in nut stores, health food stores, specialty food shops, and some supermarkets. Because of their high natural oil content, hazelnuts turn rancid rapidly. They will keep up to 4 months stored in an airtight container in the refrigerator or up to 1 year in the freezer. See also: nut.

heat lamp Also called a warming lamp, an infrared lamp is one of the main tools for sugar pulling and blowing. It is used to keep a piece of boiled and cooled sugar soft and pliable while it is being worked with. The large red spotlight bulb is generally 250 watts and 125 volts. The bulb's top portion is opaque, which forces the light and its heat down to its round bottom surface. The bulb is always elevated above the work surface, so there is room to work with the sugar beneath it. To hold the bulb above the surface it is placed at the top of a warming case or in a flexible gooseneck type of lamp. See also: blown sugar, pulled sugar, and warming case.

hojuelas de naranja Colombian sweet orange puffs made from a sweet pastry dough flavored with fresh orange juice. The dough is rolled out and cut into a variety of shapes, deep-fried in hot oil, drained, and dusted with confectioners' sugar before serving. Colombia.

hold a ribbon See ribbon.

honey A sweet, thick liquid made by honeybees, honey has been used for centuries as a sweetener. Glucose and fructose make up 75 to 80 percent of honey. The remainder is water and trace amounts of minerals. The flavor varies, depending on the area where the honey is produced and the type of flowers that the bees have fed upon. Honey can be mild or strong in flavor and light or dark in color. Generally the color corresponds to the intensity of flavor; the darker the color, the stronger the flavor. Honey is usually named by the flower that is the main source for the nectar, such as sage, clover, buckwheat, alfalfa, linden, or orange blossom. There are three types of honey: comb honey, with the liquid in the chewy, waxy comb; chunk honey, which contains small pieces of the honeycomb; and liquid honey, which is also called extracted, because it has been extracted from the comb. Liquid honey is pasteurized to help prevent it from crystallizing.

   Honey adds flavor, sweetness, texture, and moisture to baked goods. It is widely used in desserts, pastries, and confections throughout the world. Because honey attracts moisture, it is used as an interfering agent in candy making to keep sugar from crystallizing as it cooks, and it gives candies and baked goods extended shelf life. Honey is available in glass jars and plastic bottles. It is best stored tightly covered in a cool, dry place. Honey crystallizes with age; to liquefy crystallized honey, heat the opened jar or bottle in a microwave oven or in a pan of warm water over medium heat. See also: fructose and glucose.

honeydew melon A large melon with firm, smooth skin that ranges in color from creamy off-white to yellow green. Honeydew melon has thick, juicy, pale-green flesh that is very sweet. The slightly oval-shaped melons, which weigh between 4 and 8 pounds, are used like cantaloupe as an ingredient in desserts and pastries, such as fruit salads, ice creams, sorbets, parfaits, and fruit tarts. Honeydew melons are available practically year-round, because of foreign imports, with the peak in the summer months. Choose fragrant, firm melons that feel heavy for their size, with a slight soft wrinkling on their skin. A ripe honeydew melon should give slightly at both ends when pressed. Underripe honeydew melon stored at room temperature will become softer and juicier. Store ripe honeydew melon in the refrigerator for up to a week. See also: cantaloupe, fruit, and melon.

hot fudge A thick, rich topping composed of chocolate, butter, and sugar that is used hot to top ice cream and desserts. United States.

huevos Quimbos Sweet egg cookies named after the Quimbaya, an extinct tribe of Colombian Indians. Egg yolks are beaten until very thick, then spread in a buttered square pan and baked until set. When cool, the cookies are cut into a variety of shapes, a sugar syrup flavored with rum is poured over them, and they are left to soak for about an hour before being drained and served. Colombia.

hydrogenated vegetable shortening See solid shortening.

Iago A pastry named for the villain in Shakespeare's *Othello*. Iagos are composed of two 3-inch round biscuits, similar to ladyfingers, sandwiched together with coffee-flavored pastry cream, brushed with apricot glaze, and covered in coffee-flavored and -colored fondant. Iagos are usually served on a platter accompanied by other similar pastries, Desdemonas, Othellos, and Rosalindas, all named for Shakespearean characters. United Kingdom. See also: Desdemona, fondant, glaze, ladyfingers, Othello, pastry cream, and Rosalinda.

ice cream A smooth frozen dessert of milk and/or cream, sugar, often eggs, and flavoring. According to the U.S. Food and Drug Administration (FDA), in order to be called ice cream the mixture must contain at least 10 percent butterfat and 20 percent milk solids. Some air is necessary in the mixture to soften it so that it will not freeze as hard as a rock. Ice cream may contain as much as 100 percent "overrun," which means up to 50 percent air. The amount of air is not usually listed on the container. The FDA specifies that a gallon of ice cream must weigh a minimum of 4.5 pounds. If a mixture has more than 50 percent air, it would weigh less than the required guidelines. Commercially produced ice creams, especially the less expensive ones, often contain stabilizers and emulsifiers, and some contain artificial flavorings. There are two main types of American-style ice cream: a cooked custard-based ice cream and an uncooked version, called Philadelphia-style. French ice cream is based on a cooked egg custard, to which cream and flavorings are added. Italian ice cream, called gelato, has less air than either American or French ice cream, so it is denser, firmer, and richer. Ice cream often has nuts added for both flavor and texture. To make ice cream, the mixture is blended, cooled if necessary, chilled, and then processed in an ice cream machine until it reaches the desired consistency. Ice milk is similar to ice cream but contains less milk solids and less butterfat.

French vanilla ice cream is the most popular flavor. Besides being a dessert on its own, ice cream is used in many other desserts, such as parfaits, sundaes, bombes, baked Alaska, ice cream sandwiches, ice cream cakes, and banana splits. Iced desserts originated in China thousands of years ago. The Chinese taught the technique to the Arabs, who developed the art of making frozen syrups. Marco Polo brought the secrets of these frozen desserts back to thirteenth-century Italy. In the eighteenth century, a French cook to Charles I of England began to serve iced desserts to the English court. These became very popular and have remained so ever since. France. See also: baked Alaska, ice cream machine, and parfait.

FRENCH VANILLA ICE CREAM

Approximately 1 quart

2 cups milk
2 cups heavy cream
5 vanilla beans
8 large egg yolks, at room temperature
¾ cup granulated sugar

Place the milk and cream in a 3-quart heavy-bottomed saucepan. Using a sharp knife, split the vanilla beans lengthwise. Scrape out the seeds, and add the beans and seeds to the liquid. Heat the mixture over medium heat until just below the boiling point. Remove from the heat, cover, and let the mixture infuse for 30 minutes.

In the bowl of a stand mixer, using the wire whip attachment, or in a mixing bowl, using a hand-held mixer, whip the egg yolks and sugar together until they are pale yellow colored and hold a slowly dissolving ribbon when the beater is lifted, about 5 minutes.

Meanwhile, reheat the cream mixture to just below the boil.

Reduce the mixer speed to low and slowly add 1 cup of the hot cream mixture. Blend well, then return the mixture to the saucepan. Place the pan over low heat and cook, stirring constantly with a wooden spoon, until the mixture thickens and reaches 185°F on a candy thermometer, 10 to 15 minutes. At this point, a line drawn through the custard on the back of the spoon should leave a clearly defined path.

Strain the custard through a fine sieve into a bowl. Cover tightly and chill in the refrigerator for several hours, or overnight.

Process the mixture in an ice cream machine according to the manufacturer's instructions.

Store the ice cream in a covered container in the freezer for up to a month. If it is frozen solid, soften it in the refrigerator for a few hours until it is soft but not mushy before serving.

ice cream machine Ice cream machines are also called ice cream makers or ice cream freezers. There are several types available, ranging from simple to elaborate, but all are basically composed of a canister, surrounded by a freezing agent, with a paddle, called a dasher, in the center that stirs the ice cream mixture until it chills. The freezing agents differ according to the type of machine used: ice mixed with rock or table salt, a liquid chemical coolant, or a self-contained refrigeration unit. The stirring action keeps the ice cream mixture from forming ice crystals as it freezes, making a smooth product.

There are two types of hand-operated ice cream makers. The traditional machine is a wooden bucket that holds a canister with a dasher inside. The dasher is usually made of plastic. Ice and rock salt are placed between the bucket and the canister. The proportions of ice and salt will determine the texture of the ice cream; too much salt will make it grainy, too much ice will make it soft and mushy. The dasher and canister are turned by a hand crank at the side of the bucket. Newer models of this type use a plastic bucket, and some replace the rock salt with table salt. This type of ice cream maker produces a gallon of ice cream. The prechilled canister freezer, Donvier, has a hollow metal canister containing a liquid coolant that must be chilled at 0°F in the freezer for 24 hours before use. It is placed in a plastic bucket and a central dasher is inserted. A hand crank is attached to the dasher through a hole in the lid. This crank must be turned every 2 to 3 minutes for about 20 minutes to produce frozen ice cream. This type of ice cream maker is available in pint and quart sizes.

There are three types of electric ice cream machines. The traditional bucket type is available in an electric version, with a motor at the top to turn the canister. The smallest electric machine is a simple round or oval-shaped canister with a dasher and a lid. It is plugged in and placed in the freezer compartment of the refrigerator; this machine requires no ice or salt. In this model, the dasher turns while the canister does not move.

This type of machine makes 1 quart. The most elaborate and expensive electric ice cream machine is a countertop model with a self-contained refrigeration unit. It is made of plastic with a stainless steel bowl. This type is the easiest to use. The ice cream base is poured into the canister and covered with the lid, and the machine is turned on. It works rapidly and produces very smooth ice cream. It makes from $1^1/2$ to 2 quarts.

ice cream mold Square, round, rectangle, loaf, log, and dome are only some of the many shapes of ice cream molds available. Many seasonal or special shapes, such as Santa Claus and cartoon characters, can be found. They come in a wide variety of sizes, ranging from individual to large enough to serve twelve; most molds hold from 1 to 2 quarts. They are made of stainless steel, tinned steel, aluminum, plastic, or pewter. Some molds have covers. One square mold has a three-dimensional design on the bottom, which leaves its impression on top of the ice cream after it is unmolded. Other molds, resembling chocolate molds, are of two three-dimensional parts that are filled and clipped together. The sides are removed to unmold the ice cream. Molds for making bombes are usually dome- or cone-shaped, but some resemble a football or a melon with textured grooves on top. A cassata mold is a tall cylinder with a flat top and sloped sides. A parfait mold is a tall rounded cone shape with a tight-fitting lid. Just about any type of container can be used to mold ice cream, as long as it can stand up to the cold temperatures of the freezer. Sorbets and other frozen desserts can, of course, also be molded in ice cream molds. To unmold, place the mold in warm water just up to the top edge until the ice cream begins to soften. Then place a plate or serving dish over the top of the mold and invert the ice cream onto the dish. See also: bombe, chocolate mold, parfait, and sorbet.

ice cream scoop A hand-held utensil, shaped something like a small shovel, used to remove ice cream from its container. There are three main types of ice cream scoops. The traditional scoop has a round bowl and either a lever on the side of the handle or a spring mechanism on the base of the handle. When the lever is pushed in toward the handle or the handle is squeezed together, it moves an arc-shaped strip of metal from side to side along the bottom of the bowl, pushing the scoop of ice cream out of the bowl. This scoop is also available with an oval quenelle shape bowl. A nonstick scoop has a half-moon–shaped bowl and a thick handle that contains antifreeze, which makes it easy to scoop and release the ice cream. A spade has a wide flat blade with a handle that may contain a nonstick fluid. Ice cream scoops are generally made of metal. They come in a range of sizes to make scoops from $1^1/4$ to $2^1/2$ inches in diameter.

icing A sweet covering and filling for cakes and pastries, used in all types of desserts, pastries, and confections, icing is made primarily of sugar with various flavorings. Eggs, milk, and water or other ingredients, such as fat (usually butter), are often added. There are many types of icing, both cooked and uncooked, including water icing, royal icing, boiled icing, fondant icing, and seven-minute icing. The term *icing* is interchangeable with *frosting*. See also: buttercream, fondant, and frosting.

icing comb See pastry comb.

icing stencil This tool is used for imprinting a design in the icing of a cake. It is a round flat plastic disc that has words or phrases cut out of it, such as "Happy Birthday." The stencil is pressed onto the top of a cake, leaving the indentation of the words, which provides a pattern to follow. To produce professional-looking writing, gently squeeze icing out from a pastry bag and tip, following the pattern.

île flottante See floating island.

indianerkrapfen A classic Austrian individual pastry that consists of a cupcake-size vanilla-scented sponge cake hollowed out and filled with sweetened whipped cream. The pastry is completely coated with a shiny chocolate glaze. Austria.

instant espresso powder See espresso powder.

invert sugar Sucrose is inverted, or broken down, into its two single sugar components, glucose and fructose, when a sugar syrup is heated and combined with a small amount of acid, such as cream of tartar. This breakdown reduces the size of the sugar crystals, thereby helping to prevent crystallization and produce a smooth finished product. Invert sugar is used to make candies and confections. It can be bought in liquid form in cake decorating and candy making supply shops. Honey is a natural source of invert sugar, and corn syrup contains invert sugar. See also: corn syrup, crystallization, fructose, glucose, honey, and sugar.

Ischl Also called Ischl tartlet, this is a classic Austrian cookie made with a buttery ground almond or hazelnut dough, accented with cinnamon. After baking, two of the cookies are sandwiched together with strawberry, raspberry, or apricot jam; the top cookie, which has a cut-out center so the jam shows through, is dusted with confectioners' sugar before it is placed on the jam. The traditional shape for Ischl tartlets is round, but occasionally they are made in heart shapes. Austria.

Italian meringue See meringue.

jaggery Also called palm sugar, jaggery is semirefined sugar made from the sap of the Palmyra palm tree; occasionally it is made from sugarcane as well. It is a coarse, crumbly brown sugar sold in cakes or blocks. Jaggery has a strong flavor. It is widely used in Indian, Southeast Asian, and Indonesian cuisines. See also: sugar.

jalebis A classic Indian sweet of batter piped into pretzellike shapes through a pastry bag directly into hot oil and deep-fried until golden. Jalebis are fragile, loosely formed confections made with a combination of all-purpose and rice flours. They have a light, airy interior and crisp exterior. After cooking, they are coated with sugar syrup, which adds sweetness but does not make them sticky. Jalebis are best eaten within 2 hours of preparation, as they become heavy and soggy on sitting. India.

jalousie Literally translated from the French as "Venetian blind," jalousie gets its name from its appearance. A jalousie is a long rectangular pastry made with puff pastry. The top of the pastry is cut across its width into strips or bars, allowing the filling to show through. The classic filling is almond paste spread with jam, but apricot jam, other fruit preserves, and cooked apples are also used. Jalousies can be made individual size or as large pastries. France.

jam Fruit cooked with sugar until it is a thick mixture. If the fruit used to make the jam does not contain enough pectin, a natural jelling agent present in fruits, to set the jam, liquid or granular pectin is added. Jam is used as a spread on sweet breads for afternoon tea, in dessert glazes and sauces, and as an ingredient in and filling for desserts, pastries, and confections. See also: conserve, jelly, marmalade, pectin, and preserves.

Jamaican pepper See allspice.

japonaise See broyage, dacquoise, meringue, and Succès.

jar wonton Chinese deep-fried pastries. A filling of dates, nuts, lemon zest, and orange juice is enclosed inside the square dough wrappers used for the savory Chinese wontons. The dough wrappers are rolled around the filling in a tube shape and the ends are twisted to keep the filling from falling out. The pastries are deep-fried in hot oil, drained, cooled slightly, and dusted with confectioners' sugar before serving. China.

jelly A clear, glossy mixture of fruit juice and sugar cooked together until it holds its shape. If the fruit does not have enough pectin, a natural jelling agent present in fruits, to set, liquid or granulated pectin can be added. Jelly has a soft yet firm texture. It is used as a spread on sweet breads for afternoon tea, to make dessert glazes, and as a filling in desserts, pastries, and confections. See also: conserve, jam, marmalade, pectin, and preserves.

jelly-roll cake A sponge cake baked in a shallow rectangular pan and then rolled up tightly while still warm. When cool, the cake is unrolled, spread with jam, rerolled, and dusted with confectioners' sugar. The cake can be spread with other fillings, such as whipped cream, lemon cream, whipped ganache, buttercream, or chestnut purée, to form the basis of other desserts. When cut crosswise into slices, the jelly roll resembles a pinwheel. These slices can be used to line the molds for charlottes and other desserts. United States and France. See also: Bûche de Noël, buttercream, charlotte, ganache, and roulade.

jelly-roll pan See baking sheet.

Jonathan apple A favorite apple for pies and other baked desserts, Jonathans tend to lose their shape when baked whole. They have vivid red skin and juicy, spicy, sweet-tart flesh. Jonathan apples are available from September to March. See also: apple.

juicer Also called a citrus juicer and a juice extractor, this kitchen utensil is used to extract the juice from citrus fruit halves. There are several designs of this tool, but most have a center pointed ridged cone that sits on a shallow wide cup or on a perforated base that sits on top of the cup. The cup has a handle on one side and a pour spout on the opposite side. This type of citrus juicer is made of plastic, glass, ceramic, or aluminum and is operated manually. An electric citrus juicer has a short, wide cylinder that holds the perforated plate with the ridged cone. It is made of plastic, with a pour spout on one side and a handle on the opposite side. Some models may have a clear plastic top that covers it when not in use. With the machine plugged in or turned on, the cone spins when a half citrus fruit is pushed down on it. The juice drips through the perforations into the bottom container. A hand-operated citrus juicer, also called a mechanical or freestanding citrus juicer, is made of cast aluminum or chromed steel. It has a rounded top that is raised and lowered with a 6-inch-long rotating lever attached to one side of the center column. A ridged cone is attached to the base. As the top is brought down it squeezes the juice from the citrus fruit half on the cone. The juicer can sit over a glass or other container to catch the juice. All types of juicers are available in cookware shops, the cookware section of department stores, and supermarkets. See also: citrus reamer.

jumble, jumbal A crisp, delicate sugar cookie baked in a ring shape, often scented with rose water and flavored with sour cream. Jumbles date back hundreds of years. They were very popular in the eighteenth century. Coconut and walnuts were particular favorites for flavor variations. United States. See also: rose water.

junket A type of custardlike pudding, junket is made from milk, sugar, and flavorings that are jelled with rennet, a substance used to curdle milk. Junket has a soft, delicate texture, similar to cream cheese. It is served cold, often with fresh fruit, or occasionally with clotted cream, on top. United Kingdom. See also: clotted cream.

kaak A classic Lebanese yeast-risen pastry made from a sweet dough enriched with milk, eggs, and butter. Walnut-sized pieces of the pastry dough are rolled into ropes, formed into rings, and baked until golden brown. While hot, the pastries are dipped in a glaze of milk and sugar, then left to dry before serving. Kaak can also be topped with sesame seeds before baking. Lebanon. See also: sesame seed.

kab el ghzal Translated literally as "gazelles' horns," these are classic Moroccan pastries typically served with mint tea. A sweet filling of ground almonds, cinnamon, confectioners' sugar, and orange flower water is mixed and rolled into cylinders. A pastry dough of flour, confectioners' sugar, butter, and orange flower water is rolled out and cut into rectangles, and a cylinder of almond filling is wrapped inside each rectangle. The ends of the dough are pinched together, then the "package" is stretched into a crescent shape. The crescents are pierced with a fork and baked until pale-golden. Sprinkle the pastries with orange flower water and cool, then roll in confectioners' sugar. Morocco. See also: orange flower water.

kadaif, kataïfi A popular Middle Eastern confection served at many celebrations, kadaif is composed of long thin noodlelike strands of a flour and water dough—also called kadaif—that are placed in a deep baking dish and coated with melted butter. A filling of either a creamy rice mixture or a mixture of pistachios, walnuts, or almonds is enclosed in two layers of the noodles. An occasional variation of kadaif uses a cheese similar to Italian ricotta for the filling. After baking, the confection is topped with more nuts and a sweet syrup is poured over the top, as for baklava, then it is cut into squares to serve. To make kadaif as an individual pastry, the filling is rolled inside a bundle of the noodlelike strands. A classic way of arranging the bundles is to form a spiral in a round baking pan. After baking, the sugar syrup is poured over the pastries. Kadaif can be served either hot or cold. Greece and Turkey.

kadin göbegi Turkish fritters (literally, "lady's navel") made from a sweet dough similar to choux pastry. A mixture of flour, butter, water, and salt is cooked to a thick paste, then eggs are beaten in until the mass is smooth, shiny, and thick. Walnut-sized pieces of the dough are formed into balls. Then the cook dips her finger into almond extract and presses it into the center of each ball of dough to make an indentation. The balls are deep-fried in hot oil until golden brown, drained, and soaked in sugar syrup flavored with fresh lemon juice. Dollops of whipped cream are piped into the center indentations of the cooled fritters before serving. Turkey. See also: choux pastry and fritter.

kanom mo kaeng Thai baked custard squares. *Kanom* is the Thai word for dessert, *mo* means pot, referring to the cooking pot, and *kaeng* means soup or curry, referring to the consistency of the dessert. Coconut cream, beaten eggs, brown sugar, and salt are cooked together in a double boiler until very thick. The mixture is poured into a greased baking dish and baked until very firm, then broiled briefly to brown the top. The custard is cooled slightly before serving. The top is sprinkled with sautéed shallots, which have a burnt salty taste that contrasts well with the heavy sweetness of the custard. This dessert derives from the widespread Portuguese influence in Thailand during the thirteenth and fourteenth centuries, although the locally available coconut cream replaces the dairy cream used in the Portuguese recipes. Thailand.

karakot An Uzbek fruit and almond confection. Stewed fruit mixed with sugar, finely ground almonds, and vanilla is cooked in water, then thickened with egg yolks. Stiffly whipped egg whites are folded into the mixture, then it is spread in a shallow rectangular baking pan and baked in a low oven to dry out. It is cut into thin slices and traditionally served with lemon tea. Uzbekistan.

kashata na nazi Ugandan coconut candy. A mixture of sugar, moist coconut, cinnamon, and salt is cooked together until firm, then turned into a rectangular pan and left to cool. When set, it is cut into squares. The candy is traditionally served at teatime and as a snack. Uganda.

khourabia The Armenian version of shortbread, baked in a crescent shape. Stuffed khourabia is a popular variation. A mixture of ground walnuts mixed with cinnamon and sugar is pressed into the center of a ball of khourabia dough, then the dough is pinched together to enclose the filling and baked until light golden. Turkey.

kiping Rice wafers from Lucban in the Quezon Province of the Philippines. The wafers are made from a thin paste of rice flour and water, which is tinted with brightly colored dyes, such as fuschia or emerald green. The colored batter is poured onto banana leaves and steamed, then peeled off before it hardens and left to dry. The dried leaf-shaped wafers are deep-fried in hot oil and dipped into sweet syrup or coated with thin coconut jam. Traditionally made for the Lucban town festival, the wafers can be assembled by stitching them together with thread into many decorative items that are first displayed as works of art before they are eaten. Philippines.

kirschwasser Also called kirsch, kirschwasser is a colorless fruit brandy distilled from morello cherries, a small black cherry grown extensively in Europe, and the cherry pits. It is widely used to flavor desserts, pastries, and confections. Kirschwasser originated in the Black Forest region of Germany, where particularly flavorful cherries are grown, and it is used to flavor the well-known Black Forest cherry torte. Germany. See also: Black Forest cherry torte and eau-de-vie.

kissel A classic Russian custardlike dessert made with a purée of red berries, most often cranberries, that are cooked with sugar and thickened with cornstarch, arrowroot, or potato flour. Kissel can be served warm or cold, topped with whipped cream, yogurt, or custard sauce. Russia.

kiwifruit, kiwi fruit, kiwi Also called Chinese gooseberry, kiwifruit is shaped like an egg. A fuzzy thin brown skin covers its bright green flesh. Tiny edible black seeds radiate throughout the fruit from the cream-colored center core. The fruit is juicy with a unique sweet-tart flavor that is a cross between melon, strawberry, and citrus. Kiwifruit is used raw as an ingredient in many desserts, pastries, and confections and in some dessert sauces. Grown in California and New Zealand, kiwifruit is available year-round. Choose firm fruit that gives slightly when pressed, with no bruises. If it is hard, ripen at room temperature. To speed up the process, place the kiwifruit in a tightly closed paper bag; once ripened, refrigerate until ready to use. Peel the skin off just before use. See also: fruit.

kluay budt chee A Thai dessert of sliced bananas stewed in a mixture of coconut milk, salt, and sugar. After cooking, the bananas are sprinkled with roughly chopped peeled mung beans and served either hot or cold. If the dessert is served cold, it has a thicker consistency, because the coconut milk thickens as it cools. The name of the dessert translates literally as "nun bananas," because of its white color—the color of the clothing worn by Thai nuns. Thailand. See also: coconut.

knead The technique for working dough or other substances, such as marzipan, until smooth and supple. Kneading also develops the gluten structure in bread dough, helping it to hold in the gas bubbles released by the leavening agent and aiding in rising. Kneading can be done by machine, with a bread hook attachment on an electric mixer or in a food processor, or by hand. To knead by hand, gather the dough into a ball on a smooth work surface. Push it away from you with the heel of your hand while pressing it down, then gather it back into a ball, folding it over itself. Give the dough a quarter-turn, and repeat the process until the desired smooth, elastic texture is reached. See also: gluten.

koeksister A snail-shell doughnut, a South African specialty that came from Malaysia. Flour, butter, salt, and baking powder are combined with eggs to make a soft dough that is rolled out and cut into small triangles. These triangles are coiled around a finger to resemble a snail shell. The pastries are deep-fried in hot oil until golden, drained, then brushed with a sweet syrup flavored with lemon and cinnamon and rolled in sugar. South Africa.

kolachy, kolache A sweet flaky pastry usually made with a cream cheese and butter dough, occasionally with a yeast-risen dough. Kolachys have several different traditional fillings, including poppy seed, cream cheese, jam, nuts, and berries or other chopped fresh fruit. To make kolachy, the dough is rolled out and cut into squares, a spoonful of filling is placed in the center of a square of pastry dough, then two opposite corners of the square are folded over the center and pressed down to cover the filling. Some variations fold all four corners of the dough into the center. After baking, the pastries are often drizzled with a confectioners' sugar icing while warm. Poland, the Czech Republic, and Slovakia.

konditorei The German word for a pastry or confectionery shop.

koulourakia Classic Greek Easter cookies traditionally baked on Holy Thursday before Easter Sunday. The buttery, rich, golden cookies are flavored with brandy. They have a twisted, corkscrew shape, formed by first shaping the dough into a long rope, then folding the rope in half and twisting it together. The tops of the cookies are brushed with beaten egg and sprinkled with sesame seeds before baking. Greece.

kourambiedes Also called Greek butter cookies, these buttery, rich cookies are rolled in confectioners' sugar while still warm, and again before serving. They are made in a variety of shapes: round, S-shaped, oval, half-moon, and pear. Finely chopped or ground walnuts are often mixed with the dough. Rose water is sprinkled on the cookies while they are hot from the oven or just before serving. **Kourambiedes** are traditionally served at weddings, holiday celebrations, and any festive occasion. At Christmastime, a whole clove is inserted in the top of each cookie to symbolize the spices brought by the Magi. Greece. See also: cookie and rose water.

KOURAMBIEDES

Greek Butter Cookies

About 4 dozen cookies

8 ounces (2 sticks) unsalted butter, softened
1 pound confectioners' sugar, sifted, plus ½ cup sifted
    confectioners' sugar
1 large egg yolk, at room temperature
2 tablespoons brandy or Cognac
1 teaspoon vanilla extract
2½ to 2¾ cups all-purpose flour
1 teaspoon baking powder
Rose water (optional)

Position the oven racks in the upper and lower thirds of the oven and preheat to 350°F. Line three baking sheets with parchment paper.

In the bowl of a stand mixer, using the flat beater attachment, or in a mixing bowl, using a hand-held mixer, beat the butter until it is fluffy, about 5 minutes. Gradually beat in ½ cup confectioners' sugar. Blend in the egg yolk, brandy or Cognac, and vanilla extract, stopping to scrape down the sides of the bowl with a rubber spatula a few times.

Sift together 2½ cups of the flour and the baking powder. With the mixer on low speed, beat in the dry ingredients in 4 or 5 additions, blending well after each addition and stopping to scrape down the sides of the bowl with a rubber spatula as necessary. If the dough is sticky, add the remaining flour.

Break off walnut-sized pieces of the cookie dough and roll into balls, half-moons, or S-shapes. Place the rolled cookies on the baking sheets, leaving 1 inch space between them.

Bake the cookies for 6 minutes. Switch the positions of the baking sheets and bake for 5 to 6 minutes longer, until light golden.

Transfer the baking sheets to racks. Lightly sprinkle the warm cookies with the rose water, if using. Let the cookies cool slightly.

Spread half of the remaining confectioners' sugar on a baking sheet. Place the warm cookies on the confectioners' sugar, and sift the remaining sugar over them. Let cool completely, then roll the cookies in the confectioners' sugar.

The cookies will keep stored, still in the confectioners' sugar, in an airtight container at room temperature for 1 week.

krakelinge Classic South African figure eight–shaped cookies of Dutch origin. The cookies are made from a sweet dough flavored with ground cinnamon. The dough is kneaded until soft, then rolled out into a rectangle. Long narrow strips are cut from the rectangle, then shaped into figure eights. The tops of the cookies are brushed with beaten egg whites and sugar mixed with ground almonds, then they are baked until golden. South Africa.

kransekage Literally "wreath cake," this is an elaborate special-occasion Danish and Norwegian cake made almost completely of marzipan. It is a towering confection of many layers of concentric rings of cookielike marzipan cakes built up in graduated sizes. Randomly piped zigzags of royal icing are the decoration for the cake, which is usually served for special birthdays or weddings. Denmark and Norway.

krokant A chewy nut brittle rich with almonds or hazelnuts, butter, and vanilla. The sugar for krokant is cooked to a high temperature, giving the confection a rich, intense flavor. **Krokant** is eaten either unadorned or dipped in chocolate and it is used as an ingredient to make other desserts, pastries, and confections. It is also used to decorate the tops and sides of various cakes. Germany and France.

∾∾∾∾∾∾∾∾∾∾

KROKANT

About one hundred 1-inch squares

3 tablespoons flavorless vegetable oil, for the pan

1 cup granulated sugar
½ cup light corn syrup
3 tablespoons water
½ vanilla bean, split lengthwise
2 cups sliced unblanched almonds or toasted and skinned
     hazelnuts, finely chopped
¼ teaspoon salt
4½ tablespoons unsalted butter, cut into small pieces
12 ounces bittersweet chocolate to be tempered
     (see page 297) (optional)

Generously coat the back of a baking sheet, a metal rolling pin, and a pizza wheel with the vegetable oil.

In a 2-quart heavy-bottomed saucepan, combine the sugar, corn syrup, and water. Bring to a boil over high heat, brushing down the sides of the pan with a pastry brush dipped in warm water twice to prevent the sugar from crystallizing. Add the split vanilla bean and cook, stirring constantly with a long-handled wooden spoon, until the mixture registers 240°F on a candy thermometer, 4 to 5 minutes.

Add the almonds or hazelnuts, salt, and butter, and stir constantly until the mixture registers 290°F, 5 to 6 minutes longer. Remove the pan from the heat and immediately pour the mixture onto the oiled baking sheet. With the oiled rolling pin, roll out the mixture ⅛ inch thick; with a fork, remove the vanilla bean. It is necessary to work very fast because the mixture sets up rapidly and becomes too brittle to cut. Use the pizza wheel to score the krokant into 1-inch squares. Let the krokant cool completely.

Separate the krokant into squares with your fingers. Any scraps can be ground to a fine powder in a food processor for use in other recipes. Stored between sheets of waxed paper in a tightly covered container, krokant will keep for 2 weeks at room temperature.

To make chocolate-dipped krokant, temper the chocolate. Line a baking sheet with parchment or waxed paper.

Place a piece of krokant in the tempered chocolate, coating it completely. With a dipper or a plastic fork with the two middle tines broken off, lift the piece from the chocolate, gently shake off the excess chocolate, and place the krokant on the paper. Repeat with the remaining krokant. After every 4 pieces, press the tines of a fork onto the top of each chocolate-dipped piece to form a line design.

Place the baking sheet in the refrigerator to set the chocolate for 15 minutes. Place the finished krokant in paper candy cups. Stored between sheets of waxed paper the krokant will keep for 1 week in a tightly covered container at room temperature.

krumkake A traditional Norwegian rolled Christmas cookie. The 5-inch round wafer-thin cookies are made on a specially designed iron that looks like a waffle iron, similar to a pizzelle iron. The surface of the iron is intricately carved with religious and seasonal designs that are imprinted onto each cookie as it bakes. While still warm, the cookies are rolled into cigarette shapes around a dowel or into cone shapes. As the cookies cool, they become crisp. Krumkakes are often filled with whipped cream just before serving. Cardamom is frequently used to flavor the batter. Norway. See also: cardamom, krumkake iron, pizzelle, and pizzelle iron.

krumkake iron Two 5-inch flat round engraved cast-aluminum plates are hinged together to form an iron. Each plate has a long handle. Krumkake batter is placed in the center of one plate, and the plates are brought together. To cook the krumkake, the iron is placed on a ring that sits over a stove burner. Krumkake irons are available in both standard or electric models (which make two krumkakes at a time) at cookware shops and through mail order catalogs. See also: krumkake and pizzelle iron.

kuchen The German word for cake or pastry. Kuchen is a cake or pastry made with a sweetened yeast-risen dough that is either topped with a mixture of sugar and spices or nuts or filled with fruit or cheese before baking. Kuchen is the classic coffee cake and is served for both breakfast and dessert. Germany. See also: coffee cake.

kugel A classic Jewish dish, kugel is a baked noodle pudding. Sweet versions are made with raisins, nuts, sour cream, and spices, while savory versions, which are served as side dishes, contain meat, vegetables, or potatoes. Kugel is served either warm or cold. Germany and Israel.

kugelhopf A sweet raisin-filled yeast-risen bread that is a specialty of the Alsace region in France, although it originated in Austria. There are many variations of kugelhopf, with a number of countries, including Poland and Germany, claiming the cake for their own. Kugelhopf is baked in a specially designed tall fluted tube pan, which gives the cake its characteristic angled, ridged pattern. After baking, kugelhopf is dusted with confectioners' sugar. It is usually served as a coffee cake for breakfast or afternoon tea. Austria. See also: kugelhopf mold and tube pan.

kugelhopf mold A deep round ring mold with fluted sides and a narrow center tube. The design of the pan produces the cake's characteristic angled, ridged pattern. The pan is available in sizes ranging from 6- to 12-cup capacity, with the 8- and 9-inch (10- and 11-cup capacity) diameters the most popular. Kugelhopf molds are made of aluminum, glass, tinned steel, or black steel; some have nonstick linings. They are available in cookware shops and through mail order cookware catalogs. See also: tube pan.

kulich A Russian Easter cake, similar to Italian panettone and French brioche, kulich is a tall, cylindrical, light, yeast-risen cake loaded with candied orange peel, raisins, and spices. Kulich is garnished with confectioners' sugar, chopped candied orange peel, and nuts. It is traditionally served with paskha and brightly colored eggs. Russia. See also: brioche, panettone, and paskha.

kyauk kyaw A Burmese clear, two-layer, fudgelike candy made with agar-agar. The strands are soaked to soften, then cooked with coconut milk and sugar. The mixture is flavored with rose water, poured into a square mold that has been rinsed with cold water, and left to set. The candy is cut into squares, diamonds, or rectangles and eaten out of hand. Burma. See also: agar-agar.

lactose Also called milk sugar, lactose is the sugar that occurs naturally in milk. It is not as sweet as any of the other natural sugars. Lactose is used in commercial candy making.

Lady Baltimore cake A moist, pure white, three-layer cake made with a filling of chopped pecans, raisins, and other dried fruit, such as figs, and a billowy white frosting, usually made with boiled icing. The cake, which uses egg whites only, not yolks, in the batter, has a delicate fine-grained texture. Lady Baltimore cake is a traditional cake that was originally a specialty of the city of Charleston, South Carolina. There are many stories, one of which is that it was supposedly created by a character in the novel *Lady Baltimore*, written by Owen Wister at the turn of the century. The immense popularity of the book made the cake famous. United States. See also: boiled icing and Lord Baltimore cake.

ladyfinger plaque See langues de chat plaque.

ladyfingers These classic cakelike cookies are made from a delicate sponge-cake batter. Egg whites are whipped to firm peaks, and folded into thickly beaten egg yolks. The dry ingredients are then folded into this airy mixture. The batter is piped through a pastry bag onto a baking sheet into finger shapes about 3^1/$_2$ inches long and 1 inch wide. The fingers are dusted with confectioners' sugar, then baked until set. They can also be baked in a shallow pan with indentations to help form the **lady-fingers**. This pan can also be used for langues de chat cookies and for éclairs. Ladyfingers have a tender, soft interior and a delicate, crisp exterior. In France, ladyfingers are called *biscuits à la cuillière*, which means spoon cookies, because they were originally formed with a spoon. They are served as an accompaniment to ice cream, mousses, puddings, and fresh fruit. Ladyfingers are also used to line the molds for charlottes and trifles and they are used in the Italian dessert tiramisù. Ladyfingers will dry out if exposed to air for very long, but they will become sticky if exposed to too much moisture. Ladyfingers are best eaten the day they are made, but can be stored in an airtight container at room temperature for up to 1 week or frozen. France. See also: charlotte, langues de chat, pastry bag, tiramisù, and trifle.

LADYFINGERS

Twenty-four 3½- by 1-inch fingers

4 large eggs, separated, at room temperature
½ cup superfine sugar
1½ teaspoons vanilla extract
½ teaspoon cream of tartar
1 cup all-purpose flour, sifted
Pinch of salt
Confectioners' sugar for dusting

Position the oven racks in the upper and lower thirds of the oven and preheat to 350°F. Line two baking sheets with parchment paper.

In the bowl of a stand mixer, using the wire whip attachment, or in a mixing bowl, using a hand-held mixer, beat the egg yolks and ¼ cup of the sugar together on medium-high speed until the mixture is pale yellow colored and holds a slowly dissolving ribbon when the whip is held above the batter, about 5 minutes. Blend in the vanilla extract.

In a grease-free mixing bowl, whip the egg whites with the cream of tartar on medium-high speed until they are frothy. Gradually sprinkle on the remaining ¼ cup sugar and continue to whip the egg whites until they are stiff, but not dry.

Blend the flour and salt.

Gently stir ¼ of the whipped egg whites into the yolk mixture. Then alternately fold in the flour and the remaining egg whites.

Fit a 12- or 14-inch pastry bag with a #5 large plain tip. Push the pointed end of the pastry bag into the tip to keep the batter from running out as it is being filled. Stand the pastry bag tip down in a tall jar or glass and fold the top of the bag over the edge of the jar or glass, forming a cuff. Fill the pastry bag with the batter, fold the cuff up, remove the pastry bag from the jar, and release the part of the pastry bag that was pushed into the tip.

Hold the pastry bag 1 inch above the surface of the baking sheet and gently squeeze the pastry bag to pipe out fingers 3½ inches long and 1 inch wide, leaving 1 inch between them.

Dust the tops of the ladyfingers twice with confectioners' sugar. Bake the ladyfingers until they are light golden and set, about 15 minutes. Transfer the baking sheets to racks to cool completely.

The ladyfingers are best eaten the same day they are made. They can be held in an airtight container at room temperature for up to a week, or they can be frozen.

ladylock mold See cream horn mold.

Lane cake A specialty of the American South that originated in Alabama, this is a white layer cake with a rich custard filling loaded with chopped dried fruits, nuts, and coconut. The cake is completely covered with boiled icing, a fluffy, glossy white frosting. United States. See also: boiled icing.

langues de chat Translated literally from the French as "cat's tongues," these are long, thin, narrow, delicate cookies often served with sorbet, iced desserts, and sweet wines. They can be sandwiched together in pairs with ganache, jam, or buttercream to make individual pastries. Langues de chat are made by piping the batter through a pastry bag into finger-like shapes onto a baking sheet or a specially designed pan, a langues de chat plaque. France. See also: langues de chat plaque.

langues de chat plaque A flat rectangular tinned-steel pan with ten 3-inch-long shallow indentations to form the finger-shaped langues de chat. The pan can also be used to bake ladyfingers and éclairs. See also: éclair, éclair plaque, ladyfingers, and langues de chat.

lard Pork fat that has been rendered, that is, melted very slowly over low heat until the fat has separated from any connective tissue and become liquid. This liquid is strained through filter paper or fine cheesecloth to remove any remaining solids. The fat used to make lard can come from any part of the animal, but leaf lard, which comes from around the kidneys, is considered to be the best. Because of its rich flavor and its ability to produce a tender, flaky texture, lard is used to make many pastry doughs. Lard is used in many cuisines for deep-frying. Commercially produced lard is processed in a variety of ways to make it firmer in texture and milder in flavor. Some processed lard contains preservatives that enable it to be stored at room temperature. Fresh lard should be stored in the refrigerator or frozen. Lard can be found in most supermarkets. See also: fats and oils.

lattice Strips of pastry dough arranged in a crisscross or woven pattern, usually on top of a pie. A lattice is an attractive, decorative alternative to a regular top crust for a pie.

lattice dough cutter Used to form a lattice design in rolled-out pastry dough, this is a round thin flat two-piece stencil. The bottom of the stencil is solid plastic with diamond-shaped cavities. The rolled-out dough is placed over this part, and the top piece of the cutter is placed over the dough. The top piece has the lattice design stamped into it, with all of the diamond-shaped cavities left open. It looks like a series of thin intersecting lines. This top piece is pressed into the dough to cut out the lattice design, and the diamond-shaped pieces of the dough are pushed away, leaving the thin strips that form the lattice. A one-piece lattice dough cutter made of metal is also available. It stands about 2 inches high. Rolled-out pastry dough is placed on top of the cutter and a rubber rolling pin is rolled over the dough. This presses the dough into the form, which cuts out the diamond shapes, making the lattice pattern. See also: lattice dough roller.

lattice dough roller This tool is used to form a lattice design in rolled-out pastry dough. It has a 5-inch-wide roller attached by short metal arms to a short wooden handle. It is also available in an all-plastic model. The roller has 17 half-moon–shaped notched blades that are rolled over the pastry dough, cutting out slits that form diamonds when the dough is stretched. The roller is easy to use and creates a uniform pattern. It is available at cookware shops, at restaurant supply shops, and through mail order cookware catalogs. See also: lattice dough cutter.

leaf stencil This tool is used to form wafer cookie dough into thin leaf shapes. It looks something like an offset spatula, with a flat aluminum sheet, $5^{1}/_{4}$ inches long by 3 inches wide, attached to a handle. The leaf stencil is cut out of the flat surface. The wafer cookie dough is pressed through the stencil onto the cookie sheet, then baked. Leaf stencils are designed to make either one large leaf design, $4^{1}/_{2}$ inches long by $2^{1}/_{4}$ inches wide, or two smaller leaves, $1^{1}/_{2}$ inches wide by $2^{3}/_{4}$ inches long.

leaven To increase the volume and lighten the texture of a dough or batter by introducing an agent such as whipped egg whites. The fermentation of yeast and the chemical reactions of agents such as baking powder and baking soda, or a combination, produce the same results. Gas that is produced by the leavening agent becomes trapped in the dough or batter and expands when heated, causing the rising of the dough or batter. In the case of whipped egg whites, air, not gas, is trapped inside the dough or batter, creating air pockets which set when heated. See also: baking powder, baking soda, leavener, and yeast.

leavener, leavening agent A substance that produces gas that results in the lightening and raising of a dough or batter, such as yeast, a bit of fermented dough, whipped egg whites, baking powder, or baking soda. When mixed with liquid, leavening agents produce carbon dioxide gas, which causes the dough or batter to rise before and/or during baking. Egg whites cause rising by trapping air, instead of gas, which sets when heated. See also: baking powder, baking soda, and yeast.

lebkuchen The German name for thick cakelike gingerbread made with honey and spices. Lebkuchen was one of the first versions of European gingerbread. Lebkuchen dough is used in a variety of ways. Lebkuchen cookies are cut from rolled out dough with cookie cutters, or the dough is pressed into intricately carved molds. The dough is also used to make gingerbread houses. Marzipan is often used as a filling, placed between two layers of cutout lebkuchen dough before baking. Candied citrus peel and almonds are occasionally mixed with the dough. The most well-known lebkuchen are the elaborately decorated gingerbread hearts, found at regional fairs throughout the fall and into the Christmas season. Nuremberg lebkuchen are made from a different dough, based on whipped eggs and sugar, and have a soft interior as a result. The dough is spicy but is made without honey, and finely ground nuts replace the flour. Nuremberg lebkuchen are baked on rice paper rounds or rectangles. After baking, they are glazed with sugar or chocolate icing. Germany. See also: gingerbread and rice paper.

leche flan The Philippine version of crème caramel, made with evaporated milk and lime zest. Philippines. See also: crème caramel, evaporated milk, and zest.

leche frita Spanish fried custard squares with a crunchy exterior and a creamy interior. Lemon zest and cinnamon are added to a thick creamy custard. The custard is baked and cooled, then cut into squares and deep-fried in hot oil. The squares are dusted with a mixture of cinnamon and confectioners' sugar before serving. Spain. See also: custard.

lecithin An emulsifier used in chocolate and confectionery that helps to make products smooth and moist. It acts as a stabilizer by preventing the fat from separating out of a mixture. Lecithin is a naturally occurring fatty substance found in egg yolks and vegetables.

leckerli Classic Swiss rectangular-shaped honey and spice cookies. The most well-known leckerli come from Basel; they are enriched with mixed candied fruit and nuts, glazed with a confectioners' sugar icing, and cut into short, thick, finger-shaped rectangles that become crunchy when cool. Switzerland.

lekvar A Hungarian specialty, lekvar is thick, intensely flavored, spreadable preserves made of fruit, with its skin left on, cooked with sugar. Prunes or apricots are traditionally used to make lekvar. It is used as a filling in a variety of pastries, cookies, and desserts. Lekvar is available in jars or cans in most supermarkets, in specialty food shops, and through mail order cookware catalogs. Hungary.

lemon A citrus fruit that grows on a short, thorny tree. Lemons are native to India and Malaya. They were brought to Europe with the returning Crusaders. Today lemons are grown in temperate climates throughout the world. Lemons are oblong and oval-shaped, from 2 to 4 inches long, with thick bright yellow skin that encloses pale-yellow, tart, juicy pulp. The yellow rind contains the fruit's perfume and essential oil. Lemon zest (the colored part of the rind) and juice are used extensively as ingredients in desserts, pastries, and confections, and the extract is also used, but less extensively. The juice is used to keep the flesh of some cut fruits, such as apples, bananas, and pears, from turning brown when exposed to air. Fresh lemons are available year-round. Choose fragrant fruit that is plump and feels heavy for its size, with firm, smooth skin and no soft spots. Store lemons at room temperature for up to 10 days or in the refrigerator for up to a month. Lemon juice and lime juice can be used interchangeably, but they taste different. See also: citrus fruit, extract, fruit, lemon curd, lime, and zest.

lemon curd A soft, thick, spreadable cooked cream of egg yolks, butter, sugar, lemon juice, and lemon zest. **Lemon curd** continues to thicken as it is cooled and chilled before using. It is a traditional accompaniment to scones for afternoon tea. Lemon curd is also used as a filling for tarts and cakes and as a spread for various sweet breads and biscuits. United Kingdom.

LEMON CURD

2 cups

2 large lemons
5 large egg yolks, at room temperature
½ cup granulated sugar
2 ounces (4 tablespoons) unsalted butter, melted

Zest the lemons and mince the zest very fine. Squeeze the juice from the lemons, and strain the juice to remove the seeds.

In the top of a double boiler, combine the egg yolks and sugar. Stir together over medium heat to dissolve the sugar, about 3 minutes. Add the lemon juice, lemon zest, and melted butter and stir constantly with a wooden spoon until the mixture thickens and coats a spoon, about 12 minutes.

Pour the mixture into a bowl and cover it tightly with plastic wrap. Let cool to room temperature, then refrigerate until thoroughly chilled.

Lemon curd will keep for up to a month in a tightly covered container in the refrigerator.

lemon meringue pie A classic American specialty, this dessert consists of a prebaked flaky pastry shell with a rich lemon curd filling and a thick layer of meringue topping, briefly baked in a hot oven until lightly golden colored. United States. See also: lemon curd, meringue, and pie.

levulose See fructose.

licorice An herb native to the Middle East used to flavor candies and confections. The root of the licorice plant is dried and ground to a fine powder, or juice is extracted from the root. Licorice has a slightly bittersweet taste, similar to that of anise and fennel. It is used to flavor many popular black-colored candies. Licorice has been used for thousands of years both for its medicinal qualities and as a sweet flavoring.

lime A citrus fruit native to Asia Minor. Today limes are grown in tropical climates throughout the world. The small round fruit has a thin, bright greenish-yellow skin that encloses a juicy, aromatic, acid pulp.

The green rind contains the fruit's perfume and essential oil. Lime zest (the colored part of the rind) and juice are used as ingredients in desserts, pastries, and confections. The juice is sometimes used to keep the flesh of some cut fruits, such as apples, bananas, and pears, from turning brown when exposed to air. Limes are used to make marmalade. There are two main varieties of lime: the Persian, which is the most common, and the Key lime, which produces the fragrant juice used to make Key lime pie. Key limes are grown in Florida and are usually found only in specialty food shops. Limes are available year-round. Choose fragrant fruit that is plump and feels heavy for its size, with firm, smooth, evenly colored skin. Store limes in the refrigerator for up to 2 weeks. Lime juice and lemon juice can be used interchangeably, but they taste different. See also: citrus fruit, fruit, lemon, and marmalade.

linzertorte This tartlike pastry is a Viennese specialty. It is made with a buttery, spicy ground almond or hazelnut pastry dough that is fitted into a shallow tart or cake pan, filled with raspberry preserves, and topped with lattice strips of the dough. After baking, **linzertorte** is dusted with confectioners' sugar. Many variations of linzertorte are made using different preserves for the filling. Austria.

&&&&&&&&&&

LINZERTORTE

One 9½- by 1½-inch round torte

1 cup all-purpose flour
1½ cups finely ground almonds
1½ teaspoons ground cinnamon
¼ teaspoon ground cloves
½ cup granulated sugar
8 ounces (2 sticks) unsalted butter, cut into small pieces, softened
2 large egg yolks, at room temperature
1¼ cups raspberry preserves
Confectioners' sugar for garnish

Combine the dry ingredients in the bowl of an electric mixer, a mixing bowl, or a food processor fitted with the steel blade. Add the butter and egg yolks. Using the flat beater attachment or a handheld mixer, blend all the ingredients until the dough forms a smooth ball, about 2 to 4 minutes; if using the food processor, pulse until the mixture forms a smooth ball, about 1 minute. Wrap the dough in plastic wrap and chill for at least 4 hours, or overnight. (The dough can be frozen for several months. If it is frozen, defrost for at least 24 hours in the refrigerator before using.)

Before rolling the dough, knead it slightly to soften. It can be difficult to work with and may crack. Cut off one third of the dough, and refrigerate it while you work with the remaining dough. Roll out the dough between sheets of lightly floured waxed paper to a 1/4-inch-thick 12- to 13-inch round. Remove the top sheet of waxed paper. Grasp the edges of the bottom piece of waxed paper and turn the dough upside down into a 9½-inch fluted tart pan with a removable bottom. Peel off the waxed paper. Use your hands to fit the dough into the pan, making sure it fits snugly against the bottom and up the sides; if necessary, patch any cracks. Trim off the excess dough.

Spread the bottom of the pastry shell evenly with the raspberry preserves.

Between sheets of lightly floured waxed paper, roll out the remaining pastry dough into a 1/4 inch thick 12-inch by 6-inch rectangle. Using a fluted-edge pastry wheel cutter, cut the dough into 8 or 10 ½-inch-wide strips. Using an offset spatula to transfer the strips to the tart pan, form a lattice on top of the torte by laying the strips in a woven pattern. Roll the remaining pastry dough into a long rope about 1/4 inch thick. Place this around the outer edge of the tart where the ends of the strips and edges of the shell meet, and use a fork to press the rope into the edge of the tart to give it a finished look. Chill the linzertorte in the refrigerator for 15 minutes before baking.

Center a rack in the oven and preheat to 375°F.

Place the torte on a baking sheet and bake for 30 minutes, or until the pastry is golden brown and the preserves are bubbling. Transfer to a rack to cool for 15 minutes. Then carefully remove the sides of the tart pan, and let the linzertorte cool to room temperature.

Dust the top of the linzertorte lightly with confectioners' sugar before serving.

Linzertorte can be held at room temperature, well wrapped with foil, for up to 3 days.

Variation: White linzertorte is a delicious variation: Replace the ground almonds with ground hazelnuts, replace the cinnamon and cloves with the finely minced zest of 1 lemon, and replace the raspberry preserves with apricot preserves.

loaf pan This pan is designed for baking rectangular cakes and bread, including quick breads. The standard size is 9 inches long by 5 inches wide by 3 inches deep, but there are several sizes and types. The expanding loaf pan has two separate pieces that slide into each other so that it can expand from $8^3/4$ to $15^1/4$ inches long. A loaf plaque holds four small loaf pans, each measuring 5 inches long by $2^1/2$ wide, in a frame. Loaf pans are also available in long thin rectangular shapes. Loaf pans are made from a variety of materials, including glass, aluminum, tinned steel, black or blue steel, and ceramic.

Lord Baltimore cake A light-textured golden cake baked in three layers and filled with a mixture of boiled icing blended with crushed macaroons, chopped pecans or almonds, and candied cherries. The cake is frosted with billowy white boiled icing. The story is that this cake was created to use up the egg yolks leftover from making Lady Baltimore Cake. United States. See also: boiled icing and Lady Baltimore cake.

loukoumáthes, loukoumades Greek deep-fried yeast-risen honey pastries. These light and airy puffs are deep-fried in hot oil until golden brown, then soaked briefly in a rich, sweet syrup of honey, water, lemon juice, and rose water. The puffs are served warm with a sprinkling of cinnamon and sugar. Greece. See also: honey and rose water.

ma'amoul Arabic stuffed sweet balls. A dough made of milk and semolina or all-purpose flour is combined with orange flower water to make a thick paste, then kneaded until smooth and shaped into walnut-sized balls. A filling made of ground almonds and walnuts or pistachio nuts blended with sugar or of dates cooked until soft is inserted into the center of each ball and the ball is pinched to enclose the filling. The stuffed balls are baked until delicately colored. When cool, the pastries are heavily dusted with confectioners' sugar. Egypt, Syria, and Lebanon.

macadamia nut Although this nut is an Australian native, today it is grown primarily in Hawaii. Macadamia nuts grow on a small evergreen tree named for its cultivator, Scottish chemist John McAdam. These small, round nuts have extremely hard light-brown shells and, therefore, are most often available shelled. They can be bought raw, toasted, or toasted and salted. The high degree of fat in the nuts gives them their buttery rich flavor. It also causes them to turn rancid quickly, so they are best stored in a tightly sealed container or wrapped in plastic in the freezer, where they will keep for up to a year. They are used to flavor and give texture to numerous desserts, pastries, and confections. Macadamia nuts are available in most major supermarkets, health food stores, and specialty nut stores.

macaroon This classic cookie, made with almonds or almond paste, sugar, and egg whites, has a crisp, chewy exterior and a soft interior. Although macaroons made with almonds, such as **almond paste macaroons**, are the most common, macaroons can be flavored with chocolate, coffee, citrus peel, or other nuts such as hazelnuts. Coconut macaroons are a popular variation. In France, macaroons are made from two of the chewy almond cookies sandwiched together with a thin filling of raspberry or apricot jam, lemon curd, or chocolate. Macaroons have been documented in Italy as early as the eighth century. The first known recipe appeared in Venice, during the Renaissance. The city of Nancy in northeastern France is famous for its macaroons, which have been baked there for at least seven hundred years. Italy and France.

ALMOND PASTE MACAROONS

Forty-two 2-inch-diameter macaroons

1 tablespoon unsalted butter, softened, for the pans
1 tablespoon all-purpose flour, for the pans

1 roll (7 ounces) almond paste
¾ cup granulated sugar
2 large egg whites, at room temperature, lightly beaten
½ teaspoon almond extract
1 tablespoon all-purpose flour

Position the oven racks in the upper and lower thirds of the oven and preheat to 325°F. Line two baking sheets or jelly-roll pans with aluminum foil. Butter the foil with the softened butter, dust with the flour, and shake off the excess.

Combine the almond paste and sugar in the bowl of a stand mixer or in a mixing bowl. Using the flat beater attachment or a hand-held mixer, blend together on low speed until the mixture is crumbly, then beat on medium speed until well combined. Add the egg whites and almond extract and blend until smooth. Add the flour and mix well.

Fit a 12- or 14-inch pastry bag with a #5 large plain tip. Fill the pastry bag with the macaroon mixture. Pipe out 1-inch-diameter mounds onto the prepared pans, leaving 2 inches space between the mounds.

Bake the macaroons for 8 minutes. Switch the positions of the baking pans and bake for 7 minutes longer, or until golden. Transfer the baking pans to cooling racks to cool.

When completely cool, lift the macaroons off the aluminum foil. The macaroons are best eaten within 2 days. Store them in an airtight container at room temperature.

mace The lacy red outer covering that surrounds the nutmeg seed. Mace is separated from the nutmeg seed during processing and broken into pieces called blades. Mace is used to flavor desserts, cakes, puddings, and custards, as well as countless savory dishes. It is native to the Spice Islands in Indonesia and was used by ancient Indian civilizations long before it was known to the West. The Arab traders brought mace to Europe, where it became highly prized for its pungent flavor. Mace is widely available finely ground. It is best stored in a tightly sealed glass jar in a cool, dark, dry place and replaced every 4 to 6 months for maximum flavor. See also: nutmeg.

madeleine A small, light, seashell-shaped cake that was immortalized in the writings of French novelist Marcel Proust. They are baked in oval-shaped molds that have a ribbed scallop-shell form, which gives them their characteristic appearance. Classic **madeleines** are made from butter, flour, eggs, and sugar, and flavored with either lemon or orange. Variations include nuts, chocolate, cocoa, or almond paste. Madeleines are eaten more like cookies than cakes. Although their origins are cloudy, there is speculation that they originated in the French town of Commercy, in the region of Lorraine, in the eighteenth century. They are said to be named for Madeleine, the girl who brought them to the court and to the attention of Stanislaw Lezczynski, the Duke of Lorraine, who was the father of Marie, wife of Louis XV. France. See also: madeleine pan.

MADELEINES

3 1/2 dozen madeleines (3 1/2 inches long, 1 inch wide)

2 tablespoons unsalted butter, melted, for the pans
2 tablespoons all-purpose flour, for the pans

4 large eggs, at room temperature
1/4 teaspoon salt

continued

⅔ cup granulated sugar
1 teaspoon vanilla or lemon extract
1 teaspoon finely minced lemon zest
1 cup all-purpose flour
4 ounces (1 stick) unsalted butter, melted and slightly cooled

Position the oven racks in the upper and lower thirds of the oven and preheat to 400°F. Using a pastry brush, butter the insides of the shell impressions in two madeleine pans with the melted butter, then dust with the flour and tap out the excess.

In the bowl of a stand mixer, using the wire whip attachment, or in a mixing bowl, using a hand-held mixer, beat the eggs with the salt at medium speed until they are foamy, about 1 minute. Gradually beat in the sugar, then beat the mixture at medium-high speed until it is pale-colored and holds a slowly dissolving ribbon when the beater is lifted above the batter, about 5 minutes. Add the extract and lemon zest and blend well.

Fold in the flour in 3 additions, then fold in the melted butter in 3 additions.

Spoon the batter into the prepared pans, filling each impression three-quarters full. Place the madeleine pans on baking sheets, and bake for 5 minutes. Switch the positions of the baking sheets and bake for 5 minutes longer, or until the madeleines are puffed and lightly browned and spring back when lightly touched on top.

Transfer the pans to cooling racks and let cool for 2 minutes. Then turn the pans upside down and gently shake them to release the madeleines. Let the madeleines cool completely on the racks.

The madeleines will keep in an airtight container at room temperature for 3 to 4 days.

madeleine pan Also called a madeleine plaque or a madeleine sheet, this special flat rectangular tinned-steel or aluminum pan is used to bake madeleines. The most commonly available pan has twelve 3-inch-long by 1³/₄-inch-wide by ¹/₂-inch-deep shell-shaped indentations, which give the finished madeleines their characteristic ribbed scallop-shell shape. Other madeleine pans are available with as few as eight and as many as twenty-four indentations, slightly larger than the classic size. Madeleinette pans have twenty-four or forty indentations, which are half the classic size. See also: madeleine.

Magi-cake strip See cake strip.

maid of honor An individual almond-custard–filled tartlet traditionally served for afternoon tea. The tartlets take their name from Anne Boleyn, who was maid of honor to Catherine of Aragon, first wife of Henry VIII of England, and who became his second wife. United Kingdom.

maja blanca maiz A Philippine cake made of fresh coconut, corn kernels, milk, and sugar cooked with coconut oil to a thick paste, then blended with toasted anise seed. The mixture is poured into a cake pan coated with coconut oil and baked. When cool, the cake is cut and served with latik, which is the residue created when pure coconut milk is boiled until it turns to oil. Philippines. See also: anise seed and coconut.

mandarin Part of the loose-skinned family of hybrid oranges whose other members include clementines and tangerines, mandarins are small round citrus fruits with thin skin that slips off and segments that separate easily. Mandarins have bright orange skin and juicy, sweet-tart pulp. They can be full of seeds or be seedless. They range from tiny varieties the size of an egg to those the size of a baseball. Mandarin orange segments, juice, and peel are used raw, and the peel is often candied for use as an ingredient in many desserts, pastries, and confections. Fresh mandarin oranges are available from November to June. Choose bright-skinned, firm fruit that feels heavy for its size, with no soft spots or discoloration. Russets, rough brown spots on the skin, do not affect the quality or flavor of the fruit. Store mandarins in a cool, dry place for several days or in the refrigerator for several weeks. See also: citrus fruit, clementine, fruit, orange, tangelo, and tangerine.

mandelbrot A Jewish specialty of German origin, this is a crisp almond bread that is baked, sliced, and baked again. It is eaten like a cookie, similar to Italian biscotti. *Mandel* is the German word for almond, and *brot* means bread. Germany and Israel. See also: biscotti.

mandelspan Swedish semicircular lacy wafer cookies made from a mixture of almond paste, sugar, and eggs. The batter is spread on wafer paper, then transferred to an arched metal form to bake. When cool, the cookies are lightly frosted and dusted with confectioners' sugar. To show off their dramatic shape, mandelspan are often served on a round platter, arranged to form a crown. Sweden.

mandorla The Italian word for almond. See also: almond.

mango The oblong, oval fruit of the evergreen tree of the same name that is native to Southeast Asia. Mangoes have been grown for at least six thousand years and today are cultivated in India, Southeast Asia, South and Central America, and Florida. Mangoes have a thick, smooth, yellowish-red skin with a hard center stone surrounded by moist, juicy, creamy or fibrous golden pulp. The flavor of mango is a cross between peach, apricot, banana, and papaya. Mangoes are used raw as an ingredient in desserts and pastries, particularly fresh fruit tarts, sorbets, ice creams, parfaits, and frozen soufflés; they are puréed to make a dessert sauce; and they are used to make jams and jellies. Mangoes are available from May through September, with June the peak. Imported mangoes are often available throughout the year. Choose aromatic, plump, firm, yellow or red fruit with taut skin that gives slightly when pressed. Avoid fruit with soft spots. Unripe mangoes will ripen at room temperature within a few days. To speed up ripening, place the fruit in a tightly closed paper bag at room temperature. Once they are ripe, it is best to use mangoes immediately or refrigerate them in a plastic bag for no longer than 2 days. It is not easy to remove the center stone from a mango. The easiest way is to slice the fruit away from the stone into halves, then skin and slice or dice the halves. See also: fruit.

manjar blanco A classic South American milk pudding that is slow-cooked for several hours with sugar and cinnamon until it is very thick. Also called *dulce de leche* (milk sweet), manjar blanco is eaten as a dessert on its own, used as a sweet spread on bread, and is a filling for many pastries. Peru.

maple syrup The syrup produced by boiling the sap of the sugar maple tree until most of the water evaporates, maple syrup is sweet with a rich, aromatic flavor. Maple syrup is graded according to color. The delicately flavored pale golden syrups are classified as Grade AA or Fancy. Grade A and Grade B are slightly deeper in color with stronger flavors, while Grade C is very dark with a robust flavor. Maple butter or cream, which is thick and spreadable, is a product of the processing of the sap. It is made by evaporating almost all of the water out of the syrup, then cooling the remainder rapidly until it thickens. Maple sugar is the result of evaporating all the water out of the sap. Maple sugar is much sweeter than granulated sugar. It takes about 30 to 40 gallons of sap to produce 1 gallon of maple syrup. Maple syrup is produced primarily in the northeastern United States and Canada. Maple syrup tart is a specialty of the French-Canadian province of Quebec. United States and Canada.

Maraschino A clear cherry-flavored Italian liqueur made from marasca, a sour cherry grown in Northern Italy. The slightly bitter liqueur is used to flavor many Italian desserts and fruit compotes. Italy.

marble A hard, natural material that maintains a consistent cool temperature because it dissipates heat faster than other surfaces. In addition, marble does not hold moisture, so it stays dry. For these reasons, a marble slab is ideal for rolling out pastry doughs, especially those that have a high butter content, such as puff pastry and croissant dough. Marble boards are also very important for chocolate work, especially tempering, and for sugar work. A practical size is a board that measures 18 inches by 24 inches by ³/₄ inch high. A slab much larger is difficult to move because it is so heavy. Marble stains if it comes in contact with acid material, such as citrus juice. Marble should not be used as a cutting board both because it will dull knives and because knife cuts will hinder pastry, chocolate, and sugar work. See also: croissant, puff pastry, and tempering chocolate.

margarine A substitute for butter created by a French chemist in the late nineteenth century upon the request by Napoleon III for a low-cost fat. Margarine was originally made from animal fats, but today it is made primarily from hydrogenated vegetable oils and skim-milk solids that are processed to a spreadable consistency. Preservatives, salt, and emulsifiers are also added. Hydrogenation refers to the process of forcing pressurized hydrogen gas through liquids to transform them into solids or semisolids. The process simultaneously makes the oils saturated and removes any benefits of their unsaturated qualities. Soybean, safflower, and corn oils, all low in cholesterol, are most commonly used to make margarine. Margarine is often colored with achiote, the seeds of the annatto tree, and fortified with vitamins, primarily vitamin A and, occasionally, vitamin D. It can be used interchangeably with butter in recipes, but it will not impart the same rich flavor and the texture of the finished dessert, pastry, or confection will be altered. Since margarine is softer and more oily than butter and has a higher melting point, it does not have the same mouth feel as butter. There are several types of margarine available, both salted and unsalted. Regular margarine is approximately 80 percent fat and 20 percent water, coloring, and flavoring. Diet margarine is approximately 40 percent fat. Soft margarine is processed to be spreadable at any temperature, while whipped margarine has had air whipped into it, making it light and fluffy. Liquid margarine, which comes in squeeze bottles, is processed to remain liquid when cold. There are also butter-margarine blends that are approximately 40 percent butter and 60 percent margarine. Regular solid margarine is the best to use as a substitute for butter, because it is the closest to butter in consistency. The other types of margarine vary in consistency and if they are used instead of butter, the results may be drastically different. Margarine is available in 1-pound packages of four sticks or two tubs. It is best stored tightly wrapped or covered in the refrigerator for up to a month or frozen for up to a year. See also: butter and fats and oils.

marjolaine A classic long, rectangular cake composed of alternating layers of almond or hazelnut meringue, chocolate buttercream, and praline cream. Marjolaine is similar to dacquoise. Marjolaine was created by the legendary twentieth-century chef Ferdinand Point. France. See also: buttercream, dacquoise, meringue, and praline.

marmalade Citrus fruit peel and chunks cooked with sugar until the mixture thickens and holds its shape. The tender pieces of citrus fruit and peel become suspended throughout the mixture. Marmalade is clear and has a jellylike, firm yet soft texture. The word *marmalade* is derived from *marmelada*, Portuguese for quince jam, as quinces were the fruit originally used to make the preserve. Orange marmalade made with Seville oranges is the most popular marmalade. Marmalade is used as a spread on sweet breads for afternoon tea, to make dessert glazes and sauces, and as an ingredient and filling in desserts, pastries, and confections. See also: conserve, jam, jelly, and preserves.

marquise A term that refers to several different dessert preparations that are usually of a soft consistency, including a mousselike cake known as marquise au chocolat and a fruit ice that is blended with whipped cream. A chocolate dacquoise is also called a marquise, as is a génoise cake filled with chocolate pastry cream and covered with chocolate fondant. A marquise is generally molded and chilled to set, then unmolded to serve. France. See also: dacquoise, génoise, mousse, and pastry cream.

marsala A fortified wine from Sicily, Italy. Marsala has a rich, full-bodied flavor that ranges from dry to sweet. Sweet marsala is used as a dessert wine and as a flavoring for such desserts as the classic Italian frothy custard zabaglione. Italy. See also: zabaglione.

marshmallow A confection made from a mixture of corn syrup, egg whites, sugar, gelatin or gum arabic, flavoring, and coloring beaten to a light, fluffy, spongy consistency. Marshmallows are available in white or pastel colors in two sizes: regular, which is about $1\frac{1}{2}$ inches in diameter, and miniature, about $\frac{1}{2}$ inch in diameter. Originally marshmallows were made from the roots of the medicinal plant of the same name. Marshmallow creme, made from the same ingredients as marshmallows, is a thick whipped mixture available in jars in supermarkets. It is used as an ingredient in fudge, icings, cakes, and candies. United States.

maryann pan This specialized baking pan is also known under several other names, including shortcake pan, indented fruit tart pan, and obsttortenform. It is a round shallow textured tinned-steel or aluminum pan that resembles a tart pan. It has fluted sides and a deep hollow around the edge which makes the center appear raised. Sponge cakes or pastry shells are baked in this pan. The baked cake or pastry shell is turned upside down out of the pan, and the indented center is filled with fruit or cream. Maryann pans range from 8 to 12½ inches in diameter. They are also available in individual sizes, from 3 to 4¾ inches in diameter. They are available at cookware shops and through mail order cookware catalogs.

marzipan A firm but pliable confection made from a cooked mixture of sugar, egg whites or water, and finely ground almonds. Marzipan is often colored with food coloring and formed into flowers, fruits, and animals. It is also rolled out and used to cover and decorate cakes and pastries. Marzipan has a slightly sweeter almond taste and smoother texture than almond paste, but the two are essentially interchangeable. Pastries and confections that are covered with marzipan or have marzipan decorations should be kept covered until they are served because marzipan becomes crusty if exposed to the air for very long. Marzipan should be stored tightly covered with plastic wrap in the refrigerator or freezer, where it will last for up to 6 months. Marzipan originated in the Middle East centuries ago and traveled to Europe with Arab traders in the Middle Ages. The Europeans developed the use of marzipan to a fine art. Marzipan is widely available in most supermarkets and gourmet stores in plastic-wrapped rolls. See also: almond paste.

marzipan rolling pin See rolling pin.

marzipan tools A series of specialized tools made of long, thin plastic sticks that range in length from 4¾ to 6½ inches. The tips of the sticks are formed into precisely designed shapes, each of which has a particular use for shaping marzipan into flowers, fruits, animals, and other forms. The tools score, nick, notch, cup, crease, or gouge marzipan into various shapes and designs. One tool, called a blade and shell, is used to make fine creases without cutting through the marzipan and to mark flowers with a ridged finish. A scallop and comb is used to form both edges and eyes and smiles on marzipan figures. These tools are also used for gum paste work. The tools are available singly or in sets of as many as twelve at cookware shops, at cake decorating and candy making supply shops, and through mail order cookware catalogs. See also: gum paste.

mascarpone A rich, thick, velvety-soft cows' milk cheese from the Lombardy region of Italy. Ivory-colored mascarpone has the texture of sour cream and a delicate, sweet flavor. It is eaten as a dessert with fresh fruit, served with desserts in place of whipped cream, and used as an ingredient in desserts and pastries, often replacing cream cheese. Italy.

mazamorra morada A classic Peruvian fruit pudding; its name translates as "purple pudding." The color comes from the purple corn used to make the pudding. A variety of fruits, such as peaches, pears, pineapple, quinces, or apples, are cooked with cinnamon, cloves, lemon, and the corn, then strained to make a rich liquid. It is mixed with lemon juice and cornstarch, then cooked with dried peaches and plums, and poured into a mold to cool. The pudding is served cold, dusted with ground cinnamon. Peru.

mazarek, mazurek A meringuelike confection of beaten egg whites mixed with sugar and flavored in a variety of ways. The mixture is spread in a thin layer on rice paper on a baking sheet and baked in a slow oven to dry, but not brown. Occasionally it is baked in a round cake pan. When done, the confection is cut into squares or rectangles. Poland.

mazurka A little cake made of beaten eggs, honey, fresh lemon juice, lemon zest, and finely ground hazelnuts, walnuts, or almonds. Mazurkas are sweet, puffy, meringuelike confections baked in paper bake cups in muffin pans or on rice paper on baking sheets. They are cooled, then served garnished with a dollop of whipped cream and dusted with a pinch of freshly grated nutmeg. Mazurkas are traditionally served in Russia at Easter. Russia.

McIntosh apple One of the preferred varieties for baked goods, McIntosh apples do not hold their shape when baked whole. They have rich red skins streaked with green and medium-crisp, sweet-tart flesh. McIntosh apples are available from September to April. See also: apple.

measuring cup Two different types of measuring cup are used for measuring liquid and dry ingredients. Liquid measuring cups have a pour spout on top and a handle on the side. These are designed to have extra room at the top so liquids won't spill as the cup is moved. Liquid measuring cups are marked across the body with lines that indicate fluid ounces and cups, pints, or quarts. For accuracy, liquid measuring cups should be read at eye level. Liquid measures are available in 1-cup, 2-cup, and 4-cup sizes. They are made of glass, aluminum, or plastic. Dry measuring cups come in a nested set of graduated sizes. The usual sizes are $1/8$ cup, $1/4$ cup, $1/3$ cup, $1/2$ cup, and 1 cup. These measuring cups are flat on top and have long handles. They are designed to be filled to the top and the ingredient leveled off. To measure dry ingredients, such as flour or sugar, scoop or spoon the ingredient into the measure, then use a knife or spatula to sweep off the excess so that the top is flat. To measure brown sugar, pack it firmly into the measuring cup even with the top.

measuring spoon Measuring spoons come in a standard set of graduated sizes that include ¹/₄ teaspoon, ¹/₂ teaspoon, 1 teaspoon, and 1 tablespoon. The spoons are available in aluminum, stainless steel, and plastic. They are used for measuring both liquid and dry ingredients. To measure liquid ingredients, pour the ingredient carefully into the spoon just up to the top edge, so that it doesn't spill. For dry ingredients, scoop the ingredient up with the spoon and level it off with a knife or spatula.

Melba sauce Created by Auguste Escoffier, the great French chef, in honor of Dame Nellie Melba, the famed nineteenth-century Australian opera singer, Melba sauce is sweetened raspberry purée. Modern versions substitute red currant jelly flavored with kirsch and mixed with cornstarch. The sauce is traditionally used to top the dessert called peach Melba, but it can be used to garnish many other desserts, such as pound cake, fruit, and ice cream. See also: peach Melba.

melon A relative of the cucumber, a melon is a round or oval vine-grown edible gourd that varies in size. Melons have a firm rind and sweet, juicy flesh. They are native to Asia and have been cultivated for thousands of years. There are two main categories of melons: watermelons and muskmelons, which include those melons most commonly used in desserts and pastries—cantaloupe, casaba, Crenshaw, and honeydew. Melons are used raw as an ingredient in desserts and pastries such as fruit salads, ice creams, sorbets, and parfaits. Melons are available from June through October. Choose fresh-smelling, fragrant melons that are firm and heavy for their size, with no soft spots. One indication of ripeness is that the blossom end of the melon gives slightly when pressed. Slightly underripe melons do not ripen once picked, but they can be made softer and juicier by placing them in a perforated paper bag with a slice of apple at room temperature. Once they are ripe, store melons in the refrigerator for 5 to 7 days. Melons taste best at room temperature, so remove them from the refrigerator at least 30 minutes before use. See also: cantaloupe, casaba melon, Crenshaw melon, fruit, honeydew melon, and watermelon.

melon baller A hand-held 7- to 8-inch-long utensil used to cut melons or other fruits into small balls. It can also be used to scoop out and form truffle mixtures into balls. The most common type has a wood or plastic handle that holds a round, oval, or fluted sharp-edged stainless steel bowl at each end. The bowls are different sizes, ranging from ¹/₄ inch to 1¹/₄ inches in diameter. Some melon ballers have only one bowl. Melon ballers are available at cookware shops, at supermarkets, and through mail order cookware catalogs.

melting moments Named for their melt-in-the-mouth quality, these round cookies are British classics. Rich and buttery, the sweet confections are often served for afternoon tea. They are usually shaped into balls, rolled in crushed cornflakes or dried sweetened coconut, and topped with a candied cherry or a slice of angelica before baking. United Kingdom.

meringue A delicate mixture of egg whites and sugar whipped together until firm. The mixture is formed into various shapes used for making pastries and desserts. Both the mixture and the desserts made from it are called meringue. The two main types of meringue are soft and hard. The difference between them lies in the amount of sugar added to the egg whites. Soft meringue has a minimal amount of sugar and is beaten to a soft peak stage. It is used as a topping for pies and baked Alaska, to form oeufs à la neige, and in mousses. Hard meringue has a larger proportion of sugar to whites. It is generally shaped by piping the mixture through a pastry bag into disks, cases to hold fruit or sorbet, or individual shells and kisses. These are dried in the oven at a low temperature, then left to set in the turned-off oven until completely cool. This technique produces a delicate, crisp, crumbly meringue. Adding finely ground nuts, such as almonds or hazelnuts, turns the meringue into dacquoise, broyage, Succès, japonaise, or Progrès. French meringue, a type of hard meringue, is also called warm meringue. The egg whites and sugar are warmed together in a bowl set over a pan of warm water, like a bain-marie. The heat helps the sugar to dissolve and the egg whites to be beaten to their full volume. Swiss meringue, also called cold meringue, is another type of hard meringue. It is made by whipping the egg whites until frothy, then slowly adding the sugar as the whites are whipping. Italian meringue uses a hot cooked sugar syrup that is beaten into the whipped egg whites; the mixture is then beaten until it is cool and shiny. Italian meringue is a very stable meringue that holds its shape well. It is widely used in buttercream icings and meringue decorations, for dacquoise, as the basis for frozen desserts such as soufflés and sorbets, and as the topping for pies and baked Alaska. It is versatile and can be used in most cases where either soft or hard meringue would be used. Meringue is very sensitive to humidity and will soften and break down if there is too much moisture in the air. Superfine sugar produces the best-quality meringue, because it dissolves rapidly and completely and leaves no trace of grittiness. See also: bain-marie, baked Alaska, broyage, dacquoise, Pavlova, Spanish windtorte, Succès, sugar, and vacherin.

meringue powder A dried egg white–based powder used to replace fresh egg whites in making royal icing and both soft and hard meringues. Meringue powder contains sugar, egg whites, salt, vanillin, and gum. When mixed with water, the icing that results has the same consistency as icing made with fresh egg whites. The advantage to using meringue powder is that the icing made from it can be rebeaten without breaking down and also avoids any danger of salmonella. See also: meringue.

Mexican wedding cake This is not a cake at all, but a rich, buttery, round cookie, loaded with chopped pecans or almonds. The cookies are rolled in confectioners' sugar while still warm and again when cool. Many countries claim a variation of these cookies; for example, Russian tea cakes. Mexico.

m'hanncha Literally, "the snake," this is a classic Moroccan confection. A filling of ground almonds, confectioners' sugar, cinnamon, melted butter, and either orange flower water or rose water is mixed together into a thick paste, then rolled into $1/2$-inch-thick cylinders. These cylinders are rolled up inside buttered phyllo pastry dough. The cylinders are coiled in concentric circles on a buttered baking pan, brushed with beaten egg, then baked until golden brown. The pastry is cooled slightly, then sprinkled with cinnamon and confectioners' sugar, and cut into serving pieces. M'hanncha is traditionally served for special celebrations such as anniversaries and weddings. Morocco. See also: phyllo dough.

milk An opaque white liquid secreted by female mammals to feed their young. Cows' milk is the milk most commonly used in the United States. Milk is very nutritious, containing protein and many vitamins and minerals. This nutritive value also makes milk very attractive to many microorganisms that cause disease, so it is routinely pasteurized (a process of heating and sterilizing the milk to destroy the microbes, then cooling it quickly). Pasteurization removes the likelihood of disease and gives milk an extended shelf life. Most milk is also homogenized, which is a process that breaks up and evenly distributes the fat globules throughout the milk to keep them from separating and rising to the top to form cream. Milk is widely used as an ingredient in many desserts, pastries, and confections, such as creams, caramels, custards, ice creams, and sauces. Many different varieties of milk products are available. Raw milk is not pasteurized and, therefore, it carries the potential for causing disease. It is usually available only in health food stores. Ultrapasteurized milk has been heated to a much higher temperature and heated slightly longer than pasteurized milk. The process extends shelf life, but, it imparts a slightly cooked flavor to the milk.

Milk is labeled according to the amount of fat it contains. Whole milk contains at least 3.5 percent milk fat. Low-fat milk, which has had most of the milk fat removed, contains between 1 and 2 percent milk fat. Nonfat or skim milk contains less than 0.5 percent fat. It cannot be used interchangeably with whole or low-fat milk in recipes because of its significantly lower fat content.

Buttermilk was originally the milky liquid left over after churning butter. Today it is made commercially by adding special bacterial cultures to skim milk, which produce a tangy flavor and thickened texture. Some processors add butter flakes to the buttermilk to re-create the old-fashioned style. Evaporated milk is canned homogenized milk that has had half of its water removed through evaporation. It is available in both whole and skim varieties. Sweetened condensed milk is evaporated milk with the addition of sugar, in a proportion of about 40 to 45 percent of the mixture. If unopened, evaporated milk and sweetened condensed milk will last indefinitely. Powdered milk, also called nonfat dry milk, has had all of its water removed through evaporation. It is usually made from skim milk, but powdered whole milk is available. Powdered dry milk is easily reconstituted in water. Instant nonfat dry milk is also available.

Store all fresh and fluid milk in the refrigerator. All milk products are marked with a pull date to show when they should be withdrawn from sale. This date allows for some storage time in the refrigerator. Canned milk can be stored in a cool place indefinitely if unopened. Once opened, transfer it to another container and store it tightly covered in the refrigerator. Powdered milk will also keep indefinitely unopened. Once opened, store it in a dry place. Once powdered milk is reconstituted, it should be stored in a tightly covered container in the refrigerator. Powdered milk made from whole milk has a high fat content, making it prone to rancidity. It should be refrigerated in both its dry and reconstituted forms.

mille-feuille The name of this classic French pastry translates as "a thousand leaves"; it is also called a Napoléon. It is made of three rectangular strips of crisp puff pastry that are alternated with two layers of pastry cream or of sweetened whipped cream and raspberry or strawberry jam. The traditional decoration for the top of the pastry is either white fondant topped with spiderweb lines of chocolate or a heavy dusting of confectioners' sugar. After the pastry is assembled, it is cut crosswise into individual slices. Mille-feuille are fragile and should be refrigerated until just before serving. They are best if served within 4 hours of preparation. France. See also: fondant, pastry cream, and puff pastry.

mincemeat A rich preserve of finely chopped fruits, primarily apples, raisins, and candied citrus peel, nuts, rum or brandy, brown sugar, spices, and beef suet. Mincemeat takes its name from the fact that it was originally made with lean beef, although none is used in modern versions. Commercially made mincemeat is available in jars in supermarkets, usually around the Thanksgiving and Christmas holidays. Homemade mincemeat should be allowed to mellow for at least a month before using to develop a deep, rich flavor. Mincemeat is best known as the filling for mincemeat pie, although it can also be used in cakes, puddings, and cookies. United Kingdom.

mint An aromatic perennial herb native to the Mediterranean, with hundreds of different species. Peppermint and spearmint are the most commonly used and widely available mints. Mint is available fresh and dried, as an extract, and as an essential oil or essence. Mint extract and essential oil are widely used to flavor desserts, pastries, and confections, such as peppermints, ice cream, and chocolate-covered mints, and for making tea, cordials, and liqueurs. Fresh mint is also used to decorate desserts and pastries. Spearmint has bright green leaves that are set close together and notched on the ends. Peppermint has dark stems, smoother leaves, and the more pungent flavor of the two. Both peppermint and spearmint grow wild throughout the world. They are commercially grown in the United States, Europe, and Asia. Fresh mint can be stored for up to a week in the refrigerator by placing its stems in a glass of water, covering the leaves with a plastic bag, and changing the water daily. Dried mint is best stored in a tightly sealed container in a cool, dark, dry place. Replace it every 6 months for freshness. Mint extract, oil of peppermint, and oil of spearmint should be stored in tightly capped glass bottles in a cool, dark, dry place. See also: essence and extract.

mirliton Also called mirliton de Rouen, this French individual tartlet is a specialty of Rouen in northwest France. The tartlets are made with puff pastry shells filled with a rich almond cream mixture, flavored with orange flower water, and topped with confectioners' sugar before baking. Often mirlitons are decorated with a design of three almond halves. A variation includes a spoonful of apricot preserves under the almond cream filling. A mirliton is also a crisp almond cookie favored with orange flower water. France.

mix The technique for combining two or more ingredients by blending or stirring so that the resulting mixture is well integrated and the ingredients are evenly distributed.

mixing bowl A round container used for combining ingredients. Mixing bowls are available in a wide range of sizes and materials, including glass, plastic, ceramic, porcelain, stainless steel, and copper. Some have rolled top rims. Sizes range from $^1/_2$ quart up to 17 quarts. The choice of the size depends on the amount of ingredients and how they are to be combined—whether by, for example, blending gently or by tossing. Extra room in the bowl is always helpful. Some bowls are tall with slanted sides and flat bottoms, others are more shallow and curved. Some have two small loops that hang from the rim, called hang rings, so they can be hung from a rack. Although most mixing bowls do not have handles, some heavy plastic models have molded handles and pour spouts. Mixing bowls are available singly or in nested sets at cookware shops, at supermarkets, and through mail order cookware catalogs. See also: copper egg white bowl.

mocha The flavor created by the combination of coffee and chocolate, which is widely used in desserts, pastries, and confections.

moh sein buong A classic Myanmarese (Burmese) steamed sponge cake. This light-textured cake is made with rice flour. It is steamed in a tall mold in two layers, one white and one brown; the color of the darker layer comes from palm sugar. The steamed cake is sprinkled with grated coconut and crusted toasted sesame seeds mixed with salt. It is traditionally served on banana leaves. Moh sein buong is popular both for breakfast and as a snack. Myanmar.

molasses During the process of refining sugarcane, the sugar crystals are removed, and the remaining juice is molasses. The juice is boiled to various stages, resulting in different grades. Light molasses come from the first boiling. The second boiling produces dark molasses, while the third boiling produces the dark, intensely flavored, almost bitter, blackstrap molasses. Light and dark molasses are the types most often used in the United States. Light molasses is used as a syrup for pancakes. Dark molasses is used in gingerbread and many other baked goods. Both light and dark molasses are available in most supermarkets. Blackstrap molasses is available predominantly in health food stores. If sulfur is used in the refining process, the molasses is labeled sulfured, also called robust-flavor; if not, it is labeled unsulfured, also called mild flavor. Molasses has a distinct, rich flavor. Some cooks prefer unsulfured because of its deeper flavor. Molasses adds sweetness, moisture, and color to many baked goods and extends their shelf life. See also: treacle.

mold The technique for forming an ingredient into a particular shape. Molding can be done by hand, as with kneading bread, or by placing the ingredient, such as chocolate, into a container and chilling or freezing it until firm. A mold is also the container that shapes the ingredient. Molds come in a large variety of shapes, sizes, and materials and are used to shape many ingredients, including chocolate, butter, batters, mousses, and ice cream. Molds are also named after the foods they shape; for example, a kugelhopf mold, used to bake that sweet bread. See also: chocolate mold.

molded cookie This style of cookie is formed either by pressing the dough into a mold to form its shape, then tapping the dough out of the mold before baking, or by baking a batter in a shaped pan, as for the shell-shaped madeleine. See also: cookie, dough, and madeleine.

Mont Blanc A classic cold dessert of sweetened chestnut purée that has been put through a food mill or ricer to form fine strands. The strands are mounded into a fluffy, high mass that is topped with crème Chantilly. The dessert is intended to resemble Mont Blanc, the high snow-capped peak in the Alps on the French-Italian border. The Italian version, called Monte Bianco, adds Cognac or brandy and sprinkles the top of the dessert with shaved chocolate. France and Italy. See also: crème Chantilly.

Montmorency cherry See cherry.

morello cherry See cherry.

mousse From the French word meaning froth or foam, a mousse is a light, soft, creamy confection. Dessert mousses are made from melted chocolate or fruit purées lightened with beaten egg whites and whipped cream. Often gelatin is added to fruit mousses to help them set. Classic chocolate mousses usually contain both butter and egg yolks, which give them a dense, creamy texture. Lighter mousses, such as **dark chocolate mousse**, are more airy confections that eliminate the butter and egg yolks and rely on egg whites and cream for their volume. Most mousses are chilled and served cold, but there are hot variations. In addition to dessert mousses, there are many savory mousses, made from ground or puréed chicken, fish, pork, cheese, or vegetables and enriched with cream and beaten egg whites. France.

ᘓᘔᘓᘔᘓᘔᘓᘔ

DARK CHOCOLATE MOUSSE

1 ½ quarts; 6 to 8 servings

8 ounces bittersweet or semisweet chocolate, finely chopped
2 cups heavy whipping cream
3 tablespoons Grand Marnier or other orange-flavored liqueur *or*
    2 teaspoons vanilla extract
3 large egg whites, at room temperature
½ cup plus 1 tablespoon granulated sugar
1 teaspoon vanilla extract
2 tablespoons shaved bittersweet or semisweet chocolate,
    for garnish

Melt the chopped chocolate in the top of a double boiler over hot, not simmering, water, stirring frequently with a rubber spatula to ensure even melting.

Meanwhile, in a small saucepan, heat ½ cup of the cream to a boil.

Remove both pans from the heat. Remove the top pan of the double boiler, and wipe the outside dry. Pour the hot cream into the chocolate, and stir together until thoroughly blended.

Transfer the chocolate mixture to a 2-quart mixing bowl, and blend in the orange liqueur or vanilla extract. *continued*

In the chilled bowl of a stand mixer or in a chilled mixing bowl, using a chilled wire whip attachment or the chilled beaters of a hand-held mixer, whip 1 cup of the cream to soft peaks. Fold the cream into the chocolate mixture in 4 additions, blending thoroughly.

In a grease-free mixing bowl, using grease-free beaters, whip the egg whites until frothy. Gradually add the sugar, and continue whipping the egg whites until they hold stiff, but not dry, peaks, about 4 minutes. Fold the whipped egg whites into the chocolate mixture in 3 additions, blending thoroughly. Pour the mousse into a 1 1/2-quart soufflé dish or other serving bowl, or into individual serving bowls or glasses, and smooth the top. Cover the mousse with plastic wrap and refrigerate for at least 2 hours, or until set.

In a chilled mixing bowl, using chilled beaters, whip the remaining 1/2 cup cream until frothy. Add the vanilla extract and whip the cream until it holds soft peaks.

Fit a pastry bag with a #3 large closed star tip and fill the bag with the whipped cream. Decorate the top of the mousse with a border of piped shells or rosettes. Sprinkle the shaved chocolate over the whipped cream decorations and the top of the mousse. The mousse is best served within 6 hours of preparation.

mousse cake A rich, flourless cake baked in a water bath, such as **bittersweet chocolate mousse cake**. The resulting creamy, soft texture is similar to that of mousse. A mousse cake is also made by molding mousse on top of a cake layer or between layers of cake, such as génoise, in a springform pan or flan ring. This version is chilled, then unmolded and decorated before serving. United States. See also: flan ring, génoise, mousse, and springform pan.

BITTERSWEET CHOCOLATE MOUSSE CAKE

One 9- by 3-inch round cake; 12 to 14 servings

1 tablespoon unsalted butter, softened, for the pan

2 cups heavy whipping cream
2 teaspoons vanilla extract

1 pound bittersweet chocolate, finely chopped
2 tablespoons instant espresso powder dissolved in ¼ cup warm water
6 large eggs, at room temperature
½ cup granulated sugar

Generously butter the inside and bottom of a 9-inch springform pan with the softened butter. Wrap the bottom of the pan with foil that extends up over the seam. Tuck the foil in tightly. Center a rack in the oven and preheat to 350°F.

In a chilled bowl, using chilled beaters, whip 1 cup of the cream until fluffy. Add 1 teaspoon of the vanilla and whip the cream until it holds soft peaks. Refrigerate until needed.

Melt the chocolate with the espresso in the top of a double boiler over hot, not simmering, water, stirring frequently with a rubber spatula to ensure even melting.

Meanwhile, in the bowl of a stand mixer, using the wire whip attachment, or in a mixing bowl, using a hand-held mixer, whip the eggs until frothy. Gradually add the sugar, and continue to beat until the mixture is very thick and pale-colored and holds a slowly dissolving ribbon when the beaters are lifted, about 5 minutes.

Remove the top pan of the double boiler and wipe the outside dry. Using a rubber spatula, stir the chocolate mixture until it is shiny, about 2 minutes. Pour the mixture into the beaten eggs and blend thoroughly. Fold in the whipped cream.

Pour the batter into the prepared springform pan. Place the springform pan in a roasting pan or a 12- by 2-inch round cake pan. Pour hot water into the larger pan until it reaches halfway up the sides of the springform pan.

Bake the cake for 1 hour. Turn the oven off and let the cake sit in the oven for 15 minutes.

Remove the pans from the oven, and remove the cake pan from the water bath. Cool the cake in the pan on a rack for 30 minutes.

When the cake is cool, carefully remove the sides of the springform pan.

Whip the remaining 1 cup of cream until frothy. Add the remaining 1 teaspoon vanilla, and whip until the cream holds soft peaks. Slice the cake into serving pieces and top each slice with a dollop of whipped cream.

This cake is best served slightly warm or at room temperature. It can be made up to 6 hours in advance and held at room temperature. If the cake is refrigerated, the texture becomes denser and firmer. The cake will keep for 3 days, well covered, in the refrigerator.

muffin A small quick bread made with various flours. Muffins, such as **banana walnut muffins**, often contain fruits and nuts. Muffins are usually leavened with baking powder or baking soda. The ingredients for muffins should be mixed just until combined and the batter should remain lumpy. If the batter is overmixed, the gluten in the flour will develop, causing the muffins to have air pockets inside and to be flat on top. Muffins are baked in a specially designed pan with rounded cavities to hold the batter. Muffins develop slightly arched tops as they bake. They are generally sweet and are served for breakfast or tea or as a snack. English muffins are yeast-leavened rolls that are round and flat, with pebblelike depressions inside. They are usually split in half and spread with butter while warm. They are served for breakfast and afternoon tea. The name muffin is thought to have derived from an old French word, *moufflet*, which means "soft" in reference to bread. United States. See also: batter, gluten, and muffin pan.

BANANA WALNUT MUFFINS

Twelve 2½-inch-diameter muffins

3 ounces (6 tablespoons) unsalted butter, melted and cooled
½ cup granulated sugar
1 large egg, lightly beaten
1 teaspoon vanilla extract
½ teaspoon salt
1½ cups all-purpose flour
1 teaspoon baking soda
1 teaspoon baking powder
1 large ripe banana, mashed
½ cup roughly chopped walnuts
½ cup roughly chopped dried apricots (optional)

Center a rack in the oven and preheat to 350°F. Line a 12-cavity muffin pan with bake cups.

In the bowl of a stand mixer or in a large mixing bowl, combine the melted butter, sugar, egg, vanilla, and salt, using the flat beater attachment or a rubber spatula, blend briefly.

Sift together the flour, baking soda, and baking powder. Add to the egg mixture, and stir or blend with the flat beater just to combine. The batter should be lumpy. Fold in the banana, walnuts, and the apricots, if using.

Spoon the batter into the muffin pan, filling each cavity three-quarters full.

Bake the muffins for 15 to 20 minutes, until golden brown. Let cool slightly before serving.

The muffins will keep in an airtight container at room temperature for 3 days. They can be refrigerated for up to a week or frozen for up to 2 months. If frozen, defrost in the refrigerator overnight before serving. The muffins can be warmed for 8 to 10 minutes in a 350°F oven.

muffin pan A rectangular metal baking pan with six or twelve cup-shaped cavities that is used for baking muffins and cupcakes. The cavities measure about 3 inches wide and 1¼ to 1½ inches deep. Generally the cavities are lined with paper bake cups, then filled three-quarters full with the batter before baking. Muffin pans are made in a variety of materials, with aluminum or tinned steel the most common. Some muffin pans have nonstick surfaces. Muffin pans are also available in mini-size, with twelve to twenty-four cavities, each measuring about 1¼ to 1½ inches in diameter, and in giant size, measuring 3½ to 4 inches in diameter and 2 inches deep. See also: bake cup.

mürbeteig The German word for rich, buttery, sweet shortcrust pastry dough. This tender dough is used to make tart shells and cookies. Germany.

Muscovado sugar See sugar.

mut dua Candied coconut, a Vietnamese specialty made for celebrations and festive events. A fresh whole coconut is split open and drained, and the meat is removed and thinly sliced. The coconut meat is boiled briefly, then cooked slowly in a mixture of sugar, water, and vanilla extract until it has absorbed the cooking liquid. Vietnam.

nammura A Middle Eastern confection of cream of wheat mixed with butter, plain yogurt, baking powder, and a sweet lemon-flavored syrup. The mixture is spread into a greased baking pan, the top is scored into a diamond pattern, and a blanched almond is placed in the center of each piece. The confection is baked in a moderate oven until set, then the diamonds are cut through, and the confection is baked again until golden brown. While warm, the confection is soaked with more of the sweet lemon syrup. Lebanon and Syria.

Nanaimo bar A popular Canadian sweet, named for a city on Vancouver Island, Nanaimo bars are a multicolored, pastry with three rich layers. The bottom layer consists of a mixture of butter, chocolate, sugar, dried flaked or shredded coconut, graham cracker crumbs, and walnuts. It is pressed into an 8-inch square baking pan and baked briefly, then chilled until cool. A rich buttercream filling flavored with vanilla or Grand Marnier makes up the middle layer and the top layer is dark chocolate. The pastry is chilled to set the filling and the chocolate layer, then cut into bars or squares for serving. Canada.

nanas goreng An Indonesian specialty sweet of pineapple fritters. Thin slices of fresh pineapple are dipped in a batter of rice flour, sugar, salt, egg, baking soda, and water, then deep-fried in hot oil until golden brown. The pineapple slices are drained, then served warm with coffee or tea or as a snack. Indonesia. See also: fritter.

Napoléon See mille-feuille.

navel orange A member of the family of sweet oranges, navel oranges take their name from a characteristic navel-like depression at their blossom end. Navel oranges have a thick, dark-orange peel that slips off, and they easily separate into segments. The favorite orange for eating, navels are seedless with sweet, juicy pulp. They are used as an ingredient in many desserts, pastries, and confections. Navel oranges are available from October to May. Choose bright-skinned, firm fruit that feels heavy for its size, with no soft spots or discoloration. Russets, rough brown spots on the skin, do not affect the quality or flavor of the fruit. Store navel oranges in a cool, dry place for several days or in the refrigerator for several weeks. See also: citrus fruit, fruit, and orange.

nectarine A type of peach with a smooth, taut skin without down. Ripe nectarines have bright, red-blushed, golden-yellow skin and firm, sweet, juicy, golden flesh. Nectarines are used both raw and cooked as an ingredient in desserts and pastries, such as cakes, cobblers, fruit tarts, fruit salads, and ice cream. They are available from April through September, with the peak in July and August. Choose fragrant, evenly colored, firm fruit that gives slightly when pressed. Avoid any fruit with bruises, soft spots, or withered skin. Slightly underripe nectarines will ripen at room temperature within a few days. To speed up the process, place them in a tightly closed but perforated paper bag with an apple. Store ripe nectarines in a plastic bag in the refrigerator for up to a week. Bring them to room temperature and wash before using. Once cut, nectarines will turn brown from exposure to air; rub them with a sliced lemon or lime or sprinkle or dip them in water mixed with lemon, lime, or orange juice and pat dry with a towel. Nectarines can be used interchangeably with peaches in most desserts and pastries. See also: fruit and peach.

Newtown Pippin apple One of the favorite apples for use in baked goods and for baking whole because it holds its shape. Also called pippins, these apples have pale yellow-green skin and crisp, juicy, tart flesh. Pippins are available from winter through spring. See also: apple.

Nocello An Italian walnut-flavored, straw-colored liqueur used to flavor desserts, pastries, and confections. Italy.

noisette The French word for hazelnut. See also: hazelnut.

noix The French word for walnut and for nut. See also: nut and walnut.

nonfat dry milk See powdered milk.

nonfat milk See milk.

nonpareil Tiny multicolored or white sugar pellets used to decorate desserts, pastries, and confections. In England these are called "hundreds and thousands." Nonpareil is also the name of a small flat chocolate disk covered with these multicolored or sometimes only white sugar pellets. France.

nougat This confection is popular in Italy and the South of France, where it is often sold at open-air markets. It is made from a cooked sugar syrup, often with the addition of honey, that is mixed with firmly beaten egg whites, then blended with nuts and candied fruits. Nougat is usually formed in a baking pan between sheets of rice paper and weighted with heavy objects so that the confection will be compact. There are many varieties of nougat that are specialties of different countries and regions. Various nuts are used, as are different sweeteners and flavorings. Nougat is very sensitive to humidity and becomes sticky and soft if exposed to too much moisture. It is easier to cut if it stands for 12 hours after cooking. France and Italy. See also: rice paper and torrone.

nougatine A crisp nut brittle made with a mixture of caramelized sugar and hazelnuts or almonds. No liquid is used when cooking the sugar for **nougatine,** so the sugar must be stirred constantly to avoid burning and to prevent lumps from forming. After cooking, nougatine is quickly rolled out on an oiled marble slab or other surface and cut into pieces before it cools. It is also used to form various shapes such as cups or the base for croquembouche. Nougatine can be crushed to be used as an ingredient in other candies and in cakes and ice cream. France. See also: croquembouche.

NOUGATINE

Sixty 1-inch squares

3 tablespoons flavorless vegetable oil

1¾ cups granulated sugar
¼ teaspoon freshly squeezed lemon juice
1 cup lightly toasted almonds, finely chopped
12 ounces bittersweet chocolate to be tempered (see page 297)
    (optional)

Coat the back of a baking sheet, a metal or marble rolling pin, and the blade of a pizza wheel with the vegetable oil.

Heat ½ cup of the sugar in a 1-quart heavy-bottomed saucepan over medium-high heat, stirring constantly with a wooden spoon: the sugar will first become grainy, then begin to melt. When it is smooth and liquid, sprinkle on another ½ cup sugar, 1 tablespoon at a time, and stir constantly until it becomes liquid. Slowly sprinkle on the remaining ¾ cup sugar, 1 tablespoon at a time, and stir constantly until it is liquid.

Take the pan off the heat, and quickly stir in the lemon juice. Add the almonds and stir briskly to coat them completely with the caramel. Immediately pour the mixture onto the oiled baking sheet. With the oiled rolling pin, roll out the mixture to about ⅛ inch thick. The mixture sets up quickly and will become too brittle to cut, so it is necessary to work fast. Score the nougatine into 1-inch squares with the oiled pizza wheel. (Or score the nougatine into other shapes as desired.) Let cool completely. Break the nougatine into the pieces with your fingers. Any scraps or irregular pieces can be ground to a fine powder in a food processor for use in other recipes or to garnish the chocolate-dipped nougatine below. Nougatine will keep for 2 weeks in a tightly covered container at room temperature.

To make chocolate-dipped nougatine, temper the chocolate. Line a baking sheet with parchment or waxed paper.

Place a piece of the nougatine into the tempered chocolate, coating it completely. With a dipper or a plastic fork with the two middle tines broken off, lift the nougatine from the chocolate, gently shaking off the excess chocolate, and place the nougatine on the paper. Repeat with the remaining nougatine. After every 4 pieces, sprinkle a pinch of the ground nougatine on top of each piece.

Place the baking sheet of nougatine in the refrigerator for 15 minutes to set the chocolate. Place the nougatine in paper candy cups. The nougatine will keep between layers of waxed paper for a week in a tightly covered container at room temperature.

nut The edible one-celled fruit of a tree or bush, enclosed in a dry, hard shell. Technically only acorns, chestnuts, and hazelnuts qualify as true nuts, but the term is broadened to include seeds as well, specifically, almonds, Brazil nuts, cashews, macadamia nuts, peanuts, pecans, pine nuts, pistachio nuts, and walnuts. Nuts add flavor and crunchy texture to countless desserts, pastries, and confections. They are also used to decorate desserts, pastries, and confections. Nuts are used whole, chopped, and ground. Most nuts have a thin bitter outer skin, which can be removed either by toasting the nuts or by blanching.

The rich, buttery flavor of nuts is enhanced by toasting. To toast nuts, place them on a jelly-roll pan in a preheated 350°F oven. For almonds and most other nuts, toast until light-golden, 12 to 15 minutes, stirring every 5 minutes. Remove the pan from the oven and let cool on a rack. Toast hazelnuts until the skins begin to split, about 15 minutes. Remove the pan from the oven, let it sit for 10 minutes, then rub the hazelnuts between your hands or in a kitchen towel to remove most of the skins.

Grinding nuts is best accomplished in a food processor. To absorb the natural oil that is released during grinding, add 1 to 2 tablespoons of the sugar called for in a recipe to each cup of nuts. Pulse the mixture until the desired texture is reached. Don't overprocess or you will get nut butter. Nuts can be chopped on a cutting board with a chef's knife.

Most nuts are available both unshelled and shelled. Shelled nuts can be found raw, toasted, and toasted and salted. When buying unshelled nuts, look for those that feel heavy in the shell and, except for peanuts, do not rattle. Store unshelled nuts in a cool, dry place. They will usually keep from 3 to 6 months. Most nuts are high in fat and have a high natural oil content, which causes them to turn rancid rapidly. For this reason, shelled nuts are best stored in airtight containers in the refrigerator or freezer, where they will keep from 3 months to a year. This high oil content also enables nuts to be ground to a thick paste, such as praline paste made with hazelnuts, used to flavor desserts, pastries, and confections. Because of their tendency to turn rancid, buy nuts from a market that has high turnover. See also: blanch and specific nuts (almond, Brazil nut, cashew, chestnut, hazelnut, macadamia nut, peanut, pecan, pine nut, pistachio nut, and walnut).

Nutella This Italian product is made from hazelnuts, sugar, cocoa, and oil and has a spreadable consistency. It is used in desserts, pastries, and confections to impart the distinct flavor of gianduja. Nutella comes in jars and is available in the specialty food section of markets and delicatessens and in some cookware shops. Once opened, Nutella should be kept tightly sealed and stored in the refrigerator. Italy. See also: gianduja.

nutmeg This spice is the kernel of the fruit of an evergreen tree that is native to the Spice Islands in Indonesia. The kernel is enclosed in a hard shell that is covered with a delicate red membrane called mace. When dried, the oval-shaped kernel turns dark brown and becomes heavily creased. Nutmeg gives a pungent, spicy flavor to baked goods. Its primary use is in pies, cakes, custards, and quick breads. For use, it's preferable to grate whole nutmeg, using a special nutmeg grater. Freshly grated nutmeg gives a more aromatic flavor than preground nutmeg. If it is ground in advance, it loses its flavor rapidly. Nutmeg is best stored in a tightly covered glass jar in a cool, dark, dry place. Whole nutmeg has a shelf life of several years; ground nutmeg should be replaced every 6 months. See also: mace, nutmeg grater, and nutmeg grinder.

nutmeg grater A nutmeg grater is a small, tapered, tinned-steel grater with a curved fine-rasp surface across which a whole nutmeg is rubbed to produce a fine powder. There is often a compartment on top of the grater, covered with a flap, that holds a whole nutmeg.

nutmeg grinder A nutmeg grinder, also called a nutmeg mill, resembles a pepper mill. It contains a squat round cavity that houses a curved cutting blade below a spring-held plate, topped by a horizontal crank handle. A whole nutmeg is placed inside the cavity against the plate, and the handle is turned, pushing the nutmeg against the blade and grinding it to a fine powder.

obsttortenform See maryann pan.

oeufs à la neige See floating island.

offset spatula This hand-held tool has a stainless steel flexible blade with a bend or angle near the handle that is stepped down approximately 1 inch from the handle, forming a Z-like shape. The tip of the blade is round and blunt. Offset spatulas come in several sizes, from very small to large, with the length of the blade ranging from 3 to 12 inches. The special shape of the offset spatula makes it particularly good for evenly spreading batter in a shallow pan since the handle, and your hand, will not hit the sides of the pan. Offset spatulas have a wide variety of other uses in pastry and confectionery work, such as filling and icing cakes, and they are invaluable for decorative work and in tempering chocolate. See also: roulade and tempering chocolate.

ohagi Japanese sweet rice eggs. Sweet and regular short-grain rice are cooked together, then mashed into a paste and formed into egg shapes. Bean paste, sugar, and salt are cooked to a thick paste, and balls of this sweet bean paste are flattened and wrapped around the rice eggs. They can also be rolled in toasted ground sesame seeds. Japan.

oil See fats and oils.

oil of peppermint See mint.

oil of spearmint See mint.

olallieberry, olallie berry A hybrid berry, an olallieberry looks like a long, large blackberry. Dark purple olallieberries are sweet and juicy. They are used both fresh and cooked in many desserts, pastries, and confections and to make jams and jellies. Olallieberries are available primarily on the West Coast of the United States for a very short season in late May and early June. Choose fragrant, plump, deeply colored, juicy berries. Store fresh olallieberries in a single layer in the refrigerator for up to 2 days, and rinse just before use. See also: berry.

olive oil Pressed from ripe olives, olive oil is highly prized and widely used throughout the world, particularly in the Mediterranean countries. Although it is used primarily in cooking and as a salad oil, there is a long-standing tradition of baking with olive oil. There are many grades of olive oil, relating to the degree of acidity. Cold-pressed extra-virgin olive oil comes from the first pressing and is lowest in acidity. Other grades in descending order include superfine, fine, virgin, and pure. Olive oil contains no cholesterol and is high in monounsaturated fat. For desserts, pastries, and confections, choose a light, clean-flavored oil. It can be substituted for other vegetable oils, such as canola, corn, peanut, safflower, soybean, and sunflower, although the flavor will be different. Olive oil has a low smoke point, so it is not the best choice for frying. Store it tightly capped in a dark place at room temperature for up to 6 months or in the refrigerator for up to a year. It will turn cloudy and become thick in the refrigerator, but will clarify and liquefy at room temperature. Widely available in supermarkets and specialty food shops. See also: fats and oils and smoke point.

onde-onde Indonesian poached sweet rice flour balls coated with coconut. Sweet rice flour, coconut milk, and salt are mixed to a paste, then rolled into $1^{1}/_{2}$-inch-diameter balls. A cavity is indented in the center of the balls, and a spoonful of brown sugar is placed in each cavity. The balls are pinched to seal in the sugar, and rolled in sweet rice flour. They are poached in boiling water, drained, and rolled in shredded coconut. Indonesia.

orange The round citrus fruit of an evergreen tree native to China and Southeast Asia. Today oranges are cultivated in temperate climates throughout the world. The thick, bright orange rind encloses a segmented, tart-sweet, juicy pulp. There are three main varieties of oranges: loose-skinned, which includes clementines, mandarins, and tangerines; bitter; and sweet, which is divided into the categories of navel, Valencia, and blood oranges. The loose-skinned and sweet oranges are the ones used for desserts, pastries, and confections. Orange segments, juice, and peel are used raw, and the peel is candied for an ingredient in many desserts, pastries, and confections. Oranges are used to make conserves, jams, jellies, marmalades, and liqueurs. The most well known bitter orange, Seville, is used to make marmalade. Fresh oranges are available year-round, with the peak from December to May for most varieties. Choose bright-skinned, firm fruit that feels heavy for its size, with no soft spots or discoloration. Russets, rough brown spots on the skin, do not affect the quality or flavor of the fruit. Store oranges in a cool, dry place for several days or in the refrigerator for several weeks. See also: blood orange, citrus fruit, clementine, fruit, mandarin, navel orange, Seville orange, tangerine, and Valencia orange.

orange flower water Distilled from orange flowers, this is a clear, sweet, fragrant liquid used to flavor desserts, pastries, and confections. It is very strong and should be used sparingly. Widely used in the Middle Ages, today it is found primarily in Indian, Greek, Turkish, and other Middle Eastern cuisines. It is available in cookware shops and specialty food stores. Store tightly capped in a cool, dark, dry place, where it will keep indefinitely. See also: essence and extract.

ostia Italian edible wafer paper made from wheat starch. Ostia is used to line the molds and baking pans for pastries, desserts, and confections, such as panforte and torrone. Ostia can be replaced by Asian rice paper. Italy. See also: panforte, rice paper, and torrone.

Othello A pastry named for Shakespeare's Othello the Moor. Othellos are composed of two 3-inch round biscuits, similar to ladyfingers, sandwiched together with chocolate pastry cream, brushed with apricot glaze, and completely covered with chocolate fondant. Usually served on a platter accompanied by other similar pastries—Desdemonas, Iagos, and Rosalindas, which are all named for Shakespearean characters. United Kingdom. See also: Desdemona, fondant, glaze, Iago, ladyfinger, pastry cream, and Rosalinda.

ovos moles d'aveiro A favorite Portuguese rich egg custard–like dessert from the town of Aveiro. This dessert is eaten on its own or used as a component part of other desserts. It is the topping for sponge cakes and the filling for cakes, tarts, and marzipan candies, and it is used as a custard sauce to accompany puddings. It is made from rice flour or the water from cooking rice (the rice is used for another dish or it is discarded), or cooked puréed rice, combined with sugar and egg yolks. The custard is cooled before it is served (or used as part of another dessert). Portugal. See also: pudim molotoff.

pain au chocolat A favorite after-school snack for French children, pain au chocolat is made from croissant dough cut into a rectangle, rolled around a bar of rich dark chocolate, then baked until flaky and golden brown. The chocolate melts inside the dough and provides an extra burst of flavor and texture. France. See also: croissant.

pain d'épice A rich French spice breadlike cake that evolved from early European gingerbread. Pain d'épice uses more honey and spices, particularly anise, than gingerbread. Candied orange peel is frequently included in the batter, and rye flour or a combination of rye flour and white flour is often used. The roots of pain d'epice can be traced through the spiced honey cakes of the Middle East encountered by the eleventh-century Crusaders to an ancient Chinese honey bread called *mi-kong*, which was eaten by the followers of Ghengis Khan. The French version of gingerbread evolved in the cities of Rheims and Strasbourg during the fifteenth and sixteenth centuries, influenced by contact with bakers from Germany. See also: gingerbread.

palatschinken Paper-thin sweet pancakes, similar to French crêpes. Palatschinken are often served in a stack of six or seven, alternating with a filling of jam or cottage cheese, and cut into wedges, or the individual pancakes are rolled up around the filling and dusted with confectioners' sugar before serving. Austria and Hungary. See also: rakott palacsinta.

palmier Also called palm leaves, palmiers are small pastries made from sugar-encrusted puff pastry. The sides of a rectangle of puff pastry are folded into the center, then folded over to make four layers, and cut across the width into thin strips. These are laid on their sides on a baking sheet, and they fan out as they bake to resemble the leaves of palm trees. Palmiers are baked until they are crisp and the sugar caramelizes to a rich golden brown. They are served with tea or coffee or as an accompaniment to ice cream and other desserts. France. See also: puff pastry.

palm sugar See sugar.

pandowdy An old-fashioned deep-dish New England fruit dessert related to cobblers, grunts, and slumps. Sliced or cut apples or other fruits are tossed with spices and butter, sweetened with molasses, maple syrup, or brown sugar, topped with a biscuitlike dough, and baked. Partway through the baking time, the crust is broken up and pressed down into the fruit so it can absorb the juices. This technique is called "dowdying." After the crust is baked, it becomes crispy. Pandowdys are served warm with heavy cream, hard sauce, or a cream sauce flavored with nutmeg. United States. See also: buckle, cobbler, grunt, hard sauce, and slump.

panettone A sweet yeast-risen bread that is a specialty of Milan, Italy, panettone has a tall cylindrical shape with a domed top. The dough is enriched with egg yolks and filled with raisins and candied orange, lemon, and citron peels. Panettone is a traditional Christmas specialty throughout Italy, but it is also served at other festive occasions, such as weddings. It is eaten as a breakfast bread, for afternoon tea, or as a dessert. The origins of panettone and its name are cloudy. Some sources claim the bread was first made in the third century. Others say the name was originally *pane de Toni* (Toni's bread), from the name of the baker who first made panettone in Milan in the fifteenth century. Italy.

panforte This Italian sweet, a cross between a cake and a candy, is a very dense, rich confection loaded with nuts, dried fruit, and spices. The top is heavily dusted with confectioners' sugar. Panforte can be either light or dark, depending on the ingredients; cocoa imparts the dark color. Panforte is usually baked in a low round pan between sheets of edible rice paper, edible wheat starch paper (ostia), or parchment paper. Panforte has become a traditional Italian Christmas confection. Its origins are murky, but it seems to date back to the very early Middle Ages, when the first references to it are found in Siena. The name translates as strong bread. Often the confection is called **panforte di Siena**. Panforte keeps very well, which may be the reason that the Crusaders took it with them on their voyages. Italy. See also: ostia and rice paper.

❦❦❦❦❦❦❦❦❦❦

PANFORTE DI SIENA

One 9½- by 1-inch round cake; 16 to 18 servings

1 cup unblanched hazelnuts
1 cup unblanched almonds
One 8- by 11-inch sheet of edible rice paper

1 tablespoon unsalted butter, softened, for the pan

1½ cups finely chopped candied orange peel
½ cup finely chopped candied lemon peel or candied citron
½ cup all-purpose flour
3 tablespoons Dutch-processed unsweetened cocoa powder
Finely minced zest of 1 small lemon
1 teaspoon ground cinnamon
¼ teaspoon ground cloves
¼ teaspoon ground coriander
¼ teaspoon freshly grated nutmeg
Pinch of ground white pepper
¾ cup granulated sugar
¾ cup honey
1 ounce (2 tablespoons) unsalted butter
Confectioners' sugar for garnish

Center a rack in the oven and preheat to 350°F.

Place the hazelnuts on a jelly-roll pan and toast in the oven for 15 to 18 minutes, until the skins split and the nuts turn light golden brown. Transfer the pan to a rack to cool for 10 minutes. Then rub the nuts between your hands or in a kitchen towel to remove most of the skins.

At the same time, place the almonds on a jelly-roll pan and toast in the oven for 10 to 12 minutes, shaking the pan every 4 minutes to prevent burning. Transfer the pan to a rack to cool. Lower the oven temperature to 300°F.

Cut a round of rice paper to fit the bottom of a 9½-inch spring-form pan. Use the softened butter to butter the bottom and halfway up the sides of the pan. Place the rice paper round in the bottom of the pan and butter it.

In the work bowl of a food processor fitted with the steel blade, combine the hazelnuts and almonds. Pulse to coarsely chop the nuts, about 45 seconds. Or use a chef's knife to chop the nuts.

In a 2-quart mixing bowl, combine the candied citrus peels, flour, cocoa, lemon zest, spices, and chopped nuts. Toss to blend well.

continued

In a 1-quart heavy-bottomed saucepan, combine the sugar, honey, and butter. Over medium-high heat bring the mixture to a boil, and brush down the sides of the pan with a pastry brush dipped in water to prevent crystallization. Then cook the mixture until it registers 246°F on a candy thermometer, about 12 minutes.

Immediately pour the cooked sugar mixture over the dry ingredients. Working rapidly, stir the sugar syrup into the mixture until thoroughly blended, then turn the mixture into the prepared pan. With damp hands, press the cake into the edges of the pan, and smooth and even the top.

Bake the panforte for 30 minutes. It will not look set, but it will firm up as it cools. Transfer the pan to a rack to cool completely.

Use a thin-bladed small knife to loosen the panforte from the sides of the pan. Release the sides of the springform pan and remove them. Dust the top of the panforte heavily with confectioners' sugar. Use a sharp knife to cut the panforte into very thin slices.

The panforte will keep in an airtight container at room temperature for up to 1 month.

panna cotta Translated from the Italian as "cooked cream," panna cotta is a simple custard dessert lightened with gelatin. The dessert is not really cooked; the ingredients are just brought to a boil to dissolve the sugar. The molds in which the custard is formed may be lined with caramel to enhance the flavor of this creamy, smooth dessert. After the ivory-colored panna cotta is chilled for several hours, it is unmolded and, usually, served with fresh fruit and a fruit sauce or with chocolate sauce. Italy.

pa-pao-fan A traditional Chinese dessert known as "eight-treasure" or "eight-precious pudding." It is a rice pudding decorated on top with eight different dried or candied fruits or nuts, such as watermelon seeds, preserved dates, candied plums, candied orange peel, candied cherries, and walnuts. This elaborate dessert is usually served only on special occasions and at banquets, accompanied by a sweet almond-flavored syrup. China.

papaya A relative of passion fruit, papaya is the large fruit of the tree of the same name, cultivated in tropical climates throughout the world. Papayas are either round or pear-shaped with thin, smooth skin that ranges in color from green to yellow to red. The creamy-smooth, golden-orange to vivid salmon-colored flesh surrounds a deep oval center cavity that holds small, spicy, edible black seeds. Ripe papaya has a full-bodied sweet-tart flavor. The variety found most often in the United States is the Solo, which is grown in Hawaii. It weighs between 1 and 2 pounds and measures about 6 inches in length. Papayas are used both raw and cooked as an ingredient in desserts and pastries, such as cakes, fruit salads, fresh fruit tarts, fools, ice creams, and sorbets. Raw papayas don't work in gelatin desserts because they contain an enzyme that prevents gelatin from setting. When the fruit is cooked, however, the enzyme is destroyed, so cooked papaya can be used with gelatin. Papayas are available practically year-round, with the peak in late spring through early fall. Choose fragrant fruit with bright yellow skin. The fruit should give slightly when pressed gently. Avoid bruised fruit with obvious brown or soft spots. Slightly underripe papaya will ripen at room temperature in a few days. To speed up the process, place the papaya in a tightly closed but perforated paper bag with a banana or an apple. Store ripe papaya in the refrigerator for up to 5 days. Peel the skin off with a vegetable peeler or knife before use. See also: fruit.

paper candy cup These fluted candy cups, sometimes called petits fours cases, are made of thin paper and are $1^1/2$ inches in diameter and $^5/8$ inch high. They are designed to hold finished candies and truffles. Glassine cups are the best to use because they do not absorb oil from the candies. Paper candy cups come in different colors, often with seasonal decorations, such as hearts or holly leaves, but dark brown cups are the most common.

paper pastry cone Made from a triangular piece of parchment paper, a paper pastry cone is used instead of a pastry bag on occasions where it is better to be able to discard the cone rather than refill it; for example, filling a mold with chocolate and decorating or piping with chocolate or royal icing. The triangles can be bought precut or can be cut as needed. They are available at cookware shops, at cake decorating and candy making supply shops, and through mail order cookware catalogs. See also: mold, parchment paper, pastry bag, piping, and royal icing.

parchment paper Greaseproof nonstick paper used to line the bottom of pans and baking sheets so that baked goods will not stick. In many cases, using parchment paper eliminates the need to butter and flour baking pans. Parchment paper is also used to make paper pastry cones for decorative work. Parchment paper is available in rolls, sheets, or triangles at cookware shops, cake decorating and candy making supply shops, and supermarkets and through mail order cookware catalogs. See also: paper pastry cone.

parfait In France, a parfait is a light water ice or a custard frozen, traditionally, in a specially designed tall cylindrical mold and topped with whipped cream. Modern frozen parfaits are molded into a brick shape that can be sliced or cut into various other shapes. These are decorated with whipped cream, nuts, and candied fruit before serving. In the United States, a parfait is a dessert of alternating layers of ice cream, sweet syrup or sauce, and whipped cream arranged in a tall glass and topped with nuts, more whipped cream, or a Maraschino cherry. Parfaits are made in many different flavors. France and United States.

Paris-Brest A classic French pastry made from choux pastry (cream puff pastry). The pastry is formed into a large ring, brushed with egg wash, topped with sliced almonds, and baked until golden brown. When cool, the pastry is split in half horizontally, filled with praline buttercream, and topped with a heavy dusting of confectioners' sugar. Other variations include filling the pastry with sweetened whipped cream blended with praline or praline-flavored ganache. **Paris-Brest** is intended to resemble a bicycle wheel, and it takes its name from a bicycle race that was run in 1891 between the cities of Paris and Brest. France. See also: buttercream, choux pastry, egg wash, ganache, and praline.

PARIS-BREST

One 10-inch round pastry; 12 to 14 servings

Praline
½ cup unblanched hazelnuts
1 tablespoon flavorless vegetable oil
½ cup granulated sugar
¼ cup water

Ganache filling
12 ounces bittersweet chocolate, finely chopped
1 cup plus 2 tablespoons heavy whipping cream
8 ounces (2 sticks) unsalted butter, softened
or
Cream filling
2 cups heavy whipping cream
2 tablespoons superfine sugar
2 teaspoons vanilla extract

Choux pastry
1/2 cup water
2 ounces (4 tablespoons) unsalted butter, cut into small
    pieces
2 teaspoons superfine sugar
Pinch of salt
1/2 cup all-purpose flour
3 large eggs, at room temperature
1 large egg lightly beaten with 1 tablespoon milk or cream,
    for egg wash
1/3 cup sliced unblanched almonds

1/2 cup confectioners' sugar, for garnish

Center a rack in the oven and preheat to 350°F.

For the praline, place the hazelnuts on a jelly-roll pan and toast in the oven for 15 to 18 minutes, until the skins split and the nuts turn light golden brown. Transfer the pan to a rack to cool for 10 minutes. Then rub the nuts between your hands or in a kitchen towel to remove most of the skins.

Use the vegetable oil to coat the inside of an 8-inch round cake pan.

Combine the sugar and water in a 1-quart heavy-bottomed saucepan and bring to a boil over high heat. Cook the mixture, brushing down the sides of the pan twice with a pastry brush dipped in warm water to prevent crystals from forming, until it begins to turn a medium caramel color, about 10 minutes.

Quickly stir in the hazelnuts and stir to coat them completely with the caramel. Remove the pan from the heat, and immediately turn the hazelnut mixture into the oiled cake pan. Let cool completely.

Break the praline into small pieces. Place the pieces in the work bowl of a food processor fitted with the steel blade and pulse the mixture to pulverize it to a powder.

For the ganache filling, if using, melt the chocolate in the top of a double boiler over hot, not simmering, water, stirring frequently with a rubber spatula to ensure even melting.

Meanwhile, in a 1-quart saucepan, bring the cream to a boil.

Remove both pans from the heat. Remove the top pan of the double boiler and wipe the outside dry. Pour the cream into the chocolate and stir together until thoroughly blended. Transfer the mixture to a 2-quart mixing bowl, cover tightly with plastic wrap, and cool to room temperature. Refrigerate until the consistency of thick pudding, 2 to 3 hours.

Center a rack in the oven and preheat to 400°F. Use an 8-inch round cake pan or cardboard cake circle as a guide to trace an 8-inch circle in the center of a sheet of parchment paper. Place the parchment paper on a baking sheet, pencil side down.

For the choux pastry, combine the water, butter, sugar, and salt in a 2-quart heavy-bottomed saucepan, and bring to a boil over medium-high heat. Add the flour all at once and stir vigorously with a wooden spoon until it is completely mixed into the mass, 1 to 2 minutes. The mixture will form a ball around the wooden spoon.

Transfer the mixture to the bowl of a stand mixer or a mixing bowl. Using the flat beater attachment or a hand-held mixer, beat the mixture on medium speed until the steam stops rising from the dough, about 4 minutes. Beat in the eggs 1 at a time, mixing well after each addition and stopping frequently to scrape down the sides of the bowl with a rubber spatula. Blend the mixture for 1 to 2 minutes longer, until smooth.

Fit a 14-inch pastry bag with a #5 large plain tip, and fill the bag with the choux pastry. Using the traced circle as a guide, pipe 3 concentric circles of choux pastry on the parchment paper. Then pipe 2 concentric circles of choux pastry centered on top of the first 3 circles. Brush the choux pastry with the egg wash, and sprinkle the sliced almonds over the top of the pastry.

Bake the choux ring for 30 to 35 minutes, until golden brown and set. Transfer the pan to a rack to cool. (The pastry can be baked and held at room temperature, wrapped in plastic wrap, for 2 days before filling, or it can be frozen.)

To complete the ganache filling, if using, place the softened butter in the bowl of a stand mixer or in a mixing bowl. Using the flat beater attachment or a hand-held mixer, beat the butter on low speed until it is fluffy, about 2 minutes. Beat in the chocolate mixture in 4 additions, stopping to scrape down the sides of the bowl a few times. Be careful not to overbeat the chocolate, or it will become grainy. Fold the ground praline into the ganache, blending thoroughly.

For the whipped cream filling, if using, place the cream in the chilled bowl of a stand mixer or in a chilled mixing bowl. Using the wire whip attachment or a hand-held mixer, beat the cream on medium speed until it is frothy. Sprinkle on the superfine sugar, add the vanilla extract, and continue to whip until the cream holds soft peaks. Fold the ground praline into the whipped cream, blending thoroughly.

Slice the Paris-Brest in half horizontally. Place the bottom half on a 10-inch cardboard cake circle. Fit a 12- or 14-inch pastry bag with a #5 large plain tip and fill with half the ganache filling or the whipped cream filling. Pipe the filling into the bottom half of the pastry in a coil, filling it completely. Refill the pastry bag with the remaining filling, and pipe another layer on top of the first layer. Dust the top half of the Paris-Brest heavily with confectioners' sugar and position it over the filling. Refrigerate the pastry until ready to serve; if the pastry is made with the ganache filling, let it stand at room temperature for 30 minutes before serving. Use a sharp serrated knife to cut the pastry into serving pieces.

parkin A British version of gingerbread made with oatmeal and treacle or golden syrup, parkin is baked both as a loaf and as cookies. It is traditionally served at celebrations on Guy Fawkes Day, November 5. Guy Fawkes figured prominently in the seventeenth-century religious conflict involving Roman Catholic priests who were banned from Protestant England. Catholic supporters in England organized "The Gunpowder Plot," in which they plotted to blow up the Houses of Parliament; Fawkes was chosen to light the gunpowder. When the plot was discovered, he was executed. United Kingdom. See also: gingerbread, golden syrup, and treacle.

paskha A traditional molded Russian Easter dessert made from a mixture of pot or cottage cheese, sugar, butter, sour cream, and loads of dried and candied fruits and almonds or other nuts. The mixture is molded in a four-sided wooden pyramid form. The dessert is decorated with candied fruit and nuts that form the letters XB of the Cyrillic alphabet, initials for the phrase meaning "Christ is risen." Paskha is traditionally served with the Russian Easter bread kulich. Russia. See also: kulich.

passion fruit A Brazilian native, passion fruit is an egg-shaped tropical fruit, so named by early Spanish explorers who felt that parts of the flower symbolized elements of the crucifixion. Passion fruit is grown in temperate and tropical climates throughout the world. Wrinkled, leathery, thick, dusky-purple skin encloses a bright, mustard-yellow, juicy pulp flecked with small, edible, crunchy black seeds. When ripe, the fruit has a strong perfumy fragrance and an intensely sweet-tart flavor. The fruit and its juice are used raw as ingredients in desserts, pastries, and confections, such as Bavarian creams, cakes, custards, mousses, ice creams, puddings, sorbets, soufflés, and sauces. Passion fruit is available from late February through September. Choose fragrant, firm but crinkled, plump fruit that feels heavy for its size. Underripe passion fruit, which has smooth skin, will ripen at room temperature in a few days.

Store ripe passion fruit in the refrigerator for up to a week or freeze in a plastic bag for several months. See also: fruit.

pasta frolla *Frolla* is the Italian word for tender, which correctly describes this rich, sweet pastry dough. Pasta frolla is one of the foundation doughs of Italian pastry making, similar to the French pâte sucrée. See also: pâte sucrée.

pasta sfogliata The Italian word for puff pastry. See also: puff pastry.

pastiera A classic Easter dessert from Naples, Italy, pastiera is a type of pie made with a crust of pasta frolla and a filling of cooked wheat grain and ricotta cheese blended with milk, butter, eggs, and sugar. The wheat grain needs to be soaked overnight to soften it before it is cooked; it can be found precooked in cans in Italian markets and health food stores. The traditional flavorings for the filling are cinnamon and orange flower water. Chopped candied orange peel and walnuts also add their chunky textures to the creamy filling. The pie is assembled in a spring-form pan, with a latticework of pastry dough on top, and the top is dusted with confectioners' sugar after it is baked and cooled. Italy. See also: orange flower water, pasta frolla, ricotta cheese, and spring-form pan.

pastillage A modeling paste similar to gum paste, but stronger and more durable, pastillage has the consistency of pie dough. It is made of confectioners' sugar, water, sometimes cornstarch, and gelatin. Pastillage is used to make decorations, such as ribbons, and to construct three-dimensional architectural forms and other shapes, such as figures and animals. Pastillage is mixed, kneaded, colored with paste or powder food coloring as desired, and allowed to rest. Then it is rolled out, cut into the desired shapes, and left to air-dry. Once the pieces are dry, they are assembled using royal icing or soft pastillage and placed around or on a cake or pastry. Pastillage plaques can be painted with edible paint or cocoa. Although pastillage is made from edible ingredients, it dries rock-hard and, therefore, is not intended to be eaten. United Kingdom. See also: gelatin, gum paste, and royal icing.

pastillas de leche A chewy, fudgelike Philippine candy made from milk cooked with sugar and lemon zest until very thick. The mixture is spread into a 1/2-inch-thick rectangle on a sugared board, then cut into 1/2- by 2-inch pieces. Each piece is rolled in sugar and wrapped in brightly colored tissue paper cut into designs of stars, letters, leaves, such as palm leaves, or flowers, such as roses. This candy is traditionally made for holiday celebrations. Philippines.

pastille A small round confection. There are two types of pastilles: those that are small hard balls made of a mixture of sugar, water, and various flavorings and colorings, such as lemon and orange, and those that are flat drops, often flavored with chocolate and sprinkled with nonpareils. United States. See also: nonpareil.

pastry A baked item made with a crust of dough. A pastry is generally sweet, such as pie or cream puffs, although there are many savory pastries, like quiche, as well. Sweet pastries are often thought of as being delicate and fancy, such as a Napoléon or a fresh raspberry tartlet. Pastry also refers to the dough used, which is generally a mixture of flour and fat, usually butter, held together with water or eggs. See also: choux pastry, crust, mürbeteig, pasta frolla, pâte brisée, pâte sablée, pâte sucrée, phyllo dough, and puff pastry.

pastry bag A cone-shaped pastry bag is used to shape batters and doughs and to decorate desserts, pastries, and confections. Its pointed end is fitted with a pastry tip, sometimes held in place with a coupler, and the bag is filled with icing, batter, dough, or whipped cream. Pressure is applied to the bag with the hand to force the filling out through the tip to create the desired designs. Pastry bags are made of nylon, polyester, canvas, plastic-lined cloth, or disposable plastic. Nylon and polyester are the most popular materials because they are easy to handle and to care for. Pastry bags are available in sizes ranging from 8 to 24 inches long. The most useful sizes are 12 and 14 inches, because these can hold a sufficient supply of a mixture without overfilling, making them easy to handle and not requiring refilling often. For ease of handling, it is best to fill a pastry bag no more than halfway. When you buy a new pastry bag, it is necessary to cut off about ¹/₂ inch of the end for the pastry tip or coupler to fit through. Wash pastry bags, turned inside out, in hot, soapy water, then stand them wide end down on a countertop to dry. Pastry bags are available in cookware shops, cake decorating and candy making supply shops, and supermarkets. See also: coupler and pastry tip.

pastry blender This hand-held tool has several strong parallel stainless steel or aluminum U-shaped wires attached to a round wooden or plastic handle. It is used to blend cold fat into flour when making pastry dough. The fat is worked into the flour until it is cut into very tiny pieces.

pastry brush Pastry brushes are used extensively for pastry and confectionery work. They look just like paintbrushes. Pastry brushes usually have wooden handles, and the best ones are those with natural bristles. Nylon bristles tear and scratch doughs and can melt if they come in contact with heat. Pastry brushes have many uses in the dessert kitchen, including brushing excess flour from doughs, buttering the insides of molds and forms, washing down the sides of the pan as sugar is cooking, applying glazes and egg washes, and applying chocolate. Goosefeather brushes have several feathers sewn together and attached by their quills. They are used for glazing delicate fruit and for applying egg washes. It is important to keep separate the brushes that are used for fat and those that are used for sugar. It is also important to wash the brushes thoroughly with hot water and soap as soon as they are used. The different sizes of brushes have different uses. It is best to have a variety of sizes, ranging from 1/2 inch wide up to 2 1/2 inches wide.

pastry cloth A large piece of lightweight canvas or plastic-coated cotton that is used as a surface for rolling out pastry dough. The canvas cloth should be rubbed with flour before rolling out the dough, to make it "nonstick," and the excess flour should be shaken off before storing the cloth. The plastic-coated cloth is nonstick and does not need to have flour rubbed into it. Some pastry cloths have circles drawn on them that act as a guide for rolling the dough to a precise size. Sometimes the pastry cloth is stretched on a wooden and wire frame that keeps it taut. Canvas pastry cloths measure 17 by 18 inches or 21 inches square; the plastic-coated cotton cloths measure 20 by 25 inches.

pastry comb Also called a cake comb or an icing comb, this tool is made of either metal or plastic, and has serrated edges, similar to saw teeth. Metal pastry combs are usually 4 inches wide and small enough to be held in the palm of the hand. They can also be triangular in shape, with teeth on all three sides. A plastic comb looks like a long 1-inch-wide ruler. Both metal or plastic pastry combs have different-sized teeth on one or more edges. A pastry comb is used to make patterns in the icing or frosting around the sides or top of cakes and pastries and to make designs in chocolate. See also: Florentine.

pastry cream A rich, thick, cooked custard that is cooled and chilled before it is used as a filling for éclairs, Napoléons, tarts, cakes, and countless other desserts. It is made with milk, eggs, sugar, and flour. A vanilla bean is normally used to provide flavor, but many other flavors can be used, such as chocolate, coffee, orange, lemon, and raspberry. **Pastry cream** is a staple of all pastry kitchens. Pastry cream is a delicate custard and is best used within 3 days of preparation. France.

PASTRY CREAM

Approximately 3 cups

2 cups milk
½ vanilla bean, split lengthwise
6 large egg yolks, at room temperature
⅔ cup granulated sugar
¼ cup all-purpose flour or cornstarch, sifted

Combine the milk and split vanilla bean in a 2-quart heavy-duty saucepan, and heat over medium heat until just below the boil.

Meanwhile, combine the egg yolks and sugar in the bowl of a stand mixer or in a mixing bowl. Using the wire whip attachment or a hand-held mixer on medium-high speed, beat until the mixture is very thick and pale-colored and holds a slowly dissolving ribbon when the beater is lifted, about 4 minutes. Beat in the sifted flour or cornstarch, stopping to scrape down the sides of the bowl with a rubber spatula as needed.

With the mixer on low speed, slowly add half of the hot milk and blend well. Then pour the mixture back into the saucepan and stir to blend thoroughly. Bring the mixture to a boil over medium-high heat, whisking constantly.

Pour the pastry cream into a 1-quart bowl. Cover the cream immediately with waxed paper or plastic wrap to prevent a skin and let cool to room temperature. Cover the pastry cream tightly and refrigerate for at least 3 hours before using.

Stir the pastry cream vigorously before using to remove any lumps. The pastry cream will keep, well covered in the refrigerator, for up to 4 days. It cannot be frozen.

Variations: Optional flavorings for pastry cream include: 4 ounces melted chocolate (bittersweet, milk, or white); 1 tablespoon instant espresso powder dissolved in 1 tablespoon warm water; the finely minced zest of 1 large orange plus 2 tablespoons orange liqueur or 2 teaspoons orange extract; and the finely minced zest of 1 lemon plus 2 teaspoons lemon extract. These flavorings are added when the pastry cream is hot. For raspberry flavor, stir in ½ cup strained raspberry purée and 1 tablespoon raspberry-flavored liqueur when the pastry cream is cold.

pastry cutter set A nested set of cutters of graduated sizes, pastry cutters are made of wide bands of tinned or stainless steel, with the top edge rolled to create a rim. The bottom edge is sharp for cutting. Pastry cutters are available in various shapes: round with plain or fluted edges, star, heart, daisy petal, oval, and boat-shaped. The sets come in covered, boxes the shape of the cutters. The sets range from six to twenty pieces, in sizes from $1/2$ inch to $5^3/4$ inches in diameter. Pastry cutters are used to cut all types of pastry and cookie dough. They are available at specialty cookware shops and through mail order cookware catalogs.

pastry flour See flour.

pastry scraper A thin, flat, flexible piece of plastic or nylon that has a half-moon-shape and fits in the palm of one hand. A pastry scraper is used for a variety of tasks in the dessert kitchen, such as scraping out bowls, tempering chocolate, cutting doughs, and cleaning and scraping work surfaces. In French this tool is called a *corne*.

pastry tip Cone-shaped pastry tips are made of metal or plastic, with the metal ones the most popular. There are two main categories of pastry tips, small and large. The small ones are used primarily for decorative work, and the large ones for piping mixtures such as batters, doughs, fillings, and toppings. The small decorative tips are between $1^1/8$ and $1^1/4$ inches long. They are available in many shapes. The different shapes produce different designs. There are standard tips, such as plain round tips and star tips, flower tips, leaf tips, and special-use tips. Small tips are also available in sets, sometimes with a pastry bag and coupler. The coupler allows the tips to be changed without having to empty the bag or use another one. The large tips are 2 inches long. They are available in many different shapes, but the ones most often used for desserts, pastries, and confections are the plain round tips and the star tips. All pastry tips have a number, which indicates the size, etched on them. Pastry tips should be washed in hot, soapy water and dried after use. They can also be soaked in vinegar to remove any stubborn matter, and they can be washed in the dishwasher. They are available at cookware shops, cake decorating and candy making supply shops, department stores, supermarkets and through mail order cookware catalogs. See also: coupler and pastry bag.

pastry wheel This hand-held utensil consists of a thin, sharp, stainless steel wheel attached to a short handle. There are several types of pastry wheels. Wheels with plain edges are used to cut pastry dough into strips or other shapes. A wavy-edged pastry wheel, or pie jagger, cuts fluted edges on pastry dough. A ribbed pastry wheel looks like a small grooved barrel attached to a handle; it makes raised, even lines on the edges of tarts and pies. A dual pastry wheel has two blades, a plain-edged and a fluted-edged one. A combination pastry crimper/sealer has two wheels, whose edges both seal and cut pastry dough. These combination crimper/sealer tools are used primarily for filled pastries and for two-crust pies. A pizza wheel, which is larger and sturdier than a pastry wheel, also works well for cutting plain edges.

pâte The French word for dough, pastry, or batter.

pâte à choux The French term for cream puff pastry. See choux pastry.

pâte brisée One of the foundation doughs of pastry making, **pâte brisée** is a shortcrust pastry that is used as pie dough and for dishes that require a pastry dough that is not sweet, primarily savories. It is made with flour, sugar, salt, chilled butter, and cold water. Pâte brisée must chill and rest for at least 2 hours before it is used, or too much extra flour will be needed to roll it out, causing it to become tough. The dough will keep for 4 days in the refrigerator or can be frozen for several months. If frozen, defrost in the refrigerator overnight before using. France.

PÂTE BRISÉE

12 ounces; enough for one 9½-inch round tart, or two 8-inch pies, or one 8-inch double crust pie

1½ cups all-purpose flour
Pinch of granulated sugar
¼ teaspoon salt
4¼ ounces (1 stick plus ½ tablespoon) unsalted butter, cut into
    small pieces and chilled
5 tablespoons cold water

Place the flour, sugar, and salt in the bowl of a food processor fitted with the steel blade, and pulse for a few seconds. Add the butter and pulse, using on/off turns, until the butter is cut into very tiny pieces, about 1 minute. Or, combine the flour, sugar, and salt in the bowl of a stand mixer or a mixing bowl and, using the flat beater attachment or a hand-held mixer, mix for a few seconds. Add the butter and blend until the butter is cut into very tiny pieces, about 1 minute.

With the processor or mixer on, add the cold water in a steady stream, and process or mix until the dough wraps itself around the blade or forms a ball, about 1 minute. Wrap the dough in plastic wrap and refrigerate for at least 2 hours before using.

The dough will keep for 4 days in the refrigerator or, if very well wrapped, can be frozen for up to 4 months. If frozen, defrost it in the refrigerator overnight before using. If the pastry dough is very cold, let it sit at room temperature until it is pliable, but not soft, before using.

pâte feuilletée The French term for puff pastry. See puff pastry.

pâte sablée Sometimes called sand pastry, because it is fragile and crumbly, **pâte sablée** is one of the foundation doughs of pastry making. It is a delicate, rich, sweet, short dough used for tarts and tartlets and as a cookie dough. Pâte sablée is made with flour, confectioners' sugar, salt, butter, egg yolks, and vanilla or lemon extract. Pâte sablée must be given a few hours to chill and rest before using, or too much extra flour will be needed to roll it out, causing it to become tough. Because it is fragile, it often must be kneaded before rolling out, or it will crack. France.

PÂTE SABLÉE

1½ pounds; enough for two 9½-inch round tart shells

2¼ cups all-purpose flour
¾ cup sifted confectioners' sugar
Pinch of salt
7 ounces (1¾ sticks) unsalted butter, cut into 1-inch pieces, softened
2 large egg yolks, at room temperature
½ teaspoon vanilla or lemon extract

In the work bowl of a food processor fitted with the steel blade, combine the flour, confectioners' sugar, and salt. Pulse for 5 seconds to mix. Add the butter and pulse until the butter is cut into very tiny pieces, about 1 minute.

In a small bowl, lightly beat the egg yolks. Beat in the extract. Then, with the food processor running, pour this mixture through the feed tube and process until the dough wraps itself around the blade, about 1 minute. Divide the dough into 2 equal portions. Wrap each portion tightly with plastic wrap and refrigerate for 3 to 4 hours before using.

Pâte sablée will keep for 4 days in the refrigerator or can be frozen, if very well wrapped, for up to 4 months. If frozen, defrost overnight in the refrigerator before using. If the pastry dough is very cold, let it sit at room temperature until it is pliable, but not soft, then knead it briefly before using.

pâte sucrée One of the foundation doughs of pastry making, **pâte sucrée** is a rich, sweet dough used for tarts, tartlets, pies, and as a pastry base for many other desserts. It is made with flour, granulated sugar, salt, butter, eggs, and vanilla. Pâte sucrée must be allowed to chill and rest before using, or too much extra flour will be needed to roll it out, causing it to become tough. France.

PÂTE SUCRÉE

1½ pounds; enough for two 9½-inch round tart shells

2½ cups all-purpose flour
⅓ cup granulated sugar
Pinch of salt
8 ounces (2 sticks) unsalted butter, cut into 1-inch pieces, softened
1 large egg, at room temperature
1 teaspoon vanilla extract

In the work bowl of a food processor fitted with the steel blade, combine the flour, sugar, and salt. Pulse for 5 seconds to mix. Add the butter and pulse until the butter is cut into very tiny pieces, about 1 minute.

In a small bowl, lightly beat the egg with the vanilla extract. With the machine on, add the mixture through the feed tube, and process until the dough wraps itself around the blade and forms a ball, about 1 minute. Divide the dough in half. Wrap each half tightly in plastic wrap and refrigerate for at least 4 hours before using.

The pastry will keep for 4 days in the refrigerator or, if very well wrapped, can be frozen for up to 4 months. If frozen, defrost overnight in the refrigerator before using. If the pastry dough is very cold, let it sit at room temperature until it is pliable, but not soft, before using.

pâtisserie This French word has three meanings: It is the word both for pastry shop and for the art of pastry making. It is also the word for the category of sweet and savory pastries, most of which are baked. Confectionery, such as chocolate and sugar work, is included in this category.

pâtissier, pâtissière The French word (masculine and feminine) for pastry cook or pastry chef.

pavé The French word for paving stone. In pastry making, pavé refers to a square or rectangular, many-layered cake composed of génoise or sponge cake with buttercream filling and frosting. It may also mean a square piece of gingerbread.

Pavlova A dessert created by an Australian pastry chef in 1926 to celebrate the visit of famed Russian prima ballerina Anna Pavlova. **Pavlova** is composed of a light, crisp, shallow round meringue shell with a soft interior, filled with whipped cream and topped with fresh fruit native to Australia, such as kiwifruit, passion fruit, and pineapple. Bananas, strawberries, raspberries, and blueberries are also used to top the dessert. Australia.

∽∽∽∽∽∽∽∽

PAVLOVA

One 9-inch round pastry; 12 to 14 servings

Meringue shell
4 large egg whites, at room temperature
¼ teaspoon cream of tartar
1 cup superfine sugar
1 tablespoon plus 1 teaspoon cornstarch, sifted
½ teaspoon distilled white vinegar
½ teaspoon vanilla extract

Filling
2 cups heavy whipping cream
3 tablespoons superfine sugar
2 teaspoons vanilla extract

1 cup fresh raspberries, strawberries, or blackberries
1 medium banana, thinly sliced
2 to 3 kiwifruit, peeled and thinly sliced

Center a rack in the oven and preheat to 400°F. Line a baking sheet with aluminum foil. Using a 9-inch cardboard round as a guide, trace a 9-inch circle onto the dull side of the foil with a pencil, then turn the foil over on the baking sheet.

In the bowl of a stand mixer, using the wire whip attachment, or in a mixing bowl, using a hand-held mixer, beat the egg whites and cream of tartar on medium-high speed until frothy. Gradually add the sugar, then continue beating until the egg whites hold firm peaks, about 3 minutes. Turn the mixer speed to low, sprinkle on the cornstarch, and blend well. Add the vinegar and vanilla extract and blend well.

Using a rubber spatula, spread the meringue mixture onto the foil, using the circle as a guide. Mound the mixture around the edges so they are slightly thicker than the center, creating a shallow bowl. Place the baking sheet in the oven, lower the oven temperature to 250°F, and dry the meringue for 1½ hours.

Turn the oven off, prop open the oven door with a wooden spoon, and leave the meringue in the oven until it is cool. (The meringue can be made 2 days in advance and stored at room temperature, covered with aluminum foil.)

For the filling, in the chilled bowl of a stand mixer, using the wire whip attachment, or in a chilled mixing bowl, using chilled beaters, whip the cream until it is thick. Gradually sprinkle on the sugar, then beat in the vanilla extract and whip the cream until it holds soft peaks.

Reserve one quarter of the cream for decoration, and spread the remaining cream into the center of the meringue shell, mounding it slightly. Arrange the fruit in concentric circles over the cream. Fit a 12-inch pastry bag with a #3 large closed star tip, and fill with the reserved cream. Pipe a border of shells around the outer edge of the fruit.

Refrigerate the Pavlova until ready to serve. It is best to assemble the dessert no more than 3 hours before serving.

peach The round fruit of the tree of the same name, native to China. Today peaches are cultivated primarily in the United States, Australia, and South Africa. A downy, thin skin encloses fragrant, sweet, juicy flesh that surrounds a hard center stone. (The nectarine is a variety of peach that has no down on its skin and tends to be smaller.) Peach skin ranges in color from creamy off-white to reddish-yellow and the flesh from off-white to pale pink to golden yellow. There are two main types of peaches, freestone and clingstone. The names aptly describe the relationship of the fruit to its stone: Freestone releases easily from the center stone, while clingstone does not. Freestone peaches are most often available fresh. Clingstone peaches are usually canned commercially. Peaches are used both raw and cooked as an ingredient in many desserts and pastries, including cobblers, fruit salad, fresh fruit tarts, sorbets, parfaits, and ice creams. They are also used to make conserves and jams. Canned and frozen peaches are available year-round. Fresh peaches are available from May through September. Choose fragrant, firm but not hard, cream or golden-colored fruit with no bruises, soft spots, or withered skin. Slightly underripe peaches will ripen at room temperature in a few days. To speed up the process, place them in a tightly closed but perforated paper bag with an apple or a banana. Store ripe peaches in a plastic bag in the refrigerator for up to a week. Bring them to room temperature before use. The fuzzy skin of peaches can be removed by blanching them in boiling water for 10 seconds, then transferring them to cold water. The skin should slip off easily. Once peeled, peaches will turn brown from exposure to air. Rub them with a sliced lemon or lime or dip them in water mixed with lemon, lime, or orange juice and pat dry with a paper towel. Peaches can be used interchangeably with nectarines in most desserts and pastries. See also: acidulated water, blanch, fruit, nectarine, and peach Melba.

peach Melba This classic dessert was created at the turn of the century by the great French chef Auguste Escoffier in honor of the Australian opera singer Dame Nellie Melba. It consists of pitted peach halves poached in syrup and cooled, which are placed on top of scoops of vanilla ice cream. They are drizzled with Melba sauce, which is made from raspberries, and decorated with sliced almonds and, occasionally, whipped cream. See also: Melba sauce.

peanut The peanut is not a nut at all, but the seed of a tropical legume, native to South America. Peanuts grow on long tendrils just below the surface of the ground, which is why they are also called groundnuts. Two light-colored nuts covered with a brown, papery skin are enclosed in a fibrous hourglass-shaped tan shell. Peanuts have a buttery flavor that is enhanced by roasting. There are two main varieties of peanuts, the Virginia peanut and the Spanish peanut. Virginia peanuts are oval-shaped and larger than Spanish peanuts, which are round. Peanuts are used as an ingredient in desserts, pastries, and confections. They are available both shelled and unshelled, roasted, dry-roasted, salted, and unsalted. Because of their high natural oil content, peanuts turn rancid rapidly. They will keep for up to 6 months stored in the refrigerator in an airtight container.

peanut oil Clear, mild-flavored, cholesterol-free peanut oil is pressed from peanuts. It can be used as an ingredient in desserts, pastries, and confections, and its high smoke point makes it a good choice for frying. Peanut oil can be used interchangeably with other vegetable oils, such as canola, corn, olive, safflower, and sunflower, although the flavor may not be the same (as it's almost flavorless). Peanut oil is widely available at supermarkets, some Asian markets, and health food stores. Store it tightly capped in a dark place at room temperature or in the refrigerator for up to a year. It will thicken and become cloudy in the refrigerator, but will clarify and liquefy at room temperature. See also: fats and oils and smoke point.

pear The bell-shaped or rounded fleshy fruit of the pear tree, native to Asia Minor. Today the pear is cultivated in temperate climates throughout the world. Pears are usually oval, rounded and full at the bottom end, tapering to a slim elongated neck, although some varieties are round. Pears have smooth skin that ranges in color from yellow-green to brown to red with pale off-white and slightly grainy flesh that surrounds a center core. Ripe pears are juicy with either a spicy-sweet or slightly tart flavor. Pears are used raw, cooked, baked, and dried as an ingredient in many desserts, pastries, and confections. They are also used to make jams and liqueurs, such as the well-known Poire William. There are hundreds of types of pears, but only a few are available in the United States. Those varieties used most often include Anjou, Bartlett, Bosc, Comice, and Winter Nelis. Dried and canned pears are available year-round. Fresh pears are available from mid-July through May, with the peak between September and January. Choose fragrant, evenly colored, blemish-free, firm fruit with stems attached. Pears should give slightly when pressed at the stem end. Slightly underripe pears will ripen at room temperature within a few days. To speed up the process, place them in a tightly closed but perforated paper bag with an apple or a banana. Store ripe pears in the refrigerator for up to a week. Since they taste best at room temperature, let them stand out of the refrigerator at least 30 minutes before use. When cut, the flesh has a tendency to turn brown from exposure to air. To prevent this, rub the surface of the pear with a sliced lemon or lime or sprinkle it with or place it in water mixed with a little lemon, lime, or orange juice, then pat dry with a paper towel before use. See also: acidulated water, Anjou pear, Bartlett pear, Bosc pear, Comice pear, fruit, Pear Frangipane Tart (page 127), Poire William, and Winter Nelis pear.

pear corer See corer.

pearl sugar Also called coarse or decorating sugar, pearl sugar is white sugar that has been processed into small round grains, resembling pearls, about four to six times larger than grains of granulated sugar. Pearl sugar is used not as a sweetener in baking, but as a garnish and topping to decorate desserts, pastries, and confections. See also: sugar.

pecan A species of hickory nut native to the American Southeast, the pecan was first cultivated by the Indians. Today the biggest producer of pecans is Georgia. A smooth, thin, 1-inch-long light-brown, oval shell encloses a nut that is golden brown outside and ivory-colored inside. Pecans have a rich, buttery flavor that is enhanced by toasting. Their most popular use is in pecan pie, although they are used in many other desserts, pastries, and confections. They are available year-round both shelled and unshelled, but the fall is the peak season. Choose unshelled nuts that feel heavy, with shells free of cracks and holes. Because of their high natural oil content, pecans turn rancid rapidly. Store unshelled pecans in a cool, dry place for up to 6 months. Shelled pecans will keep in an airtight container in the refrigerator for up to 3 months, or in the freezer for up to 6 months. See also: nut.

pecan pie A classic single-crust pie from the American South, pecan pie is rich with butter, eggs, molasses or corn syrup, brown sugar, and pecans. It is a sweet, chewy pie traditionally made in the fall and winter. Pecan pie is often served for dessert during the Thanksgiving and Christmas holiday celebrations. It is usually accompanied by whipped cream or vanilla ice cream. United States. See also: pecan and pie.

pectin A tasteless, water-soluble, naturally occurring jelling substance found in plants. Pectin is abundant in the seeds, skins, and body of certain fruits, such as apples, quinces, black and red currants, oranges, and lemons. Pectin is used to set cooked fruits, especially those low in pectin, such as strawberries and peaches, to make jams and jellies. It must be balanced with the correct amounts of both sugar and acid, such as lemon juice, in order to work properly. Pectin is also used as a jelling agent in some candies, such as Turkish delight and jelly beans. Pectin is available in most supermarkets as either a powder or a liquid. See also: Turkish delight.

penuche A fudgelike, creamy candy made with milk or cream, brown sugar, butter, vanilla, and often nuts. The name comes from the Mexican word for brown sugar or raw sugar. Mexico.

peppermint See mint.

persimmon Native to Asia, the persimmon today is grown in Japan, China, countries of the Mediterranean basin, South America, and the United States. In the United States there are two main varieties of persimmons, the Hachiya and the Fuyu. Hachiya persimmons weigh about a pound and are oval with a pointed base. Fuyu persimmons, which are smaller, are round and look like large tomatoes. Both varieties have smooth red-orange skin and flesh of the same color. When ripe, the skin of a persimmon is transparent and the creamy-textured fruit has a very sweet flavor. Hachiya persimmons are very bitter if eaten underripe. Fuyu persimmons can be eaten when firm. Persimmons are used both fresh and cooked as an ingredient in desserts, pastries, and confections, such as cookies, quick breads, ice creams, sorbets, and puddings, and they are used to make jams and jellies. Persimmons are available from October through March. Choose fragrant, plump, unblemished, bright red-orange fruit that gives with slight pressure. Underripe persimmons will ripen at room temperature within a few weeks. To speed up the process, place them in a tightly closed but perforated paper bag with a banana or an apple. Store ripe fruit in the refrigerator and use within a few days. Peel persimmons before cooking or puréeing. See also: fruit.

pestiños al anís Spanish anise-flavored fried pastries. They are made with a sweet pastry dough mixed with white wine and oil that is flavored by using it to brown lemon zest and anise seeds. The dough is rolled out thin and cut into small rectangles, then deep-fried in hot oil, which makes the rectangles puff up. After frying, the pastries are drained, dipped in a honey syrup, drained again, and dusted with confectioners' sugar before serving. Spain.

petit four A tiny individual-sized cake, pastry, cookie, or confection. Petits fours are most often thought of as miniature fancy cakes covered with icing and elaborately decorated, but tiny tartlets, molded chocolates, and sugar-coated fruits, such as dates stuffed with marzipan, are also considered to be petits fours. Petits fours secs (dry) is the French term for delicate, crisp cookies that are often served with afternoon or after-dinner coffee or tea or as an accompaniment to ice creams, sorbets, custards, and dessert wines. *Mignardise* is the French name given to an assortment of petits fours served after a formal dinner. The name petit four comes from *four*, the French word for oven. These little cakes, which bake at lower temperatures, would be baked after the large cakes, while the oven was cooling down but still retained some heat. There is also a savory category of petits fours, which are made from pastry dough, such as miniature croissants, turnovers, barquettes, and quiches. These are served at lunches and to accompany cocktails. France.

petits fours molds Miniature individual shallow mold available in many shapes, including square, oval, rectangular, round, diamond, triangular, and boat-shaped, with either plain or fluted edges. Petits fours molds are used for forming tiny tartlets and molding chocolates. The molds are about $1^1/4$ to $1^1/2$ inches in diameter and $^1/2$ inch deep. They come in a boxed set of fifty, with five each of ten designs, or are available individually. They can be found at cookware shops and through mail order catalogs.

petticoat tail The name given to a pie-shaped wedge of shortbread cut from a large round. This shape is said to resemble the petticoats worn by women during the time of the Norman Conquest of Britain, in the twelfth century. See also: shortbread.

pfeffernüsse Translated from the German as "peppernuts," these spicy Christmas cookies are flavored with black pepper and spices such as cinnamon, cloves, cardamom, ginger, and nutmeg. Traditionally the cookies are made with honey, but sugar is often used. These hard cookies contain no fat, which makes them able to be stored for a long time. Variations of these small round treats are found throughout the Scandinavian countries as well. Germany.

phyllo dough Phyllo, also sometimes called filo or fillo dough, translates from the Greek as "leaf"; phyllo dough is paper-thin, leafy sheets of dough made of flour and water. It is used in many sweet and savory Middle Eastern dishes, such as baklava and spanakopita. Phyllo dough originated in Greece and is similar to, but thinner than, streudel dough. Phyllo dough dries out rapidly when exposed to air. When working with it, it is necessary to keep the dough covered with a damp cloth. Phyllo dough is available fresh in some Greek and Middle Eastern markets and frozen in 1-pound packages in most major supermarkets. Defrost the dough in the refrigerator overnight before using. Greece. See also: baklava.

pie A pastry consisting of a sweet filling baked in a pastry crust in a shallow, sloped-sided pan. A pie may have only a bottom crust, which makes it open-face, or it may have both a top and a bottom crust. A deep-dish pie is baked in a deeper pan and has only a top crust. Pies can also have other toppings instead of a pastry crust, such as meringue or a crumb topping. Fruit is the filling most often used for dessert pies, but nuts are also used extensively. Pie crusts can be made from many types of dough, including shortcrust pastry, puff pastry, cookie crumbs, ground nuts, and meringue. Pies are served directly from the pans in which they were baked, often accompanied with fresh whipped cream or ice cream. United States. See also: chiffon pie, lemon meringue pie, pecan pie, pie plate, and pumpkin pie.

pièce montée Translated literally from the French as "mounted piece," this term refers to elaborate, lavish table ornaments generally made from various forms of sugar. These were widely used by the nobility during the Middle Ages to decorate tables for banquets and parties. These spectacular ornaments were often made in animal shapes or depicted a variety of subjects, such as historical or allegorical scenes. The pieces were constructed of various materials, including nougat, sugar flowers and ribbons, sponge cake, petits fours, dragées, and marzipan. Today more modest decorative items made of blown, poured, or pulled sugar are used only on very special occasions. See also: blown sugar, poured sugar, and pulled sugar.

pie pan See pie plate.

pie plate Also called a pie pan, this pan is used exclusively for baking pies. It is round with sloped sides and about 1¹/₂ inches deep. Pie plates are made of tinned steel, aluminum, glass, or ceramic, and some have a nonstick lining. They range in size from 8 to 12 inches, with 9 inches being the most popular. There is also a perforated pie plate that has small holes all over its bottom, which allow the steam to escape and keep the bottom of the pie crust from becoming soggy. The oval pie dishes for deep-dish pies are slightly deeper than standard pie plates. See also: pie.

pierog A Polish crescent-shaped pastry. *Pierogi* translates as "pockets" or "envelopes." To make dessert pierogi, a sweet pastry dough is rolled out and cut into circles. A filling of cottage cheese, sugar, candied orange peel, and raisins is placed on one half of each circle and the other half is folded over, forming a half-moon. The edges of the dough are sealed, and the pierogi are poached in boiling water. They are served warm, sprinkled with sugar and drizzled and accompanied by sour cream. A Russian version of pierogi is filled with cherries or apples mixed with sugar or with preserves. After poaching, these pierogi are drizzled with butter and served with sugar and sour cream as accompaniments. Poland and Russia.

pie weights Round ceramic or flat aluminum pellets used to weight down a pie crust or tart shell that is baked with no filling. The weights keep the sides from collapsing and the bottom from puffing up. The weights should always be placed on top of a piece of aluminum foil or parchment paper, or they may bake into the crust, and they should fill the shell almost full. Pie weights also conduct heat to the top and sides of the pie crust or tart shell as it bakes. Pie weights are available in 2-pound packages at cookware shops. See also: bake blind.

pignoli See pine nut.

pineapple The tropical fruit of the plant of the same name, native to South America. Today pineapples are grown primarily in China, Southeast Asia, and Hawaii. Pineapples look like large pinecones, cylindrical with spiny scales. A cluster of long, swordlike green leaves sprouts from the top of the fruit. The tough golden-yellow skin encloses rich, juicy, sweet-tart yellow flesh. Pineapple is used raw, cooked, dried, and candied as an ingredient in desserts, pastries, and confections. Raw pineapples contain an enzyme that prevents gelatin from setting. Cooking destroys the enzyme, so cooked pineapple can be used with gelatin. Pineapples do not ripen further after they are picked, so they must be left on the tree until the starch converts to sugar. Once picked, they are delicate and highly perishable. Both canned and fresh pineapples are available year-round, with the peak for the fresh fruit from March through June. Choose very fragrant, deep yellow, unblemished fruit that gives slightly when pressed. An indication of ripeness is that a leaf pulled from the center releases easily. Store ripe whole pineapple in a plastic bag in the refrigerator for up to 5 days. Pineapple must be peeled and cored before use. Once it is cut, store the fruit in a tightly sealed container in the refrigerator for up to 3 days. See also: fruit.

pineapple corer See corer.

pine nut The seed of the pinecone of different varieties of pine trees. There are two main types of pine nuts: Mediterranean and Chinese. Both nuts are ivory-colored and small, about $1/2$ inch long. Mediterranean pine nuts, which come from the stone pine, are long and slender with a delicate flavor. They are used primarily in Mediterranean and Middle Eastern cuisine. The Chinese pine nut is wider at one end and has a strong, pungent flavor. It is used in Chinese and other Asian cuisines. Both types are used in desserts, pastries, and confections. Often they are toasted to enhance their flavor. Pine nuts are also called pignoli, piñón, pignon, and Indian nuts. Because of their high natural oil content, pine nuts will turn rancid rapidly. They will keep for up to 6 months stored in an airtight container in the refrigerator or for up to a year in the freezer. Chinese pine nuts are available in Asian markets. Mediterranean pine nuts are available in bulk in nut shops, health food stores, and specialty food stores, and prepackaged in supermarkets. See also: nut.

piping A technique for forcing buttercream, choux pastry, icing, chocolate, or any other material from a pastry bag to form specific shapes or decorative designs. Piping must be done steadily and evenly while the pastry bag is held at an angle above the piping surface. The shape of the pastry tip used determines the design and shape of the piped material. A parchment paper pastry cone is often used to hold icing or melted chocolate, which is forced through a very tiny opening at the pointed end of the cone to create fine, delicate designs, writing, and scrollwork for decoration of desserts, pastries, and confections. See also: paper pastry cone, parchment paper and pastry bag.

piping chocolate Melted chocolate combined with just a few drops of water or simple sugar syrup to make it fluid enough to use for writing and piping decorations onto pastries, desserts, and confections. See also: chocolate and sugar syrup.

piping gel A colorless, tasteless, transparent substance made from sugar, corn syrup, water, vegetable gum, and benzoate of soda, piping gel is used to decorate cakes and pastries with writing and fine-line designs. It can be colored with paste or powder food coloring. Piping gel is available at cake decorating supply shops and through mail order cookware catalogs.

pippin apple See Newtown Pippin apple.

pisang goreng Indonesian fried bananas. Thinly sliced bananas are dipped in a batter of rice flour, sugar, salt, egg, baking soda, and water, then deep-fried in hot oil until golden brown. The bananas are drained, then served warm with coffee or as a snack. Indonesia.

pistachio nut The seed of a tree native to the Middle East, the pistachio nut is widely cultivated in California, Turkey, Italy, and Iran. The pale green nut, surrounded by a papery reddish-brown skin, is enclosed in a hard, tan shell. Occasionally, the shells of pistachio nuts are tinted red with vegetable dye. Pistachio nuts have a sweet, delicate flavor. They are used to flavor and decorate desserts, pastries, and confections. Pistachio nuts are available shelled and unshelled, raw, roasted, or roasted and salted. If using unshelled nuts, look for nuts with partially open shells. If the shell is closed, it indicates that the nutmeat is immature. Pistachio nuts are best stored in an airtight container in the refrigerator or freezer, where they will keep for up to 6 months. See also: nut.

Pithiviers Pithiviers is a classic round flat French cake made from two circles of puff pastry that enclose a filling of frangipane cream. The edges of the cake are scalloped and a sunburst or rosette pattern is etched on top. Galette des Rois is the name given to the cake when it is served during Twelfth Night celebrations; this version contains a bean or other token embedded in the filling, which is reputed to bring good luck to the recipient. The cake is a specialty of the town of Pithiviers in the Orléans region in the Loire Valley. France. See also: frangipane, galette, and puff pastry.

PITHIVIERS

One 10-inch round cake; 12 to 14 servings

1¼ pounds Classic Puff Pastry (page 243)
1 recipe Frangipane (page 127)
1 large egg yolk beaten with 1 teaspoon water, for glaze

Line a baking sheet with a sheet of parchment paper. Divide the puff pastry into 2 equal pieces. On a lightly floured surface, roll out 1 piece to a large circle, 11 to 12 inches in diameter. Using a 10-inch cardboard cake circle as a guide, cut out a circle of puff pastry. Transfer the pastry to the lined baking sheet, positioning it in the center of the baking sheet. Roll out the remaining puff pastry to a large circle. Using an 11-inch plate, cut out an 11-inch circle of puff pastry.

Place the frangipane cream in the center of the 10-inch circle of puff pastry, mounding it slightly. Leave a 2-inch border around the filling. Dampen a pastry brush with water and brush around the outside edge of the circle. Position the 11-inch circle over the filling, draping it over the center. Line up the edges of the 2 circles of puff pastry, and press them together to seal. Crimp the outside edges of the Pithiviers.

Use a small knife or toothpick to pierce a tiny hole in the very center of the pastry. Score the pastry, beginning at the top hole and working to the outside edges, in curved lines, forming a sunburst design; do not cut through the pastry. Brush the pastry with half of the egg glaze and refrigerate for 15 minutes.

Center a rack in the oven and preheat to 450°F.

Brush the Pithiviers with the remaining egg glaze and place it in the oven. Reduce the oven temperature to 400°F, and bake for 15 minutes. Then reduce the oven temperature to 350°F, and bake for 25 to 30 minutes longer, until puffed and golden brown. Transfer the baking sheet to a rack to cool for 15 minutes. The Pithiviers is best served warm.

pizzelle A large round cookie made from a rich batter of eggs, sugar, butter, flour, and vanilla, baked on a specially designed pizzelle iron, which looks like a waffle iron. The intricately carved surfaces of the pizzelle iron imprint designs onto the cookie as it cooks. Pizzelle become crisp as they cool. While still warm, they can be rolled into a cone shape, then filled with whipped cream when cool. Italy. See also: pizzelle iron.

pizzelle iron Two 5-inch engraved round cast-aluminum plates are hinged together to form an iron. Each plate has a long handle. Pizzelle batter is placed in the center of one plate, the plates are brought together, and the iron is placed over a stove burner to cook the pizzelle. Pizzelle irons come with different designs engraved on the plates, such as stars or flowers, and the edges can be ruffled or plain. The Scandinavian version of pizzelle is krumkake, baked on a similar iron that has the traditional engraved scroll designs. Pizzelle irons are also available in electric models. There are two types, designed to make either two regular or four miniature pizzelle at the same time. See also: krumkake iron and pizzelle.

plombières A type of ice cream made with a custard base blended with whipped cream and candied fruits and frozen in a square ice cream mold. *Plomb* is the French word for lead, the original material of the metal mold. Plombières is also a custard blended with whipped egg whites and fresh or candied fruit. France.

plum An Asian native, the plum was brought to Europe with the returning Crusaders. Plums have an oval center stone surrounded by soft, juicy, sweet-tart flesh and a thin, smooth skin. Plums are round to oval-shaped with skin and flesh ranging in color from yellowish-green to blue-red to purple. There are many varieties of plums, including the prune, which can be dried with the pit intact. Plums are used both raw and cooked as an ingredient in many pastries, desserts, and confections and they are used to make jams and jellies. Canned plums are available year-round. Fresh plums are available from May through October. Choose plump, firm fruit with evenly colored, smooth, unblemished skin that gives slightly when pressed. Slightly underripe plums will ripen at room temperature within a few days. To speed up the process, place them in a tightly closed but perforated paper bag with an apple or a banana. Store ripe plums in a plastic bag in the refrigerator for up to 5 days and rinse just before use. See also: fruit.

poach Poaching is the technique for gently cooking fruits in a liquid that is hot, but just below the boiling point. Usually the liquid is a sugar syrup, but occasionally wine is used. This technique enables the fruit to retain its shape and to absorb flavor from the poaching liquid. Cooking puddings and custards in a water bath is also a form of poaching. See also: water bath.

poe A Tahitian chilled custard. Puréed tropical fruits, such as pineapple, mango, papaya, and banana, are combined with brown sugar, vanilla seeds scraped from the pod of the vanilla bean, and arrowroot-thickened fruit juice. The mixture is placed in a buttered baking dish and baked until set and golden-colored. The dessert is served chilled, with coconut cream. Tahiti. See also: arrowroot.

Poire William A clear, colorless, pear eau-de-vie that is a specialty of Switzerland. Some brands of Poire William have a whole pear inside the bottle. To achieve this, the bottle must be placed over the small, budding fruit on the tree—then the pear grows inside the bottle. Poire William is used to flavor desserts, pastries, and confections. See also: eau-de-vie.

pomegranate A native of Iran cultivated in tropical climates throughout the world, the pomegranate is a round fruit the size of an orange, with thin, leathery red skin enclosing translucent ruby-red pulp. Hundreds of glistening red sweet-tart seeds are embedded in the pulp, separated by a bitter white membrane. The seeds are either eaten whole or squeezed for their juice. The juice is used as an ingredient in pastries, desserts, and confections, and the seeds are used as a garnish. Pomegranates are available from September through December, with the peak in October. Choose pomegranates that feel heavy for their size, with firm, unblemished, brightly colored skin. Store pomegranates in a cool, dry place at room temperature for a few weeks or in a plastic bag in the refrigerator for up to 3 months. Pomegranate seeds can be frozen in a plastic bag for up to 4 months. See also: fruit.

pomelo, pommelo, pummelo A large citrus fruit native to Malaysia, the pomelo is considered to be the ancestor of the grapefruit. Pomelos, which range from the size of a cantaloupe to as large as a soccer ball, are either pear-shaped or round. Their skin color ranges from green to yellow to pink. The flesh is either yellow or pale pink, and its texture varies greatly from very juicy to dry, with or without seeds. The taste is either sweet or very acidic. Pomelos can be used like grapefruit as an ingredient in desserts, pastries, and confections. They are available, primarily in Asian markets, in January and February. Choose aromatic, plump, brightly colored fruit that feels heavy for its size, with thin, smooth skin that gives slightly when pressed. Store pomelos at room temperature for up to 2 days or in a plastic bag in the refrigerator for up to a week. See also: citrus fruit, fruit, and grapefruit.

pommelo See pomelo.

poppy seed This spice is the tiny, kidney-shaped, blue-gray, ripe seed of the opium poppy plant, which is native to the Mediterranean area. About nine hundred thousand of the minute seeds make a pound. Poppy seeds are used as a filling for many cakes, cookies, and breads and as a topping for some baked goods, such as coffee cakes. They are also mixed with poppy seed oil and ground to a paste for use in some Turkish pastries. Poppy seeds have a nutty flavor and crunchy texture. They have been used in cooking for thousands of years, particularly in the cuisines of Eastern Europe, India, and the Middle East. Poppy seeds are available both whole and ground in supermarkets and in specialty delicatessens. They will last indefinitely if stored in an airtight container in a cool, dark place.

pot de crème cup See custard cup.

potica A Czech and Slovak special-occasion pastry, potica is made from a yeast pastry dough that is hand-stretched until it is paper-thin. A rich filling of nuts cooked in honey and milk is rolled up inside the dough, as for a strudel. After baking, the pastry is sliced crosswise, revealing a spiral of the filling inside. The Czech Republic and Slovakia.

pound cake This cake takes its name from the original recipe, which called for a pound each of eggs, butter, sugar, and flour. It is a creamed cake, meaning that the butter and sugar are creamed together before the other ingredients are added. In France, **pound cake** is called quatre-quarts, meaning four quarters, referring to the four ingredients. Today's pound cakes use the same ingredients but in different proportions, so they are less dense and heavy. Modern pound cakes usually include baking powder, and occasionally milk, to lighten the batter. Vanilla extract is the typical flavoring, but lemon, orange, or almond extracts, lemon juice, and lemon or orange zest can easily be substituted. Nuts, spices, and chocolate are also used to create delicious variations. Pound cake is typically baked in a loaf shape. Pound cake came to America with the British colonists in the seventeenth century and has become a classic American cake. Pound cake is often served with fresh fruit, ice cream, or fruit sauces, such as lemon or raspberry. It is generally served for afternoon tea or dessert. Pound cake keeps for several days at room temperature if well wrapped in aluminum foil, or it can be frozen. United States.

∽∾∽∾∽∾∽∾∽∾

POUND CAKE

One 9- by 5- by 3-inch loaf, serves 10 to 12

1 tablespoon unsalted butter, softened, for the pan
1 tablespoon cake flour, for the pan

2 cups cake flour
1 teaspoon baking powder
¼ teaspoon salt
8 ounces (2 sticks) unsalted butter, softened
1½ cups superfine sugar
4 large eggs, at room temperature
3 tablespoons milk
2 teaspoons vanilla extract

Center a rack in the oven and preheat to 325°F. Generously butter the inside of a 9- by 5- by 3-inch loaf pan with the softened butter. Dust the inside of the pan with the flour, then tap out the excess.

Sift together the cake flour, baking powder, and salt onto a piece of waxed paper.

In the bowl of a stand mixer, using the flat beater attachment, or in a mixing bowl, using a hand-held beater, beat the butter until it is fluffy, about 2 minutes. Gradually add the sugar and continue beating to cream the butter and sugar, about 2 minutes, stopping to scrape down the sides of the bowl with a rubber spatula occasionally.

Add the eggs 1 at a time, beating well after each addition. Beat in the milk and vanilla extract, and blend well.

With the mixer on low speed, slowly add the dry ingredients and beat until thoroughly blended, stopping to scrape down the sides of the bowl occasionally. Turn the batter into the prepared loaf pan, and use the rubber spatula to smooth the top.

Bake the pound cake for about 1 hour and 10 minutes, until the top is risen and the cake is golden brown. Transfer the pan to a rack to cool for 15 minutes. Run a thin-bladed knife around the inside edge of the loaf pan to loosen the cake, turn the cake out of the pan, then turn it right side up and let cool completely on the rack.

Well wrapped in aluminum foil, pound cake will keep for 4 days at room temperature, or it can be frozen. If frozen, defrost it overnight in the refrigerator before serving.

Variations: Several variations of pound cake are also delicious: Replace the vanilla extract with lemon, orange, or almond extract. Or add 1 tablespoon finely minced lemon or orange zest. Cinnamon, mace, and nutmeg can be added to taste, as can finely ground nuts or praline. Four ounces melted bittersweet chocolate can be blended into the batter to make a chocolate variation.

poured sugar Sugar cooked to the hard crack stage is poured in a steady stream into a lightly oiled shallow template cut from rolled-out modeling paste, placed on aluminum foil. The poured sugar is left to set completely at room temperature, for up to 4 hours. When the sugar is firm, the form is cut away and lifted off. Powdered food coloring can be added to the sugar during the final stages of cooking. Poured sugar pieces can be "glued" together with hard crack sugar or royal icing to form three-dimensional shapes. These three-dimensional shapes resemble pieces of stained glass. Poured sugar pieces can be sprayed with a thin layer of clear varnish to prevent them from changing color and protect them from exposure to moisture, dust, and fingerprints. They will last for several days stored in a cool, dry place. See also: Table of Sugar Temperatures and Stages (page 335).

powdered milk Milk that has had all of the water removed through evaporation. Powdered milk is usually made from skim milk, but, powdered whole milk is available. Because it has a high fat content, making it prone to rancidity, powdered milk made from whole milk must be kept refrigerated in both its dry and reconstituted forms. Nonfat dry milk, which has had all of the butterfat removed, is available as both regular and instant. Powdered buttermilk is also available. Unopened powdered nonfat milk and buttermilk can be kept in a dry place up to 6 months. Once opened, it is best to refrigerate them. Once dry milk is reconstituted, it should be stored in a tightly covered container in the refrigerator. Reconstituted dry milk does not taste the same as fresh milk. It is most suited to use in doughs and batters for baked goods, where its flavor is not prominent. See also: milk.

powdered sugar See sugar.

praline A confection made of caramelized whole almonds, praline can also be ground to a powder and used as a flavoring, filling, and decoration in desserts, pastries, candies, and confections. In French, praline powder is *pralin*. Often praline is made with hazelnuts or a combination of both almonds and hazelnuts. *Praliné* is the French name for the category of chocolate candies and confections that are flavored with praline or praline paste. In Louisiana, a praline is a specialty candy made with pecans and brown sugar, shaped into a round, flat patty. Praline derives its name from the Duke of Plessis-Praslin, whose chef created it in the seventeenth century. France and United States. See also: praline paste.

praline paste A thick paste made by grinding caramelized almonds or hazelnuts to release their natural oils. Praline paste has a texture similar to nutty peanut butter. It is used to flavor desserts, pastries, and confections. United States.

preserves Whole or coarsely chopped pieces of fruit cooked with sugar until the mixture thickens and loosely holds its shape. If the fruit used to make preserves does not have enough pectin, a natural jelling agent present in fruits, powdered or liquid pectin can be added. Preserves also refers to the general category of fruit spreads, which includes conserves, jams, jellies, and marmalades. Preserves are used to spread on sweet breads for afternoon tea, to make dessert glazes and sauces, and as an ingredient and filling in desserts, pastries, and confections. See also: conserve, jam, jelly, marmalade, and pectin.

pressed cookie To make this type of cookie, dough is pushed through a cookie press fitted with a template or through a pastry bag fitted with a fancy tip, forming a distinctive shape. See also: cookie, cookie press, and dough.

profiterole A tiny cream puff filled with crème Chantilly, ice cream, or pastry cream. Stacked in a low pyramid shape in a dessert dish and covered with chocolate sauce, they are a classic dessert. Profiteroles are also used to form the elaborate dessert croquembouche, a tall pyramid-shaped cake, and they are used in Gâteau Saint-Honoré. There are also savory versions of profiteroles with fillings of cheese or meat. These are served as an appetizer or an accompaniment to soup. France. See also: choux pastry, crème Chantilly, croquembouche, and Gâteau Saint-Honoré.

Progrès See Succès.

proof To test yeast to determine if it is alive and has the ability to leaven a baked good. The yeast is sprinkled over warm liquid, a small amount of sugar is added, and the mixture is left to stand in a warm, draft-free place for 5 to 10 minutes. If the mixture bubbles and foams, the yeast is active. Proofing is also the fermentation that occurs during the rising of a bread or pastry before baking. During this process, the yeast grows and gives off carbon dioxide gas that inflates the dough, thereby creating a light, flavorful dough. See also: yeast.

pudding A cooked dessert with flour or another grain, such as rice or tapioca, as the foundation. Ingredients such as eggs, milk, fruit, sugar, and/or spices are also added. Puddings are soft, creamy desserts, similar to custards, baked in a bain-marie in the oven or cooked in a double boiler on the stove top. Puddings require long, slow cooking to keep them from curdling. They are served warm or cold, often with a sauce. English-style puddings, such as plum pudding, are steamed in a mold. They have a firm, solid texture, similar to a cake, and are more substantial than the baked custard type of pudding. One of the most famous puddings, Yorkshire pudding, isn't a pudding at all: It's an English type of popover traditionally served with roast beef. See also: bain-marie, custard, pudding mold, and tapioca.

pudding mold Used for steamed plum pudding and other steamed puddings, this is a deep cylindrical mold with fluted or grooved sides, a scalloped top, and a center tube. Some pudding molds have a lid that is held on by two clips at the top rim, others have a wide rim and no lid. The molds are made of aluminum, tinned steel, or glazed earthenware called basins. They are available in sizes ranging from a 2-cup to a 2-quart capacity at cookware shops and through mail order cookware catalogs.

pudim molotoff This Portuguese dessert is a rich egg custard thickened with cornstarch that is turned into a mold coated with butter and sugar. The custard is baked in a water bath until it is a light golden brown. Once the custard is cooled, it is turned out of the mold, decorated with toasted almonds, and served with a sweet egg sauce. Portugal. See also: cornstarch, custard, ovos moles d'aveiro, and pudding.

puff pastry One of the foundation doughs of pastry making, puff pastry is called *pâte feuilletée* in French, meaning "pastry leaves." It is a rich, delicate, flaky pastry with a high proportion of butter in the dough. Puff pastry is made of two main elements, the pastry dough, called the *détrempe*, and chilled fat, which is traditionally butter, although oil, margarine, lard, and goose fat may be used. The fat is rolled between the layers, which are folded over and rolled out again several times, with rest periods and chilling in between the rolling and folding. This creates about 700 very thin layers of each element. When the pastry dough is baked, the fat melts and, along with the water in the dough, creates steam, which causes the many layers to rise to up to eight times their original volume. The result is a light, crisp, flaky pastry. **Classic puff pastry** is not a sweet dough, but it is used for many sweets, including Napoléons, palmiers, cream horns, and allumettes. It is also used to make tart shells and bouchées. It is used for appetizers and entrées, such as vol-au-vent and cheese straws, and to wrap around food, such as fish or meat. *Demi-feuilletage*, or half puff pastry, is the name given to the pastry created from puff pastry scraps or leftover pieces of dough that are gathered together and rolled out; it is used for tartlet or barquette shells or puff pastry decorations that don't need to rise as high.

Puff pastry has a colorful history, beginning with the cooks of ancient Greece. In 1525, puff pastry was cited in a decree by the Municipal Council of Venice, Italy, that forbade extravagant wedding feasts. Some historians believe that a seventeenth-century French landscape painter, Claude Lorraine, who served an apprenticeship as a pastry cook, was the creator of classic puff pastry. Feuillet, the chief pastry cook to the House of Condé, also is credited with its creation. Whatever its origins, the popularity of puff pastry is well established. France. See also: allumette, bouchée, cream horn, mille-feuille, and palmier.

CLASSIC PUFF PASTRY

2¼ pounds

4 cups all-purpose flour
2 teaspoons salt
15 ounces (3¾ sticks) unsalted butter, chilled
1⅛ cups ice water

Place 3½ cups of the flour and the salt in the work bowl of a food processor fitted with a steel blade. Cut 3 ounces (6 tablespoons) of the chilled butter into small pieces and add to the bowl. Pulse the mixture until the butter is cut into very tiny pieces, resembling coarse meal, about 2 minutes. With the machine running, add the ice water through the feed tube, and process until the dough forms a ball, about 30 seconds. Remove the dough from the bowl, cut a few crosshatch marks in the top, and cover with plastic wrap. Refrigerate for 40 minutes to relax the dough.

Cut the remaining 12 ounces (3 sticks) butter into pieces, and place in the bowl of a stand mixer or in a mixing bowl. Add the remaining ½ cup flour, and blend, using the flat beater attachment or a hand-held mixer, until the butter is pliable, but not soft. Stop a few times to scrape down the beater and sides of the bowl with a rubber spatula. Place the butter mixture on a large piece of waxed paper, fold the paper over the butter mixture, and form it into a 5-inch square.

Roll out the ball of dough on a lightly floured surface to a circle or square about 12 inches in diameter. Place the butter square in the center of the dough. Fold over the sides of the dough to enclose the butter, and pinch the top edges together.

Roll the dough out into a rectangle about 8 inches wide and 16 inches long. Be sure to keep the edges even. Fold the bottom third of the dough up over the center, and then fold the top third down over it, lining up the edges, forming a 3-layer package. Turn the dough so that the crease of the top fold is to your right. This is the first of 6 turns. Again roll out the dough into a large rectangle and fold in thirds keeping the edges even. Dust the baking sheet with flour and transfer the dough to the baking sheet. Press 2 fingertips into the dough to mark it, to show how many turns you have done. Cover the dough with plastic wrap and let rest in the refrigerator for at least 40 minutes.

Roll the dough out and fold it into thirds 2 more times. Transfer it to the baking sheet and make 4 fingertip indentations. Cover and refrigerate for at least 40 minutes (This point is the best time to freeze the dough if desired. Well wrapped, it will keep for several months in the freezer. Defrost it overnight in the refrigerator before completing turns 5 and 6.)

Turns 5 and 6 should be completed at least 2 hours before you plan to use the pastry dough. Puff pastry must have time to relax before baking or there will be excessive shrinkage: Roll out the dough and fold it 2 more times. Transfer it to the baking sheet, make 6 fingertip indentations, cover, and refrigerate for at least 2 hours.

Roll out the pastry dough and shape it for the desired use. After rolling out, allow it to rest for at least 15 minutes before baking to avoid excess shrinkage.

pulled sugar Sugar cooked to the hard crack stage is poured out onto an oiled marble slab and kneaded with a metal spatula until it is cool enough to be handled. The sugar is then pulled by hand, like taffy, under heat lamps until it is pliable and soft enough to form into various shapes, such as ribbons, fruits, animals, flowers, and leaves, used to decorate desserts, pastries, and confections. Pulled sugar is colored using powdered food coloring dissolved in a few drops of Cognac or kirsch. The color is added to the pliable mass and kneaded in until it is evenly distributed. As the sugar is pulled, it takes on a satin sheen. Pulling sugar works best in a dry, cool environment. Ornaments made from pulled sugar will last for several months stored in an airtight container at room temperature. See also: Table of Sugar Temperatures and Stages (page 335).

pummelo See pomelo.

pumpkin A large, round, vine-grown fruit of the squash family, native to the Americas. Pumpkins have been grown for thousands of years. They range from about a pound to over one hundred pounds in weight. Thick, hard skin that ranges in color from green to yellow to deep orange encloses yellow or orange fibrous pulp loaded with flat, broad, creamy-white seeds. The sweet flesh is used cooked as an ingredient in pastries, particularly pies and quick breads. Canned pumpkin purée is available year-round. Fresh pumpkins are available during the fall and winter, with the peak in late October. Choose pumpkins that feel heavy for their size, with evenly colored, unblemished skin. Small pumpkins generally have sweeter flesh than large ones. Store whole pumpkins at room temperature for up to a month or in the refrigerator for up to 3 months. See also: fruit and pumpkin pie.

pumpkin pie A classic American single-crust pie with a smooth, creamy filling of puréed pumpkin mixed with sugar, cream or evaporated milk, eggs, and spices such as cinnamon, ginger, nutmeg, and cloves. Pumpkin pie is usually made in the fall and winter. It is traditionally served warm or at room temperature as dessert for the Thanksgiving meal and is usually accompanied by whipped cream. United States. See also: pie and pumpkin.

punschtorte An Austrian cake so named because the layers are soaked in a punchlike syrup mixture containing rum. The cake, which is similar to a French génoise, is split into three layers, and each layer is soaked with the syrup. The layers are filled with apricot jam, and the cake is coated with pink fondant icing. Austria. See also: fondant.

quark Also called topfen, quark is an Austrian fresh, uncured, soft-curd cheese made from skim milk, similar to cottage cheese. It has a characteristic tangy taste and creamy texture. Quark is widely used as an ingredient in pastries and desserts. Austria.

quatre-quarts The French name for a pound cake made of equal weights of four ingredients: butter, eggs, flour, and sugar. See also: pound cake.

quick bread A bread or other baked good made with a quick-acting leavener such as baking powder or baking soda, which allows immediate baking instead of having to wait for yeast to rise. Eggs are also used as a leavener in quick breads, as they trap air that turns to steam when baked, causing the bread to rise. These baked goods are light and moist with a tender, crumbly texture. Quick breads are made either from a batter (muffins and coffee cakes), or from a dough (biscuits and scones). Quick breads that are sweet are served with afternoon coffee or tea or for breakfast; savory quick breads, such as zucchini bread or pumpkin bread, are served to accompany a meal. United States. See also: baking powder, baking soda, biscuit, leavener, muffin, and scone.

quince Native to Asia and cultivated for at least four thousand years, the quince looks like a cross between an apple and a pear. Thin yellow skin surrounds off-white, hard, dry flesh that has a tart apple-pear flavor. Almost always used cooked, quinces are an ingredient in desserts, pastries, and confections. Because quinces are naturally high in pectin, they are widely used to make marmalade, preserves, jams, and jellies. The name for marmalade comes from the Portuguese word for quince. When cooked, quinces turn a rosy-pink color. Quinces are available in the fall from October through December. Choose firm, evenly colored, yellow fruit, with no soft spots. Store quinces in a plastic bag in the refrigerator for a few months. Wash them just before use. See also: fruit.

quindin A classic Brazilian dessert, a quindin is a large cupcake-size macaroon with a jellylike sugar-and-egg topping. These tender sweets are baked in a water bath. Brazil.

rabadi Milk cooked down slowly until it is reduced to a quarter of its original volume to make a rich sauce with a honeylike consistency, maple color, and distinct sweet aroma. Rabadi is used as a dessert sauce in Indian cuisine and is often sweetened and topped with nuts, such as almonds or pistachio nuts, and served as a pudding. Rabadi can also be thinned with water or more milk and served as a drink. India.

rahat loukoum See Turkish delight.

rainbow sugar See crystal sugar.

raisins Grapes that are dried, either by the sun or by forced hot air. Because all of their water has been removed, raisins are very withered. They are very sweet because the grape's natural sugar caramelizes during the long drying process. Raisins are dark brown because of this caramelization. Sultanas, also called golden raisins, are treated with sulfur dioxide, before being dried by hot air. This process retains the light color of the grapes and produces very plump and moist fruit. Dried currants are made from very small Zante raisins. Thompson grapes are used to produce seedless raisins. Muscat grapes, which usually have their seeds removed before processing, are also used to make raisins. They produce the sweetest raisins. California grows about half of the world's raisins. Raisins, currants, and sultanas are used extensively in desserts, pastries, and confections. They are often soaked in rum or brandy to soften them before they are added to baked goods.

rakott palacsinta A Hungarian layered cake of thin crêpelike pancakes stacked alternately with a filling such as walnut and honey, plum jam and walnut, poppy seed, or chocolate with raisins, rum, and candied orange peel. Other fillings include apricot jam with brandy, chocolate and walnuts, or cottage cheese with confectioners' sugar, golden raisins, and lemon zest. The cake is either topped with meringue and baked until lightly browned in a slow oven or sprinkled with sugar and dotted with butter, then baked in a moderate oven until golden. After the cake is cooled, it is cut into wedges to serve. Hungary. See also: palatschinken.

ramekin, ramequin An individual straight-sided deep porcelain or earthenware baking dish, resembling a small soufflé dish. It is smooth on the inside and traditionally has a fluted exterior. Ramekins are used for baking and chilling custards, mousses, and soufflés. They are also used as serving dishes for the desserts that have been baked or chilled in them. Ramekins are available in a variety of sizes ranging from about 2 to 4^1/$_2$ inches wide and 1^1/$_4$ to 2 inches deep. They are available at cookware shops. See also: soufflé dish.

ras gulla See roshgulla.

ras malai A traditional Indian dessert of subtly flavored, delicate cheese balls or patties simmered in syrup until they puff up like dumplings. They are served cold with a thick cream sauce, garnished with almonds and pistachio nuts. India.

raspberry A member of the rose family and a relative of the blackberry, a raspberry is a small oval berry grown on thorny bramble vines. Raspberries range in color from golden to red to dark purple to black; red is the most commonly available. Raspberries are used as an ingredient in many desserts, pastries, and confections, such as fresh fruit tarts, pies, cobblers, mousses, shortcakes, sorbets, and ice creams, and they are used to make dessert sauces, jams, and jellies. Frozen raspberries are available year-round. Fresh raspberries are available from May through November in various parts of the United States. Choose very fragrant, plump, deeply colored, juicy berries without the hull. If the hulls are still attached, it means the berries were picked too soon and will be tart. Avoid berries with any signs of mold or rot. Store fresh raspberries in a single layer in the refrigerator for up to 2 days. If necessary, quickly rinse the berries just before use. See also: berry.

raspberry sauce A thick but pourable mixture of puréed fresh or defrosted frozen raspberries blended with sugar, lemon juice, and often kirschwasser, framboise, or Chambord. Raspberry sauce is used as a garnish for desserts, ice creams, and pastries. See also: Chambord, coulis, framboise, and kirschwasser.

ratafia A sweet liqueur made by macerating fruit or fruit and nut kernels in sugar and alcohol. Black cherries, black currants, raspberries, and almonds are some of the traditional ingredients used. Ratafia essence is made from oil of almonds. Ratafia and ratafia essence are used to flavor desserts, pastries, and confections. Ratafia is also a sweet almond-flavored macaroon.

ravanie, revaní A classic Greek nut cake. While still warm, the light and airy cake is soaked with a honey syrup flavored with orange or lemon juice, orange or lemon zest, and orange flower water, which infuses the cake with its rich, sweet flavors. Greece. See also: orange flower water and zest.

reamer See citrus reamer.

refrigerator cookie This type of cookie is made by shaping the cookie dough into a log, chilling it in the refrigerator until firm, then slicing rounds off the log for baking. These are also called icebox cookies. See also: cookie and dough.

rehrücken A classic delicate chocolate and almond Austrian cake baked in a specially designed long curved mold and to resemble the shape of a saddle of venison. The cake is covered with a shiny chocolate glaze and decorated with rows of blanched whole or slivered almonds, which are spiked into the top to look like the fat with which a real roast of venison is larded. Austria.

rehrücken mold This specialized baking pan, made of tinned steel or aluminum, is used to make the Austrian "mock saddle of venison" cake. It resembles a long loaf pan, except it is curved like a half-moon and has deep indentations across it. Some pans also have a deep groove lengthwise down the center, to represent the bone of the saddle of venison. The curved, ridged pattern is baked into the cake, giving it its characteristic look. A rehrücken mold is 10 to 14 inches long, 4¹/₂ inches wide, and 2¹/₂ inches deep. The molds are available at cookware shops and through mail order cookware catalogs.

Reine de Saba A French chocolate and almond cake, **Reine de Saba,** which translates as "Queen of Sheba," is a dense, rich, moist, single layer cake covered with a thin layer of ganache cream and topped with a shiny poured chocolate glaze. The cake is decorated with toasted sliced almonds. It is important not to overbake the cake, or it will not have its characteristic creamy center. France. See also: cake.

REINE DE SABA

One 9-inch round cake; 12 to 14 servings

1 tablespoon unsalted butter, softened, for the pan
1 tablespoon all-purpose flour, for the pan

Cake
6 ounces bittersweet chocolate, finely chopped
6 ounces (1½ sticks) unsalted butter, softened
1 cup plus 1 tablespoon granulated sugar
4 large eggs, separated, at room temperature
½ cup finely ground almonds
1 large egg white, at room temperature
1 cup all-purpose flour

Ganache cream
8 ounces bittersweet chocolate, finely chopped
¾ cup heavy whipping cream
6 ounces (1½ sticks) unsalted butter, softened

Chocolate glaze
8 ounces bittersweet chocolate, finely chopped
¾ cup heavy whipping cream

½ to ¾ cup toasted sliced almonds, for decoration

Position a rack in the center of the oven and preheat to 350°F. Butter the inside of a 9-inch round pan with the softened butter, and butter a 9-inch parchment paper round. Dust the pan with the flour, tap out the excess, and place the parchment paper round in the bottom of the pan, butter side up.

For the cake, melt the chocolate in the top of a double boiler set over hot, not simmering, water, stirring frequently with a rubber spatula to ensure even melting.

Meanwhile, in the bowl of a stand mixer, using the flat beater attachment, or in a large mixing bowl, using a hand-held mixer, beat the butter until light and fluffy, about 2 minutes. Add 1 cup of the sugar and blend very well. Add the egg yolks, 1 at a time, beating well after each addition. Blend in the ground almonds, stopping occasionally to scrape down the sides of the bowl with a rubber spatula.

Remove the top of the double boiler from the water and wipe the outside dry. Pour the melted chocolate into the egg mixture and blend thoroughly.

In the bowl of a stand mixer, using the wire whip attachment, or in a grease-free mixing bowl, using grease-free beaters, whip the 5 egg whites on medium-high speed until frothy. Add the remaining 1 tablespoon sugar and whip until the whites hold stiff, but not dry, peaks. Fold the flour and whipped egg whites alternately into the chocolate mixture. The batter will be very thick and dense.

Scrape the batter into the prepared cake pan and use a rubber spatula to spread it smoothly and evenly in the pan. Bake for 40 minutes, or until the top is slightly cracked and the cake has risen to fill the pan. Transfer the pan to a rack to cool for 15 minutes.

Place a 9-inch cardboard cake circle over the top of the pan. Invert the pan onto the cardboard circle and gently remove the pan. Peel off the parchment paper. (The bottom of the cake is now the top.) Let the cake cool completely, on the round on the rack.

For the ganache cream, melt the chocolate in the top of a double boiler over hot, not simmering, water, stirring frequently with a rubber spatula to ensure even melting.

Meanwhile, in a small saucepan, heat the cream to a boil over medium heat.

Remove both pans from the heat. Remove the top pan of the double boiler and wipe the outside dry. Pour the hot cream into the chocolate, and stir until very smooth. Cover tightly with plastic wrap and let cool to room temperature. Then refrigerate until the consistency of thick pudding, 2 to 3 hours.

If the ganache is chilled longer and the mixture becomes too firm, let it stand at room temperature until the correct consistency.

In the bowl of a stand mixer, using the flat beater attachment, or in a mixing bowl, using a hand-held mixer, beat the softened butter until light and fluffy, about 2 minutes. Add the chocolate mixture a few tablespoons at a time, and blend well. Do not overbeat, or the chocolate will become grainy.

Using an 8-inch or 10-inch flexible-blade spatula, coat the top and sides of the cake with the ganache cream. Smooth and even the top and sides of the cake with the spatula. Chill the cake in the refrigerator for 2 hours or in the freezer for 30 minutes.

For the chocolate glaze, melt the chocolate in the top of a double boiler over hot, not simmering, water, stirring frequently, until the chocolate is very smooth. Meanwhile, in a small saucepan, heat the cream to a boil over medium heat.

Remove both pans from the heat. Remove the top pan of the double boiler and wipe the outside dry. Pour the hot cream into the chocolate, and stir until very smooth.

Line a jelly-roll pan with parchment or waxed paper, and set a cooling rack over the paper. Place the chilled cake on the cooling rack. Starting in the center of the cake and working out to the edge, pour the chocolate glaze in a steady stream over the cake. It should flow smoothly over the top and down the sides; it may be necessary to use the flexible-blade spatula to sweep over the top of the cake to help push the glaze over the sides. Work rapidly, as the glaze begins to set up as soon as it hits the chilled cake and the spatula can leave marks in the glaze. Let the glaze set for about 10 minutes.

Place the toasted almonds on a sheet of parchment or waxed paper. Use a flexible-blade spatula to lift up the cardboard cake circle, and carefully hold up the cake with one hand. With your other hand, press the almonds into the sides of the cake just up to the top edge. Transfer the cake to a serving plate. Place 24 to 26 additional sliced almonds 1 inch apart around the outside top edge of the cake, about 1 inch in from the edge, with the points facing in.

This cake is best served within 4 hours of preparation. It can be held at room temperature, loosely covered, until served. If the cake is refrigerated, the glaze loses its gloss, and it is necessary to bring the cake to room temperature before serving. The cake will keep about 3 days well covered in the refrigerator.

religieuse Translated from the French as "nun," this classic pastry looks something like a nun in her habit. It is composed of two choux puffs filled with chocolate, vanilla, or coffee pastry cream, stacked one on top of the other and frosted with chocolate or coffee icing. Religieuse can be made as a cake in a large size or as an individual pastry. France. See also: choux pastry and pastry cream.

ribbon The term used to describe the consistency of a batter or mixture, such as eggs and sugar, that has been beaten until it is very thick and pale-colored. When the whisk or beater is lifted above the bowl, the batter drops slowly onto the mixture in the bowl in a ribbonlike pattern. This ribbon holds its shape for a few seconds before it sinks into the mixture.

rice flour Rice ground to a very fine powder, used in place of flour in pastries, cakes, custards, and cookies, such as some versions of shortbread. It is also used as a thickening agent.

rice paper An edible, almost transparent paper made from a mixture of water and rice flour or the pith of the rice paper plant or tree, which is native to China. Rice paper is flavorless and comes in rectangular, square, or round sheets. Rice paper has many uses in the dessert kitchen, such as lining the pan and the top of torrone, separating the stacked tiers of wedding cakes, and lining baking sheets. Rice paper should be kept dry, or it will dissolve. It is available in cake decorating supply shops, Asian markets, and supermarkets. See also: torrone.

rice pudding A firm baked custardlike mixture of rice cooked in milk with sugar, raisins or currants, butter, eggs, ground cinnamon, and vanilla extract. One of the characteristics of rice pudding is its creamy texture, which is the result of cooking a small amount of rice very slowly in a large amount of milk. The slow cooking allows the rice to absorb all the milk, which makes it plump and creamy. **Rice pudding** has a rich, golden color. United States.

RICE PUDDING

12 servings

1 tablespoon unsalted butter, softened, for the pan

3 cups milk
½ cup long-grain white rice
½ cup granulated sugar
⅓ cup currants
2 tablespoons finely chopped candied orange peel
½ teaspoon ground cinnamon
Pinch of salt
2 ounces (4 tablespoons) unsalted butter, softened
2 large eggs, at room temperature
2 large egg yolks, at room temperature
1 tablespoon vanilla extract

Generously butter the inside of a 9- by 2-inch round cake pan with the softened butter.

Combine the milk and rice in a 1-quart covered saucepan, and bring to a boil over medium heat. Reduce the heat to low and cook the rice for 1 hour.

Stir the sugar, currants, candied orange peel, cinnamon, salt, and butter into the rice mixture, and cook 30 minutes, or until the liquid is completely absorbed by the rice. Remove from the heat.

Center a rack in the oven and preheat to 325°F.

In the bowl of a stand mixer, using the wire whip attachment, or in a mixing bowl, using a hand-held mixer, beat the eggs and egg yolks together until thick, about 3 minutes. Stir the beaten eggs and vanilla extract into the rice mixture, blending thoroughly.

Scrape the pudding into the prepared pan, and place the pan on a baking sheet. Bake for 35 minutes, or until the pudding is golden brown on top and the sides have slightly pulled away from the pan. Transfer the pan to a rack to cool to room temperature.

Serve the rice pudding at room temperatue, or cover with foil and refrigerate for up to 3 days.

ricotta cheese A rich, sweet, fresh unripened cheese with a light nutty taste. Ricotta is white and moist with slightly grainy clumps. Italian ricotta is made from the whey (liquid) left from making cheese of sheep's milk, such as provolone and mozzarella. In the United States, it is made from cow's milk. Ricotta cheese is available as regular, made from whole milk; low-fat, made from skim milk; and part-skim, made from partially skimmed milk. The low-fat and part-skim varieties have less fat and fewer calories than regular ricotta cheese. They can be substituted for each other in recipes with no noticeable difference in texture. Ricotta may be blended with sugar and served with fresh fruit as a dessert. It is also used as an ingredient in many Italian desserts, such as cheesecake, cannoli, and cassata. Ricotta cheese is highly perishable. It should be kept refrigerated and used within a short time of purchasing. See also: cannoli, cassata, and cheesecake.

Rigó Jancsi A Hungarian chocolate pastry, **Rigó Jancsi** takes its name from a famous nineteenth-century gypsy violinist who, according to legend, broke many hearts. The pastry consists of two layers of rich chocolate cake that enclose a whipped rum- or orange-flavored ganache filling, topped with a chocolate glaze. Rigó Jancsi is cut into squares for serving. Hungary. See also: ganache.

∞∞∞∞∞∞∞∞∞∞

RIGÓ JANCSI

Twenty-four 2-inch squares

Cake
5½ ounces bittersweet chocolate, finely chopped
5 larges eggs, separated, at room temperature
½ cup plus 2 tablespoons granulated sugar
1½ tablespoons instant espresso powder dissolved in 1½ table-
　　spoons warm water
1 teaspoon vanilla extract
Pinch of salt
¼ teaspoon cream of tartar
¼ cup Dutch-processed unsweetened cocoa powder, sifted

Ganache
1¼ pounds bittersweet chocolate, finely chopped
2¼ cups heavy whipping cream
¼ cup dark rum or orange-flavored liqueur
2 teaspoons vanilla extract

Apricot filling
⅓ cup apricot preserves
2 teaspoons dark rum or orange-flavored liqueur

Glaze
3 ounces bittersweet chocolate, finely chopped
⅓ cup plus 1 tablespoon heavy whipping cream

Decoration
3 ounces bittersweet chocolate, finely chopped

Center a rack in the oven and preheat to 375°F. Line a jelly-roll pan with a sheet of parchment paper.

For the cake, melt the chocolate in the top of a double boiler over hot, not simmering, water, stirring frequently with a rubber spatula to ensure even melting. Remove from the heat.

In the bowl of a stand mixer, using the wire whip attachment, or in a mixing bowl, using a hand-held mixer, beat the egg yolks with 2 tablespoons of the sugar until very thick and pale-colored and the mixture holds a slowly dissolving ribbon when the beater is lifted, about 5 minutes. Fold in the melted chocolate, espresso, vanilla extract, and salt.

In a grease-free mixing bowl, using grease-free beaters, beat the egg whites with the cream of tartar until frothy. Gradually sprinkle on the remaining 1/2 cup sugar, and continue beating until the whites hold stiff, but not dry, peaks.

Fold the whites into the yolk mixture in 4 additions. Turn the batter out into the prepared pan, and spread it evenly and smoothly. Bake for 10 minutes, then reduce the oven temperature to 350°F and bake for 10 minutes longer, or until the top of the cake cracks slightly when touched. Transfer to a rack to cool.

When the cake is cool, dust the top with the cocoa powder.

For the ganache, melt the chocolate in the top of a double boiler over hot, not simmering, water, stirring frequently to ensure even melting.

Meanwhile, in a small saucepan, heat the cream to a boil over medium heat.

Remove both pans from the heat. Remove the top of the double boiler and wipe the outside dry. Pour the chocolate into a large mixing bowl. Add the hot cream, and stir until thoroughly blended. Stir in the rum or orange liqueur and vanilla extract and blend well. Cover tightly with plastic wrap, and let cool to room temperature. Then refrigerate until it reaches the consistency of thick pudding, 2 to 3 hours. If the ganache is chilled longer and the mixture becomes too firm, let it stand at room temperature until it reaches the correct consistency.

In the bowl of a stand mixer, using the flat beater attachment, or in a mixing bowl, using a hand-held beater, beat the chilled ganache until fluffy, about 1 minute. Do not overbeat, or the chocolate will become grainy.

Run a sharp knife around the edges of the cake. Cover the cake with a sheet of waxed paper and place another jelly-roll pan over the cake, bottom side down. Invert the cake onto the pan, and gently peel the parchment paper off the cake. Cut the cake in half crosswise. Place one-half on an 8- by 12-inch cardboad rectangle.

For the filling, in a small bowl, combine the apricot preserves and rum or orange liqueur and blend well.

Spread the apricot filling over 1 of the cake layers. Spread the beaten ganache over the apricot layer. Position the second cake layer evenly over the ganache, and press gently on the cake layer.

Cover a jelly-roll pan with a sheet of parchment or waxed paper. Place a cooling rack over the paper and transfer the assembled cake onto the rack. Refrigerate the cake while you prepare the glaze.

For the chocolate glaze, melt the chocolate in the top of a double boiler over hot, not simmering, water, stirring frequently with a rubber spatula to ensure even melting. *continued*

Meanwhile, in a medium saucepan, heat the cream to a boil over medium heat.

Remove both pans from the heat. Remove the top of the double boiler and wipe the outside dry. Pour the cream into the chocolate, and stir for about 5 minutes to blend thoroughly and cool the mixture.

Starting from I long edge, pour the glaze in a steady stream over the chilled cake, using a flexible-blade spatula to sweep over the top I or 2 times to spread the glaze. Work rapidly, as the glaze begins to set up.

For the decoration, melt the chocolate in the top of a double boiler over hot, not simmering, water, stirring frequently. Add a drop or 2 of water to the chocolate and stir to blend well. (This should slightly thicken the chocolate.) Pour the chocolate into a paper pastry cone, fold down the top edges, and snip a tiny opening in the pointed end.

Pipe several thin, parallel lines across the top of the cake about ½ inch apart. Draw the tip of a toothpick or a sharp knife at I-inch intervals across the cake in the opposite direction, at a right angle to the lines to create a feathered effect. Then repeat this motion in the opposite direction in even intervals. Wipe the toothpick or knife clean after each pull.

Refrigerate the cake for 20 minutes to set the glaze. Using a knife dipped in hot water and then dried, slice the cake into 2-inch squares. The cake will keep well covered in the refrigerator for 2 days, but it tastes best served at room temperature.

rolled cookie A cookie made by rolling out a firm dough to an even thickness with a rolling pin, then cutting it into various shapes with individual cookie cutters or a decoratively carved rolling cookie cutter before baking. See also: cookie, cookie cutter, and dough.

rolled fondant An icing made from confectioners' sugar, gelatin, glucose or corn syrup, and glycerin that is similar in texture to pastry dough. Some recipes for **rolled fondant** call for a small amount of solid white vegetable shortening. Rolled fondant is mixed, kneaded until very smooth and pliable, and rolled out with a rolling pin. It is draped over cakes that are either covered with a layer of marzipan or iced with buttercream. The fondant sets firm on top but remains moist inside. Rolled fondant gives cakes a satiny-smooth, alabasterlike surface for decorating, as well as helps to keep cakes moist for several days by sealing them from exposure to air. Rolled fondant is traditionally used in the British, Australian, and South African styles of cake decorating as the background for delicate filigree-lace designs, extension work, made-ahead pieces of extremely fine line designs of icing that extend from the sides of the cake, porcelainlike flowers, and designs made with various crimpers. Rolled fondant is most often used to cover wedding and other celebration cakes. It is also shaped into flowers and ribbons for cake decorations. United Kingdom. See also: crimper and marzipan.

ROLLED FONDANT

2½ pounds; enough to cover a 10- by 3-inch round cake

2 pounds confectioners' sugar, sifted, plus additional if necessary
¼ cup water
2 scant tablespoons powdered gelatin
½ cup glucose
2 tablespoons glycerin
2 to 3 tablespoons sifted cornstarch, for kneading
2 to 3 drops clear flavoring, such as kirschwasser
Few drops of paste food coloring (optional)

Place the sifted confectioners' sugar in the bowl of a stand mixer or in a large mixing bowl, and make a well in the center.

Place the water in a small saucepan, and sprinkle on the gelatin. Let sit for 5 minutes, then heat over very low heat just until the gelatin is dissolved, about 3 minutes.

Add the glucose and glycerin to the dissolved gelatin and blend well. Pour this mixture into the well in the sugar, and mix with the flat beater attachment or with a hand-held mixer on low speed to a doughlike consistency, about 5 minutes. Stop to scrape down the beaters a few times with a rubber spatula.

Transfer the fondant to a smooth surface lightly dusted with cornstarch, and knead for several minutes, until it is smooth and pliable. Add the flavoring and any desired color, and knead until thoroughly blended. If the fondant is too soft, knead in more sifted confectioners' sugar. If it is too stiff, add boiling water a drop at a time until it is pliable.

Use the fondant immediately, or store it in an airtight container at room temperature for up to a week or in the refrigerator for up to 3 weeks. If refrigerated, bring the fondant to room temperature before using it.

To cover a cake with the fondant, on a smooth surface dusted with confectioners' sugar, roll it out to a large round about 14 to 16 inches in diameter between ⅛ and ¼ inch thick. Gently roll the fondant up around the rolling pin, and carefully unroll it over the cake. Use your hands to smooth the fondant and fit it to the sides of the cake. Eliminate any air bubbles or folds in the fondant by pressing them down and out with your hands. Cut off the excess fondant at the bottom of the cake.

rolling cookie cutter See cookie cutter.

rolling pin A long, thick, smooth cylinder designed for rolling out dough. Some rolling pins have handles at each end of the cylinder. Standard rolling pins are 2 to 3½ inches thick and 12 to 18 inches long. A heavy-duty rolling pin is the most efficient for rolling out dough because its weight allows the rolling pin to do most of the work. Rolling pins are made of many materials: glass, ceramic, marble, Teflon, brass, copper, stainless steel, plastic, and wood. Hardwood, such as boxwood or beechwood, is the preferred material for rolling pins because of its weight and strength. Marble rolling pins are ideal for rolling doughs with a high butter content, because marble stays cool longer than other materials. Some cooks prefer to use a glass rolling pin with a hollow center they can fill with ice cubes to keep the dough cool. There are several specialized types of rolling pins. An American rolling pin is made of heavy hardwood with handles at each end and a steel shaft down the center that spins on ball bearings. This makes the rolling action smooth and consistent. A French rolling pin is a solid hardwood cylinder with no handles, 2 inches thick and 20 inches long. It is the preference of many professional bakers and pastry cooks, who believe it allows them to feel the thickness of the dough and gives them more control than a rolling pin with handles. There is also a tapered French hardwood rolling pin, which is thick in the center and tapers out to each end. This design makes it easy to rotate the pin and to roll out circles of dough. A Tarla is a versatile hardwood rolling pin covered with a thin sheet of copper, with short knob handles. It works very well with doughs with a high butter content, maintaining a coolness similar to marble. It also works well for rolling out hot brittle mixtures, such as nougatine and krokant, because it does not stick to the brittle. A caramel rolling pin is a long ribbed aluminum cylinder that is used to roll out caramel. A nougat rolling pin is a long cylinder of solid steel, used for rolling out the nut brittles nougatine and krokant. A tutové is a French heavy-duty rolling pin, made of either hardwood or plastic, that has deep horizontal ribs in the cylinder. It is designed for distributing butter evenly between layers of dough, such as puff pastry and crois-sant dough. A springerle rolling pin, used for the German anise seed cookies, has etched designs that imprint the dough as it rolls. Marzipan rolling pins are hollow cylinders made of either plastic or steel, which are textured, ribbed, or grooved to form patterns and designs on the marzipan. A plastic basket-weave rolling pin imprints a woven pattern on pastry dough, marzipan, gum paste, or rolled fondant. Flatbread rolling pins are used to make traditional notched and grooved designs in Scandinavian flatbreads. Rolling pins, especially those made of wood, should be wiped off and dried after use, never soaked in water or put in the dishwasher. See also: gum paste, krokant, marzipan, nouga-tine, puff pastry, and rolled fondant.

Rome Beauty apple The preferred apple for baking whole because it holds its shape. Rome Beauties have dark red skin and tender, juicy, sweet-tart flesh. Rome Beauty apples are available from November to June. See also: apple.

Rosalinda A pastry named for the character Rosalind in Shakespeare's *As You Like It*. Rosalindas are composed of two 3-inch round biscuits, similar to ladyfingers, sandwiched together with rose water– or kirsch-scented whipped cream, brushed with apricot glaze, and covered in pink rose water– or kirsch-flavored fondant. Rosalindas are usually served on a platter accompanied by other similar pastries: Desdemonas, Iagos, and Othellos, all named for Shakespearean characters. United Kingdom. See also: Desdemona, fondant, glaze, Iago, kirschwasser, ladyfingers, Othello, and rose water.

rosette A fried pastry made from a thin, rich batter that is formed into different shapes with a rosette iron, then deep fried in hot oil. After they are drained on paper towels, rosettes are usually sprinkled with confectioners' sugar while still warm. A rosette is also a design made from icing or whipped cream, used to decorate cakes and pastries. It is made using a pastry bag fitted with a star-shaped tip. It is created by holding the pastry bag about an inch above the surface to be decorated and, while squeezing the bag to push out the icing, making a tight swirl of the wrist in a counterclockwise direction. See also: pastry bag, pastry tip, and rosette iron.

rosette iron This specialized utensil is an L-shaped metal rod held by a wood or plastic handle. Some irons have two rods held by a single han-dle. A variety of different-shaped metal forms, such as a butterfly, a star, or a snowflake, can be fitted onto the end of the rod. The form is dipped into rosette batter, then deep-fried, forming a pastry of that shape. Cuplike forms, called timbales, are also available. These deep-fried shapes can be filled with custard, mousse, or fruit for desserts. If the tool comes with these cups, it is called a timbale iron or a rosette-timbale iron. Rosette and timbale irons are available at cookware shops, in cookware sections of department stores, and through mail order cookware catalogs. See also: rosette.

rose water Pure rose oil or essence, distilled from rose petals, is distilled to make rose water. It is an intensely fragrant, pale pink, floral water used to flavor and scent pastries, desserts, and confections. It has been in use for centuries and is widely used in the cuisines of India, Turkey, Asia, and the Middle East. It is an essential ingredient in the Turkish candy rahat loukoum, also called Turkish delight. Rose water is very powerful and should be used sparingly. See also: essence and Turkish delight.

roshgulla Also called ras gulla, this is a Bengal sweet made from fresh Indian-style cottage cheese, called chenna, kneaded with flour to make it light and spongy. The mixture is formed into small round balls and cooked in a sweet syrup flavored with rose water. The balls are cooled and served with the cooking syrup. Bangladesh. See also: rose water.

rotary beater Used like an electric mixer for whipping air into mixtures such as egg whites, cream, and light batters, a rotary beater is a hand-powered utensil. It consists of two teardrop-shaped beaters made of thin ($^1/_4$ inch wide), flat metal strips connected to a center metal shaft, topped by a gear-driven wheel with a hand crank. A handle is either on the top or the side of the wheel. The entire utensil is about a foot long and 3 to 4 inches wide. When the hand crank turns the wheel the beaters rotate. The speed of the beaters is determined by the speed at which the wheel is cranked. It takes two hands to operate this utensil, one to hold it upright and the other to crank the wheel. Good quality rotary beaters have beaters made of stainless-steel with nylon gears. Poor quality rotary beaters have beaters made of chromed steel, cast aluminum, or plastic with metal gears. Be sure to buy a rotary beater with a smooth rotary action. Poorly made rotary beaters work sporadically and the parts jam often. Rotary beaters are available in cookware shops, the cookware section of department stores, and supermarkets.

roulade A sponge cake, génoise, or a similar cake made without butter and with the addition of whipped egg whites that are folded into the batter to lighten it. The cake is baked in a jelly-roll pan and rolled up tightly while still warm. When cool, the cake is unrolled, spread with buttercream, jam, whipped cream, lemon cream, whipped ganache, or one of many other fillings, and rerolled. The cake is dusted with confectioners' sugar or covered with buttercream, whipped ganache, or whipped cream and decorated. A roulade is the basis for many cakes, such as **spicy pumpkin roulade** and Bûche de Noël, the classic Christmas cake. France. See also: Bûche de Noël, buttercream, ganache, and jelly-roll cake.

∞∞∞∞∞∞∞∞∞∞

SPICY PUMPKIN ROULADE

One 15-inch-long cake; 12 to 14 servings

1 tablespoon unsalted butter, softened, for the pan

Cake
4 large eggs, at room temperature
1⅓ cups granulated sugar
¾ cup canned pumpkin purée
1¼ teaspoons freshly squeezed lemon juice
1 cup all-purpose flour
1½ teaspoons baking powder
2½ teaspoons ground cinnamon
1½ teaspoons ground ginger
¾ teaspoon freshly grated nutmeg
½ teaspoon salt
1⅓ cups finely chopped walnuts
Confectioners' sugar, for dusting

Filling
2 cups heavy whipping cream
2 tablespoons confectioners' sugar, sifted
1½ teaspoons vanilla extract
½ teaspoon ground cinnamon
¼ teaspoon ground ginger
¼ teaspoon freshly grated nutmeg

12 walnut halves
Candied orange peel for garnish (optional)

Center a rack in the oven and preheat to 375°F. Line a jelly-roll pan with a sheet of parchment paper, and butter the paper with the softened butter.

For the cake, in the bowl of a stand mixer, using the wire whip attachment, or in a large mixing bowl, using a hand-held mixer, whip the eggs on medium-high speed until they are very thick and pale and hold a slowly dissolving ribbon when the beaters are lifted, about 5 minutes. Gradually beat in the sugar, blending well. Then blend in the pumpkin and lemon juice.

In another bowl, combine the flour, baking powder, cinnamon, ginger, nutmeg, and salt. Fold the dry ingredients into the pumpkin mixture in 3 additions, blending thoroughly after each addition. Fold in 1 cup of the walnuts. *continued*

Turn the batter out into the prepared pan. Use an offset spatula to spread the batter smoothly and evenly in the pan. Sprinkle the remaining ⅓ cup of walnuts over the batter. Bake for 15 to 18 minutes, until the cake is light golden and the top springs back when touched.

Remove the pan from the oven, and use a sharp knife to loosen the edges of the cake. Lay a kitchen towel on a work surface, cover it with a sheet of parchment paper, and dust the parchment paper lightly with confectioners' sugar. Turn the cake out onto the parchment, and gently peel the paper off the cake. Starting from a long end, immediately roll up the cake and parchment paper tightly in the towel. Let the cake cool completely, rolled in the towel.

For the filling, in a chilled bowl, using chilled beaters, whip the cream until it holds soft peaks. Add the confectioners' sugar, vanilla extract, and spices, and whip the cream until it holds firm peaks.

Unroll the cake and remove the towel. Trim off any rough edges. Use an offset spatula to spread one quarter of the cream evenly over the cake. Roll up the cake, using the parchment paper as a guide: To make a tight roll, roll the parchment paper over the top of the cake, leaving a piece to hold from underneath the cake. Wedge a ruler against the cake and push away from yourself, while pulling the bottom end of the parchment toward you.

Place the roulade on a rectangular serving plate, seam side down, and discard the parchment paper. Fit a 14-inch pastry bag with a #3 large closed star tip and fill with the whipped cream. Pipe parallel rows of cream from one end of the roulade to the other, starting from the bottom and moving toward the top. Turn the serving plate around and pipe cream up the other side of the roulade. With the remaining whipped cream, pipe a row of 12 rosettes down the center of the roulade. Place 1 walnut half in the center of each rosette, and, if desired, decorate the rosettes with candied orange peel.

Refrigerate the roulade until ready to serve. Slice the roulade into serving pieces. It is best not to assemble the roulade more than 3 hours before serving.

Royal Anne cherry See cherry.

royal icing An icing made from confectioners' sugar, egg whites or dried meringue powder, and a few drops of lemon juice, which dries to a rock-hard finish. Royal icing is used for long-lasting delicate cake decorations, such as fine line piping and flowers. The icing can be tinted with food coloring. United States.

rubber spatula A spatula with a thin, flat, flexible, rectangular solid rubber or plastic blade attached to a handle. The blade is curved at one top corner and squared at the other. Some spatulas have wooden handles and others are a one-piece design with the rubber blade and a plastic handle molded together. These one-piece spatulas can be safely cleaned in the dishwasher. There is also a rubber spoon-shaped spatula, called a spoonola, with a deeper, more rounded blade. Rubber spatulas range from $9^1/2$ to $16^1/2$ inches long, their blades from 2 to $3^1/2$ inches wide and $3^1/4$ to 5 inches long. A rubber spatula is used to scrape batters and doughs from the sides of mixing bowls and for folding, mixing, and blending ingredients.

rugelach Eastern European cookies made with a rich cream cheese dough that is cut into triangles and rolled up around a filling to form crescent shapes. The filling can be jam, poppy seed, raisins and nuts, chocolate, nuts and cinnamon, or fruit. Poland.

rum An alcoholic spirit distilled from fermented sugarcane juice or molasses, made primarily in the Caribbean countries of Barbados, Cuba, Guyana, Jamaica, Puerto Rico, and Trinidad. Rum comes in two main types: white or silver, which is clear and light-bodied, and golden or amber, which is deeply colored and flavored. Dark Jamaican rum is especially richly flavored and may have caramel added to darken its color. Rum is used to flavor many desserts, pastries, and confections. Barbados, Cuba, Guyana, Jamaica, Puerto Rico, and Trinidad.

sabayon See zabaglione.

sablé The French word for sand, sablé refers to a classic cookie or small cake made from a delicate, crumbly, sandy dough. Sablés originated in the Normandy region of France. They are flavored in different ways, with the addition of ground almonds or other nuts and orange or lemon zest. France. See also: pâte sablée.

saccharometer A specially designed instrument for measuring the density or specific gravity of sugar dissolved in water to make a syrup, which determines whether the syrup is at the correct concentration for its various uses, such as the base of a sorbet or a poaching liquid. The saccharometer consists of two parts, a glass tube and the hydrometer, which has a weighted bulb on its lower end with graduated lines across its body to indicate the density. The tube is partially filled with the sugar syrup, then the hydrometer is lowered into the solution, where it floats. The line on the hydrometer that corresponds to the surface of the syrup indicates its density. The degree of density is expressed in the decimal system, also called the Brix scale. See also: Brix scale.

Sachertorte A dense, thin, very rich chocolate cake that is either filled with or coated with apricot preserves. The cake is iced with a satiny-smooth poured chocolate glaze and "Sacher" is written on top with piping chocolate. Sachertorte is usually served with a dollop of whipped cream, *schlag* in German. This world-famous torte was created in 1832 by Franz Sacher, the Austrian pastry chef to Prince Metternich. In the 1950s a great rivalry developed between the Hotel Sacher and Demel's pastry shop in Vienna, Austria, as to the authenticity of their recipes for Sachertorte. Both claimed versions passed down from the descendants of Franz Sacher. A court decision gave the Hotel Sacher the right to top each of their tortes with a chocolate emblem that states it is the "genuine" Sachertorte. Austria. See also: chocolate glaze, glaze, piping chocolate, and schlag.

sacristain A small sweet made from a twisted stick of puff pastry that is coated with granulated sugar and chopped raw almonds before baking. France.

safflower oil Flavorless, colorless, cholesterol-free safflower oil, pressed from safflower seeds, has the highest level of polyunsaturates of any oil. It is one of the main oils used to make margarine. It can be used as an ingredient in desserts, pastries, and confections, and its high smoke point makes it an excellent choice for frying. Safflower oil can be used interchangeably with other vegetable oils, such as canola, corn, olive, soybean, and sunflower. It is widely available at supermarkets and health food stores. Store it tightly capped in a cool, dark place for up to a year. It will not turn cloudy and thicken when refrigerated as other oils do. See also: fats and oils, margarine, and smoke point.

saffron The world's most expensive spice, saffron is the dried stigma of crocus flowers. Each flower produces only three of the golden strands, which are handpicked and dried. Saffron's characteristic yellow-orange color is used to tint many Middle Eastern and Indian desserts and confections and some Western European cakes and breads. Saffron has been used for centuries; it was brought to the Western world by Arab traders and the Crusaders returning from their sojourns to the Middle East. The saffron cakes still made today in Cornwall, England, are considered a direct descendant from the Crusaders because they are very similar to the cakes made from recipes brought back by them. Saffron is available either in strands or ground to a fine powder. The strands are preferable because the powder is too often in fact actually a less-expensive spice, turmeric. The strands are crushed and added directly to a dessert or are first steeped in boiling water, which releases their delicate aroma, flavor, and red-orange color. The soaking water is then used in the dessert or confection. Saffron is best stored in an airtight container in a cool, dark, dry place. Because it loses its flavor quickly, it is best to buy saffron in small quantities.

safra Translated from the Arabic as "yellow," this is a semolina and date cake with honey syrup. A filling made of a thick paste of a date mixture spiced with cinnamon and cloves is spread between two layers of a sweet semolina mixture. The top of the cake is scored in a diamond pattern and a blanched almond or whole clove is pressed into each diamond, then the cake is baked until golden. A hot syrup of sugar, honey, water, and lemon juice is poured over the still-warm cake, and it is left to soak in the syrup. This cake is traditionally served at afternoon tea or coffee or as a snack. Libya.

salambô An individual round pastry made from a choux pastry puff and filled with kirsch-flavored pastry cream. The top is dipped in hot caramel or iced with green fondant and sprinkled with shaved chocolate. The pastry, created in the late nineteenth century, takes its name from a character in an opera. France. See also: caramel, choux pastry, fondant, and pastry cream.

Sally Lunns These rich, sweet yeast-risen buns are British classics. They are made of flour, eggs, yeast, cream, sugar, and flavorings such as lemon and nutmeg. Sally Lunns are traditionally served warm, split in half, and spread with butter or whipped cream. There is confusion as to their origin. Some sources claim that a French pastry cook named Sally Lunn invented the sweet buns in Bath, England, during the eighteenth century. Other sources claim that the name is a corruption of the name of a French cake, "sol et lune." Still other sources claim the name comes from an Alsatian sweet bread called solilmeme, a type of brioche that is richer than Sally Lunns. Whatever the origin, Sally Lunns are a popular sweet bun served in many bakeries and tea rooms throughout England. United Kingdom. See also: brioche.

salt Salt, or sodium chloride, is a naturally occurring edible white crystalline compound used to preserve and enhance the flavor of food. It is often used to heighten the flavor of desserts, pastries, and confections. Salt has been a highly prized commodity for thousands of years. It comes from salt mines or from the sea. There are many types of salt: Table salt is fine-grained and flows freely because of additives that prevent it from clumping. Iodized salt is table salt with the addition of iodine, which is a trace element essential to the human diet. Rock salt, an unrefined inedible gray salt, which comes in large chunky crystal, is valued for its ability to retain cold and heat. One of its many uses is to help freeze ice cream. Kosher salt, which has large crystals, and sea salt, which can be either coarse or fine-grained, are very flavorful salts sprinkled on rolls, breads, and pretzels before baking, among other uses. Kosher salt and sea salt contain no additives and are about half as salty as table salt. Sea salt, as its name implies, comes from seawater that has evaporated. Salt will last indefinitely if kept in a cool, dry place. Most types of salt are readily available in supermarkets, health food stores, and specialty food shops.

Salzburger nockerl A specialty dessert from Salzburg, Austria, Salzburger nockerl is a sweet soufflé flavored with lemon zest and vanilla. Traditionally it is baked in three mounds in an oblong dish and served hot, dusted with confectioners' sugar. Austria. See also: soufflé.

Sambuca A colorless, slightly sweet Italian liqueur, with a pronounced licorice flavor that comes from anise seed. Sambuca is used to flavor desserts, pastries, and confections. Italy. See also: anise seed.

sambusik Middle Eastern crescent-shaped pastries filled with a mixture of walnuts and sugar. Thin 2-inch-diameter circles of sweet pastry dough are filled with the nut mixture, then folded in half and the edges sealed to form a half-moon. The pastries are baked until light golden, then dipped into a cool honey syrup flavored with lemon and rose water. Lebanon. See also: rose water.

sanding sugar See crystal sugar.

sandkage Literally "sand cake," this is a traditional Danish cake that is tender, moist, and delicate. It is rich with butter, eggs, and sugar, and its usual flavoring is brandy. One of the cake's distinguishing characteristics is that is contains potato flour, which adds to its tenderness. Sandkage is usually baked in a loaf shape like pound cake. The cake is not iced, but garnished with a light dusting of confectioners' sugar. In Sweden the same cake is called *sandkaka*. Denmark.

sanwin makin A Myanmarese (Burmese) semolina cake or pudding from the major port city of Bassein, in the southern part of the country. Semolina flour is mixed with coconut milk, ghee (clarified butter), and sesame seeds, then flavored with cardamom and raisins. The cake is broiled briefly to brown the top, then baked until set and golden. After cooling, it is cut into slices or diamond-shaped pieces. Myanmar.

Sarah Bernhardt A classic individual pastry created in Denmark in honor of the popular nineteenth-century actress. The pastry consists of an almond macaroon topped with a cone of rich chocolate ganache, all enrobed in dark chocolate. Denmark. See also: ganache and macaroon.

savarin A rich, sweet, yeast-risen cake that is traditionally baked in a shallow ring mold. The cake is soaked with a rum or kirsch syrup after baking and brushed with apricot glaze, and the center opening is filled with pastry cream or crème Chantilly. Savarin is decorated with candied cherries and angelica or with fresh fruit. Savarin can be made in either individual or large size. It is made from the same dough that is used for babas, but without raisins. Savarin is named after the legendary culinarian Brillat-Savarin. France. See also: angelica, baba, crème Chantilly, and pastry cream.

scale A kitchen tool used to determine the accurate weight of ingredients. There are three types of scales: spring, balance, and electronic. The spring scale has a bowl or pan that sits on a platform. It reads in either ounces and pounds or grams and kilos, or both. A spring scale uses a spring device attached to a dial that registers the weight when an ingredient is placed in the weighing bowl or pan. A spring scale can be set to a zero reading while ingredients are on the platform, so that each new ingredient added can be accurately weighed. Spring scales have a tendency to lose their elasticity over time, which can result in less accurate measurement. Spring scales can measure up to $4^1/2$ pounds. They are generally made of plastic, and some have a bowl that fits over the platform, which acts as a cover when the scale is not in use.

There are two kinds of balance scales. The first type has two round trays held by arms on each side of a platform. One of the trays holds the ingredient and the other holds weights of various sizes, which, when balanced with the ingredient, show its weight. Another type of balance scale is called a beam-balance. It has a rectangular pan that sits on top of the platform, with two bars beneath it, similar to the scales found in a doctor's office. Weights are moved back and forth along these beams until they balance, which shows the weight of the ingredient. Beam-balance scales measure in ounces and pounds or grams and kilos. Balance scales can measure up to 22 pounds and are usually made of metal.

Electronic scales display a digital readout of the weight of the ingredient. They are battery operated, made of plastic, and extremely accurate. They can be reset to a zero reading while ingredients are on the platform, so that each new ingredient added can be accurately weighed. Electronic scales can weigh up to 10 pounds. Scales are available at cookware shops, at restaurant supply shops, and through mail order cookware catalogs.

schlag The German word for whipped cream, which is traditionally served with German and Austrian pastries, cakes, and coffee drinks.

scone A Scottish quick bread originally made with oats and cooked on a griddle either on the top of the stove or over an open fire. Scones were traditionally triangular-shaped. Today's scones are made with wheat flour, are baked, and come in several shapes: round, square, and triangular. Scones are soft and delicate inside and have a crisp, golden brown exterior. They are usually eaten hot, split in half, and spread with butter, jam, or clotted cream and are traditionally served with afternoon tea or breakfast. Buttermilk and **cream scones** are popular variations of the traditional scone. Confusion about the origin of the name persists. Some sources say the name comes from the Stone (Scone) of Destiny, where the kings of Scotland were traditionally crowned. Other sources say it comes from the Dutch word *schoonbrot*, meaning "beautiful bread." Scotland.

CREAM SCONES

Approximately sixteen 2½-inch round scones or twelve 3-inch triangular scones

2½ cups all-purpose flour
1 tablespoon plus 2 teaspoons baking powder
2 tablespoons granulated sugar
Pinch of salt
3 ounces (6 tablespoons) unsalted butter, cut into pieces
    and chilled
⅓ cup currants or raisins
Zest of 1 large orange
2 large eggs, at room temperature
¾ cup heavy whipping cream
1 large egg yolk beaten with 2 tablespoons cream, for egg wash

Position the oven racks in the upper and lower thirds of the oven and preheat to 450°F. Line two baking sheets with parchment paper.

In the work bowl of a food processor fitted with the steel blade, combine the flour, baking powder, 1 tablespoon plus 1 teaspoon of the sugar, and the salt. Pulse for 5 seconds to blend. Add the butter and pulse until the butter is cut into tiny pieces, resembling a coarse meal, about 30 seconds. Add the currants or raisins and orange zest.

In a small bowl, lightly beat the eggs. Blend in the cream. With the machine running, add the cream mixture through the feed tube, and process until the dough forms a ball, about 30 seconds.

Turn the dough out onto a floured work surface. Dust the dough with flour and roll it out to a thickness of ¾ inch. Brush off the excess flour. Use a 2¼-inch round cutter to cut out circles, and transfer the rounds to the lined baking sheets, leaving 1 inch space between them. Or, to make triangular-shaped scones, cut out 6-inch circles, then cut each circle into quarters. Transfer the triangles to the lined baking sheets, leaving 1 inch space between them. Gather the scraps together, reroll, and cut into scones.

Brush the tops of the scones with the egg wash, then sprinkle them with the remaining 2 teaspoons sugar. Bake the scones for 7 minutes, switch the positions of the baking sheets, and bake for 5 to 7 minutes longer until golden brown. Transfer the baking sheets to racks to cool slightly.

Serve the scones warm. They will keep for 3 days at room temperature in an airtight container or wrapped in foil. Warm in a 300°F oven before serving.

scrape down To remove batter or dough from the sides of a mixing bowl by using a rubber or plastic spatula or pastry scraper. The spatula or pastry scraper is run around the side of the bowl under the batter or dough, gathering it up, and the dough or batter is added to the bulk of the dough or batter in the bowl. See also: pastry scraper and spatula.

seafoam See divinity.

seffa A Moroccan specialty, seffa is made with couscous, a tiny grain pellet made from hard semolina wheat. For this dish, the couscous is cooked with butter, then flavored with cinnamon, sugar, and orange flower water. It is served for dessert, mounded on a platter. Morocco.

semifreddo Translated from the Italian as "half-cold," semifreddo is a chilled or frozen mousselike dessert, similar to ice cream. A semifreddo is frozen in a mold in the freezer, rather than in an ice cream machine. Air is incorporated into a semifreddo through the use of whipped cream, meringue, or whipped eggs in the mixture. A semifreddo is typically layered or mixed with chocolate, fruit, nuts, or crushed cookies and formed into a loaf or a dome shape. The mixture does not freeze thoroughly but has a simultaneous creamy and chunky texture. A complementary fruit, caramel, or chocolate sauce is often served with semifreddo. Semifreddi are made in many flavor combinations and are occasionally used as the filling for a cake made with crisp meringue layers. Italy. See also: ice cream and mousse.

serikaya dengan agar-agar A Malaysian specialty, this coconut-milk jelly candy is made with agar-agar cooked with water, cardamom, and cinnamon. Sugar, coconut milk, and salt are added, and the mixture is simmered until very thick. It is strained, then poured into a rectangular or square mold. After cooling and chilling, the candy is cut into squares. Malaysia. See also: agar-agar and coconut.

sesame balls A Chinese dessert made from a thin batter of glutinous rice powder and water, which is cooked briefly in boiling sugared water. More glutinous rice powder is added to make a soft dough, which is kneaded, then rolled into balls. A hole is made in the center of each ball and filled with sweet bean paste, then the dough is pinched to seal in the filling. The balls are rolled in sesame seeds and deep-fried in hot oil until browned, then drained and cooled slightly before serving. China.

sesame seed Cultivated as early as 3000 B.C. in the Middle East, sesame seed is the seed of an herbaceous plant that is widely grown in Indonesia and East Africa. The seeds came to the United States with African slaves, who called them benne [BEHN nee] seeds. Sesame seeds are tiny and flat with a slightly sweet, nutty taste that is enhanced when toasted. The most widely available sesame seeds are cream-colored, but there are also black and brown sesame seeds, commonly used in Japanese and Middle Eastern cooking. Sesame seeds are widely used for sprinkling on top of breads, cakes, cookies, and pastries, and they are ground and used to make halvah, a classic Middle Eastern confection. Sesame seeds have a very high natural oil content, which gives them a tendency to rancidity. They are best stored in a tightly covered container in the refrigerator. The seeds are also pressed to make oil, which is widely used in Asian and Middle Eastern cuisines. Sesame seeds are available in bulk in health food stores or in packages and jars in supermarkets and specialty food shops.

seven-minute icing A satiny, fluffy meringue icing made with egg whites, sugar, corn syrup, water, and cream of tartar beaten together in a double boiler with a whisk until the icing begins to hold peaks and reaches its billowy texture. This process generally takes about 7 minutes, which gives the icing its name. Many variations of seven-minute icing can be made with the addition of flavorings such as maple syrup, brown sugar, coconut, orange zest, or lemon zest. United States.

Seville orange A bitter orange with rough, thick skin and a very tart, seedy pulp, grown in Spain. Because of their bitter taste, Seville oranges are not eaten raw. They are used primarily for making marmalade and liqueurs, such as Cointreau, Grand Marnier, and Curaçao. See also: citrus fruit, Cointreau, Curaçao, Grand Marnier, and orange.

sfogliatelle These traditional scallop shell–shaped pastries are from Naples, Italy. Made with a type of puff pastry, these individual pastries are flaky and crisp on the outside, with a creamy filling of ricotta cheese and semolina, flavored with vanilla, cinnamon, and candied orange peel. Chocolate is a popular flavor variation for the filling. Another version of sfogliatelle, sfogliatelle frolla, is made with pasta frolla, Italian shortcrust pastry that is similar to French pâte sucrée, instead of flaky pastry. Italy. See also: pasta frolla and pâte sucrée.

sheeter This large machine is used for rolling out dough in professional kitchens. The sheeter uses a wide piece of canvas stretched horizontally between two cylinders that are several feet apart, resembling a small conveyor belt. A set of rollers, similar to the rollers on an old-fashioned washing machine, sits in the center of the sheeter, slightly above the canvas. The dough is rolled between these rollers, dropping gently to the canvas below. The width between the rollers can be adjusted to determine the thickness of the dough. A sheeter is used primarily to make large quantities of puff pastry.

sherbet See sorbet.

sholeh zard An Iranian specialty rice pudding flavored with saffron, almonds, pistachio nuts, and cinnamon. Iran. See also: rice pudding.

shoofly pie A Pennsylvania Dutch specialty, shoofly pie is a very sweet, spicy pie with a bottom pastry shell and a custard filling made of molasses and boiling water, covered with a crumb topping of brown sugar and spices. Another variation alternates the custard and the crumb topping inside the pie shell, ending with more crumbs on top, to create "gravel pie." The name is thought to come from the fact that flies have to be shooed away from the sweet molasses used in the pie. United States.

shortbread A rich cookie made with flour, sugar, butter, and salt. **Shortbread** has a high proportion of butter to flour, which makes the cookie tender and crumbly. Chopped nuts, citrus zest, or candied fruit can be added for flavor. Traditionally, shortbread is formed in a large round mold about 8 inches in diameter and cut into pie-shaped wedges after baking. These wedges were given the name "petticoat tails," because their shape is said to resemble the petticoats worn by women during the time of the Norman Conquest of Britain, in the twelfth century. Shortbread is also shaped as rectangular bars or in rounds, called "highlanders." Royal shortbread is shortbread that is half-dipped in chocolate. Shortbread cookies were originally served with tea at the Christmas and New Year's holidays, but now are made all year round. Shortbread originated in Scotland and is a refinement of the ancient Yule cake called bannock, which was a symbol of the sun. Scotland.

SHORTBREAD

Sixty 2½- by 1-inch cookies

1 pound unsalted butter, softened
1 cup superfine sugar
½ teaspoon salt
4 cups all-purpose flour

In the bowl of a stand mixer, using the flat beater attachment, or in a mixing bowl, using a hand-held mixer, beat the butter until light and fluffy, about 3 minutes. Beat in the sugar until thoroughly blended, about 2 minutes.

Blend the salt into the flour, and add the flour to the butter mixture in 4 additions, scraping down the sides of the bowl with a rubber spatula after each addition. Mix for 1 to 2 minutes longer, until the dough is smooth and soft.

Lightly flour a jelly-roll pan or a 10- by 15-inch cookie sheet. Pat and roll the dough out in the pan to a thickness of ⅜ inch. It will almost fill the pan. Use a ruler and a sharp knife to score pieces that are 1 inch wide and 2½ inches long, cutting 10 across a short side and 6 down. Use a fork to pierce each piece 3 times on the diagonal. Cover the dough with plastic wrap and refrigerate for at least 1 hour.

Position the racks in the upper and lower thirds of the oven and preheat to 325°F. Line two baking sheets with parchment paper.

Cut the chilled shortbread through the lines and transfer to the lined baking pans, leaving 1 inch space between them. Place the baking sheets in the oven, reduce the oven temperature to 300°F, and bake for 30 minutes. Turn the pans around and switch their positions, and bake 10 to 15 minutes longer, until the shortbread is light golden on the bottom and sand-colored on top.

Transfer the baking sheets to racks to cool. The shortbread will keep for 5 days in a well-covered container at room temperature.

shortbread mold Scottish shortbread is traditionally formed in a round mold about 8 inches in diameter, then cut into pie-shaped wedges after baking. Modern shortbread molds are round or square ceramic plates, similar to a pie pan, that are marked into 8 wedges or squares. The molds have decorative designs etched into them, which imprint the shortbread. There are also round wooden shortbread molds, with an etched design of the thistle of Scotland. The dough is pressed into the floured mold and flattened, then the mold is inverted and tapped to release the dough. When the shortbread is baked, it retains the shape of the mold and the imprinted design. Wooden and ceramic molds are available in 4-inch, 6-inch, and 8-inch diameters at cookware shops and through mail order cookware catalogs. See also: cookie mold and shortbread.

shortcake An American dessert, shortcake traditionally consists of a sweet, crumbly, cakelike biscuit, although sponge cake or angel food cake is sometimes substituted. The biscuit is split in half horizontally, filled with fresh fruit, and then topped with sweetened whipped cream. Strawberries are the fruit used most often, but any fresh fruit can be used. United States. See also: angel food cake, biscuit, and sponge cake.

sieve See strainer.

sift Sifting is a technique for aerating dry ingredients, such as flour, cornstarch, and confectioners' sugar, to lighten the ingredient and break up any lumps. The ingredient is placed in a sifter, strainer, or drum sieve and pushed through the mesh screen. This process separates the ingredient and adds air to it. Sifting results in a finer texture in baked goods.

sifter A manually operated kitchen utensil used to aerate flour and other dry ingredients, such as confectioners' sugar, cornstarch, and cocoa powder, that tend to clump together. Sifting is also a method for mixing dry ingredients together evenly. Made of stainless steel, aluminum, or plastic, a sifter is a tall, wide cylinder with a squeeze handle or a handle and crank lever on the side. Arched rods or a rotary blade inside the cylinder push the ingredient against and through a mesh screen at the bottom. The rods, or blade, are operated either by squeezing the handle or by turning the crank lever. Some sifters have as many as three mesh screens through which the ingredients pass. There is also a battery-powered sifter that is operated by merely pushing a button on the handle. Sifters are available in sizes ranging from 1- to 8-cup capacity at cookware shops, in cookware sections of department stores, at supermarkets, and through mail order cookware catalogs. See also: drum sieve.

silver leaf Edible silver leaf is made from pure silver. The leaves are extremely thin. They come in packages of twenty-five $3^3/_4$-inch-square leaves, arranged between sheets of tissue parchment paper. Silver leaf has no taste. It dissolves easily from the moisture in one's hands if touched; therefore, it must be handled carefully with a sable brush. Silver leaf is available from gilders' and sign-painters' suppliers and art supply stores. Silver leaf is best stored in a cool, dry place where it will last indefinitely. Silver leaf has been used in Indian cuisine to decorate desserts, pastries, and confections for thousands of years. See also: gold leaf, gold powder, gold ribbon, and silver powder.

silver powder Edible silver powder is made from pure silver, ground to dust. Silver powder, which has no taste, is used to decorate desserts, pastries, and confections. It is extremely light and has a tendency to "fly," so it should be handled carefully. A sable brush is the best tool to use to gild a surface with silver powder. Silver powder is available from gilders' and sign-painters' suppliers, art supply stores, and cake decorating supply shops. Silver powder is best stored in a cool, dry place in a well-covered container, where it will last indefinitely. See also: gold leaf, gold powder, gold ribbon, and silver leaf.

simnel cake A rich English spice cake loaded with dried fruits and candied orange peel. A layer of almond paste or marzipan is sandwiched between two layers of the cake batter before it is baked. A second layer of almond paste or marzipan is placed on top of the baked cake and baked briefly, then the cake is spread with apricot glaze. Small marzipan balls, resembling eggs, are used to decorate the top edge of the cake. Simnel cake is often served for Easter and Mother's Day celebrations. Bury is the name of another type of simnel cake. It is made from a sugar dough enriched with candied orange peel, dried fruits, and spices, rolled out into a thin round, and decorated with sliced almonds in the shape of a cross. United Kingdom.

skim milk Also called nonfat milk, skim milk contains less than 0.5 percent fat. See also: milk.

slump A Colonial New England deep-dish fruit dessert topped with a biscuitlike crust. A slump is a type of cobbler, similar to a grunt, but slumps are usually baked rather than steamed. Often they have both a bottom and top crust, similar to the dough used for dumplings, which stays moist and soft inside while becoming crispy on the outside. Slumps are traditionally served with heavy cream. The name may derive from the fact that the dessert does not keep its shape when served and "slumps" when placed on a plate. United States. See also: buckle, cobbler, grunt, and pandowdy.

smoke point The temperature at which heated fats and oils begin to break down and give off smoke and acrid gas. Because vegetable oils have a higher smoke point than solid fats such as butter and margarine, they are most often used for frying. See also: butter, canola oil, corn oil, fats and oils, lard, margarine, olive oil, peanut oil, safflower oil, solid shortening, soybean oil, and sunflower oil.

snickerdoodle An American specialty cookie that originated in nineteenth-century New England. Buttery, sweet snickerdoodles are flavored with dried fruits, nuts, and spices such as nutmeg and cinnamon. The surface of snickerdoodles is dusted with cinnamon and sugar before baking, which produces a crinkly top. These whimsically named cookies can have either a soft or a crunchy interior. United States.

soaking syrup See sugar syrup.

soft ball stage The stage at which a small amount of hot sugar syrup dropped in cold water forms a soft, sticky ball that flattens when removed from the water. The temperature range for soft ball stage is from 234° to 240°F on a candy thermometer. See also: Table of Sugar Temperatures and Stages (page 335).

soft crack The stage at which a small amount of hot sugar syrup dropped in cold water separates into strands that are firm but pliable when removed from the water. If bitten into, a piece of the cooled syrup will stick to the teeth. The temperature range for soft crack stage is from 270° to 290°F on a candy thermometer. See also: Table of Sugar Temperatures and Stages (page 335).

solid shortening An artificially created fat for use in baking. Solid shortening is made by hydrogenation, a process of forcing pressurized hydrogen gas through liquid vegetable oil to transform it into a solid or semisolid form, such as margarine. Although solid shortening is 100 percent fat, it has virtually no cholesterol and is low in saturated fat. Emulsifiers are added to solid shortening to help stabilize the suspension of fat in liquid and to keep the shortening moist, which helps make it spreadable. Crisco, available both unflavored and butter-flavored, is one of the most familiar solid shortenings. Solid shortening is interchangeable with butter in recipes; however, it does not have the same rich flavor, and the texture of the finished product will be different from one made with butter. Solid shortening is also used for frying because it has a high smoke point. It is available in cans, tubs, and stick form. It is best stored tightly covered at room temperature for several months. See also: butter, fats and oils, margarine, and smoke point.

soomsoom mah assal A Middle Eastern confection of honey and lemon juice cooked to a thick syrup. Toasted sesame seeds and chopped walnuts or almonds, or shredded coconut, are added and blended with the honey syrup. The mixture is transferred to a greased baking pan, cooled, and cut into squares. Lebanon and Syria.

sopaipillas Sweet pastry fritters made from pastry dough rolled out thin and cut into strips. The pastry strips are deep-fried in hot fat, drained, then dusted with confectioners' sugar before serving. Argentina. See also: fritter.

sorbet The French word for sherbet. Sorbet is made primarily of fruit juice or fruit purée, sugar, and water. Liqueur or an infusion, such as tea, can take the place of the juice or purée to provide the flavor. Sherbet often has egg whites, milk, or gelatin added to it. Sorbet has a smooth texture and is sometimes called a water ice because it contains no fat. In Italian it is *sorbetto*. Sorbets are served both between the courses of a meal, as a palate refresher, and as a dessert—such as **blueberry sorbet**. Sorbets were the first iced desserts and were introduced by the Chinese long before ice cream appeared in the eighteenth century. Arab traders learned about sorbets from the Chinese and introduced them to the Italians. The name is a derivation of the Italian word *sorbetto*, which comes from the Turkish word *chorbet*, meaning drink. China. See also: granita and water ice.

BLUEBERRY SORBET

I quart

3 pints fresh blueberries
½ cup plus 2 tablespoons water
¾ cup granulated sugar
Finely minced zest of I large lemon
Juice of ½ large lemon, strained
2 tablespoons kirsch

Rinse the berries and place them in a 2-quart heavy-bottomed saucepan with 2 tablespoons of the water. Cook the berries over low heat, stirring occasionally, until they are softened, about 15 minutes. Transfer the berries to a food processor or blender and purée. There should be 3 cups of purée.

In a small saucepan, combine the remaining ½ cup water and the sugar. Bring to a boil and cook for 5 minutes. Remove from the heat, and let cool for 10 minutes.

Add the cooled sugar syrup to the berry purée. Stir in the lemon zest, lemon juice, and kirsch. Cover the mixture and chill in the refrigerator for at least 2 hours.

Process the sorbet in an ice cream maker according to the manufacturer's directions. Store the sorbet in a tightly sealed container in the freezer for up to a month. If it is frozen solid, soften it in the refrigerator before serving.

sorghum Also called sorghum molasses and sorghum syrup, sorghum is a sweet, rich, tangy syrup, produced from the juice of the stems of the cereal plant of the same name. The juice is boiled down to produce the strong, sweet syrup, which is thinner and less sweet than molasses. Sorghum is sometimes confused with light molasses or wild honey. Sorghum can be substituted for molasses in desserts and baked goods. United States. See also: molasses.

soufflé An airy and fragile mixture, a dessert soufflé is based on a sweet egg custard, such as pastry cream, that rises as it bakes from the air beaten into egg whites blended into the custard base. When the mixture is heated, air and steam are trapped inside the custard, causing it to rise. Soufflés are famous for rising to almost double their size, over the top of the dish in which they are baked. As soon as a soufflé is removed from the oven, it begins to collapse, so it must be served immediately. Sweet soufflés are flavored with chocolate, fruit purées, or liqueurs and are often served with a complementary sauce. They are baked in a straight-sided round soufflé dish that is coated with butter and sugar, which gives the outside of the soufflé a light, sweet crust. Savory soufflés are based on a thick white sauce and contain purées of vegetables, meat, or fish, or grated cheese; they are generally served as a first course or an entrée for lunch or dinner. Chilled and iced soufflés are made of chilled or frozen mousse or ice cream. The mixture is molded in a soufflé dish with a parchment paper or aluminum collar that extends above the rim of the dish to support the mixture. When the mixture is frozen and the collar is removed, the soufflé stands up over the edge of the dish, resembling a puffed baked soufflé. France. See also: pastry cream and soufflé dish.

soufflé dish A deep round straight-sided porcelain or earthenware baking dish used for baking or chilling soufflés, custards, and mousses. It is smooth on the inside and traditionally has a fluted exterior; most soufflé dishes are plain white. Soufflé dishes are also used as serving dishes for the desserts that have been baked or chilled in them. They are available in various sizes ranging from 4 to $8^{1}/_{2}$ inches in diameter and $2^{3}/_{4}$ to 4 inches high at cookware shops, in cookware sections of department stores, and through mail order cookware catalogs. The $1^{1}/_{2}$- and 2-quart sizes are the most popular. See also: soufflé.

sour cream See cream.

soybean oil Bland, pale yellow, cholesterol-free soybean oil is extracted from soybeans. High in both mono- and poly-unsaturates, soybean oil is the main ingredient in many brands of margarine. Because soybean oil has a high smoke point, it is particularly good for frying. It can be used as an ingredient in desserts, pastries, and confections. Soybean oil is virtually interchangeable with other vegetable oils, such as canola, corn, olive, peanut, safflower, and sunflower. It is widely available in supermarkets. Store soybean oil tightly capped in a dark place at room temperature for up to 6 months or in the refrigerator for up to a year. If it becomes cloudy in the refrigerator, let it stand at room temperature to clarify. See also: fats and oils, margarine, and smoke point.

Spanish windtorte A classic Austrian confection, Spanish windtorte is an elaborately decorated meringue shell filled with fresh berries and whipped cream. The sides of the meringue shell are decorated with piped shell shapes and rosettes and with crystallized violets, and the top of the confection is crowned with a decorated meringue disk. In Austria, the meringue mixture of egg whites and sugar is called "Spanish wind," hence the cake's name. Austria. See also: vacherin.

spatula A flexible utensil used to blend mixtures together and to spread icings, fillings, and batters. There are several different types of spatulas: Rubber spatulas have a flat, flexible, rectangular blade made of solid rubber or plastic attached to a wooden or plastic handle. There is also a rubber spoon-shaped spatula, called a spoonola, with a deeper and more rounded blade. Rubber spatulas are used to scrape batters and doughs from the sides of mixing bowls and for folding, mixing, and blending ingredients together. A flexible-blade spatula has a long, narrow, flexible stainless steel blade with a rounded end, set into a wooden handle. This type of spatula has many uses, including icing cakes and pastries; spreading frostings, fillings, and batters; transferring cakes and pastries from one place to another; and releasing desserts from molds. Flexible-blade spatulas come in a wide variety of sizes. An offset spatula has a flexible metal blade that is stepped down about 1 inch from the wooden handle, forming a Z-shape. It is used to spread batters in jelly-roll pans, to spread icings and frostings on cake layers, to move cakes, cake layers, and pastries, and in tempering chocolate. Offset spatulas come in several sizes from very small to large, with the length of the blade ranging from 3 to 12 inches. Wooden spatulas also have many uses in the pastry, dessert, and confectionery kitchen. Wooden spatulas in a variety of sizes and shapes are part of the traditional batterie de cuisine. Those with long handles are good for keeping hands a safe distance from hot mixtures, such as caramels and brittles, as they cook. See also: Batterie de Cuisine (331), flexible-blade spatula, offset spatula, rubber spatula, and wooden spoon and spatula.

spearmint See mint.

speculaa A rich, spicy, crisp gingerbread cookie that is a Christmas specialty of Holland; similar versions are also made in Belgium, Germany, and Austria. Traditionally the dough is pressed into wooden molds elaborately carved into various shapes such as St. Nicholas, animals, and windmills. The Dutch word *speculaa* means mirror, and the molds are shaped "to mirror" images of the world. Holland. See also: cookie mold.

sponge cake An airy, light-textured cake leavened solely by the air beaten into the eggs it contains. A sponge cake has very little or no fat. There are many varieties of sponge cake, including génoise, ladyfingers, and angel food cake. Sponge cake is used as the base for many cakes and desserts. Most often baked as a round cake, it can also be baked in a rectangular pan and then rolled up to form a jelly-roll cake. Sponge cake can be flavored in many ways: with, for example, lemon zest, orange zest, ground almonds, ground hazelnuts, or chocolate. See also: angel food cake, biscuit, génoise, ladyfingers, and roulade.

spoom See spuma.

springerle Classic imprinted German anise seed Christmas cookies that originated in Swabia, a historical region of Southwest Germany, in the fifteenth century. Springerle are formed either by rolling out the dough and then imprinting it with a carved rolling pin or by rolling the dough into elaborately carved wooden cookie molds. Because the dough used to make springerle has no fat and is very firm, the cookies hold the detailed impressions from the rolling pin or molds very well. After the cookies are formed, they are dried at room temperature overnight before baking, to help set the designs. An ancient tradition is to hand-paint the cookies and use them as ornaments to decorate Christmas trees. Germany.

springerle rolling pin. See rolling pin.

springform pan A deep round straight-sided two-piece baking pan with expandable sides, secured by a clamp, and a removable bottom. When the clamp is opened, the sides of the pan expand and release the bottom. This feature makes it easy to remove a cake from the pan, as it is not necessary to turn it upside down. Springform pans are generally $2^1/_2$ to 3 inches deep and can be found in many different diameters, ranging from 4 inches to 12 inches. Some have bottoms that are tubes. Springform pans are used most frequently for baking cheesecakes and other cakes, such as mousse cakes, that must be handled carefully when they are removed from the pan. See also: cheesecake and mousse cake.

spuma Meaning froth or foam, spuma is a creamy frozen Italian dessert made with a sugar syrup blended with either fruit juice or wine, such as Champagne, muscatel, sauternes, sherry, or port. When the mixture is partially frozen, an Italian meringue is folded in, which gives it an airy and frothy consistency. The French version of this dessert is called spoom. Italy. See also: meringue.

spumone, spumoni An Italian molded frozen dessert composed of two layers of ice cream, generally chocolate and vanilla, that enclose a layer of sweetened whipped cream blended with candied fruits and toasted nuts and flavored with rum or brandy. Often whipped egg whites are blended into the ice cream before it is molded. Spumone is cut into slices for serving, revealing the layers. It is often served with a dessert sauce. Italy.

spun sugar Also called angel's hair, spun sugar is used to decorate desserts, pastries, and confections. Sugar, water, and cream of tartar are cooked to the hard crack stage (310°F). Then a fork or whisk is dipped into the syrup and flicked or waved back and forth over an oiled rolling pin to form fine, threadlike strands, which can be gathered up and wrapped around or draped over a cake or pastry. Spun sugar can also be formed over an oiled bowl to make a crown or cage or over a waxed paper–covered surface. When the spun sugar strands are cool and hard, they can be broken into pieces or crushed and then sprinkled onto a dessert or pressed into small bowls to form baskets for holding desserts. Because humidity causes spun sugar to soften and disintegrate, it is best made in a cool, dry environment. Decorations made from spun sugar should be used within a few hours of preparation, or they will melt. See also: candy thermometer and Table of Sugar Temperatures and Stages (page 335).

star fruit See carambola.

stiff, but not dry The point to which egg whites are beaten for many desserts: until they just hold firm peaks and are still glossy, moist, and not too finely grained.

stir The technique for mixing ingredients together in a circular motion until they are thoroughly combined. Stirring is accomplished using a spoon, rubber spatula, or a whisk.

stollen A German Christmas specialty, stollen is a rich, sweet, yeast-risen bread, loaded with dried fruits. The most familiar stollen is from Dresden. Classically, stollen is shaped as a long loaf with a ridge down the center, tapered at each end. Stollen keeps well and can be made up to 3 weeks before serving. It is rich and, therefore, is usually served in thin slices with breakfast or afternoon tea. Germany.

strain A technique for filtering, pressing, sifting, and puréeing liquid or dry ingredients, which removes lumps and results in a smooth texture. See also: drum sieve, sift, and strainer.

strainer Also called a sieve, a strainer has many uses in the pastry and dessert kitchen: sifting small amounts of dry ingredients, puréeing fruit and fruit sauces, straining glazes, and draining and rinsing fruit. A strainer is made of wire or nylon mesh held by a frame of various shapes. A china cap is a conical strainer made of stainless steel or aluminum. A colander is a bowl-shaped, perforated metal or plastic strainer. Some have small feet or a bottom ring and, usually, two handles. A bowl strainer is the most commonly used strainer. It has a round plastic or metal rim that holds the bowl-shaped mesh and, often, a long handle. There are 1 or two small hooks at the side opposite the handle, which allow the strainer to be balanced over a pan or a bowl. The mesh is metal or nylon and is available in different grades from very fine to coarse. Bowl strainers come in many sizes ranging from 2^1/$_2$ to 8 inches in diameter. Strainers are available at supermarkets, cookware shops, cookware sections of department stores, and restaurant supply shops and through mail order cookware catalogs. See also: drum sieve and strain.

strawberry A member of the rose family and a relative of both the blackberry and the raspberry, a strawberry is a vine-grown juicy, brilliant red, conical fruit, covered with tiny seeds and topped with a cap of green leaves. Strawberries have been cultivated since the thirteenth century. Today's berries are the result of centuries of experimentation and cross-breeding. French wild strawberries, fraises des bois, which are tiny and intensely sweet, are relatives of the American strawberry. Ripe strawberries are naturally sweet. Strawberries are used as an ingredient in many desserts, pastries, and confections, such as fresh fruit tarts, pies, cobblers, mousses, shortcakes, sorbets, and ice creams, and they are used to make dessert sauces, jams, and jellies. Frozen strawberries are available year-round. Fresh strawberries are available from February through November in various regions of the United States. Choose fragrant, plump, unblemished, shiny, bright red fruit with the green caps still attached. Check the bottom of the plastic basket for crushed or moldy berries, and avoid them. Fresh strawberries are delicate and should be handled with care. Store fresh strawberries in the refrigerator for up to 3 days and rinse first, then hull just before use. See also: berry.

strawberry huller This hand-held tool is used to remove the leaves and cores from strawberries. It looks something like a wide V-shaped pair of metal tweezers, with gripping surfaces on each rounded end. It is 2^1/$_4$ inches long. Some taper slightly from the top end to about 1^1/$_4$ inches wide at the widest point. To use, grasp the strawberry leaves with the huller, squeezing the sides together to hold them. Then twist and pull the huller to remove the leaves and their core from the berry. Strawberry hullers are available at cookware shops, supermarkets, and cookware sections of department stores and through mail order cookware catalogs.

Strega Translated as "witch," Strega is a golden-colored Italian liqueur made from over seventy herbs, spices, and flowers. The golden-yellow color comes from the saffron flower. Rich and sweet, with a mild vanilla flavor, Strega is used in many Italian desserts, pastries, and confections. Italy.

streusel The German word for "sprinkle," streusel is a crumbly topping made of butter, flour, sugar, and spices. Finely chopped nuts are occasionally included in the mixture. Streusel is sprinkled on the top of sweet breads, cakes, muffins, and coffee cakes before they are baked. It makes a rich, crisp crust as it bakes, adding both taste and texture to the baked goods it tops. Germany.

stripper A hand-held 6-inch-long utensil that is used to cut $^1/_4$-inch-wide strips of the rind of citrus fruits. It has a metal blade with an arched sharp hole in the center, held by a plastic or wood handle. When the arched hole is pressed against citrus fruit and the tool is pulled down with some pressure, it cuts strips of the peel. The length of the strip can be varied according to whether the stripper is pulled from the top to the bottom or around the fruit. These strips are used as is for decoration, or they can be candied. Sometimes this tool is sold as a combination zester/stripper. Strippers are available at cookware shops, supermarkets, cookware sections of department stores, and restaurant supply shops and through mail order cookware catalogs. See also: zester.

stroopwafel A Dutch cookie composed of two very thin, crisp, 4-inch-diameter cinnamon and nutmeg flavored sweet wafers imprinted with a cross-hatch pattern, sandwiched together with molasses or caramel-flavored syrup. Holland.

strudel A classic long rectangular pastry made of many layers of a paper-thin dough wrapped around a sweet filling. The dough is rolled and stretched very thin, then sprinkled with bread crumbs to absorb the liquid released from the filling as it bakes. The pastry is rolled up around the filling, brushed with butter, and baked until golden and crisp. After baking, strudel is sliced crosswise into individual pieces about $1^1/_2$ inches wide. The traditional strudel dough is difficult to handle, and it must be made from flour with a high gluten content so it will be strong and won't tear as it is stretched. Many cooks use phyllo dough as a very acceptable substitute for handmade dough. The classic filling is made with apples and raisins, but many others are also popular, including cherry, plum, poppy seed, cream cheese or cottage cheese, and nuts. Savory strudels, eaten as first courses or entrées, are made with fillings of beef or cabbage enhanced with onions and spices, cheese, and vegetable. The name comes from the German word for whirlwind. Strudel was inspired by the paper-thin pastry dough Phyllo, used for Turkish baklava. There has been tremendous cross-cultural influence on the cuisines of Eastern Europe by the migrations throughout the centuries. The Austro-Hungarian Empire stretched to the east in its heyday from the thirteenth to the early twentieth centuries. There is a great rivalry between the Hungarians and the Austrians as to the origin of strudel. Apparently the Hungarians did create strudel and its dough, but the Austrians, particularly the Viennese, enthusiastically embraced the pastry and elevated strudel making to a high art. Hungary. See also: phyllo dough.

Succès A classic French cake composed of two round layers of crisp almond meringue filled and covered with rich praline buttercream. Toasted sliced almonds are pressed into the sides of the cake and the top is heavily dusted with confectioners' sugar. Succès is also the name of the crisp meringue layer used to make the cake. France. See also: buttercream, dacquoise, Japonaize, meringue, and praline.

sucrose See sugar.

sugar Once a highly prized luxury, sugar did not come into widespread use in Europe and America until the seventeenth century, although the Arabs had been using sugar since the fifth century B.C. There are many forms of sugar. Sucrose, the most commonly used form, is a complex sugar derived from sugarcane or sugar beets. Fructose and glucose are the two simple sugars that make up sucrose. Fructose, also called fruit sugar or levulose, is found in honey as well as in fruits. Glucose is found in honey and in some fruits and vegetables. Dextrose, also called grape sugar, and corn sugar are other terms for glucose. Lactose is milk sugar, and maltose is malt sugar.

A sweet crystalline substance that is almost wholly sucrose, granulated or table sugar is very highly refined. The color of sugar ranges from light to brown, depending on the amount of molasses remaining in it or added to it during processing. Sugar adds tenderness, sweetness, texture, stability, and extended shelf life to desserts, pastries, and confections. Granulated sugar also comes in cubes and various other textures. Superfine sugar, called castor or cater sugar in the United Kingdom, is more finely granulated than table sugar. It works particularly well in meringues, because it dissolves so rapidly that it leaves no trace of grittiness. Granulated and superfine sugar can be substituted for each other. Coarse sugar, also called decorators' sugar or pearl sugar, is white sugar that has been processed into small, round grains, resembling pearls, about four to six times larger than grains of granulated sugar. It is used for garnishing cookies and other baked goods, pastries, and confections. Crystal sugar is similar to coarse sugar, except it is in the form of pellet-shaped crystals instead of grains. It is used in the same way as coarse sugar.

Confectioners' sugar, also called powdered sugar, is granulated sugar that has been ground to a powder. It usually has a small amount of corn-starch mixed with it to prevent caking due to the absorption of moisture. It should always be sifted before use. Confectioners' sugar, called icing sugar in the United Kingdom, and *sucre glace* in France, dissolves easily. Confectioners' sugar is used in icings and frostings, and to dust and decorate the tops of various desserts and pastries. It is also widely used in confectionery. Granulated sugar that has been combined with vanilla beans, then ground to a powder, is called vanilla sugar. It is available in small packets or you can make your own by burying split vanilla beans in sugar and tightly covering the container. Let the mixture stand for at least 24 hours, then grind in a food processor fitted with the steel blade.

Brown sugar is white sugar processed with molasses, which gives it a soft, moist texture. Brown sugar has a distinctive, rich flavor. It is available in light and dark, the difference being the amount of molasses added to it during processing. If brown sugar is exposed to the air it will dry out, but hardened brown sugar can be kept soft or softened by placing it in an airtight container with a slice of apple. Brown sugar must be tightly packed for measuring because otherwise it traps air between its crystals. It can be substituted for granulated sugar but will impart a more full-bodied flavor and deep color.

Raw sugar is the same color as light brown sugar but is grainier. It is the residue left after processing sugar to remove the molasses. Much of the molasses remains in the granules, giving raw sugar its amber color and rich flavor. Because raw sugar may contain mold and bacteria, it must be purified for sale in the United States. Turbinado sugar is raw sugar that has been cleaned by washing it with steam. Its amber-colored coarse crystals have the same robust taste as brown sugar. Light-brown Demerara sugar, named for the area in Guyana that it comes from, is a popular type of raw sugar. It has coarse crystals that dissolve slowly. This characteristic makes it highly valued to sweeten hot cereal and coffee because as the sugar crystals dissolve the cereal or coffee becomes sweeter. Barbados sugar, also called Muscovado sugar, is a finer grained raw sugar than Demerara. It comes in both dark and light styles. It has a strong molasses flavor and is available mostly in Britain.

Palm sugar, also called jaggery, is made from the sap of the Palmyra palm tree. It is a coarse brown sugar sold in cakes or lumps. Palm sugar is widely used in Indian, Southeast Asian, and Indonesian cuisines. Brown sugar can be substituted for palm sugar. Sugar is also made from dried dates that are ground to a powder. Date sugar is not as sweet as sucrose. It is used primarily to sweeten fresh fruit, cereal, and drinks and occasionally for baking.

The most widely used form of liquid sugar is corn syrup, which comes from corn kernels. Available in light and dark forms, corn syrup is a thick, pourable liquid. Because corn syrup attracts moisture, it is valued in candy making for preventing other sugars from crystallizing, and it adds moisture to candies and baked goods. Honey, maple syrup, molasses, treacle, and golden syrup are other types of liquid sugar. Lactose is sugar that occurs naturally in milk. It is not as sweet as the other liquid sugars.

Sugar is pure carbohydrate. It is best stored at room temperature in a cool, dry place. Liquid sugar, such as corn syrup, should be stored in the refrigerator after opening. See also: dextrose, fructose, glucose, golden syrup, honey, lactose, maple syrup, molasses, pearl sugar, treacle, and vanilla sugar.

sugar bloom A white crust of sugar crystals that forms when moisture condenses on the surface of chocolate or other candies. Sugar bloom is generally caused by storing loosely wrapped chocolate or candies in the refrigerator, which exposes them to too much moisture. Sugar is drawn out of the chocolate or candies and dissolves in the moisture on the surface. When the moisture evaporates, the sugar crystals remain.

sugar pan The classic pan for cooking sugar is a straight-sided deep flat-bottomed unlined heavy-gauge copper pan with a pour spout and a hollow handle. Sugar pans are available in many sizes, ranging from 3-cup to 3-quart capacity. Copper is the best material for conducting heat evenly and rapidly, and it stands up extremely well to the high temperatures needed for cooking sugar mixtures. If the pan were lined, with tin as an example, the lining might begin to melt before the sugar mixture reached its correct temperature. The easiest way to remove sugar that sticks to the pan after cooking is to fill the pan with water and bring it to a boil. To clean copper, use a solution of salt and vinegar or lemon juice. Rub this vigorously all over the pan, rinse off, and dry the pan with a soft towel.

sugar substitutes The two main types of sugar substitutes are saccharin and aspartame, which are, respectively, three hundred and two hundred times sweeter than sugar. Although these artificial sweeteners have intense sweetening power, they cannot be used interchangeably with granulated sugar in baked goods, because sugar provides structure and texture to baked goods and the sweetness of the artificial sweeteners breaks down during the prolonged high heat needed for baking. Baked goods are made from well-balanced formulas, and if their structure is altered, the result will not be the same. Saccharin also has a bitter aftertaste when heated. Sugar substitutes can be used to sweeten cold dishes. Be sure to read the label on the package to know the equivalent quantity of sugar substitute for regular sugar. For most brands, one package granulated, which is $1/4$ teaspoon, is equal to 2 teaspoons granulated sugar, and $1^1/2$ teaspoons liquid is the equivalent of $1/4$ cup granulated sugar. Sugar substitutes are available in granulated form, in both individual packets and bulk, and in liquid form in most supermarkets.

sugar syrup A combination of sugar and water cooked until the sugar dissolves, then boiled for about 1 minute. Sugar syrup is also called simple sugar syrup or simple syrup. It is used to soak cakes and pastries, to dilute fondant, to poach fruit, and as a glaze. It is added to sorbets and frostings and is widely used in confectionery as the basis of many candies. If flavoring, such as vanilla or lemon extracts or liqueurs, is added to the syrup, it is called soaking syrup. Sugar syrup can be made in various densities. Thin syrup is 3 parts water to 1 part sugar; medium syrup is 2 parts water to 1 part sugar; and heavy syrup is equal amounts of sugar and water. As sugar syrup cooks, it goes through various stages of density and color changes, ranging from clear to dark brown—better known as caramel. The stages of density correspond to specific temperature readings on a candy thermometer, but they can be tested by dropping a ball of the syrup into a glass of cold water. The various characteristics that the ball exhibits show the stage of the sugar. The thread stage (223° to 234°F) forms a loose, thin 2-inch-long thread in the water that can't be gathered into a ball. The soft ball stage (234° to 240°F) forms a soft, sticky ball that flattens when removed from the water. The firm ball stage (244° to 248°F) forms a firm yet pliable, sticky ball that holds its shape briefly, but deflates when left at room temperature for a few minutes. The hard ball stage (250° to 266°F) forms a rigid, sticky ball that holds its shape against pressure. The soft-crack stage (270° to 290°F) separates into strands that are firm but pliable. If a piece is bitten into, it will stick to the teeth. The hard crack stage (300° to 310°F) separates into brittle threads that shatter easily. The sugar is no longer sticky at this stage. Beyond this stage, the sugar syrup turns to caramel (320° to 360°F), ranging from very pale to golden to medium brown to dark brown to black. See also: caramel, caramelize, and Table of Sugar Temperatures and Stages (page 335).

summer coating See confectionery coating.

sunflower oil Light, colorless, virtually flavorless, cholesterol-free sunflower oil, which is extracted from sunflower seeds, has a high level of polyunsaturates. It can be used as an ingredient in desserts, pastries, and confections. Sunflower oil has a low smoke point, so it is not the best choice for frying. It can be used interchangeably with other vegetable oils, such as canola, corn, olive, peanut, safflower, and soybean. It is widely available at supermarkets and health food stores. Store sunflower oil tightly capped in a cool, dark place for up to a year. If it turns cloudy in the refrigerator, let it stand at room temperature to clarify. See also: fats and oils and smoke point.

sungkaya A Thai steamed coconut custard. Coconut milk, eggs, and sugar are blended together, then steamed in a bowl or half a coconut until firm. The custard is chilled before serving. Thailand.

sweet couscous See seffa.

sweetened condensed milk A blend of homogenized whole milk and sugar, which makes up 40 to 45 percent of the mixture, that is heated to evaporate over half of the water, leaving a sweet, sticky mixture. If unopened, sweetened condensed milk will last in a cool place indefinitely. Once opened, transfer the contents to a clean container and store tightly covered in the refrigerator for up to a week. See also: milk.

Swiss meringue See meringue.

syllabub Dating back to Elizabethan England, this thick, custardlike dessert is made with cream or milk beaten with white wine, sugar, lemon juice, and, occasionally, sherry or brandy. Syllabub can also be used as a filling or topping for cakes and cookies. United Kingdom.

syrnik A Ukrainian cake made with a type of farmer's cheese, farina (cream of wheat), and eggs. The rich and creamy cake is flavored with butter, sugar, and lemon and filled with raisins. Ukraine.

taffy A candy, similar to caramel, usually made from molasses or brown sugar and water, cooked to either the hard ball or soft crack stage, to produce a concentrated mixture. This mixture is blended with butter, which gives it a firm, chewy texture. Other ingredients, such as nuts and flavorings, are often added as well. The taffy is cooled slightly, then pulled into long ropes, which are doubled, twisted, and pulled again several times. The pulling incorporates minute air bubbles that lighten the taffy's texture and color and give it an opaque sheen. Taffy is generally cut into small square-shaped pieces with an oiled knife or scissors. The finished candy is soft and chewy. Saltwater taffy is an American candy that was especially popular in the late nineteenth century. It was originally made with a small amount of saltwater. To prevent taffy from becoming too soft and sticky from contact with moisture, wrap the pieces in waxed paper and store them in an airtight container at room temperature. In Britain, taffy is known as toffee or toffy and has a more brittle, crunchy consistency. United States. See also: caramel, toffee, and Table of Sugar Temperatures and Stages (page 335).

tamis The French word for sieve, sifter, or strainer. See also: drum sieve.

tangelo A citrus fruit hybrid created from a cross between a tangerine and a pomelo or a grapefruit. Juicy, sweet-tart tangelos are virtually seedless. Their loose, easily removed skin ranges in color from yellow to deep orange and they range in size from tiny to as big as a large apple. There are many varieties of tangelos, with the best known the Mineola, which has a nipple-shaped end. Tangelos are used like oranges, and the peel is often candied as an ingredient in many desserts, pastries, and confections. Tangelos are available from November to April. Choose bright-skinned, firm fruit that feels heavy for its size, with no soft spots or discoloration. Russets, rough brown spots on the skin, do not affect the quality or flavor of the fruit. Store tangelos in a cool, dry place for several days or in the refrigerator for several weeks. See also: citrus fruit, fruit, grapefruit, pomelo, and tangerine.

tangerine A member of the loose-skinned mandarin family of hybrid oranges, a tangerine is a small, round citrus fruit with rough, deeply colored orange skin and juicy, sweet flesh. The fruit takes its name from the city of Tangier in Morocco, where it was developed. Tangerine segments, juice, and peel are used raw and the peel is often candied as an ingredient in desserts, pastries, and confections. Tangerines are available from November to June. Choose bright-skinned, firm fruit that feels heavy for its size, with no soft spots or discoloration. Russets, rough brown spots on the skin, do not affect the quality or flavor of the fruit. Store tangerines in a cool, dry place for several days or in the refrigerator for several weeks. See also: citrus fruit, fruit, mandarin, orange, and tangelo.

tapioca A starch derived from the root of the tropical manioc or cassava plant, tapioca is used like cornstarch to thicken fruit fillings, custards, and puddings. Tapioca is also made into a pudding itself, with a texture similar to a creamy rice pudding. It is the preferred thickener for fruit fillings and sauces that are to be frozen because it does not break down when thawed. Tapioca is available in the form of tiny pearls or beads, which soften when cooked, or as a flour, which is ground from the pearls. Tapioca comes in various sizes and flavors and as regular or instant. Pearl tapioca is available at most supermarkets. The other forms can be found at health food stores or at markets specializing in Asian or Latin American food. All forms of tapioca will last indefinitely if stored in a cool, dark, dry place. See also: custard and pudding.

tart An open-face pastry consisting of a straight-sided shallow pastry shell and a filling. The pastry shell can be baked blind and then filled, or the filling and the pastry shell can be baked together, depending on the type of tart. The pastry shell for a **fresh fruit tart** is baked first, then filled with pastry cream, topped with fresh fruit, and glazed. Tarts can be either sweet—such as fresh fruit tarts, custard tarts, or nut tarts—or savory, with a filling of cheese or vegetables or meat—such as a quiche. For sweet tarts, the shell is usually made from a slightly sweet pastry dough, such as pâte sucrée, although puff pastry is occasionally used. Tarts come in many sizes, including individual and mini, which may be called tartlets. They are made in many different shapes, including round, square, and rectangular, but round is most common. Tarts are made in specially designed pans that have fluted sides and removable bottoms or are baked in flan rings. They are served freestanding, out of their baking pans. In Britain, a tart is called a flan. In German-speaking countries, tarts are called tortes or kuchen. See also bake blind, flan, flan ring, glaze, linzertorte, pastry cream, pâte sucrée, puff pastry, tarte Tatin, tartlet, and tart pan.

∞∞∞∞∞∞∞∞∞

FRESH FRUIT TART

One 9½-inch round tart; 12 servings

1 recipe Pâte Sucrée (page 225)
½ recipe Pastry Cream (page 221)
1½ pints fresh strawberries, washed, dried, hulled, and cut in half
    lengthwise, or 2 cups fresh raspberries, blackberries, or
    blueberries, or 3 kiwifruits, 3 carambolas, 3 medium bananas,
    4 tangerines, 3 oranges, or 2 to 3 cups cut-up fresh fruit
1 recipe Apricot Glaze (page 142)
Fresh mint sprigs for garnish (optional)

    Center a rack in the oven and preheat to 400°F.
    Roll out the pâte sucrée on a lightly floured work surface to a 12-inch round about ⅛ inch thick. Carefully roll the pastry dough up the rolling pin, then gently unroll the dough into a 9½-inch fluted tart pan with a removable bottom. Carefully fit the pastry dough into the bottom and up the sides of the tart pan. Trim off the excess dough.
    Place the tart pan on a jelly-roll pan. Line the tart shell with a large piece of aluminum foil, and weight the foil with tart weights or dried beans or rice. Bake the tart shell for 10 minutes. Remove the foil and weights from the shell and bake 10 to 12 minutes longer, until golden brown and set. Transfer the tart shell to a rack to cool. (The tart shell can be baked up to 2 days ahead and held at room temperature, wrapped in foil.)
    Remove the sides of the tart pan from the tart shell and place the shell on a serving plate. Spread the pastry cream evenly in the shell. Use a rubber spatula to smooth the top. Cover the pastry cream with overlapping circles of the strawberries, or arrange the other fruit in concentric circles on top of the cream.
    Lightly brush the berries with the apricot glaze. Decorate the tart with a few sprigs of fresh mint if desired.   continued

Serve the tart immediately or refrigerate until ready to serve. The tart should be assembled no more than 3 hours before serving, or the pastry cream will make the tart shell soggy.

Tartarian cherry See cherry.

tarte Tatin A classic French caramelized upside-down apple tart. This tart is baked with the shortcrust pastry dough on top of the apples. When baked, it is turned out of the pan so the pastry is on the bottom. The pan is coated with caramel before the apples are added, and as the tart bakes, the butter and sugar that coat the apples caramelize as well, heightening the tart's rich flavor. **Tarte Tatin** is traditionally served with crème fraîche. This tart takes its name from, and was made famous by, two sisters named Tatin, in the Sologne (Loire) region of France, who served it at their hotel during the late nineteenth and early twentieth centuries. Tarte Tatin is very popular throughout France. Its full name is La tarte des Demoiselles Tatin. France. See also: caramelize and crème fraîche.

TARTE TATIN

One 10-inch round tart; 12 to 14 servings

Pastry dough
1 cup all-purpose flour
¼ teaspoon granulated sugar
⅛ teaspoon salt
3 ounces (6 tablespoons) unsalted butter, cut into pieces and
    chilled
3 tablespoons cold water

Filling
½ cup granulated sugar
⅓ cup water
2 ounces (4 tablespoons) unsalted butter, cut into 1-inch cubes
8 medium Granny Smith or Golden Delicious apples, peeled, cored,
    halved, and thickly sliced
⅓ cup superfine or granulated sugar

Finely minced zest of 1 large lemon
¾ teaspoon ground cinnamon
1 cup crème fraîche, for garnish (page 86)

For the pastry dough, place the flour, sugar, and salt in the work bowl of a food processor fitted with the steel blade. Pulse for 5 seconds to blend. Add the butter and pulse until it is cut into tiny pieces, about 1 minute. With the machine on, add the cold water through the feed tube, and process until the pastry forms a ball around the blade, about 30 seconds. Wrap the pastry dough in plastic and refrigerate for at least an hour, or until firm, enough to roll.

For the filling, combine the ½ cup sugar and the water in a 1-quart heavy-bottomed saucepan and bring to a boil over high heat. Cook the sugar syrup to a golden caramel color, occasionally washing down the sides of the pan with a pastry brush dipped in warm water to prevent crystallization. Pour the caramel into a 10-inch glass pie plate, round cake pan, or cast-iron skillet, and tilt the pan to completely cover the bottom with the caramel. Set aside.

Heat the butter in a large sauté pan until it is foaming. Add the apples, the ⅓ cup sugar, the lemon zest, and cinnamon. Cook over medium heat, stirring frequently with a wooden spoon, until the apples are golden and soft, but still hold their shape, about 15 minutes. Transfer the apples to a baking sheet to cool briefly.

Center a rack in the oven and preheat to 400°F.

Arrange the apple slices in tight concentric circles over the caramel in the pie plate or cake pan.

Roll out the pastry dough on a lightly floured surface to an 11- to 12-inch round about ¼ inch thick. Loosely roll the pastry dough up around the rolling pin, then unroll it over the apples. Trim off the excess pastry dough, and tuck in the edges of the dough to completely cover the apples. Pierce the pastry dough in several places.

Bake the tart in the oven for 45 minutes, or until the pastry is browned. Remove the tart from the oven and run a knife around the edges to loosen the dough. Cool the tart on a rack for about 10 minutes.

Place a serving plate over the pie pan, cake pan, or skillet and carefully invert the tart onto the plate. Gently remove the pan. If any apples stick to the caramel, use a spatula to remove them from the pan and arrange on top of the tart. Serve the tart warm or at room temperature with crème fraîche as an accompaniment.

tartlet An individual-size or miniature tart. See also: tart and tartlet pan.

tartlet pan Smaller than tart pans, tartlet pans are available in different sizes and shapes, including round, oval, rectangular, and square. They are made of tinned or black steel and most do not have removable bottoms. They come plain or fluted, with straight or sloping sides. Tartlet pans range from 2 to 4^1/$_2$ inches in diameter and from ^{3}/$_4$ to 1^1/$_2$ inches high. Tiny petits fours molds can also be used to shape tartlets. Barquette molds are oval tartlet pans. Tartlet pans are available in cookware shops and through mail order cookware catalogs. See also: barquette mold and petits fours molds.

tart pan The classic pan for baking tarts is round, made of tinned or black steel, with fluted, slightly sloping sides and a removable bottom. Tart pans are also available in other shapes, such as square, a wide rectangle, and a long thin rectangle. Tart pans range from ^{3}/$_4$ to 1^1/$_4$ inches high and from 4^1/$_2$ inches to 12^1/$_2$ inches in diameter. Flan rings are also used to form tarts. Tarts pans are available in cookware shops, the cookware section of department stores, and through mail order cookware catalogs. See also: flan ring.

tart weights See pie weights.

tayglach A Jewish confection of honey-sweetened dough rolled into ^{1}/$_2$- to 1-inch-thick logs, cut into 1-inch pieces, and baked until golden. The logs are poached in a ginger-flavored sugar and honey syrup. After poaching the dough is rolled into individual balls, then the balls are rolled in chopped nuts or shredded coconut. Germany and Israel.

tea A light meal served in the late afternoon, generally between three-thirty and five o'clock, that originated in England. For afternoon tea, the traditional fare popularized in England consists of sandwiches, scones, muffins, and/or crumpets, with butter or clotted cream and jam, and various pastries, cakes, and cookies, such as shortbread. Afternoon tea is thought of as a dainty affair, in contrast to high tea, which is a heavier, more substantial meal, with meat or fish dishes as well, that takes the place of the evening meal. High tea is generally served starting at six o'clock. High tea is most popular in Northern England and Scotland. Anna, the seventh Duchess of Bedford, invented afternoon tea in the early nineteenth century (some sources say 1830, others say 1840), because the story goes, she became hungry in the late afternoon when there were hours to wait before dinner would be served. As the century went on, afternoon tea became more elaborate. Women would change into special tea dresses, and the plates, cups, and silverware used were more delicate. Afternoon tea was embraced enthusiastically in Europe, especially France, where there are many tearooms and pastry shops that serve tea. United Kingdom.

tempering chocolate A process that fixes the unstable cocoa butter molecule, which has several different melting points, at its most stable point. This keeps the cocoa butter from rising to the surface of the chocolate and forming unattractive gray or white streaks and spots known as chocolate bloom. Chocolate that is out of temper also has a grainy texture. Tempering gives chocolate a shiny, unblemished appearance and a smooth texture. Chocolate always comes tempered from the manufacturer. When it is melted, it goes out of temper and must be retempered to use it for molding or dipping. Tempered chocolate breaks with a crisp sharp snap, sets up quickly, and is easy to remove from molds because it shrinks when cool. The tempering process involves heating the chocolate so that it melts completely, cooling it by stirring to below the melting point of cocoa butter (about 78°F), and heating it again to an exact temperature. This process stabilizes the cocoa butter crystals. There are many methods for tempering chocolate. The **classic method for tempering chocolate** gives the most reliable and longest lasting results. The **quick method for tempering chocolate**, which is easier, also produces good results, but the chocolate is less stable and, as a result, it will not stay in temper as long. See also: chocolate, chocolate bloom, chocolate thermometer, confectionery coating, double boiler, marble, offset spatula, pastry scraper, rubber spatula, and tempering machine.

ⵥⵥⵥⵥⵥⵥⵥⵥ

CLASSIC METHOD FOR TEMPERING CHOCOLATE

1 pound good-quality chocolate

Chop the chocolate into small pieces. Place in the top of a double boiler and melt over hot, not simmering, water, stirring frequently with a rubber spatula to ensure even melting. The temperature of the chocolate should not exceed 120°F, or it will burn. Remove the double boiler from the heat, then remove the top pan and wipe the outside very dry.

To begin cooling the chocolate, stir it several times. Pour about two thirds of the chocolate onto a marble board. Spread the chocolate out using an offset spatula, then gather it back into a pool in the center of the marble with a plastic pastry scraper. Repeat this process 3 or 4 times, or until the chocolate registers 78°F on a chocolate or instant-read thermometer.

Return the chocolate to the pan with the remaining chocolate, and stir together until thoroughly blended, 2 to 3 minutes. Take the temperature of the tempered chocolate. It should be between:

88° and 91°F for bittersweet or semisweet chocolate
85° and 88°F for milk chocolate   *continued*

84° and 87°F for white chocolate

If the temperature of the chocolate is slightly low, replace the pan in the bottom of the double boiler and warm over low heat briefly, until it reaches the correct temperature. If the temperature of the chocolate is higher than it should be, pour about two thirds of the chocolate onto a clean marble board and repeat the tempering process.

To hold tempered chocolate at the correct temperature, place the top pan of the double boiler over water that is 2 degrees warmer than the chocolate. The water may need to be changed during the period of time that the chocolate is being used; as the chocolate cools, it will thicken and will need to be tempered again. Stir the chocolate frequently so it will not build up on the sides of the pan and become too cool.

To ensure success, be sure to use chocolate that contains cocoa butter. Compound, or summer, coating chocolate does not contain cocoa butter (and does not need to be tempered).

QUICK METHOD FOR TEMPERING CHOCOLATE

1 pound good-quality chocolate

Chop the chocolate into very tiny pieces. Set aside about one third of the chocolate. Melt the remaining chocolate in the top of a double boiler over hot, not simmering, water, stirring often with a rubber spatula to ensure even melting. The temperature of the chocolate should not exceed 120°F, or it will burn.

Remove the double boiler from the heat, then remove the top pan and wipe the outside dry. Stir in the reserved chopped chocolate in 3 to 4 additions, making sure each addition is completely melted before adding more. Adding the chopped chocolate brings down the temperature of the melted chocolate so that it should be tempered. To test if the chocolate is at the correct temperature, place a dab under your lower lip: If it feels comfortable, not too hot and not too cool, it is correct.

Hold the chocolate at the correct temperature by placing the top pan of the double boiler over water that is 2 degrees warmer than the chocolate.

tempering machine A machine designed specifically for melting and tempering chocolate. Tempering machines come in many different sizes and capacities, with small machines available for home use. The machine melts the chocolate, tempers it, and holds it at the correct temperature for dipping and molding truffles and candies. The small tempering machines have a plastic or metal casing that holds the electrical components, with a control panel on the front that has a temperature control knob, an on-off switch, and a switch that controls the bowl motor. A stainless steel bowl sits on top of the casing and is divided in half crosswise by a large plastic scraper, which holds a probe and a chocolate thermometer. Finely chopped chocolate is placed behind the scraper, the machine is set to a specific temperature, and the bowl is set to revolve. As the bowl rotates, the melted chocolate moves to the front of the scraper. Tempering machines are easy to use. Simply turn on the machine, put in finely chopped chocolate, and set the temperature according to the manufacturer's instructions. It takes approximately an hour to temper chocolate in the machine and perfect results are guaranteed. A unique feature of these machines is that chocolate can be held at a constant temperature to keep it liquid for several hours or even overnight. This means that additional chocolate can be tempered faster than by starting with chopped chocolate. The bowls of the tempering machines lift out for cleaning, and extra bowls and scrapers are available. See also: tempering chocolate.

thala guli These sesame seed and palm sugar balls are a traditional candy from Sri Lanka. Sesame seeds are ground in a mortar until they are crushed and release their oils, then palm sugar is grated in and salt is added. This mixture is kneaded until it holds together, then formed into walnut-sized balls. The balls are wrapped in rectangular pieces of waxed paper, and the ends of the paper are twisted, and cut into fringe. These popular candies are served at the end of a curry meal or as a snack. Sri Lanka. See also: sugar.

thong muan Translated from the Thai as "rolled gold," this dessert is composed of flour, coconut milk or cream, eggs, sugar, water, and lime juice mixed together into a thin batter and cooked on a utensil similar to a pizzelle or krumkake iron to a crisp wafer. While still warm, the wafers are rolled into tight cigarette shapes, similar to brandy snaps. This sweet is the result of the French influence in Thailand. The locally available coconut milk or cream replaces the dairy milk or cream that the French traditionally use. Thailand. See also: brandy snap, krumkake iron, and pizzelle iron.

thread stage The stage at which a small amount of hot sugar syrup forms a loose, thin thread when dropped from a spoon into cold water. The temperature range for thread stage is from 223° to 234°F on a candy thermometer. See also: Table of Sugar Temperatures and Stages (page 335).

timbale See rosette iron.

tiramisù An Italian dessert very popular in the United States and Italy, tiramisù is similar to a trifle. Made in a deep bowl, it is composed of layers of coffee-and-brandy-soaked ladyfingers or sponge cake, alternated with first a custard filling of zabaglione and then sweetened mascarpone, the Italian cheese that is a cross between cream cheese and sour cream. Some variations add chopped chocolate to the filling. Tiramisù is garnished with whipped cream, cocoa powder, and, occasionally, ground cinnamon. *Tiramisù* translates as "pick me up." Italy. See also: ladyfingers, mascarpone, sponge cake, trifle, and zabaglione.

toffee A brittle, crunchy, buttery candy made from a mixture of sugar, butter, and water cooked until they caramelize at the soft crack stage. The mixture is poured out onto an oiled surface, such as marble or stainless steel, or onto an oiled baking pan, rolled out thin, scored into pieces, and left to cool completely. After cooling, the candy is separated into its pieces. Toffee that is rich with butter and flavored with brown sugar is called butterscotch. **English toffee** is a well-known favorite type of toffee that is dipped in chocolate, then rolled in chopped almonds. To prevent toffee from becoming soft and sticky from contact with moisture, store the pieces in an airtight container between layers of waxed paper at room temperature. United Kingdom. See also: butterscotch and Table of Sugar Temperatures and Stages (page 335).

ENGLISH TOFFEE

Sixty 1½- by 4½-inch pieces

3 tablespoons flavorless vegetable oil
10 ounces (2½ sticks) unsalted butter, cut into small pieces
1 cup granulated sugar
½ teaspoon salt
¼ cup water
2½ cups unblanched almonds, finely chopped
12 ounces bittersweet, semisweet, or milk chocolate to be
    tempered (see page 297)

Use the vegetable oil to generously coat the back of a baking sheet or a marble board, a metal rolling pin, and a pizza wheel or a large chef's knife.

In a 3-quart heavy-bottomed saucepan, combine the butter, sugar, salt, and water, and stir over low heat to melt the butter. Raise the heat to medium and cook the mixture, stirring constantly with a long-handled wooden spoon, until it registers 260°F on a candy thermometer, about 10 minutes. Add ½ cup of the chopped almonds and cook, stirring constantly, until the mixture turns golden brown and reaches 305°F on the candy thermometer.

Remove the pan from the heat and immediately pour the mixture onto the oiled pan or marble. Quickly spread it out thin (⅛ inch thick) with the rolling pin into a large rectangle. Using the pizza wheel or chef's knife, score the toffee into narrow finger shapes 1½ inches long and ½ inch wide. Let the toffee cool completely. Break the toffee into pieces along the scored lines.

Temper the chocolate. Line three baking sheets with waxed paper. Place the remaining 2 cups chopped almonds in a mound on one of the baking sheets.

Place a piece of toffee in the tempered chocolate, coating it completely. Using a dipping fork or a plastic fork with the two middle tines broken off, lift the piece from the chocolate, gently shake off the excess chocolate, and set the toffee in the mound of almonds. Roll the toffee in the almonds to coat it completely, then transfer it to another lined baking sheet. Repeat this process with all the pieces of toffee. When the baking sheets become full, place each one in the refrigerator for 15 minutes to set the chocolate.

The toffee will keep for a month stored between layers of waxed paper in an airtight container in the refrigerator. It is best eaten at room temperature.

topfen See quark.

torrone The Italian version of nougat, usually made with honey, toasted almonds, pistachios, and other nuts, such as hazelnuts. Italy. See also: nougat.

TORRONE

Sixty-four 1-inch squares

Two 8- by 11-inch sheets edible rice paper
3 tablespoons light corn syrup

½ cup honey
1 cup granulated sugar
½ cup water
2 large egg whites, at room temperature
Pinch of cream of tartar
1 teaspoon vanilla extract
1 cup roughly chopped toasted sliced almonds
1 cup roughly chopped toasted and skinned hazelnuts
1 cup roughly chopped toasted pistachio nuts

Use 1 sheet of the rice paper to line an 8-inch square baking pan, spreading the paper up the sides of the pan.

In a 3-quart heavy-bottomed saucepan, combine the corn syrup, honey, sugar, and water. Cook over medium heat, stirring constantly with a long-handled wooden spoon, until the sugar is dissolved, about 5 minutes. Brush down the sides of the pan with a pastry brush dipped in warm water to prevent the sugar from crystallizing. Raise the heat to medium high, place a candy thermometer in the pan, and cook the mixture, without stirring, until it registers 290°F on the thermometer, about 15 minutes. Brush down the sides of the pan with a pastry brush dipped in water twice while the mixture is cooking.

Meanwhile, in the bowl of a stand mixer, using a wire whip, or in a mixing bowl, using a hand-held mixer, beat the egg whites on medium speed until they are frothy. Add the cream of tartar, increase the speed to medium high, and beat the egg whites until they hold stiff, but not dry, peaks, 3 to 5 minutes.

With the mixer speed at medium, slowly pour the hot sugar syrup into the egg whites, taking care not to let the sugar syrup drip down the sides of the bowl. Raise the mixer speed to high and beat until the mixture is stiff and cool. Blend in the vanilla and stir in the nuts.

Turn the mixture out into the prepared pan and spread it smoothly and evenly over the bottom and into the corners of the pan. Place the remaining sheet of rice paper on top of the candy, place a cutting board or plate on top of the rice paper, and weight it with a heavy item, such as a heavy pan. Let the torrone stand for 12 hours at room temperature.

Use a sharp thin-bladed knife to release the edges of the candy from the pan. Invert the candy onto a cutting board, then reinvert, so the top side is facing up. Using a serrated knife cut the candy into 1-inch squares, leaving the paper on it. Stored between sheets of waxed paper in a tightly covered container, the candy will keep for 1 week at room temperature or 3 weeks in the refrigerator.

torta The Italian word for tart, cake, pie, and pastry and the Spanish word for loaf, cake, and a dish made with pastry. It is also the Portuguese word for a light sponge cake or a tart.

torta delizia A classic Italian cake that consists of layers of sponge cake filled with jam or pastry cream. The outside of the cake is completely covered with an almond macaroon paste that is piped on with a pastry bag and star tube. The cake is briefly baked in a hot oven to lightly brown the almond paste, then a sweet glaze is brushed over the cake to make it shiny. This cake is very sweet and is meant to be eaten in small portions, much like a confection. Italy.

torta di mandorle A specialty of Venice, Italy, this almond tart is found in many shapes and sizes throughout the city. **Torta di mandorle** is composed of a sweet pastry shell filled with rich, creamy frangipane that is completely covered with unblanched whole almonds. The tart is baked until it is golden. After it is cool, the top of the tart is dusted heavily with confectioners' sugar. The tart is usually baked in a large rectangular shape, but round and square shapes as well as individual size tarts are also made. Italy.

TORTA DI MANDORLE

Venetian Almond Tart

One 14- by 4-inch tart, 12 to 14 servings

1 recipe Pâte Sucrée (page 225)
1 recipe Frangipane (page 127)
1 cup (4½ ounces) unblanched whole almonds
¼ to ⅓ cup confectioners' sugar, for garnish

Center a rack in the oven and preheat to 375°F. Line a jelly-roll pan with parchment paper and center a 14- by 4½-inch flan form on the pan.

Roll out the pâte sucrée on a lightly floured work surface to a rectangle about 16 by 6 inches and ⅛ inch thick. Carefully roll the pastry dough up around the rolling pin, then gently unroll the dough into the flan form. Carefully fit the pastry dough into the bottom and up the sides of the flan form. Trim off the excess pastry dough.

Pour the frangipane into the tart shell. Use a rubber spatula to smooth the top. Cover the top of the frangipane with the unblanched whole almonds in tight, crosswise lines.

Bake the tart for 30 minutes, until the filling is slightly puffed and golden brown. Transfer the tart to a rack to cool.   *continued*

Gently pull up on the flan form to remove it from the tart. Use 2 large spatulas to transfer the tart to a 14- by 4-inch cardboard. Dust the top of the tart heavily with the confectioners' sugar.

Serve the tart immediately or store it for up to 3 days at room temperature, tightly wrapped in aluminum foil.

torta diplomatica A rich, delicate Italian cake, torta diplomatica is composed of bottom and top disks of puff pastry alternated with a pastry cream filling and a layer of sponge cake moistened with rum sugar syrup. The sides of the cake are coated with more pastry cream. Crushed baked puff pastry is pressed into the sides, and the top of the cake is dusted with confectioners' sugar. Italy. See also: pastry cream, puff pastry, and sponge cake.

torte The German word for cake. Tortes are usually made with flour, sugar, eggs, and butter, but often ground nuts or bread crumbs are substituted for some or all of the flour. Tortes have a moist quality that keeps them fresh for several days. A torte may be either a multilayered cake or a dense-textured single-layer cake, such as **chocolate amaretti torte**. Torte also refers to a few tartlike confections, such as linzertorte. Tortes originated in Central Europe. See also: linzertorte.

CHOCOLATE AMARETTI TORTE

One 9- by 2-inch round torte; 12 to 14 servings

2 teaspoons unsalted butter, melted, for the pan
2 teaspoons all-purpose flour, for the pan

Torte
4 ounces bittersweet chocolate, finely chopped
1/2 cup finely ground amaretti biscuits
1/2 cup all-purpose flour
8 ounces (2 sticks) unsalted butter, softened
1 cup granulated sugar
5 large eggs, separated, at room temperature

Confectioners' sugar for garnish
12 to 14 fresh mint leaves (optional)
12 to 14 fresh raspberries or 6 to 7 fresh strawberries, washed,
    dried, hulled, and cut in half lengthwise (optional)

Center a rack in the oven and preheat to 350°F. Brush the inside of a 9- by 2-inch round cake pan with the melted butter. Dust the pan with the flour and shake out the excess. Place a 9-inch parchment paper round in the bottom of the pan and brush with the butter.

For the torte, melt the chocolate in the top of a double boiler over hot, not simmering, water, stirring frequently with a rubber spatula to ensure even melting. Remove from the heat.

Combine the amaretti and flour, and set aside.

In the bowl of a stand mixer, using the flat beater attachment, or in a mixing bowl, using a hand-held mixer, beat the softened butter until light and fluffy, about 2 minutes. Add the sugar and blend well. Beat in the egg yolks 1 at a time, mixing well and stopping to scrape down the sides of the bowl after each addition.

Beat in the flour mixture in 3 additions, scraping down the sides of the bowl after each addition. Add the melted chocolate and blend well.

In a grease-free bowl, using grease-free beaters, whip the egg whites until they are stiff, but not dry. Fold the whites into the chocolate mixture in 3 or 4 additions.

Pour the batter into the prepared pan, and bake for 40 to 45 minutes, until a tester inserted 2 inches in from the outer edge comes out clean. Transfer the pan to a rack to cool for 15 minutes. Place a 9-inch cardboard cake circle over the top of the cake pan and invert the cake onto the cardboard. Peel the parchment paper off the cake. (The bottom of the torte is now the top.) Let the torte, on the cake round, cool completely on the rack.

To decorate the torte, dust the top heavily with confectioners' sugar. With a sharp knife, mark the outer edge of the torte into serving pieces. If using, place a mint leaf in the center of each piece, about 1 inch in from the outer edge. Place a raspberry or a strawberry half at the base of each mint leaf. If not using mint, place a raspberry or strawberry half in the center of each serving piece, about 1 inch in from the outer edge.

The torte will keep for 3 days well wrapped in the refrigerator. It is best served at room temperature.

tortoni Often called biscuit tortoni, this Italian frozen dessert is a combination of ice cream or sweetened whipped cream and rum or sherry mixed with chopped almonds or crumbled macaroons. It is often served in individual paper cups. The dessert takes its name from the owner of a well-known eighteenth-century Paris café of the same name. Italy.

toscatårta A classic Swedish almond-topped butter cake. After a light, buttery, sponge-type cake is baked, it is topped with a cooked mixture of butter, sugar, flour, milk, and almonds, and placed under the broiler for a few minutes to brown the topping. The cake is traditionally served warm. Sweden.

treacle A sweet, heavy, cane-sugar syrup, similar to molasses. The syrup is boiled to remove some of the sucrose, which makes it more concentrated, darkens its color, and deepens its flavor. Treacle, a British specialty, undergoes more refining than molasses, which makes it thinner and lighter in color. However, treacle and molasses can be substituted for each other in recipes. Dark treacle or black treacle is "regular" treacle, whereas light treacle is called golden syrup. Treacle has a distinct, rich flavor. It gives sweetness, moisture, color, and longer life to many baked goods. Treacle is available primarily in specialty food stores. United Kingdom. See also: golden syrup and molasses.

trifle A well-known English dessert made in a deep bowl, trifle is composed of liqueur-soaked sponge cake or ladyfingers spread with jam, topped with custard, and decorated with whipped cream and almonds. United Kingdom. See also: ladyfingers and sponge cake.

trois frères mold A shallow, scalloped, round tube mold made of tinned steel. It is used for baking cakes or for molding cold desserts. The mold was created in the nineteenth century and named for the three French pastry chef brothers who invented it. This mold is made in 6-ounce and $1^1/_2$-quart capacities, ranging from 4 to 8 inches in diameter. It is available at cookware shops and through mail order cookware catalogs.

truffle See chocolate truffle.

truffle dipper See chocolate dipping forks.

truffle grid A rectangular form made of flat metal wires, tightly cross-woven, suspended on small $1/_2$-inch-high feet. A truffle grid looks like a cooling rack, but it has a tighter weave of wires. It is used to give texture to the outside chocolate coating of truffles. While still liquid, the dipped truffles are rolled over the grid, creating a rough texture. A truffle grid can also be used as an icing rack to hold cakes or petits fours while fondant or chocolate icing is poured over them. See also: chocolate truffle.

tuaca A golden-colored, slightly sweet Italian liqueur, flavored with vanilla and accented with orange, almond, and coconut. Tuaca is said to date back to the Renaissance. It is used to flavor desserts, pastries, and confections. Italy.

tube pan A round baking pan that has a hollow tube in the center, which conducts heat to the center of the cake so that it bakes evenly. Most tube pans have high slightly slanted sides. An angel food cake pan usually has several small "feet" around the rim, which allow air to circulate around the pan as it stands upside down to cool. Alternatively, the center tube is taller than the sides of the pan for the same effect. Some angel food cake pans have removable bottoms. Other special pans that are also tube pans include a kugelhopf pan or mold and a Bundt pan, which have deeply grooved sides that create patterns in the finished cakes. There is also a tube pan that has fluted sides. Tube pans have between 9- and 12-cup capacities. They are 8 to 10 inches in diameter and 3½ to 4 inches high. They are available at cookware shops and through mail order cookware catalogs. See also: Bundt pan and kugelhopf mold.

tuile A classic delicate, thin, crisp almond cookie. **Tuiles** are formed into their characteristic arched shape by placing them over a rolling pin or into a curved mold while still warm, then left to set. When cool, the cookies resemble the curved roof tiles for which they are named. Tuiles are made in many flavor variations, including vanilla, lemon, and orange. Other nuts can replace the traditional almonds. Tuiles are often served as an accompaniment to ice cream, sorbet, or mousse. France. See also: tuile cookie mold.

TUILES
Curved Almond Cookies

Approximately 24 cookies

1 tablespoon unsalted butter, softened, for the pans

3½ tablespoons unsalted butter, softened
½ cup granulated sugar
2 large egg whites, at room temperature
⅓ cup all-purpose flour
⅓ cup almond meal (see page 4)

½ teaspoon almond extract
⅓ to ½ cup sliced unblanched almonds

Center a rack in the oven and preheat to 425°F. Line two baking sheets with aluminum foil. Use the softened butter to butter the foil.

In the bowl of a stand mixer, using the flat beater attachment, or in a mixing bowl, using a hand-held mixer, beat the butter until light and fluffy, about 2 minutes. Add the sugar and beat until well blended, stopping to scrape down the sides of the bowl occasionally with a rubber spatula.

Add the egg whites and beat until well combined. Fold in the flour in 3 additions, then fold in the almond meal and almond extract.

Drop teaspoons of the batter onto the prepared baking sheets, leaving 3 inches space between them. With the back of a spoon dipped in cold water, flatten the batter into circles about 2 to 3 inches in diameter. Sprinkle the sliced almonds on top of the circles.

Place one sheet of the cookies in the oven and bake for 6 to 8 minutes, until the outer edges are golden brown and the centers are set. Remove the baking pan from the oven. Working very quickly, use a small offset spatula to lift the cookies from the baking pan. Drape the cookies over a rolling pin or place them in a tuile cookie mold, and let them cool in their curved shape. If the cookies become difficult to remove from the baking pan, return the pan to the oven for 30 to 45 seconds.

Bake the second pan of cookies and repeat the shaping process. Let cool.

The cookies will keep for 5 to 6 days in an airtight container at room temperature.

tuile cookie mold This mold has six smooth, narrow, curved tinned-steel troughs that create the perfect arched shape for tuiles. As soon as the cookies are removed from the oven, they are transferred to the mold, which holds them as they cool, creating their characteristic curved tile shape. The mold measures 12 by 14 inches. It is available at specialty cookware shops and through mail order cookware catalogs.

tulipe Translated from French as "tulip," this is a ruffled pastry shell made from a delicate cookie batter. While still warm, the cookie is placed either in or over the back of a cup, small bowl, or muffin tin cup and molded to fit the container. The cookie is left to cool so it will hold the shape of the object. The cooled tulipe is filled with fresh berries, mousse, sorbet, ice cream, or whipped cream and served as a dessert. France.

Turbinado sugar See sugar.

Turkish delight Also called rahat loukoum, meaning "a rest for the throat," Turkish delight is a chewy, gelatinous confection with a rubbery texture. It is made of fruit juice, sugar, honey, glucose, and cornstarch or gelatin and is traditionally tinted pink or green. Chopped nuts, such as pistachio nuts, pine nuts, almonds, or hazelnuts, are often added to the confection for texture. Turkish delight is cut into squares and covered with confectioners' sugar. Turkey.

turnover A round or square pastry case folded in half over a filling, creating a half-moon or a triangle. The filling can be either sweet, such as fruit, or savory, such as minced chicken. Turnovers are either baked or fried. They can range in size from one-bite finger food to 8 inches in diameter. The sweet versions are served for dessert, the savory renditions as appetizers or entrées. United States.

turntable A turntable looks like a lazy Susan and is used in decorating and assembling cakes. A turntable elevates the cake above counter height and brings it closer to eye level, making the work more accurate. A sturdy, footed, 4-inch-high cast-iron base holds a thin flat metal plate. Round plates are available in 12-, 14-, and 16-inch diameters, and a rectangular plate that measures 12 by 16 inches is also available. An adjusting metal screw in the base controls the stability of the plate, making it easy to regulate the speed at which the plate can be rotated. Cakes are placed on the metal plate and decorations are piped onto them while the plate is rotated as necessary by hand. This allows for uniform decorations. Cakes can also be assembled on the turntable, one layer at a time. Rotating the turntable slowly makes it easy to apply the icing or filling evenly to the cake layer. Plastic turntables are also available, but are not as sturdy or stable as the metal ones, especially when handling large cakes. Turntables are available at cookware shops, at cake decorating supply shops, and through mail order cookware catalogs.

tutové See rolling pin.

ugli fruit A citrus fruit hybrid that is a cross between an orange, a tangerine, and a grapefruit or pomelo, ugli fruit is native to Jamaica. Ugli fruit looks like a pear-shaped grapefruit, with thick, lumpy, loose skin ranging in color from lime green to pale orange. The practically seedless, juicy, bright-yellow to orange pulp is tart-sweet and zesty. Ugli fruit and its peel, which removes easily, can be used like oranges, tangerines, and grapefruit as an ingredient in desserts, pastries, and confections. The fruit is available in specialty markets from January to June. Choose fragrant fruit that feels heavy for its size, with orange-tinted, unblemished skin that gives slightly when pressed. Store ugli fruit at room temperature for up to 4 days or in the refrigerator for up to 3 weeks. See also: citrus fruit, fruit, grapefruit, orange, pomelo, and tangerine.

unmold To remove a cake, ice cream, candy, or other item from the container or mold that gives it its shape. Different methods are used depending on what is being unmolded. For soft items such as ice creams, custards, and desserts made with gelatin, briefly dip the base of the mold in hot water. The food should move slightly inside of the mold and the sides may begin to melt slightly. Place a plate over the mouth of the mold and invert the mold onto the plate. Gently shake or tap the mold to release the dessert, then lift off the mold. Occasionally it may be necessary to run a thin-bladed knife between the edge of the mold and the dessert. Also, leaving the mold to stand for a few minutes while inverted often works by allowing gravity to help. Cakes, muffins, and other baked goods are inverted onto a cooling rack, then their pans are lifted off. Many recipes call for allowing baked goods to sit in the pan for 10 to 15 minutes to begin cooling before they are inverted. This time allows steam to build up, which helps to release them from the pan. Tarts that are baked in pans with removable bottoms are easily released by pushing up on the bottom and allowing the sides to fall away. Tarts baked in a flan ring can be unmolded by lifting off the ring. To release candies from their molds, turn the molds upside down and manipulate the molds with a back-and-forth motion. Or gently tap the mold against a countertop or with your fingers to release the candy. To remove candy from two-part molds, take off the clips that hold the mold together and gently pull away both sides of the mold. See also: baking pan, cake pan, chocolate mold, cooling rack, flan ring, and tart pan.

unsalted butter See butter.

upside-down cake A batter cake baked with fruit or another topping covering the bottom of the pan, which has first been coated with a mixture of butter and brown sugar that caramelizes during baking. After the cake is baked, it is inverted onto a serving platter so that the glazed fruit or topping is then on top of the cake. Pineapple upside-down cake is the most well known. United States.

vacherin A French dessert composed of a round hard meringue base with several meringue rings stacked on it and glued together with soft meringue, then dried to form a container; this container is filled with crème Chantilly and fresh fruit, or ice cream, and decorated with crystallized flowers or fresh fruit. Some vacherins are constructed with a merginue top, others are left open. A variation of vacherin is made with rings of almond paste, instead of meringue, stacked on the meringue base. The name comes from the cheese of the same name, which the meringue container is said to resemble in shape and color. The Austrian dessert known as Spanish windtorte is an elaborately decorated vacherin. France. See also: crème Chantilly, meringue, and Spanish windtorte.

Valencia orange A member of the sweet family of oranges, Valencia oranges are appreciated for the quality of their juice. They have thin, light-orange skin that is often streaked with yellow. The sweet, juicy flesh is practically seedless. Valencia oranges are used as an ingredient in desserts, pastries, and confections. They are available from January through October. Choose firm fruit that feels heavy for its size, with no soft spots or discoloration. Russets, rough brown spots on the skin, do not affect the quality or flavor of the fruit. Store Valencia oranges in a cool, dry place for several days or in the refrigerator for several weeks. See also: citrus fruit, fruit, and orange.

vanilla bean The pod of a climbing orchid vine native to southern Mexico, vanilla beans have been used as a flavoring for hundreds of years. The Aztecs used the beans to flavor chocolate. The plants are widely grown in tropical climates, such as Tahiti and Madagascar, which produce the most moist and flavorful beans. The pods are picked green, then cured. The curing process begins with a boiling-water bath, then the beans are wrapped and left to sweat in the sun. This sweating process is alternated with drying, which produces the characteristic dark brown color and shriveled appearance of the long, thin beans and causes the outside of the pods to become encrusted with frosty white crystals, called vanillin. Vanillin gives the beans their fragrant flavor and aroma.

Vanilla beans are used extensively to flavor desserts, pastries, and confections. To use the bean for flavoring, it is split open and steeped in liquid. The tiny black grains that fill the inside of the bean contain the potent vanilla flavor, which is released during the steeping. After use, the beans can be thoroughly rinsed and dried, then buried in a well-covered container of granulated or confectioners' sugar for several days to make vanilla sugar. Vanilla beans dry out if exposed to air. To keep them plump and flexible, store them wrapped in plastic in a tightly covered container in a cool, dry place, where they will last for several months.

vanilla extract Produced by steeping vanilla beans in an alcohol-and-water solution, pure vanilla is concentrated and, therefore, only a small amount is needed for flavoring. Vanilla is expensive to produce, which has led to the proliferation of synthetically produced vanilla. According to the U.S. Food and Drug Administration, to be labeled as pure vanilla extract, a product must be made from vanilla beans. If synthetically produced vanillin is used as a flavoring, the label must state that the product is artificially flavored. If a combination of pure and artificial vanillas are used to produce the flavor, the label states that the product is "vanilla-flavored." Mexican vanilla, which is much cheaper than the vanilla available in the United States, often contains coumarin, which is a potentially toxic substance. Consequently, Mexican vanilla is banned by the FDA. Vanilla extract will last indefinitely if stored in a tightly covered glass or plastic bottle in a cool, dark, dry place. See also: extract, vanilla bean, and vanillin.

vanilla kipferl Classic Viennese crescent-shaped butter cookies. The cookies are made from a pastry dough rich with ground almonds, butter, sugar, and vanilla and rolled in confectioners' sugar after baking. They are traditionally made during the Christmas holiday season. Austria.

vanilla sugar Granulated or confectioners' sugar that has been infused with the fragrant flavor of vanilla. To make vanilla sugar, score a vanilla bean lengthwise, place it in a tall jar, and cover it with sugar. Cover the jar and let stand for at least 24 hours so the sugar can absorb the vanilla flavor. Replenish the sugar as it is used. The vanilla bean will continue to perfume the sugar for several months. Vanilla sugar is also made commercially and is available in small packets. Vanilla sugar can be substituted in almost any recipe that calls for sugar. See also: sugar.

vanillin Powdery white crystals that form on the outside of vanilla pods during their curing process. Vanillin gives the beans fragrant flavor and aroma. Vanillin is also synthetically produced as a by-product of the paper industry. It is treated with chemicals that give it an artificial taste. Synthetically produced vanillin is often used to flavor vanilla extract. If so, the label on the vanilla extract must state this. Because of its artificial taste, synthetically produced vanillin is easily detected when used to flavor desserts, pastries, and confections. See also: vanilla bean and vanilla extract.

vark The Indian word for tissue-thin silver or gold leaf, which is used to decorate sweets and desserts for special occasions and celebrations, such as weddings and religious festivals. India. See also: gold leaf and silver leaf.

vegetable oil See canola oil, corn oil, fats and oils, olive oil, peanut oil, safflower oil, soybean oil, and sunflower oil.

vegetable oil spray Made of water, vegetable oil, lecithin, and preservatives, vegetable oil spray is a nonstick mixture used in place of butter or margarine for greasing pans to help baked goods release easily. Lecithin, a primary ingredient, is made from soybeans and aids in easy release. Vegetable oil sprays are used primarily to reduce the amount of fat used in baking. They are made from the oils considered to be the lowest in cholesterol, such as canola, corn, or safflower. There are several brands of vegetable oil sprays available, including Wesson, Mazola, and Pam, which come in both regular and butter flavor. Vegetable oil sprays are available in pump-style spray bottles and aerosol cans in supermarkets. They must be shaken vigorously before use. Vegetable oil sprays should be stored in a cool, dry place where they will last for up to a year. See also: Baker's Joy, fats and oils, and lecithin.

Victoria sandwich cake Named for Queen Victoria, this English cake also goes by the name of Victoria sponge. It is composed of two layers of buttery sponge cake filled with either raspberry or strawberry jam and sweetened whipped cream or buttercream. **Victoria sandwich cake** is usually served for afternoon tea. United Kingdom. See also: sponge cake.

⊗⊗⊗⊗⊗⊗⊗⊗⊗

VICTORIA SANDWICH CAKE

One 8-Inch round cake; 10 to 12 servings

2 tablespoons unsalted butter, melted, for the pans
2 tablespoons all-purpose flour, for the pans

6 ounces (1½ sticks) unsalted butter, softened
¾ cup plus 2 tablespoons granulated sugar
3 large eggs, at room temperature
1½ cups all-purpose flour
2 teaspoons baking powder
½ teaspoon salt
Finely minced zest of 1 lemon
1½ cups heavy whipping cream
½ cup raspberry jam
½ cup toasted sliced almonds

Center a rack in the oven and preheat to 350°F. Brush the inside of two 8- by 2-inch round cake pans with the melted butter, then dust with the flour, and shake out the excess. Line the bottom of each pan with an 8-inch round of parchment paper, and brush the rounds with butter.

In the bowl of a stand mixer, using the flat beater attachment, or in a mixing bowl, using a hand-held mixer, beat the softened butter until light and fluffy. Add ¾ cup of the sugar and beat until well blended. Add the eggs 1 at a time, beating well after each addition.

Sift together the flour and baking powder, and add the salt.

Add the dry ingredients to the butter mixture In 3 additions, stopping to scrape down the sides of the bowl with a rubber spatula after each addition. Add the lemon zest and blend well.

Divide the batter evenly between the prepared cake pans, and smooth the tops with a rubber spatula. Bake for 20 minutes, or until the layers are lightly browned and the tops spring back when touched. Transfer the pans to racks to cool.

Place an 8-inch cardboard cake circle over each cake pan, and invert the layers onto the cardboard circles. Gently peel the parchment paper off the layers and reinvert them onto other cardboard circles. (The layers can be baked 2 days in advance and held at room temperature, well wrapped in plastic wrap.)

In a chilled bowl, using chilled beaters, whip the cream until it begins to thicken. Gradually add the remaining 2 tablespoons sugar and whip until the cream holds firm peaks.

Slice the 2 layers in half horizontally. Place the bottom half of 1 layer on a cardboard cake circle. Spread with one third of the raspberry jam and spread one quarter of the whipped cream over the jam. Place a second layer on top, and repeat with the jam and whipped cream. Add the third layer, spread with jam and whipped cream, then top with the final layer. Cover the sides and the top of the cake with the remaining cream.

Spread the toasted almonds on a sheet of waxed or parchment paper. Using an offset spatula, gently lift the cake up, and hold it from underneath with one hand. With your other hand, press the almonds into the sides of the cake up to the top edge.

Refrigerate the cake until ready to serve. The cake can be assembled up to 4 hours before serving.

wafer A very thin, crisp biscuit or cookie. Although round is the most common shape, wafers can be made in various shapes, such as fans. They can be imprinted with a variety of designs; some are made on carved irons, such as a krumkake iron or pizzelle iron. Wafers are often rolled into cigarette shapes while still warm and, occasionally, filled with whipped cream or jam. Wafers are used primarily as an accompaniment to ice creams and ices. Wafers have been documented as far back as the twelfth century, when they were baked on carved irons held over an open fire. Wafers are made from a batter similar to that for waffles and are considered to be the forerunners of waffles. Brandy snaps, krumkake, and pizzelle are modern variations of wafers. United Kingdom. See also: biscuit, brandy snap, krumkake, krumkake iron, pizzelle, pizzelle iron, and waffle.

waffle Made from a thin batter, waffles are crisp cakes baked until golden between the hinged plates of specially designed engraved irons that give them a honeycomb surface. Waffles are made primarily from flour, sugar, eggs, butter, and milk, with various flavorings such as vanilla, orange, lemon, cinnamon, nutmeg, nuts, or chocolate. Most batters are leavened with baking powder, although yeast is used occasionally. Waffles are usually eaten hot, topped with confectioners' sugar, butter, jam, preserves, marmalade, honey, maple syrup, fruit sauces, or whipped cream. Fresh fruit and ice cream are also used as garnishes for waffles. Waffles can be thin and crisp or fluffy, like thick Belgian waffles, which have deep pockets in their surface. Waffles can be made in a variety of shapes, including square, rectangular, round, and heart-shaped. They are served for both breakfast and dessert. United States. See also: waffle iron.

waffle iron An appliance for cooking waffles made of two hinged metal plates that close together. Each plate has protruding studs that fit between those on the other plate, forming the characteristic honeycomb or grid appearance in the surface of the waffles. Waffle irons are available both as electric models and as irons to be used on top of the stove. Electric waffle irons cook both sides of the waffle simultaneously. The stove-top models must be turned over after one side is cooked. Stove-top waffle irons can be used on either gas or electric stoves. Waffle irons are made of cast aluminum and are available with a nonstick surface, which makes cleanup easy. Waffle irons come in a variety of shapes, including round, rectangular, square, and heart-shaped. Belgian waffle irons make thicker waffles with deeper pockets than regular waffle irons. See also: waffle.

wagashi Japanese confections made from various combinations of adzuki beans, sugar, rice powder, flour, and vegetable gelatin, which are blended into a doughlike consistency. The different mixtures are fashioned into various whimsical designs, such as leaves wrapped around small balls, layers of chrysanthemum blossom wafers enclosing a filling of adzuki bean jam, cherry blossoms, chestnuts, and jelled cubes enclosing a tiny fish. These bite-sized delicacies are served for special occasions accompanied by green tea. Japan.

walnut The fruit of the walnut tree, which is native to Asia and is cultivated in Asia, Italy, France, and North America. Of the many varieties of walnuts, the most popular are English walnuts and black walnuts. The butternut, also called a white walnut, is a relatively unknown but highly prized species. English walnuts, which have a mild flavor, are the most commonly available. They are widely grown because they are the easiest to shell. Black walnuts have a richer, stronger flavor but are very difficult to shell. Walnuts are enclosed in a hard, two-part light-brown shell. The color of the shell indicates the quality of the nut. The lighter the shell, the higher the grade of walnut. The two-part wing-shaped nut is surrounded by a thin brown skin, which is usually not removed. Walnuts have a rich, buttery flavor that is enhanced by toasting. They are widely used ground, chopped, or whole to flavor and decorate desserts, pastries, and confections. Walnuts are available year-round both unshelled and shelled. Choose unshelled walnuts without holes or cracks in their shells. Store unshelled walnuts in a cool, dry place for several months. Because of their high natural oil content, which causes them to turn rancid easily, shelled walnuts should be stored in an airtight container in the refrigerator for up to 3 months or in the freezer for up to a year. Walnuts are available in supermarkets, nut stores, and health food stores. See also: nut.

warming case Used for working with pulled or blown sugar, a warming case is a three-sided Plexiglas case that is open in the front. The case has a wooden base and top that supports a heat lamp used to keep sugar soft and pliable while it is being pulled or blown. The case traps warmth in the working area, helping to keep the sugar warm longer. See also: blown sugar, heat lamp, and pulled sugar.

water bath A two-part setup in which a pan or bowl that holds a shallow amount of hot water into which another smaller pan or bowl is set so that its contents will be protected from the heat source or from intense heat. A water bath insulates and provides a consistent source of heat for melting ingredients, such as chocolate and butter, evenly, and for holding ingredients at a constant temperature without burning. The technique of cooking in a water bath can be done either on top of the stove or in the oven. It is used for cooking and baking delicate custards and cheesecakes, as it keeps them from curdling and cracking and for keeping cooked or baked dishes or sauces warm. See also: bain-marie.

water ice A frozen dessert of sugar and water, blended with a flavoring such as fruit juice or fruit purée, liqueur, or an infusion such as coffee or tea. A water ice is smooth and contains no fat or egg whites. Water ices are served on their own or as an accompaniment to pastries and cakes. See also: granita and sorbet.

watermelon The fruit of a vine native to Africa, watermelon is a large melon, either round or oblong, with a hard rind that ranges in color from pale off-white to dark green. The rind can be solid, speckled, or striped. The crisp, sweet, juicy pulp ranges from pinkish-red to yellow to creamy off-white. All watermelons have small black, brown, green, white, or speckled seeds scattered throughout—even the seedless varieties, whose few tiny seeds are edible. Watermelon is used as an ingredient in desserts such as fresh fruit salad and ice creams and sorbets. Watermelon is available almost year-round through foreign imports, with the peak from June to August. Because the melons can be so large, they are often sold cut in half or quarters. Choose cut watermelon that has firm, juicy red flesh with dark seeds. Small white seeds indicate that the melon is immature. Choose whole watermelons that feel heavy for their size and sound hollow when tapped on the side. Look for smooth, slightly dull, evenly colored, firm rind that gives slightly to pressure.

Avoid melons with soft spots, cuts, or bruises. Store cut melons tightly wrapped in plastic in the refrigerator for up to 3 days. Store whole melons in the refrigerator for up to a week. See also: fruit and melon.

wedding cake A symbolic, usually elaborately decorated, cake that is the centerpiece of a wedding feast or celebration. Wedding cakes are often composed of tiers of graduated sizes and topped by an ornamental bride and groom. Fresh, sugar, or crystallized flowers are often used to decorate the cake, as are garlands of icing, lace made from icing, and marzipan. Traditionally, the top tier of the cake is saved and frozen for the bride and groom to eat on their first anniversary. Many countries and cultures have their own particular wedding cakes, such as France's croquembouche or a heavy fruitcake traditional in Britain and its former colonies of South Africa, Australia, and New Zealand. There are many rituals associated with cutting the wedding cake and sharing it with the wedding guests. In Britain, for example, pieces of the cake are wrapped and given to the guests to take home and eat at a later time. See also: cake and croquembouche.

whip The technique of beating rapidly in a circular motion to incorporate air into a substance, such as cream or egg whites, which expands its volume. Whipping is accomplished either by hand with a whisk or rotary beater or by machine with an electric mixer. Whipping is stirring that is done rapidly and vigorously. See also: rotary beater and whisk.

whisk A hand-held kitchen utensil made of several thin stainless-steel looped wires attached to a wooden or stainless steel handle, forming a teardrop shape. The stainless steel wires come in a range of thicknesses, making some whisks more flexible, some sturdier. Miniature whisks are about 7 inches long. Standard whisks are between 10 and 14 inches in length. Flat whisks are sometimes used for folding cake batters and other mixtures. The wires in a balloon whisk form a bulb shape, making it comparatively wide at the bottom; a pastry whisk is more elongated, with a narrow bulb shape. Both of these whisks have a variety of uses in the dessert kitchen, such as whipping cream and egg whites, blending batters, and stirring custards as they cook. Balloon whisks incorporate more air into a mixture than any other whisk. They are especially prized for whipping egg whites. See also: copper egg white bowl and whip.

white chocolate A blend of cocoa butter (from the cocoa bean), sugar, milk solids, lecithin, and vanilla. Because white chocolate contains no chocolate liquor, the liquid pressed from the cocoa bean during processing, the U.S. Food and Drug Administration has ruled that technically it cannot be called chocolate. It is usually labeled "confectionery coating." It has a soft consistency and cannot be used interchangeably with other chocolates in recipes. White chocolate is not the same as summer coating, which contains no cocoa butter. See also: chocolate and confectionery coating.

Winesap apple One of the favorite apples for baked goods and baking whole because it holds its shape. Winesap apples have dark red skin and juicy, tart, pale yellow flesh. Winesap apples are available from November to June. See also: apple.

wintergreen A native North American evergreen plant with red berries and small white bell-shaped flowers. The plant is also called checkerberry. The round, deep green, highly aromatic leaves produce piquant oil of wintergreen, which is used as a flavoring in confectionery. United States.

Winter Nelis pear A stocky pear with practically no neck, a Winter Nelis pear has brownish-green skin dotted with russet and firm, creamy white, spicy flesh. Winter Nelis pears are used both raw and cooked as an ingredient in desserts, pastries, and confections. It is a favorite pear for baking and poaching because it holds its shape. Winter Nelis pears are available from November to May. Choose fragrant, firm, blemish-free fruit that gives slightly when pressed at the stem end. Slightly underripe Winter Nelis pears will ripen at room temperature within a few days. To speed up the process, place them in a tightly closed but perforated paper bag with an apple or a banana. Store ripe Winter Nelis pears in the refrigerator for up to a week. See also: fruit and pear.

wooden spoon and spatula These utensils are invaluable for stirring hot candy mixtures and custards as they cook. Wood does not conduct heat, so the utensils stay cool. Nor does wood scratch the surfaces with which it comes in contact. Wooden spoons and spatulas with a straight or flat edge cover more surface on the bottom of the pan than those that are round, although the round ones are preferred for small pans. Wooden spoons and spatulas in a variety of sizes and shapes are part of the traditional batterie de cuisine. Those with long handles work well to protect hands from hot mixtures, such as caramels and brittles, as they cook. Wooden spoons and spatulas should not soak in water or be washed in the dishwasher, which would cause them to splinter and deteriorate over time. Those made of hardwood, such as boxwood, will last longer than those of softer woods. See also: Batterie de Cuisine (page 331), and spatula.

XXX, XXXX The symbols used on the labels of confectioners' sugar to indicate its fineness. The more Xs, the finer the grade of sugar. The number of Xs indicate the number of holes per inch on the screens used to form the size of the sugar crystals. For example, four Xs indicate four holes per inch. Confectioners' sugar is sometimes called 10 X, referring to the number of holes on the screens that it passes through during processing. See also: sugar.

yeast A microscopic single-celled fungus that induces fermentation and leavening by releasing carbon dioxide, yeast has been used as a leavening agent for bread for at least six thousand years. Although yeast is always in the air, it was the work of the French scientist Louis Pasteur in the 1850s that led to the understanding of the fermentation process and ultimately to the development and cultivation of the yeast we use today. Baker's yeast is widely used as a leavening agent in baked goods. Yeast feeds on the sugar or starch (flour) in a dough, converting it to carbon dioxide, which becomes trapped inside the dough's structure and causes it to rise. Besides food, yeast needs two other elements to grow: a warm, draft-free environment (about 80°F) and moisture, in the form of liquid. There are two types of yeast widely available in supermarkets, compressed fresh yeast in small, solid cakes and active dry yeast, in granules that need liquid to be activated. Active dry yeast is available in premeasured packets and jars in most supermarkets and in bulk at some health food stores. It comes in two forms, regular and a quick-rising type, which raises dough up to 50 percent faster. Yeast is a living organism. For this reason, pay close attention to the expiration date on the package. After that date, the yeast loses its potency. Unopened packages or jars of dry yeast should be stored in a cool, dry place. Once opened, they must be kept refrigerated until used. Fresh yeast is far more perishable than dry yeast and should be stored in the refrigerator until used. It will usually last just a week or so. Both compressed yeast and active dry yeast may be frozen for longer periods, if very well wrapped. All yeast should be at room temperature to use.

To determine if yeast is still active, it should be proofed: To proof active dry yeast, sprinkle it over warm water (not more than 110°F), leave it for 1 minute, then stir it to dissolve and add a pinch of sugar. Leave this mixture in a warm place for 5 to 10 minutes. To proof cake yeast, mash it into warm water, add a pinch of sugar, and proceed as with the dry yeast. In either case, if the yeast is still active, the mixture will bubble and foam above the surface of the liquid. If the mixture is not foamy, discard it and replace with fresher yeast. See also: leaven, leavener, and proof.

yield The amount or quantity that a recipe makes.

yogurt Milk that has been fermented and coagulated with lactic bacteria to produce a thick, custardlike, creamy consistency and a tangy taste. Yogurt originated in the Balkans hundreds of years ago. It is thought to have been created by accident by nomadic tribes who carried milk in gourds hung over the backs of camels. The movement and the exposure to the warmth of the sun encouraged the bacteria to develop, which thickened the milk. Yogurt is widely used in Middle Eastern, Mediterranean, and Indian cuisines. Cows' milk is primarily used to make yogurt, although other animals' milk can be used. Plain yogurt, made with no additional flavoring, is used in baking, often to replace cream or sour cream. It is also used as a dessert and is often combined with fresh or dried fruit. Yogurt may be made with whole milk, low-fat milk, or nonfat milk. It is highly perishable and must be stored in the refrigerator. It is best to use yogurt by the pull date on the carton. Yogurt can also be homemade by heating milk to a boil, cooling it to 95° to 100°F, adding a spoonful of commercial yogurt as a starter, and holding the mixture at a steady temperature of about 70°F for several hours.

York Imperial apple One of the preferred apples for baked goods and baking whole because it holds its shape. York Imperial apples have bright red skin streaked with yellow and firm, off-white, sweet-tart flesh. York Imperial apples are available from October to May. See also: apple.

zabaglione A classic Italian dessert, zabaglione is a light, frothy, airy custard made by whipping together egg yolks, sugar, and sweet marsala wine over heat. Occasionally, Champagne, sauternes, or port is used in place of the marsala. A specially designed deep copper pan with a rounded bottom is often used to cook the custard, but zabaglione can also be made in the top of a double boiler over simmering water. Traditionally, zabaglione is made just before it is served. Zabaglione is served as a dessert by itself, and it is used as a sauce to accompany cake, ice cream, fruit, or pastry. In France it is called *sabayon*. Italy.

zaletti Venetian diamond-shaped cornmeal cookies. In addition to the crunchy cornmeal, raisins soaked in dark rum, lemon zest, and vanilla extract lend their textures and flavors to these buttery-rich, popular cookies. **Zalettini** are small versions of the large cookies. Italy.

ZALETTINI

36 to 42 cookies

¾ cup raisins
About ½ cup dark rum
1½ cups plus 2 tablespoons all-purpose flour
5½ ounces (11 tablespoons) unsalted butter, softened
½ cup plus 1 tablespoon granulated sugar
2 large eggs, at room temperature
1 teaspoon lemon extract
1 teaspoon vanilla extract
Finely minced zest of 1 small lemon
2 teaspoons baking powder
1 cup plus 3 tablespoons fine yellow cornmeal
¼ teaspoon salt

Place the raisins in a small bowl and add rum to cover them. Cover the bowl with plastic wrap and let the raisins soak for at least 30 minutes.

Position the racks in the upper and lower thirds of the oven and preheat to 375°F. Line two baking sheets with parchment paper.

Drain the raisins and pat them dry with paper towels. Toss them with 2 tablespoons of the flour, and set aside.

In the bowl of a stand mixer, using the flat beater attachment, or in a mixing bowl, using a hand-held mixer, beat the butter until soft and fluffy, about 2 minutes. Add the sugar and creme the mixture until well blended. Add the eggs 1 at a time, beating well after each addition, and stopping frequently to scrape down the sides of the bowl with a rubber spatula. Add the lemon and vanilla extracts and lemon zest and blend well.

Sift together the remaining 1½ cups flour and the baking powder, and blend in the cornmeal and salt. Add dry ingredients to the butter mixture in 3 additions, mixing well after each addition. Stir in the raisins and mix thoroughly.

Pinch off walnut-sized pieces of the dough and roll into flat logs about 3 inches long, 1 inch wide, and ½ inch thick. Place the zalettini on the lined baking sheets at least 1 inch apart. Bake the zalettini for 15 to 20 minutes, until lightly browned. Transfer the baking pans to racks to cool. The zalettini will keep for 5 to 7 days in an airtight container at room temperature.

zerde An Azerbaijani silky-smooth, sweet pudding made with milk, sugar, and butter, and flavored with rose water and saffron. After the pudding is cooked, it is cooled, then dusted with cinnamon before serving. Versions of this dessert, decorated with pomegranate seeds, currants, or toasted pine nuts, are also found in Turkey. Azerbaijan. See also: rose water and saffron.

zest The colored outer rind of citrus fruit, which contains the fruit's sweet flavor and perfume in its essential oils. Zest is removed with a special tool called a zester, which separates it from the bitter white pith. Citrus zest is used to flavor creams, custards, cakes, and other desserts, pastries, and confections. The zest is also candied and used as a confection or a flavoring. See also: zester.

zester This 6-inch-long hand-held utensil is designed to remove the aromatic outer rind or zest from citrus fruits, such as lemons and oranges, without removing the inner white pith, which is bitter. A zester has five small sharp holes in the end of a short metal strip attached to a handle made of plastic or wood. The holes are placed against a citrus fruit and pulled from top to bottom, which removes the zest in tiny threads. Sometimes this tool is sold as a combination zester/stripper. See also: stripper and zest.

zimtsterne Translated as "cinnamon stars," these classic cookies are traditionally made at Christmastime throughout all the German-speaking countries. They are made from a flourless dough that contains no fat, a combination of finely ground almonds and a cinnamon-flavored meringue. Before baking, the stars are spread with a meringue icing thinned with lemon juice or kirsch. Often the icing is sprinkled with colored sugar crystals. The flavor of zimtsterne improves with age. They can be kept in an airtight container for as long as 3 months. Germany.

zuccotto A classic Florentine dessert, zuccotto is assembled in a dome-shaped mold. The name derives from *zucco*, the Italian word for pumpkin. It is thought that the shape resembles that of the dome of Florence's famed cathedral, the Duomo. Thin slices of sponge cake or ladyfingers moistened with liqueur are used to line the mold, which is filled with a mixture of whipped cream, sugar, chopped chocolate, and toasted hazelnuts. Cake or ladyfingers are also used to seal the top of the mold. The dessert is chilled for several hours, then unmolded and dusted with a mixture of confectioners' sugar and cocoa powder before serving. Italy.

Zugor kirschtorte A Swiss specialty cake, **Zugor kirschtorte** is composed of two crisp hazelnut meringue layers that enclose two layers of génoise that have been brushed with kirsch sugar syrup; pink-tinted kirsch-flavored buttercream is alternated with the meringue and génoise layers. The sides of the torte are spread with more buttercream, then coated with ground toasted hazelnuts. The top of the torte is heavily dusted with confectioners' sugar, scored in a diamond pattern, and decorated with pale green marzipan leaves and candied cherries or marzipan cherries. The cake takes its name from the town of Zug, located in the northeastern part of Switzerland. Switzerland. See also: buttercream, génoise, hazelnut, kirschwasser, marzipan, and meringue.

ᘓᘓᘓᘓᘓᘓᘓᘓᘓᘓ

ZUGOR KIRSCHTORTE

One 9-inch round cake; 12 to 14 servings

½ cup unblanched hazelnuts
¼ cup granulated sugar
⅓ cup water
2 tablespoons kirsch
Two 9-inch Hazelnut Meringue Disks (see Mocha Dacquoise,
    page 95)
One 9-inch round Génoise (page 138)
1 recipe Classic French Buttercream (page 31), flavored with
    3 tablespoons kirsch and colored with 3 drops red paste
    food coloring
½ to ¾ cup confectioners' sugar, for dusting
2 ounces marzipan
Green paste food coloring
Red paste food coloring

Center a rack in the oven and preheat to 350°F.

Place the hazelnuts in a cake pan and toast them in the oven for 15 to 18 minutes, until the skins split and the nuts turn light golden brown. Transfer the pan to a rack to cool for 10 minutes.

Rub the hazelnuts between your hands or in a kitchen towel until most of the skins flake off. Place the hazelnuts in the work bowl of a food processor fitted with a steel blade. Add 1 tablespoon of the sugar and pulse until the nuts are finely ground, about 1 minute.

Combine the remaining 3 tablespoons sugar and the water in a small saucepan and bring to a boil over high heat. Remove from the heat and let cool, then add the kirsch to the sugar syrup.

Trim the edges of the hazelnut meringue disks to even them. Slice the génoise horizontally into 3 equal layers. Only 2 layers are needed for the torte; reserve the remaining layer for another use.

Place 1 of the meringue disks on a 9-inch cardboard cake circle.

Spread the disk evenly with a thin layer of the French buttercream, using a flexible-blade spatula. Position a layer of génoise over the buttercream and brush the layer with half of the sugar syrup. Spread the génoise layer with a layer of buttercream (about the same thickness as the cake layer). Position the second génoise layer over the buttercream and brush with the remaining sugar syrup. Spread this layer with more buttercream, then position the second meringue disk over the buttercream, bottom side up. Spread the meringue disk with buttercream, and cover the sides of the cake with the remaining buttercream. Use the spatula to smooth and even the buttercream.

Heavily dust the top of the torte with confectioners' sugar, completely covering the buttercream. Use a long flexible-blade spatula or the back of a long knife to score the top into a diamond design: Gently press the blade into the confectioners' sugar at ½-inch intervals across the top. Then turn the cake halfway around and repeat the pattern across the first lines.

Spread the ground hazelnuts on a piece of waxed paper. Use a flexible-blade spatula to lift up the cake, and hold it carefully from underneath with one hand. With your other hand, press the hazelnuts into the sides of the cake just up to the top edge. Carefully set the cake down on a serving plate. Use a small knife to mark the serving pieces around the top outside edge of the cake.

Divide the marzipan in half. Place one half on a smooth work surface sprinkled with confectioners' sugar. Use a toothpick to dab a few drops of green paste food color into the marzipan. Knead the marzipan to distribute the color evenly, using more confectioners' sugar as needed to keep it from sticking; the color should be fairly light. Roll the marzipan out to a thickness of about ⅛ inch. Use a small leaf cutter or a knife to cut out 12 marzipan leaves.

Place a leaf, pointed end facing out, in the center of each serving piece, 1 inch in from the outside edge.

Color the remaining marzipan, using red paste food coloring. Pinch off pieces of the marzipan about the size of a small cherry, and roll each piece into a ball. Place a ball at the base of each leaf.

Refrigerate the torte for at least 2 hours to mellow. Remove it from the refrigerator and let stand at room temperature for 30 minutes before serving. Cut the torte with a serrated knife or with a sharp knife dipped in hot water and dried. The torte will keep, well covered, in the refrigerator for up to 3 days.

zuppa Inglese This classic Italian dessert, literally, "English soup," is similar to English trifle. It is a cold dessert composed of rum- or kirsch-soaked sponge cake or ladyfingers layered in a deep bowl with pastry cream, whipped cream, toasted almonds, and candied fruit. Zuppa Inglese was created in the nineteenth century by Italian pastry cooks who were influenced by the English puddings that were popular in Italy at the time. Italy. See also: ladyfingers, sponge cake, tiramisù, and trifle.

BATTERIE DE CUISINE

This is a list of the **basic** equipment and utensils you need to get started making pastries, desserts, and confections:

aluminum foil	
angel food cake pan:	10- by 4-inch with removable bottom
baking sheets:	two 12- by 15- by 1-inch
cake pans:	one 8- by 2-inch round
	one 9- by 2-inch round
	one 8- by 8- by 2-inch
	one 9- by 13- by 2-inch
cake slicer	
candy thermometer	
chef's knives:	8-inch and 10-inch blades
cookie cutters	
cooling rack(s)	
double boiler	
drum sieve or sifter	
flexible-blade spatula:	8-inch and 10-inch blades
hand-held mixer	
loaf pan:	9 by 5 by 3 inches
measuring cups (wet and dry)	
measuring spoons	
mixing bowls:	a variety of sizes ranging from $\frac{1}{2}$-quart to 3-quart capacity
muffin pan	
offset spatula	
parchment paper	
paring knife	
pastry bag:	12 inches or 14 inches
pastry brushes:	two 1-inch-wide
pastry scraper	
pastry tips:	#3 closed star, #5 plain tip
pie pan:	9-inch diameter
rolling pin	
rubber spatulas:	two $9\frac{1}{2}$ inches long with 2-inch-wide blade

| | two 16½ inches long with 3½-inch-wide blade |
| ruler: | 18 inches |

saucepans:	½-quart, 1-quart, 2-quart, and 3-quart capacity
scissors	
springform pan:	9- by 3-inch

| tart pan: | 9½-inch diameter with removable bottom |

| vegetable peeler |

| waxed paper |
| whisk |

| wooden spatulas, two |
| wooden spoons, two |

| zester |

This is a list of the equipment and tools that would be **nice to have** to supplement the basics:

bake cups:	2- by 1¼-inch
barquette molds:	3- to 4- by 1³/₃- by ½-inch
bench scraper	
Bundt pan:	10- by 3½-inch

cardboard cake circles:	a variety of sizes to correspond to the sizes of your cake pans
cheesecake pan	
chocolate dipping forks	
chocolate molds (shallow and hollow)	
chocolate thermometer	
cookie mold	
cookie press	
cookie stamp	
corer	
coupler	
crimper	
custard cups	

| dredger |

| flan ring |
| food processor |

| goosefeather pastry brush |

| ice cream scoop |

| madeleine pan |

marble board
melon baller

---

paper candy cups	
pastry brush:	2-inch-wide
pastry wheel	
pie weights	

---

scale	
stand electric mixer	
strainer:	4-inch diameter
strawberry huller	
stripper	

---

tartlet pans
tube pan

This is a list of **extra** equipment that would increase your capability for making a variety of desserts, pastries, and confections (many of these items are found in most professional pastry, dessert, and confectionery kitchens):

air pump for blown sugar
alcohol burner for pulled sugar

---

brioche pan, large:	8-inch diameter
brioche pans, individual:	2¹/₂-inch diameter

---

cake breaker
cake leveler
cake lifter/decorating stencil
cake strip
cake tester
cannoli forms
caramel rulers
charlotte mold
cherry pitter
chocolate tempering machine
coeur à la crème mold
copper egg white bowl
cream horn mold
croissant cutter
croquembouche mold

---

docker
dough divider
doughnut cutter

éclair plaque
entremet ring

---

fondant funnel

gum paste tools and cutters

heat lamp for pulled and blown sugar

ice cream machine
ice cream mold
icing stencil

ladyfinger plaque
langues de chat plaque
lattice dough cutter
lattice dough roller
leaf stencil

maryann pan
marzipan tools

pastry blender
pastry cloth
pastry comb
pastry cutter set
petits fours molds
pudding mold

ramekins
rehrücken mold
rice paper

shortbread mold
soufflé dish
strawberry huller
stripper
sugar pan, copper

truffle grid
tuile cookie mold
turntable

waffle iron
warming case for pulled and blown sugar

TABLE OF SUGAR TEMPERATURES AND STAGES

An accurate candy thermometer is the most reliable way to determine when sugar has cooked to the correct temperature. This table shows the stages that correspond to the standard temperature ranges of cooked sugar, the characteristics of each stage, and the uses for each stage. To test for these stages without a candy thermometer, drop a teaspoonful of the sugar syrup into a glass of cold water, then retrieve the syrup by pressing it gently between your thumb and forefinger.

TEMPERATURE RANGE	STAGE	CHARACTERISTICS AND USES
223–234°F 106–112°C	**Thread**	Forms a loose, thin thread. Used for sugar syrups.
234–240°F 112–115°C	**Soft ball**	Forms a soft, sticky ball that flattens when removed from the water. Used for buttercreams, fudge, and caramels.
242–248°F 116–120°C	**Firm ball**	Forms a sticky, firm but pliable ball that holds its shape briefly, then deflates when left at room temperature for a few minutes. Used for buttercreams, caramels, Florentines, nougat, Italian meringue, and toffees.
250–266°F 121–130°C	**Hard ball**	Forms a rigid, sticky ball that holds its shape against pressure. Used for caramels, nougat, divinity, and toffees.
270–290°F 132–143°C	**Soft crack**	Separates into strands that are firm but pliable. If you bite into a piece of the cooled syrup, it will stick to your teeth. Used for butterscotch, krokant, nougat, torrone, taffy, and rock sugar candy.

300–310°F 148–153°C	**Hard crack**	Separates into brittle threads that shatter easily; the sugar is no longer sticky. Used for brittles, toffee, glazed fruit, blown sugar, pulled sugar, poured sugar, and spun sugar.
320–360°F 160–182°C	**Caramel**	Becomes transparent and undergoes color changes ranging from light golden to dark amber. Used for caramel-coated molds, praline, brittles, and nougatine.

TABLE OF TEMPERATURE EQUIVALENTS FOR FAHRENHEIT AND CELSIUS

DEGREES/FAHRENHEIT	DEGREES/CELSIUS (CENTIGRADE)
32 (water freezes)	0
41	5
50	10
59	15
68	20
77	25
86	30
95	35
104	40
113	45
122	50
131	55
140	60
149	65
158	70
167	75

DEGREES/FAHRENHEIT	DEGREES/CELSIUS (CENTIGRADE)
176	80
185	85
194	90
203	95
212 (water boils)	100

TO CONVERT FAHRENHEIT TO CELSIUS (CENTIGRADE):

subtract 32 and multiply by 5/9 (0 5556)

or:

subtract 32, multiply by 5, and divide by 9

Example: 223°F = 106°C

$$223$$
$$\underline{-32}$$
$$191 \times 0.5556 = 106$$

or

$$223$$
$$\underline{-32}$$
$$191 \times 5 = 955 \div 9 = 106$$

TO CONVERT CELSIUS (CENTIGRADE) TO FAHRENHEIT:

multiply by 9/5 (1.8) and add 32

or:

multiply by 9, divide by 5, and add 32

Example: 120°C = 248°F

$$120$$
$$\times \underline{9/5} \ (1.8)$$
$$216 + 32 = 248$$

or

$$120 \times 9 = 1080 \div 5 = 216 + 32 = 248$$

TABLE OF WEIGHT AND MEASUREMENT EQUIVALENTS

U.S. MEASURING SYSTEM	METRIC SYSTEM
Capacity	**Approximate Capacity**
1/4 teaspoon	1.25 milliliters
1 teaspoon	5 milliliters
1 tablespoon	15 milliliters
1/4 cup	60 milliliters
1 cup (8 fluid ounces)	240 milliliters
2 cups (1 pint; 16 fluid ounces)	470 milliliters
4 cups (1 quart; 32 fluid ounces)	0.95 liter
4 quarts (1 gallon; 64 fluid ounces)	3.8 liters
Weight	**Approximate Weight**
1 dry ounce	15 grams
2 ounces	30 grams
4 ounces (1/4 pound)	110 grams
8 ounces (1/2 pound)	230 grams
16 ounces (1 pound)	454 grams

LIQUID MEASUREMENT

Measurement	Fluid Ounces	Ounces by Weight	Grams
2 tablespoons	1 fluid ounce	1/2 ounce	14 grams
1/4 cup	2 fluid ounces	1 3/4 ounces	50 grams
1/3 cup	2 2/3 fluid ounces	2 ounces	70 grams
1/2 cup	4 fluid ounces	4 ounces	113 grams
2/3 cup	5 1/3 fluid ounces	5 ounces	142 grams
3/4 cup	6 fluid ounces	6 1/4 ounces	177 grams
1 cup	8 fluid ounces	8 ounces	227 grams

Measurement	Equivalent
1/4 cup (2 fluid ounces)	5 tablespoons
1/3 cup (2 2/3 fluid ounces)	7 tablespoons
1/2 cup (4 fluid ounces)	11 tablespoons
/3 cup (5 1/3 fluid ounces)	14 tablespoons
3/4 cup (6 fluid ounces)	16 tablespoons
1 cup (8 fluid ounces)	20 tablespoons

DRY MEASUREMENT

Measurement	Equivalent
3 teaspoons	1 tablespoon
2 tablespoons	$1/8$ cup
4 tablespoons	$1/4$ cup
$5^1/3$ tablespoons	$1/3$ cup
8 tablespoons	$1/2$ cup
$10^2/3$ tablespoons	$2/3$ cup
12 tablespoons	$3/4$ cup
16 tablespoons	1 cup

GRANULATED SUGAR

Measurement	Ounces	Grams
1 teaspoon	$1/6$ ounce	5 grams
1 tablespoon	$1/2$ ounce	15 grams
$1/4$ cup	$1^3/4$ ounces	50 grams
$1/3$ cup	$2^1/4$ ounces	65 grams
$1/2$ cup	$3^1/2$ ounces	100 grams
$2/3$ cup	$4^1/2$ ounces	130 grams
$3/4$ cup	5 ounces	145 grams
1 cup	7 ounces	200 grams

BROWN SUGAR

Measurement	Ounces	Grams
1 tablespoon	$1/4$ ounce	7 grams
$1/4$ cup	$1^1/4$ ounces	35 grams
$1/3$ cup	$1^3/4$ ounces	50 grams
$1/2$ cup	$2^3/4$ ounces	75 grams
$2/3$ cup	3 ounces	85 grams
$3/4$ cup	$3^1/2$ ounces	100 grams
1 cup	5 ounces	145 grams

FLOUR (UNSIFTED)

Measurement	Ounces	Grams
1 tablespoon	$1/4$ ounce	7 grams
$1/4$ cup	$1^1/4$ ounces	35 grams
$1/3$ cup	$1^1/2$ ounces	45 grams
$1/2$ cup	$2^1/2$ ounces	70 grams
$2/3$ cup	$3^1/4$ ounces	90 grams
$3/4$ cup	$3^1/2$ ounces	100 grams
1 cup	5 ounces	145 grams

NUTS

I cup, shelled	Ounces	Grams
Almonds, sliced	3 ounces	85 grams
Almonds, unblanched whole	4¹/₂ ounces	130 grams
Cashews	4¹/₂ ounces	130 grams
Hazelnuts	4¹/₂ ounces	130 grams
Macadamia nuts	4 ounces	110 grams
Peanuts	4 ounces	110 grams
Pecans	4 ounces	110 grams
Pistachio nuts	5 ounces	145 grams
Walnuts	3¹/₂ ounces	100 grams

BUTTER

Measurement	Ounces	Grams
1 tablespoon	¹/₂ ounce	15 grams
2 tablespoons	1 ounce	30 grams
4 tablespoons (¹/₂ stick; ¹/₄ cup)	2 ounces	60 grams
8 tablespoons (1 stick; ¹/₂ cup)	4 ounces (¹/₄ pound)	115 grams
2 sticks	8 ounces (¹/₂ pound)	230 grams
4 sticks	1 pound	454 grams

COMPARATIVE VOLUME OF STANDARD BAKING PAN SIZES

PAN SIZE	VOLUME
Round cake pans	
5- by 2-inch	$2^2/_3$ cups
6- by 2-inch	$3^3/_4$ cups
7- by 2-inch	$5^1/_4$ cups
8- by $1^1/_2$-inch	4 cups
8- by 2-inch	7 cups
9- by $1^1/_2$-inch	6 cups
9- by 2-inch	$8^2/_3$ cups
10- by 2-inch	$10^3/_4$ cups
12- by 2-inch	$15^1/_2$ cups
14- by 2-inch	21 cups
9- by 3-inch Bundt	9 cups
10- by $3^1/_2$-inch Bundt	12 cups
9- by 4-inch kugelhopf	12 cups
9- by 3-inch tube	10 cups
10- by 4-inch tube	16 cups
9- by $2^3/_4$-inch springform	10 cups
10- by $2^3/_4$-inch springform	12 cups
9- by 3-inch cheesecake	14 cups
$2^3/_4$- by $1^1/_4$-inch muffin cup	$1/_2$ cup
Pie plates	
8- by $1^1/_4$-inch	3 cups
9- by $1^1/_4$-inch	$3^1/_2$ cups
9- by $1^1/_2$-inch	4 cups
9- by 2-inch	6 cups
Square pans	
8- by 8- by $1^1/_2$-inch	6 cups
8- by 8- by 2-inch	8 cups
9- by 9- by $1^1/_2$-inch	8 cups
9- by 9- by 2-inch	10 cups
10- by 10- by 2-inch	12 cups
12- by 12- by 2-inch	16 cups

Rectangular and loaf pans

$10^1/_2$- by $15^1/_2$- by 1-inch jelly-roll pan	10 cups
$12^1/_2$- by $17^1/_2$- by 1-inch jelly-roll pan	12 cups
11- by 7- by 2-inch rectangle	8 cups
13- by 9- by 2-inch rectangle	15 cups
8- by 4- by $2^1/_2$-inch loaf	4 cups
$8^1/_2$- by $4^1/_2$- by $2^1/_2$-inch loaf	6 cups
9- by 5- by 3-inch loaf	8 cups

Unusual-shaped pans

8- by $2^1/_2$-inch heart	$8^1/_2$ cups
$9^1/_4$- by $6^5/_8$-inch oval	6 cups

Note: To determine the volume of any pan, use a liquid measure to pour water into the pan until it reaches the top.

CONVERTING TO AND FROM METRIC

When This Factor Is Known	Multiply By	To Find
Weight		
Ounces	28.35	Grams
Pounds	0.454	Kilograms
Grams	0.035	Ounces
Kilograms	2.2	Pounds
Measurement		
Inches	2.5	Centimeters
Millimeters	0.04	Inches
Centimeters	0.4	Inches
Volume		
Teaspoons	4.93	Milliliters
Tablespoons	14.79	Milliliters
Fluid ounces	29.57	Milliliters
Cups	0.237	Liters
Pints	0.47	Liters
Quarts	0.95	Liters
Gallons	3.785	Liters
Milliliters	0.034	Fluid Ounces
Liters	2.1	Pints
Liters	1.06	Quarts
Liters	0.26	Gallons
	Divide By	
Milliliters	4.93	Teaspoons
Milliliters	14.79	Tablespoons
Milliliters	236.59	Cups
Milliliters	473.18	Pints
Milliliters	946.36	Quarts
Liters	0.236	Cups
Liters	0.473	Pints
Liters	0.946	Quarts
Liters	3.785	Gallons

PROFESSIONAL PASTRY AND CONFECTIONERY SCHOOLS

BASIC TRAINING AND CONTINUING EDUCATION

L'Academie de Cuisine
5021 Wilson Lane
Bethesda, MD 20814
Tel: (301) 986–9490 or (800) 445–1959
Fax: (301) 652–7970

Baltimore International Culinary College
17 Commerce Street
Baltimore, MD 21202–3230
Tel: (410) 752–4710 or (800) 624–9926
Fax: (410) 752–3730

California Culinary Academy
625 Polk Street
San Francisco, CA 94102
Tel: (415) 771–3536 or (800) 229–2433, ext. 241
Fax: (415) 771–2108

The Cooking & Hospitality Institute of Chicago, Inc.
361 West Chestnut
Chicago, IL 60610
Tel: (312) 944–0882

Le Cordon Bleu Ecole de Cuisine et de Pâtisserie
8, rue Leon Dehomme
75015 Paris
France
Tel: (33–1) 48.56.06.06
Fax: (33–1) 48.56.03.96

114 Marylebone Lane
London W1M 6HH
England
Tel: (44–71) 935–3503
Fax: (44–71) 305–7621

ROOB–1, 28–13 Sarugaku-CHO
Shibuya-ka, Tokyo
150 Japan
Tel: (81–3) 54.89.01.41
Fax: (81–3) 54.89.01.45

Le Cordon Bleu Paris Cooking School
Suite 400
1390 Prince of Wales Drive
Ottawa, Ontario
K2C 3N6 Canada
Tel: (613) 224–8603
Fax: (613) 224–9966

The Culinary Institute of America
433 Albany Post Road
Hyde Park, NY 12538–1499
Tel: (914) 452–9600, or
(800) 285–4627 (admissions),
or
(800) 888–7850 (continuing education)
Fax: (914) 452–8629

Ecole de Gastronomie Française Ritz-Escoffier
15 Place Vendôme
75001 Paris
France
Tel: (33–1) 42.60.38.30
Fax: (33–1) 40.15.07.65

Ecole Lenôtre
Boîte Postale 6-40, rue Pierre Curie
78373 Plaisir Cedex
France
Tel: (33–1) 30.81.46.34/46.35
Fax: (33–1) 30.54.73.70

The French Culinary Institute
462 Broadway
New York, NY 10013–2618
Tel: (212) 219–8890
Fax: (212) 219–9292

George Brown College School of
Hospitality
P.O. Box 1015, Station B
3000 Adelaide Street East
Toronto, Ontario M5T 2T9
Canada
Tel: (416) 867–2225 or (800)
263–8995

Johnson & Wales University
8 Abbott Park Place
Providence, RI 02903
Tel: (401) 456–1000

Merkblatt Patisserie
Gastgewerbefachschule der Wiener
Gastwirte
Judenplatz 3–4
1010 Wien (Vienna)
Austria
Tel: (222) 5330643–30
Fax: (222) 5333704–19
(Classes offered only in German)

The National Center for Hospital-
ity Studies at Sullivan College
Sullivan Centre Campus
Watterson Expressway at Bards-
town Road
P.O. Box 33–308
Louisville, KY 40232
Tel: (502) 456–6504 or (800)
844–1354
Fax: (502) 454–4880

New England Culinary Institute
250 Main Street
Montpelier, VT 05602–9720
Tel: (802) 223–6324
Fax: (802) 223–0634

New York Restaurant School
27 West 34th Street
New York, NY 10001
Tel: (212) 947–7097
Fax: (212) 967–3441

The Pastry Institute of
Washington, D.C.
6856 Eastern Avenue NW
Washington, DC 20012
Tel: (202) 726–0790
Fax: (202) 723–8970

Peter Kump's New York
Cooking School
307 East 92nd Street
New York, NY 10128
Tel: (212) 410–4601
Fax: (212) 348–6360

The Restaurant School
4207 Walnut Street
Philadelphia, PA 19104
Tel: (215) 222–4200
Fax: (215) 222–4219

CONTINUING EDUCATION

The Chocolate Gallery School of
Confectionery Arts
34 West 22nd Street
New York, NY 10010
Tel: (212) 675–2253
Fax: (212) 675–2545
Director: Joan Mansour

Cocoa Barry Training School
1500 Suckle Highway
Pennsauken, NJ 08110
Tel: (609) 663–2260
Fax: (609) 665–0474
Director: Pascal P. Janvier

**Ecole Gastronomique Bellouet
Conseil**
48, rue de Sèvres
75007 Paris
France
Tel: (33–1) 40.56.91.20
Fax: (33–1) 45.66.48.61
Director: Jöel Bellouet

**International School of
Confectionary Arts**
9209 Gaither Road
Gaithersburg, MD 20877
Tel: (301) 963–9077
Fax: (301) 869–7669
Directors: Ewald and Susan Notter

La Varenne Ecole de Cuisine
Château du Fëy
89300 Villecien
France
Tel: (33) 86.63.18.34
Fax: (33) 86.63.10.33
  or
P.O. Box 25574
Washington, DC 20007
Tel: (202) 337–0073 or (800)
537–6486
Fax: (703) 823–5438
Director: Anne Willan

New School for Social Research
Culinary Arts Division
100 Greenwich Avenue
New York, NY 10011

Tel: (212) 225–4141
Executive Director: Gary A.
 Goldberg

Richardson Researches, Inc.
23449 Foley Street
Hayward, CA 94545
Tel: (510) 785–1350
Fax: (510) 785–6857
Director: Terry Richardson

**Richemont Bakery and
Confectionary School**
Rigistrasse 28
6006 Lucerne
Switzerland
Tel: (41–41) 51.58.62
Fax: (41–41) 51.48.80
Director: Walter Boesch

Scottsdale Culinary Institute
8100 East Camelback Road
Scottsdale, AZ 85251
Tel: (602) 990–3773, or
(800) 848–2433
Fax: (602) 990–0351
Admissions Director: Darren S.
Leite

MAJOR SOURCES FOR EQUIPMENT AND INGREDIENTS WORLDWIDE

Albert Uster Imports, Inc.
9211 Gaither Road
Gaithersburg, MD 20877–1419
Tel: (301) 258–7350 (East Coast),
(510) 569–0280 (West Coast),
or
(800) 231–8154
Fax: (301) 948–2601
*Pastry and confectionery
equipment and ingredients*

**American Chocolate Mould
Company, Inc.**
3194 Lawson Boulevard
Oceanside, NY 11572
Tel: (516) 766–1414
Fax: (516) 293–2239
*Chocolate tempering machines and
chocolate molds*

Bridge Kitchenware
214 East 52nd Street
New York, NY 10022
Tel: (800) 274–3435
Fax: (212) 758–4387
Professional culinary equipment

Broadway Panhandler
520 Broadway
New York, NY 10012
Tel: (212) 966–3434
Pastry and confectionery equipment

The Chocolate Gallery
34 West 22nd Street
New York, NY 10010
Tel: (212) 675–2253
Fax: (212) 675–2545
*Cake decorating, candy making, and
gum paste supplies and ingredients*

David Mellor
4 Sloane Square
London SW 1W 8EE
England
Tel: (44–71) 730–4259
Professional culinary equipment

Dean & DeLuca
560 Broadway
New York, NY 10012
Tel: (212) 431–1691 or (800)
221–7714
Fax: (212) 334–6183
*Pastry and confectionery ingredients
and equipment*

E. Dehillerin
18–20, rue Coquillière
75001 Paris
France
Tel: (33–1) 42.36.53.13
Professional culinary equipment

G. Detou
58, rue Tiquetonne
75002 Paris
France
Tel: (33–1) 42.36.54.67
Fax: (33–1) 40.39.08.04
Pastry and confectionery ingredients

Divertimenti
45–47 Wigmore Street
London W1H 9LE
England
Tel: (44–71) 935–0689
Professional culinary equipment

Easy-Leaf
947 N. Cole Avenue
Los Angeles, CA 90038
Tel: (213) 469–0856
Pure gold leaf, gold powder, gold ribbon, pure silver leaf, gilders' tips, and brushes

The French Kitchen & Tableware Supply Company
42 Westbourne Grove, Paddington
London W2 5SH
England
Tel: (44–71) 221–2112
Fax: (44–71) 792–0069
Culinary equipment

Hillard's Chocolate System
275 East Center Street
Bridgewater, MA 02379
Tel: (508) 587–3666
Fax: (508) 587–3735
Chocolate tempering machines

The King Arthur Flour Baker's Catalogue
P.O. Box 876
Norwich, VT 05055
Tel: (800) 827–6836
Fax: (802) 649–5359
Culinary equipment and ingredients

Kitchens (Catering Utensils) Limited
4 & 5 Quiet Street
Bath BA1 2JS
England
Tel: (0225) 330524
Culinary equipment

The Kitchen Witch Gourmet Shop
127 North El Camino Real, Suite D
Encinitas, CA 92024
Tel: (619) 942–3228
Culinary equipment and ingredients

Kolb Bäckereimaschinen AG
Hauptstrassem 51
9463 Oberriet
Switzerland
Tel: (41) 071.78.22.55
Professional culinary equipment

La Cuisine Kitchenware
323 Cameron Street
Alexandria, VA 22314
Tel: (703) 836–4435 or (800) 521–1176
Fax: (703) 836–8925
Culinary equipment and ingredients

Maid of Scandinavia
3244 Raleigh Avenue
Minneapolis, MN 55416
Tel: (800) 328–6722
Fax: (612) 927–6215
Culinary equipment and ingredients

MORA
13, rue Montmartre
75001 Paris
France
Tel: (33–1) 45.08.19.24
Professional culinary equipment

Paprikás Weiss Importer
1572 Second Avenue
New York, NY 10028
Tel: (212) 288–6117
Fax: (212) 734–5120
Pastry and confectionery ingredients

C. A. Paradis, Inc.
1314 Bank Street
Ottawa, Ontario, K1S 3Y4
Canada
Tel: (613) 731–2866
Culinary equipment

Parrish's Cake Decorating Supplies, Inc.
225 West 146th Street
Gardena, CA 90248
Tel: (213) 324–2253 or (800) 736–8443
Fax: (213) 324–8277
Cake decorating and candy making equipment and supplies

J. B. Prince Company
20 West 38th Street
New York, NY 10018
Tel: (212) 302–8611
Fax: (212) 819–9147
Professional culinary equipment and tools

G. B. Ratto & Company
International Grocers, Inc.
821 Washington Street
Oakland, CA 94607
Tel: (800) 325–3483
Fax: (510) 836–2250
Pastry and confectionery ingredients

Russell Food Equipment Ltd.
450 Preston Street
Ottawa, Ontario, K1S 4N6
Canada
Tel: (613) 238–6555
Professional culinary equipment

Sepp Leaf Products
Suite 381
381 Park Avenue South
New York, NY 10016
Tel: (212) 683–2840/1
Fax: (212) 725–0308
Pure gold leaf, gold powder, gold ribbon, pure silver, gilders' tips, and brushes **[orders from professionals/wholesale only]**

Williams-Sonoma
Mail Order Department
P.O. Box 7456
San Francisco, CA 94120–7456
Tel: (415) 421–4242 or (800) 541–2233
Fax: (415) 421–5253
Culinary equipment and ingredients

Wilton Industries, Inc.
2240 West 75th Street
Woodbridge, IL 60517
Tel: (708) 963–7100 or (800) 772–7111
Cake decorating and candy making equipment and supplies

BIBLIOGRAPHY

Alejandro, Reynaldo. *The Philippine Cookbook*. New York: Coward-McCann, Inc., 1982.

Amendola, Joseph. *The Baker's Manual*. Rochelle Park, NJ: Hayden Book Company, 1982.

———, and Lundberg, Donald B. *Understanding Baking*. New York: Van Nostrand Reinhold Company, 1970.

Bacon, Josephine. *The Pâtisserie of Vienna*. London: Macdonald Orbis, 1988.

Bagget, Nancy. *The International Cookie Cookbook*. New York: Stewart Tabori & Chang, 1988.

Barron, Rosemary. *Flavors of Greece*. New York: William Morrow and Company, Inc., 1991.

Benning, Lee Edwards. *The Cook's Tales*. Old Saybrook, CT: Globe Pequot Press, 1992.

———. *Oh, Fudge!* New York: Henry Holt and Company, 1990.

Beranbaum, Rose Levy. *The Cake Bible*. New York: William Morrow and Company, Inc., 1988.

———. *A Passion for Chocolate*. New York: William Morrow and Company, Inc., 1989.

Bickel, Walter, ed. *Hering's Dictionary of Classical and Modern Cookery*. London: Virtue and Company Ltd., 1985.

Bloom, Carole. *Truffles, Candies, & Confections*. Freedom, CA: Crossing Press, 1992.

Braker, Flo. *The Simple Art of Perfect Baking*. New York: William Morrow and Company, Inc., 1985.

Brennan, Jennifer. *The Cuisines of Asia*. New York: St. Martin's/Marek, 1984.

Brown, Cora; Brown, Rose; and Brown, Bob. *The South American Cookbook*. New York: Dover Publications, Inc., 1971.

Buck, Pearl. *Pearl S. Buck's Oriental Cookbook*. New York: Simon and Schuster, 1972.

Bush, Carroll D. *Nut Grower's Handbook*. New York: Orange Judd Publishing Company, Inc., 1953.

Casas, Penelope. *The Foods and Wines of Spain*. New York: Alfred A. Knopf, 1991.

Child, Julia; Bertholle, Louisette; and Beck, Simone. *Mastering the Art of French Cooking*. Vol. 1. New York: Alfred A. Knopf, 1969.

———, and Beck, Simone. *Mastering the Art of French Cooking*. Vol. 2. New York: Alfred A. Knopf, 1970.

Claiborne, Craig. *An Herb and Spice Cook Book*. New York: Bantam Books, 1963.

———. *Craig Claiborne's New York Times Food Encyclopedia*. New York: Times Books, 1985.

Coady, Chantal. *Chocolate: The Food of the Gods*. San Francisco: Chronicle Books, 1993.

Cook's and Diner's Dictionary. New York: Funk & Wagnalls, 1968.

Copage, Eric V. *Kwanzaa*. New York: William Morrow and Company, Inc., 1991.

Cost, Bruce. *Ginger East to West*. Berkeley: Aris Books, 1989.

Coyle, L. Patrick. *The World Encyclopedia of Food*. New York: Facts on File, Inc., 1982.

Cunningham, Marion. *The Fannie Farmer Baking Book*. New York: Alfred A. Knopf, 1984, 1990.

———. *The Fannie Farmer Cookbook*. 13th edition. New York: Alfred A. Knopf, 1990.

David, Elizabeth. *Spices, Salt and Aromatics in the English Kitchen*. Baltimore: Penguin Books, 1970.

Derecskey, Susan. *The Hungarian Cookbook*. New York: Harper & Row, 1972.

Ettlinger, Steve. *The Kitchenware Book*. New York: Macmillan Publishing Company, 1992.

Field, Carol. *Celebrating Italy*. New York: William Morrow and Company, Inc., 1990.

———. *The Italian Baker*. New York: Harper & Row, 1985.

FitzGibbon, Theodora. *The Food of the Western World*. New York: Quadrangle/New York Times Book Company, 1976.

Foods of the World (series). Alexandria, Va.: Time-Life Books, 1968.

France, Wilfred J., ed. *The New International Confectioner*. London: Virtue and Company Ltd., 1979.

Frey, Iris Ihde. *Crumpets and Scones*. New York: St. Martin's Press, 1982.

Friedlander, Barbara. *The Secrets of the Seed: Vegetables, Fruits and Nuts*. New York: Grosset & Dunlap, 1974.

Generet, Alex, and Line, Yetty. *Le Guide Marabout de la Pâtisserie et des Desserts*. Verviers, Belgium: Marabout, 1976.

Good Cook/Techniques and Recipes (series). New York: Time-Life, Inc., 1981.

Harris, Jessica B. *Tasting Brazil*. New York: Macmillan Publishing Company, 1992.

Healy, Bruce, and Bugat, Paul. *Mastering the Art of French Pastry*. New York: Barron's, 1984.

Herbst, Sharon Tyler. *Food Lover's Companion*. New York: Barron's, 1990.

———. *The Joy of Cookies*. New York: Barron's, 1987.

Hillman, Howard. *Kitchen Science*. Boston: Houghton Mifflin, 1989.

Hogrogian, Rachel. *The Armenian Cookbook*. New York: Atheneum, 1971.

Horn, Jane, ed. *Cooking A to Z*. Santa Rosa, CA: Cole Group, 1992.

Humphrey, Sylvia Windle. *A Matter of Taste*. New York: Macmillan Company, 1965.

Iaia, Sarah Kelly. *Festive Baking*. New York: Doubleday, 1988.

Jaffrey, Madhur. *Madhur Jaffrey's Indian Cooking*. New York: Barron's, 1983.

Karoff, Barbara. *South American Cooking*. Reading, MA: Aris Books/Addison-Wesley Publishing Company, Inc., 1989.

Lang, Jenifer Harvey, ed. *Larousse Gastronomique: The New American Edition*. New York: Crown Publishers, Inc., 1988.

Lemnis, Maria, and Vitry, Henryk. *Old Polish Traditions in the Kitchen and at the Table*. Warsaw: Interpress Publishers, 1981.

Leung, Mai. *The Chinese People's Cookbook*. New York: Harper & Row, 1979.

Loh, Lily. *Lily Loh's Chinese Seafood & Vegetables*. Solana Beach, CA: Solana Publishing Company, 1991.

Malgieri, Nick. *Great Italian Desserts*. Boston: Little, Brown and Company, 1990.

———. *Nick Malgieri's Perfect Pastry*. New York: Macmillan Publishing Company, 1989.

Mariani, John F. *The Dictionary of American Food & Drink* (revised edition). New York: Hearst Books, 1994.

Marks, Copeland. *The Exotic Kitchens of Indonesia*. New York: M. Evans and Company, Inc., 1989.

———. *The Indonesian Kitchen*. New York: Atheneum, 1981.

———. *Sephardic Cooking*. New York: Donald I. Fine, Inc., 1992.

———, and Thein, Aung. *The Burmese Kitchen*. New York: M. Evans and Company, Inc., 1987.

Mashiter, Rosa. *A Little English Book of Teas*. San Francisco: Chronicle Books, 1989.

McGee, Harold. *On Food and Cooking*. New York: Collier Books, 1984.

Merchant, Ismail. *Ismail Merchant's Indian Cuisine*. New York: St. Martin's Press, 1986.

Merson, Annette. *African Cookery*. Nashville, TN: Winston-Derek Publishers, Inc., 1987.

Morse, Kitty. *Come with me to the Kasbah: A Cook's Tour of Morocco*. Casablanca, Morocco: Editions SERAR, 1989.

Morton, Marcia, and Morton, Frederic. *Chocolate: An Illustrated History*. New York: Crown Publishers, Inc., 1986.

Nabwine, Constance, and Montgomery, Bertha Vining. *Cooking the African Way*. Minneapolis: Lerner Publications Company, 1988.

Norman, Jill. *Aromatic Herbs*. New York: Bantam Books, 1990.

———. *Chocolate*. New York: Bantam Books, 1990.

———. *Spices: Roots and Fruits*. New York: Bantam Books, 1989.

———. *Spices: Seeds and Barks*. New York: Bantam Books, 1990.

———. *Sweet Flavorings*. New York: Bantam Books, 1989.

Ojakangas, Beatrice. *Great Old-Fashioned American Desserts*. New York: E.P. Dutton, 1987.

Ortiz, Elisabeth Lambert. *The Encyclopedia of Herbs, Spices & Flavorings*. New York: Dorling Kindersley, Inc., 1992.

———. *The Food of Spain and Portugal*. New York: Atheneum, 1989.

———, with Endo, Mitsuko. *The Complete Book of Japanese Cooking*. New York: M. Evans and Company, Inc., 1976.

Passmore, Jacki. *The Encyclopedia of Asian Food and Cooking*. New York: Hearst Books, 1991.

Pâtisserie et Entremets. Lausanne, Switzerland: Ecole Hôtelière de la Société Suisse des Hôteliers, 1973.

Peck, Paula. *The Art of Fine Baking*. New York: Simon and Schuster, 1961.

Pépin, Jacques. *La Methode*. New York: Times Books, 1979.

———. *La Technique*. New York: Pocket Books, 1976.

Philippou, Margaret Joy. *101 Arabic Delights*. Brighton, England: Clifton Books, 1969.

Purdy, Susan G. *Have Your Cake and Eat It Too*. New York: William Morrow and Company, Inc., 1993.

———. *A Piece of Cake*. New York: Atheneum, 1989.

———. *As Easy as Pie*. New York: Collier Books, 1984.

Radecka, Helena. *The Fruit and Nut Book*. New York: McGraw-Hill, 1984.

Reich, Lilly Joss. *The Viennese Pastry Cookbook*. New York: Collier Books, 1970.

Riely, Elizabeth. *The Chef's Companion*. New York: Van Nostrand Reinhold, 1986.

Roden, Claudia. *A Book of Middle Eastern Food*. New York: Vintage Books, 1974.

Rombauer, Irma S., and Becker, Marion Rombauer. *Joy of Cooking*. 18th edition. Indianapolis: Bobbs-Merrill Company, Inc., 1967.

Routhier, Nicole. *The Foods of Vietnam*. New York: Stewart Tabori & Chang, 1989.

Roux, Michel, and Roux, Albert. *The Roux Brothers on Pâtisserie*. New York: Prentice Hall Press, 1986.

Rubash, Joyce. *Master Dictionary of Food & Wine*. New York: Van Nostrand Reinhold, 1990.

Sahni, Julie. *Classic Indian Cooking*. New York: William Morrow and Company, Inc., 1980.

————. *Classic Indian Vegetarian and Grain Cooking*. New York: William Morrow and Company, Inc., 1985.

Salloum, Mary. *A Taste of Lebanon*. New York: Interlink Books, 1989.

Schneider, Elizabeth. *Uncommon Fruits & Vegetables: A Commonsense Guide*. New York: Harper & Row, 1986.

Simon, André L. *Concise Encyclopedia of Gastronomy*. Woodstock, NY: Overlook Press, 1982.

————, and Howe, Robin. *The Dictionary of Gastronomy*. Woodstock, NY: Overlook Press, 1978.

Simpson, Helen. *The London Ritz Book of Afternoon Tea*. New York: Arbor House, 1986.

Solomon, Charmaine. *The Complete Asian Cookbook*. Rutland, VT: Charles E. Tuttle Company, 1992.

Stobart, Tom. *The Cook's Encyclopedia*. New York: Harper & Row, 1981.

Taik, Aung Aung. *The Best of Burmese Cooking*. San Francisco: Chronicle Books, 1993.

Tannahill, Reay. *Food in History*. New York: Stein and Day, 1973.

Trewby, Mary. *A Gourmet's Guide to Herbs & Spices*. Los Angeles: HP Books, 1989.

Uvezian, Sonia. *The Best Foods of Russia*. New York: Harcourt Brace Jovanovich, 1976.

Von Bremzen, Anya, and Welchman, John. *Please to the Table*. New York: Workman Publishing, 1990.

Wells, Patricia. *The Food Lover's Guide to France*. New York: Workman Publishing, 1987.

————. *The Food Lover's Guide to Paris*. 3rd ed. New York: Workman Publishing, 1993.

Willan, Anne. *Look & Cook Fruit Desserts*. New York: Dorling Kindersley, Inc., 1992.

Wolfert, Paula. *Couscous and Other Good Food from Morocco*. New York: Harper & Row, 1973.

Wright, Jeni. *Pâtisserie of Italy*. London: Macdonald Orbis, 1988.

INDEX OF RECIPES